DATE			

·CONIFERS·

·CONIFERS·

KEITH·D·RUSHFORTH

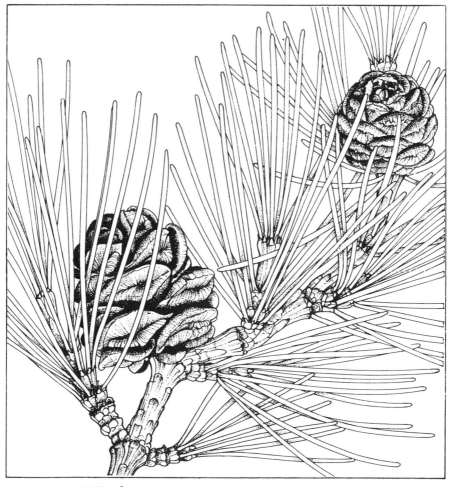

 Facts On File Publications
New York, New York ● Oxford, England

First published in the United States in 1987
by Facts On File, Inc.,
460 Park Avenue South,
New York, New York 10016

CIP Data available on request.

ISBN 0-8160-1735-2

Printed in Great Britain

10   9   8   7   6   5   4   3   2   1

Contents

To Heather, Rebecca and Timothy

Colour Plates

1. *Abies forrestii* — Forrest fir, young female cones in early summer
2. *Abies procera* — Noble fir, mature cone
3. *Cedrus atlantica glauca* — Atlas cedar, male cones in autumn
4. × *Cupressocyparis leylandii* 'Haggerston Grey' — Leyland cypress
5. *Cupressus corneyana* — Bhutan cypress, 40 m tall with a bole diameter of 2 m, at Drukyel Dzong, NW Bhutan, 2,600 m, KR762
6. *Glyptostrobus pensilis* — Chinese Swamp cypress, growing in water near Guangzhou (Canton), China
7. *Juniperus chinensis* 'Aurea' — Golden Chinese juniper, two genetically identical trees!
8. *Juniperus squamata* — Flaky juniper, Lingshi, NW Bhutan, 4,050 m, KR907
9. *Juniperus wallichiana* — Wallich juniper, 15 m tall, Soe Tajitang, NW Bhutan, 3,500 m, KR802
10. *Keteleeria fortunei* — Fortune keteleeria, Cape d'Arguilar, Hong Kong, KR420
11. *Metasequoia glyptostroboides* — Dawn redwood
12. *Picea omorika* — Serbian spruce
13. *Picea likiangensis* — Likiang spruce, male cones
14. *Picea asperata* — Dragon spruce, female cone just after pollination in early summer
15. *Pinus bungeana* — Lacebark pine
16. *Pinus culminicola* — Potosi pinyon, on summit of Cerro Potosi, NE Mexico, 3,550 m, KR440
17. *Pinus engelmannii* — Engelmann pine, Galeana, NE Mexico, 2,100 m, KR495
18. *Pinus hartwegii* — Hartweg pine, Nevada de Colima, W Mexico, 3,150 m, KR648
19. *Taxodium distichum* — Swamp cypress, 'knees' or 'pneumatophores' formed on the roots when growing beside water
20. *Thuja plicata* 'Zebrina' — Variegated Western red cedar

Figures

Acknowledgements

I would like to thank Dr Chris Page, of the Royal Botanic Garden, Edinburgh, for comments on the general taxonomic treatment, especially that of the Taxales; to the late Laurie Gough for discussions on Junipers; Michael Frankis for some very interesting observations on the Pines; and Dr John Gibbs, Clive Carter and Bob Strouts, of the Forestry Commission, for their helpful advice on Chapter 7. Thanks are also due to Joanna Langhorne for her line drawings and to the Hillier Arboretum, with others, who provided reference material for the figures. Also I would like to register my appreciation to my family for their forbearance of my passion for trees, and to all the people who, in one way or another, have helped me learn more about conifers.

·CHAPTER 1·
Introduction

Conifers are plants which can evoke strong emotions. They include the main evergreen plants available to the gardener and, as such, can be very useful in the garden. Equally, if mis-used they can be drab and dismal. This book is intended to outline the large range of conifers which are available to beautify gardens in the temperate parts of the world and to give ideas on using these plants in the garden.

Understanding and getting the best from conifers involves knowledge of their natural history. As wild plants, they include species which are dominant plants over much of the world's surface, especially in the northern forests which stretch across Europe, Asia and North America. They have characteristics which fit them for survival in often difficult conditions, where broadleaved trees cannot compete.

There are many joys in growing conifers. Most are evergreen but they include many different colours of leaves, from 'selected' plants with golden, silver, glaucous blue or variegated foliage, to naturally-occurring forms with leaves which are often silvery on the underside, or with bold needles sometimes 30 cm, or even 50 cm in length. Five genera, however, are deciduous, and these have autumn tints to the dying leaves and, particularly in the larches, bright and early new spring foliage and attractively coloured winter twigs.

There are species which will quickly form trees, including the tallest trees in the world, whilst some species are slow-growing and very long-lived. The habit, or appearance of the tree, is shapely and formal in some, whilst equally shapely but informal in others; it is possible to have the two effects by choosing different forms of the same species.

Some species are attractive in flower or fruit. The fruits are very often brightly coloured for long periods; in some Silver firs, this may be from early summer with the immature cones till long after mid-winter.

The many selected forms of dwarf conifers add another dimension. These associate well with many rock garden plants, or with heathers, or as dot plants in a lawn. Many are very picturesque in their Lilliputian habits.

One of the major uses of conifers in many gardens is as hedging or shelter plants. Here the ability of some species to make neat hedges may be used for formal screens, or a less formal effect may be attained using larger-growing species.

Conifers are occasionally condemned as dull, particularly the way in which the foliage of many of them may look rather unexciting in early spring when the broadleaved trees are just leafing out. For some of the commoner species this would be a valid criticism but for two facts. Prior to the deciduous trees reclothing themselves with a fresh set of leaves, the evergreen foliage of the conifer has probably been the only green in the garden, and a few weeks later, come late June, when the new foliage of the broadleaved tree has matured and dulled, the conifers will make their own splash of new growth. It is important when designing a garden setting to remember the way in which plants vary throughout the year, and to include both broadleaved and coniferous elements in the design. The very dullness of the foliage of some species at certain times of the year can be a great asset, when used to provide a dark backcloth to a light flower or foliage otherwise set against the sky.

In the succeeding chapters, conifer natural

history, particularly as it relates to their garden use, is discussed in Chapter 2, siting them in the garden in Chapter 3, Dwarf conifers in Chapter 4, propagation in Chapter 5, planting and replanting — a valuable exercise when a dwarf conifer outgrows its 'dwarf' position, in Chapter 6 and pests and diseases in Chapter 7. Finally, in the gazetteer section in Chapter 8, individual genera, species and cultivars are discussed. All the hardy conifers are examined in detail, with a botanical description, discussion of cultivars and assessment of garden worth.

·CHAPTER 2·
Biology of Conifers

What is a Conifer?

The name conifer is applied in common usage to plants belonging to three different orders of the Gymnospermae. The Gymnospermae differ from the Angiospermae, the other class of seed-bearing plants, in having the seeds, or ovules, borne naked on scales, rather than enclosed in ovaries. The names of these two classes of plants translate from the Greek as 'naked seed' and 'hidden seed'.

The three botanical orders which make up our conception of conifers are the Coniferales, the Taxales and the Ginkgoales. Also included in the living Gymnosperms but not part of our understanding and usage of the term conifer are the two orders — Cycadales, which are similar in gross appearance (but not in floral detail!) to some ferns and many palms, and Gnetales, which look like some angiosperms. These are not discussed further in this book.

The word conifer is derived from the shape of the fruit, or cone, of many species; it is equally applicable to the shape of the tree, particularly in the young stage. However, like many words, its current usage has extended beyond the strict definition of its original derivation, and many species of conifer have neither a cone-shaped fruit nor a conical growth habit.

Typically, conifers have fruits which are composed of many scales arranged in a helix and bearing the seeds, but the differences from this general idea are the basis for the acceptance of different orders, families, genera and species.

Classification

Botanical classification has as its most basic unit a species and these are grouped together with similar species in a genus. Both the genus and species names, and any botanical entities within the species, are in Latin, which is the international language of botany. A genus will contain one or more species; the unifying characters will be those associated primarily with the flowers and fruits.

Above a genus in the botanical hierarchy comes the family, which contains one or more genera possessing several characters in common and by which the family can be separated from other families. Above the family is the order, in which a number of families are grouped. Family names end in -aceae and order names in -ales. Sometimes it is appropriate to consider distinct elements in a family and these may be termed subfamily, tribe or subtribe. Similarly, in a genus subdivisions are: subgenus, section, subsection and series. Once a particular level of classification has been delimited, the individual units within that classification are called *taxa* (singular: *taxon*).

Normally a species can be expected to differ from its nearest relatives in three or four major, non-interrelated characters but the best definition of a species is 'whatever a competent botanist considers is a species'. The traditional criterion of a species being interfertile between members of the species and, under natural circumstances, at least partially intersterile with members of another species is subject to too many qualifications to be useful in practice.

Within the many individuals which comprise a species, there will be some variation. The form of the species which is first described is considered the 'typical' or type form. Where other forms occur, the traditional approach was to call all the variants 'varieties' of the species, but this term has become rather confused with the use of the same word for individual garden selections. There is a growing tendency, therefore, for the highest level of variation from the type of a species to be a sub-species, particularly where the variation is correlated with the distribution or ecology of the plant. A subspecies may be expected to differ from its species by one or two significant characters or by a larger number of more minor ones. If there is no indication of a separate geographical or ecological distribution, the plant will be a variety or *varietas*. Forms or *forma* are groups of plants which differ from the species in only one or two marked characters, such as abnormally large or small leaves, or cones, or similar feature which may be determined by only a few genes.

Specially selected individuals are termed 'cultivars' — the word is derived from *culti*vated *vari*ety. Strictly, a cultivar name can only be applied to one individual plant and others vegetatively propagated from it. Seedlings raised from this plant will not be genetically the same and, therefore, do not belong to that cultivar. Cultivar names first described before 1959 may be in Latin, but all names given after then must be in a vernacular language and are termed fancy names. Cultivar names are written with capital letters for the first letter of each word; they are either placed in single quotes or preceded by the abbreviation cv.

An example of a plant name is:

Picea pungens forma *glauca* 'Hoopsii', where *Picea* is the genus name, *pungens* is the specific epithet, *glauca* refers to the form of the species with blue wax-covered foliage and 'Hoopsii' is a cultivar selected for its very silvery blue foliage.

Names are given according to taxonomy and nomenclature, which are two different subjects. Taxonomy is the study and practice of classification. It involves choosing characters which assist in the understanding of the subject. Nomenclature is far more bureaucratic and is concerned with the application of the correct name in a given situation. In the gazetteer section you will find that each Latin plant name has after it the name of the person or 'authority' who first gave it that name. This is important because on many occasions the same name has been used in a genus for two or more very different plants. Giving the name of the authority defines in which sense the name is being used. Where the name was first given in either a

different genus or at a different taxonomic rank, the authority includes in brackets the name of the person who first coined the name. The first name given to a plant has priority *at that level* over later names, even if it was first given in another genus or species. This means that a plant can have one name as a species but another as a subspecies or varietas. Corsican pine is one such species; in Britain it is usually treated as a varietas of the European Black pine — as *Pinus nigra* var. *maritima*, but more logically it should be treated as a subspecies, in which case it is *P. nigra* subsp. *laricio*, which is the name more often used on the continent; *maritima* has priority at the varietas level over *laricio* even though *maritima* was first used as a variety of Scots pine (*P. sylvestris*). If treated as a species in its own right, Corsican pine is *P. laricio*. Alternative names or synonyms are often used for a species; these are given in brackets in the Gazetteer section.

From the above, you will appreciate that the species concept is in some measure artificial; botanists do not always agree upon the significance of certain characters and they may, quite legitimately, give more or less consideration to certain characters and then treat the plant at a different level, perhaps under a different name.

Synopsis of Conifers

The Coniferales are the largest group of conifers. There are five different families, containing some 48 genera and over 600 species.

The Podocarpaceae have the seeds supported on a fleshy development of the peduncle. The Araucariaceae have a single seed set on the ovuliferous scale. The Cupressaceae are characterised by the decussately-arranged cone scales and the foliage being in decussate pairs or whorls of three; the number of erect ovules per scale varies from two to 20 plus. The Taxodiaceae is close to the Cupressaceae but with the leaves spirally set, except in *Metasequoia*, and the fertile scales bearing two to six erect or inverted ovules. The Pinaceae is characterised by the fertile scales bearing only two inverted ovules and there being a prominent bract scale associated with each ovuliferous scale (in *Pinus* fused in the mature cone with the ovuliferous scale).

Order	Family	Genus	Approx. no of species
Ginkgoales	Ginkgoaceae	*Ginkgo*	1
Coniferales	Araucariaceae	*Agathis*	13
		Araucaria	18
	Cupressaceae	*Actinostrobus*	3
		Austrocedrus	1
		Callitris	14
		Calocedrus	3
		Chamaecyparis	8
		× *Cupressocyparis*	3
		Cupressus	25
		Diselma	1
		Fitzroya	1
		Fokienia	1
		Juniperus	60
		Libocedrus	5
		Microbiota	1
		Neocallitropsis	1
		Papuacedrus	2
		Pilgerodendron	1
		Platycladus	1
		Tetraclinis	1
		Thuja	5
		Thujopsis	1
		Widdringtonia	3
	Pinaceae	*Abies*	55
		Cathaya	1
		Cedrus	4
		Keteleeria	10
		Larix	15
		Picea	37
		Pinus	120
		Pseudolarix	1
		Pseudotsuga	8
		Tsuga	10
	Podocarpaceae	*Acmopyle*	2
		Dacrycarpus	9
		Dacrydium	25
		Decussocarpus	12
		Falcatifolium	5
		Halocarpus	3
		Lagarostrobus	2
		Lepidothamnus	3
		Microcachrys	1
		Microstrobus	2
		Parasitaxus	1
		Phyllocladus	5
		Podocarpus	94
		Prumnopitys	10
		Saxegothaea	1

Order	Family	Genus	Approx. no of species
	Taxodiaceae	*Athrotaxis*	3
		Cryptomeria	2
		Cunninghamia	2
		Glyptostrobus	1
		Metasequoia	1
		Sciadopitys	1
		Sequoia	1
		Sequoiadendron	1
		Taiwania	2
		Taxodium	3
Taxales	Taxaceae	*Austrotaxus*	1
		Pseudotaxus	1
		Taxus	10
	Cephalotaxaceae	*Amentotaxus*	4
		Cephalotaxus	9
		Torreya	7

The Taxales are a much smaller group with two families of six genera and about a score of species. The seeds are always single, and enclosed in a fleshy aril. In the Taxaceae the aril is open at the apex. In the Cephalotaxaceae, the aril totally encloses the seed.

The Ginkgoales contain just a single family with but one species, which has single seeds outwardly like some of the Taxales, but also has very distinctive, broad flat leaves.

Flowers and Fruits

Conifers reproduce by means of the seeds produced in the female cones. The young cones, or flowers of conifers, are of only one sex, that is the flowers are either male or female. Most species are monoecious, that is they have flowers of both sexes carried on the one plant. Species in the yew family, and many junipers, are dioecious, that is the flowers of the two sexes are borne on separate plants. The fruit is the mature female cone.

Male Cones

The pollen-producing flowers, usually called the male cones, or more correctly, the microsporangiate strobili (i.e. small spore cones), consist of a number of stamens set in a catkin-like cluster. Often these are yellow, crimson or violet in colour. They disperse large numbers of the very small pollen grains. In many species the pollen grains have two air sacs to enable the pollen to be more readily carried on the wind. No conifer is pollinated by insects, at least not deliberately.

At anthesis, the pollen falls onto the ovules which are open to the air on the scales of the

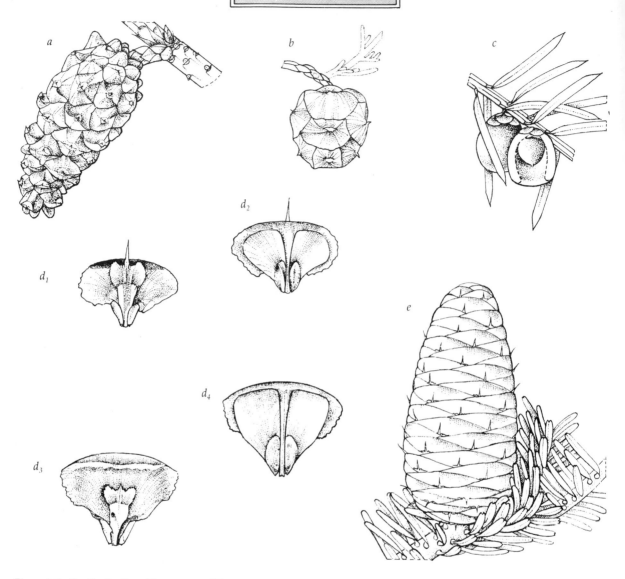

Figure 2.1 Conifer Fruits. a Mature cone of Pinus sylvestris. *b Cone of* Cupressus sempervirens. *c Fruit of* Taxus baccata *cut away to reveal seed. d Cone scales of* Abies, *showing bracts scale (d_1, d_3), seeds with wings (d_2, d_4) and ovuliferous scale (d_{1-4}). e Mature cone of* Abies.

female cones, or megasporangiate strobili (i.e. big spore cones). The pollen grain germinates on the ovule and grows into it, leading to the fusion of the nucleus of the pollen cell with the egg cell.

Fertilisation may occur within a few weeks of pollination, but in *Pinus* and some other genera it does not take place for a full year. *Ginkgo* is unique in having motile sperm cells which 'swim' towards the ovule; fertilisation in *Ginkgo* may not occur until after the ripe fruit has fallen to the ground.

Male cones are usually found on the lower branches or on the undersides of the shoots. Where they occur on the same branch as female cones, they will be found at the basal end. In the Cypress family, they are terminal on weak shoots, but in most other groups they develop from resting buds.

Female Cones

The female flowers are usually carried on the strongest growths, and are most frequent in the upper third of the tree. In most genera they develop from resting buds which do not produce any leaves. In the true conifers, that is the order Coniferales, the female flower consists of a central axis which has pairs of scales set in a helical or opposite arrangement. The paired scales consist of a sterile bract scale with, above it, a fertile scale. The fertile or ovuliferous scale carries the ovules on the upper surface either singly, in pairs or up to a score together on each scale, depending upon the genus. The bract and ovuliferous scales may be quite distinct, as in *Pseudotsuga* and *Abies*, or become visually indistinguishable, as in *Pinus*. In the yew family the ovule is solitary and is not set on a bract, whilst in the *Ginkgo* family two ovules are carried at the end of a long stalk. In both of these families, the fruit develops as a single seed partially or wholly enclosed in a fleshy covering or aril. The fruits may take one or two years to develop, although in some *Juniperus* and two species in *Pinus* three seasons are required to ripen the mature cone. In the true conifers, the cones become woody, except in the Junipers where the cone scales become fleshy or fibrous.

Seed Dispersal and Germination

Some species rely upon birds or animals to scatter the seeds and these are those with either single seeds with fleshy coats, such as yew, or species with large wingless seeds, such as some pines. Most species, however, have seeds with relatively large wings to maximise wind dispersal. The cones of some pine species are designed to open only after a forest fire has occurred; a benefit of this is that a large number of cones may be 'held' on the tree, representing up to 20 years' seed production, and only released when competing ground vegetation has been destroyed.

Germination in nearly all conifers is epigeal, i.e. the cotyledons are extracted from the seedcase, raised above the ground and act as the first leaves. (The other form of germination is hypogeal, in which the cotyledons remain buried in the seedcase in the soil and a shoot with only true leaves emerges. Only some species in the genus *Araucaria* and all the species in *Torreya* and *Keteleeria* have this form of germination.) In either case, the process is started by the seed absorbing water, and extending the radicle or root before any top growth is made. The number of cotyledons varies. Usually it is two or three, except in the Pinaceae where any number up to 23 can be expected.

Leaves

The typical needle is the commonest leaf type associated with conifers, and is several times longer than its width. This leaf is found on all the Pinaceae, Taxaceae and Cephalotaxaceae, and is represented in the other families except the *Ginkgo* family. Typically, it is pointed and sharp, as shown by some spruces, but as often it has a rounded blunt or notched apex and is flattened with two distinct surfaces. In *Pinus* the leaves in a cluster or fascicle together make a cylinder, so each one is a segment representing either a half, third or fifth of a circle.

Scale leaves are found on most of the Cypresses and in some of the Podocarpaceae and Taxodiaceae. These are small, rather acute shaped leaves which clasp and conceal the stem. The tip may either be adpressed, or free. When a free tip is elongated, it becomes a needle, as is shown by some of the junipers and in *Sequoiadendron*; these leaves are decurrent on the stem, just like the scale leaves; some junipers can carry both leaf types on the same twig. In many of the cypress family, such as in *Thuja* or in *Chamaecyparis*, but not in *Cupressus* itself, the scale leaves are arranged in sets of two pairs at right angles to each other, i.e. orthogonally. In these plants, the pair which is above and below the shoot is usually smaller and more scale-like, whilst the lateral pair is often flattened.

Large broad leaves are the exception, being found only in *Ginkgo*, although in some of the Podocarpaceae and Araucariaceae the leaves are only slightly longer than broad. The veins in these leaves are always simple and run along the entire length of the leaf; secondary and crossing veins, as produced by all broadleaved plants, are not found.

The other true leaf commonly found, although not immediately recognisable, is the small brown scale which subtends either the needle fascicle of *Pinus*, or which is found on the shoots of *Sciadopitys* or *Phyllocladus*.

These last two genera do not have normal leaves. Rather, in *Phyllocladus* photosynthesis is carried out on modified shoots (phylloclades), which are green and flattened. In *Sciadopitys*, the exact nature of the photosynthesising structure is unresolved; opinions differ as to whether it is either a phylloclade or a modified short shoot with two needles joined together.

The remaining leaf type is the juvenile or primordial leaf, normally only produced as the first few centimetres of growth on young seedlings. These are often longer than adult leaves. A number of the cultivars in the cypress family are juvenile forms, where the plant has not attained the mature foliage type. A few species, e.g. *Pinus canariensis*, regularly produce juvenile leaves, even on old trees.

The leaves in most conifers are set spirally around the shoot. In the cypress family, and also in *Metasequoia, Agathis, Amentotaxus* and some Podocarps, they are set in opposite pairs; in some junipers and in the juvenile foliage of a few other members of the cypress family, they may be in whorls of three, as well as in pairs, particularly on vigorous shoots.

Needle retention varies with the species. In the five deciduous genera it is only one summer. The oldest living needles I have counted were on an *Abies nordmanniana* and were 26 years old, but the circumstances were exceptional — the lower branches of old trees with side light in a moist Scottish glen. Most species will only retain their leaves for 3-5 years, although yew, Silver firs and spruces will often keep them for up to ten years. Foxtail pines, such as *Pinus aristata*, regularly keep their needles for 15 years, exceptionally to over 30 years. Monkey puzzle (*Araucaria araucana*) leaves may also be retained for 15 or so years; the base of the leaf enlarges where it is attached to the ever-expanding stem.

The outer layer of the leaf, the cuticle, protects the leaf from drying out, a danger in many of the environments where conifers flourish. Conifers from moist, tropical regions do not have such well developed cuticles. The leaf, however, has to obtain carbon dioxide, which, with water and trapped energy from sunlight, is used in photosynthesis to make sugars and release oxygen. The main source of carbon dioxide is from the atmosphere, and breathing pores, called *stomata* (singular *stoma*) perform this gaseous exchange. The stomata are often set in rows, sometimes on both surfaces of the needle, more often only on the lower surface. To reduce water loss from the stomata, they are often covered in wax. Conversely, this wax layer may assist the run-off of water under wet conditions. The internal structure of the leaves includes the vascular tissue, which conducts water, nutrients and the products of photosynthesis around the leaf and connects with the xylem and phloem (see page 20). Many species also have resin ducts, or resin canals in the leaves.

Figure 2.2 Leaf Characters

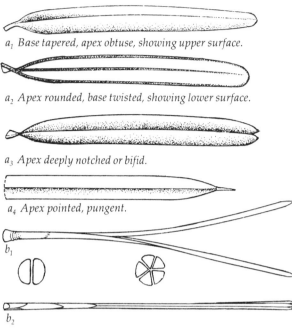

a_1 *Base tapered, apex obtuse, showing upper surface.*

a_2 *Apex rounded, base twisted, showing lower surface.*

a_3 *Apex deeply notched or bifid.*

a_4 *Apex pointed, pungent.*

b_1

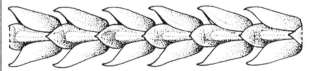

b_2

b_1 *and* b_2 *Pine needles, including leaf sheath at base and cross-section.*

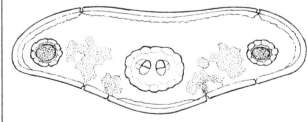

c Foliage of Thujopsis dolabrata, *showing facial and lateral pairs of leaves.*

d Leaf section of Abies, *showing 2 resin canals, central vascular bundle and cuticle.*

Buds and Flushing

The buds on some conifers, particularly those in the pine family, are covered with budscales and are similar in general appearance to the buds of broadleaved trees. Several other families, especially the cypress family, do not have distinct buds. They make the new growth from meristematic (or growth) tissue in the axils of the leaves.

The buds in the pine family expand in early spring when they burst or *flush*. The buds contain the leaf primordia for all the leaves which the shoot will produce that year; this number is laid down during the summer of the previous year. The tree can adjust the extent to which the shoot elongates and the size of the needles produced but has little control during the season of growth on the number of leaves. In 'good' years, i.e. ones better than the tree expected when the buds were developed, the needles will be spaced further apart and longer than in a 'normal' year; conversely in 'bad' years, they will be closer together and shorter. Most members of the pine family have little ability to produce 'free growth', i.e. not predetermined growth, after the first few years as seedlings. New lateral buds are formed during the early spring period. The buds laid down can develop into four different types; vegetative buds, dormant buds, female cone buds and male cone buds. Externally they appear fully developed by mid-summer, but growth continues in the buds until early winter.

This fixed or predetermined growth explains why conifers are slow to react to the application of fertiliser and can be difficult to transplant. As the planned new leaves are laid down in sequence along the shoot, additional fertiliser received by the plant after mid-summer of one year cannot be adequately reflected in the laying down of new leaf primordia until spring of the next year, which means extra leaves in the summer of the third growing season after application. The length of time for which the needles are carried, and re-cycling of nutrients within the tree, result in a positive effect on growth lasting for five or more years. Equally, the shock of being transplanted as a mature tree can take several years to work its way through the tree's system. The effect of this can be mitigated by moving larger trees at the end of the summer when the growth for the next year has been determined but there is still plenty of time to make new roots before root growth ceases in early winter. It is essential, however, not to let the tree suffer from moisture stress before it has had the opportunity to make new roots.

The same controls act upon the formation of male and female cone buds. Where these are an important part of the amenity offered by the tree, it is necessary to realise how much their production is affected by the tree's condition, and often, therefore, the weather conditions two to three years before they make a display.

Branching

The way a tree holds its branches changes as the branch ages and also varies with the position of the branch on the tree.

The branches in the upper crown are usually held at a slight upward angle but as the branch becomes older it may grow more horizontally, and ultimately bend downwards; the tip of downward-growing branches are reclinate and point up, so that the branch is curved down, out and up along its length. Serbian spruce (*Picea omorika*) exhibits this tendency very well with, in old trees, the branches hanging down along the trunk before arching out and up. In some species, particularly species of *Chamaecyparis* and *Tsuga*, the leading shoot (and young branches) are floppy and point down, only to become erect (or horizontal) as they develop.

Many cultivars have been selected which exaggerate the natural characters, so that some upright cultivars have the branches growing at a very acute angle to the leading shoot, such as *Pinus sylvestris* 'Fastigiata', whilst pendulous ones either have downward-growing branches, or weaker branchlets unable to support themselves, e.g. *Sequoiadendron giganteum* 'Pendulum'.

The order of the branch, that is how successive branches relate to each other and to the main stem, also affects how a branch grows, and should be borne in mind when describing branchlets. A first order branch is the primary growing point, i.e. the central leading shoot of the seedling tree (although when used in a plant description it can refer to the main branch being examined). The branches which arise from this axis are second order branches; those growing out of them are third order, and so on. Very few trees have more than five orders of branches, although with some of the cypresses it can be difficult to work out! The order of a branch determines how it grows. First order ones are always the main stems of trees, second order ones the major branches, third order the smaller branches and fourth and fifth order ones the branchlets. On many trees, the female cones are carried on a different order of branching than the male cones; in spruces the female cones are found on the second and third order branches, whilst the male cones usually occur on the fourth and fifth order branchlets. The later orders of branches have much less vigour than the first and second orders and this can greatly affect the appearance of the tree. In Brewer spruce (*Picea breweriana*) the weeping foliage is much admired but only the third and fourth order branchlets hang down; the second order branches are more or less horizontal and create the spreading framework to display the branchlets. This also shows why Brewer spruce trees must be several years old before developing their characteristic habit.

Bark

The bark of all conifers consists of two layers. The inner bark or phloem is involved in the conduction of materials between the roots and the top of the tree, mainly taking sugars back down to the roots. The outer bark is a protective layer. In young trees it is often smooth, becoming scaly and ridged. In some species, especially in *Sequoia* and *Sequoiadendron*, it is thick and fibrous and acts as a defence against fire damage. In others, e.g. *Abies squamata*, the bark is attractively flaky.

Wood

Conifer wood, or xylem, consists mainly of tracheids. These are elongated spindle-shaped cells and are dovetailed together. The tracheids produced during the early part of the growing season are for the conduction of water and nutrients from the roots, and may also be used for the winter storage of the products of photosynthesis. Those laid down in the summer provide strength. The sides of the tracheids are set with many pores, called pits, which allow the transfer of sap from one cell to the next. The pits have mechanisms to cut off the movement of sap, and these are often specific to families or certain groupings of conifers. The yew family has the tracheids strengthened by a spiral thickening of the cell wall. Large vessels for water conduction, as found in the broadleaved trees, are absent. The medullary rays, which allow transport between the wood produced in different years, are usually only one cell thick. In some genera, such as *Pinus*, resin ducts are found in the wood and are visible as small dots in a transverse section. The heartwood of many conifers is quite durable and distinct from the sapwood. The tracheids are long, 3-11 mm, and make the timber useful for paper production.

The amount of spring and summer wood produced, and the proportion of each, will vary with the weather conditions prevailing during that year and, to some extent, the previous growing season.

This provides a measure of the climatic conditions and is used in dendrochronology. By comparing the growth characteristics of a number of pieces of known age, it allows the age of an individual piece of wood to be determined; dendrochronology also allows predictions to be made about the climate at the time when the wood was laid down. Very similar, although not identical, growth records are found for Britain and western Europe.

When a stem is leaning, additional strength is required in the timber to support the tree. In conifers, this extra strength is made on the lower, or compression, side of the stem and is called compression wood. Although bolstering the stem, compression wood cuts badly and decreases the value of a piece of timber.

Roots

The roots of conifers are similar to the roots of most other woody plants. The root system of the young tree starts from the radicle or primary root of the seedling. To begin with, this grows down into the earth but lateral roots soon develop. During the first year of the plant's life the primary root will tend to be larger than all the laterals produced. It is only on very dry sites, where deep rooting is essential if the plant is to find sufficient moisture, that the primary root will grow to any great depth and become a 'classical' taproot of mythology. Normally, the root will grow down to the level in the soil where shortage of oxygen prevents the roots surviving. On most sites this will mean that during the summer season, as the soil dries out, the roots will grow deeper but as the winter rains raise the water table, the lower portion of the root system will be killed, to regrow next season. In successive years the lateral roots will become dominant, with the result that in most trees it is impossible to determine which was the seedling's 'taproot'.

Species differ in the natural development of their root systems. Spruces (*Picea*) have a tendency to be shallow-rooted, whilst Silver firs (*Abies*) will be deeper rooting but the site conditions will determine how shallow or how deep the roots of each tree can naturally extend.

When a tree is planted out, either in the forest or garden, initially it will use the root system it had in the nursery but will then produce a new root system. In spruce forests experiments have shown that after about eight years the root system of the tree will consist of from three to eleven major lateral roots, which will remain the tree's supporting roots throughout the rest of its life. A number of minor lateral roots will also exist but these apparently cease to grow in size after a few years, although they may increase in length.

The function of the root system is twofold: support for the top portion of the tree and to extract nutrients and water from the soil.

Support for the aerial parts is provided by the roots being in intimate contact with a very large volume of soil. There is no precise knowledge of how far an individual root will extend but measurements on a number of different species have shown that they usually extend up to a radius of between one and two times the tree's height, although this is very approximate and will depend much on chance growth and the soil conditions. The depth of the system will usually be 50-90 cm; only on light gravel soils and exceptionally elsewhere will it be deeper. A tree of only 10 m with roots spreading for a similar radius will, in theory, be in contact with an area of soil 20 m in diameter and 0.5 m in depth, and this soil will weigh over 400 tons. Very rarely do trees completely blow out of the ground. If a tree is blown down it is usually because the main roots have become rotten and no longer maintain contact between the trunk and the smaller roots which are in close contact with the soil.

The collection of nutrients and water from the soil is the other function of the root system. This is mainly carried out by the smaller roots. There are two ways in which the nutrients enter the roots, these are by the roots absorbing the nutrients in water solution from the soil by osmosis, and by association, called a mycorrhizal association, with a fungus.

Water, with dissolved nutrients, is carried into the root tissue by osmotic pressure. This is a natural chemical phenomenon by which water will flow across a semipermeable membrane from a weak solution towards a stronger one. The sap in the roots contains more ions, i.e. dissolved nutrients, than the surrounding soil (when this does not occur, as in a saline soil, most land plants are unable to absorb water through the roots and die). Water and nutrient absorption takes place primarily in the younger roots, where the covering layer is thinner and more permeable. (However, there is evidence that even roots with quite a thick bark can still absorb water and nutrients by osmosis.) In young roots there is a zone of very fine hairlike growths (root-hairs) just behind the

growing tip which have a very thin membrane and also increase the area of root in contact with the soil, thereby adding to the uptake of nutrients and water. Root hairs have only a very short life.

Many conifers form an intimate association with a fungus, to make mycorrhiza (plural mycorrhizae), literally fungus root. These associations are of benefit to both the plant and the fungus. The fungus receives sugars and other products of photosynthesis from the tree; in return, the fungus extends out into the soil and collects water and nutrients for the root. As the fungal strands are very fine and extend much further than roots, they can collect more nutrients than the tree's roots could find. Mycorrhizal associations are especially important to trees on very poor sites, and have been found to decrease in number on sites where fertiliser has been added (thereby to a limited extent minimising the impact of the fertiliser). A probable explanation for the reduction in significance of the mycorrhizal associations on nutrient-rich soils is that on these soils there is no imbalance in the production by the leaves of carbohydrate or sugar production over protein production, as occurs where nutrients are lacking; therefore excess sugars do not occur in the roots, so there is no surplus to feed the fungus.

Two main types of mycorrhizal association exist: endotrophic mycorrhizae and ectotrophic mycorrhizae. Ectotrophic mycorrhizae are most common on conifers. The fungus forms a sheath over the young roots and causes the root to stop growing; usually, these roots become forked. In endotrophic mycorrhizae, there is no sheath of fungus over the roots, but the fungal strands, or hyphae, grow into or between the cells of the root. In each case the hyphae extend from the root into the soil. The fungus-plant association is symbiotic, but only as long as it suits either side. If the tree becomes too weak to provide the necessary sugars, there is evidence that the fungus may become parasitic; if the nutrient supply is so good (e.g. when fertilised), the tree may discard the fungus.

In the garden, mycorrhizae are useful in providing the tree with nutrients, and probably hastening decay of organic matter in the soil. The mycorrhizal fungus will produce fruit bodies around the tree on which it thrives and these should not be confused with decay fungi fruit bodies.

Ecology

Throughout the world conifers are found on a number of different sites but the main common feature is the ability of most species to tolerate moisture stress and to conserve water. This is the character which unites the Saharan cypress (*Cupressus dupreziana*) with Mexican pines (*Pinus* spp.) and the northern boreal forests of Europe, Asia and America.

Moisture stress occurs in three forms, characterised by low rainfall, hot summer temperature leading to high evaporation and dry winter cold.

The largest portion of the world's surface dominated by conifers is the boreal forest. This stretches across the continents of the northern hemisphere and continues south down mountain chains at high altitude. The main features of the climate in the boreal forests is a long and very cold dry winter, with associated drying winds, and short cool summers. Total rainfall is usually low, but because of the short cool summer little water is lost by the plant through evaporation.

Despite the enormous areas occupied, the boreal forests contain very few species. For a species to thrive in the boreal forest it needs to be able to control water loss and to exploit to the full the short growing season. Water conservation is very important because the very low humidity makes it evaporate easily, even when frozen, and any evaporation of water will further cool the plant. Most conifers in these forests have thick cuticles to protect the leaves but also most regulate the cell contents so that they can survive freezing to temperatures of −55°C and below.

The tree needs, also, to be able to capitalise on the short summer when conditions are favourable for growth. This favours evergreen species as they can start photosynthesis as soon as the temperature warms up sufficiently in the spring. The tree species found farthest north, however, is the Siberian larch (*Larix russica*) and this is deciduous; it can survive in conditions where winter cold and desiccation are too severe for evergreen conifers and broadleaved trees, such as birches, and is reported to 71°N. Because of its need to exploit good growing conditions quickly, Siberian larch (and some other species) will start into growth in January or even December in cultivation, only to be damaged by following frosts; in its native habitat the seasons are clearly marked and spring is short and frostfree.

The same testing conditions occur further south along mountain chains. This is because as the air pressure drops, the air expands and cools. The rate of cooling is constant with increasing altitude and the temperature falls by approximately 1°C for every 170 m increase in altitude. High mountain ranges are, therefore, cooler than the plains below, and often windy. Another characteristic of mountain ranges in low latitudes is a very high level of ultra-violet light. The thick protective cuticles and waxy coverings of the leaves protect against this, as well as restricting water loss. Interestingly, one difference in leaf structure between boreal species and those from mountain chains nearer the Equator lies in the distribution of stomata; in boreal species they are clustered in lines on the lower sides of the needles and covered with a thick layer of protective wax, but in montane species stomata and wax are present on both upper and lower leaf surfaces.

In regions of low rainfall, conifers can survive by controlling moisture loss. In some places, such as in central Asian mountain chains, their survival is restricted to north-facing slopes where snowfall collects but is only slowly melted, providing moisture through the summer. Evergreen species are better adapted to these regimes, as their thick leaves reduce water loss whilst letting photosynthesis occur when conditions are suitable. Growth in these conditions is slow, both because of the shortage of water and as a consequence of the water-loss control mechanisms. Nelson pine (*Pinus nelsonii*) from north-east Mexico is a three-needled pinyon pine. It controls water loss from the needles by having the stomata only on the inside surfaces and holding, almost sticking, the three needles together so that they appear as a single needle; the amount of carbon dioxide which can be absorbed must be small, but sufficient for the volume of water available on the dry limestone knolls on which the species is found. The Mediterranean is another region of the world where conifers abound in the low summer rainfall.

Conifers also dominate regions where there appears to be sufficient rainfall. These include the temperate rain forests of the Pacific north-west coast of North America and the pine forests of the south-east USA. In these areas there is more than 100 cm of rainfall per annum. However, they are generally areas with hot summer climates and high potential evaporation from both the soil and plant tissues. This leads to periods in the year when moisture is not freely available to the plant and it is the ability of the conifers to tolerate the dry periods which gives them the competitive edge over other plants.

Many conifer species are capable of growing on barren or nutrient-poor sites and this ability, combined with their drought tolerance, favours conifers in places such as the sandy barren parts of south-east USA.

Conifers are also found in various habitats because they can tolerate low light conditions. They can therefore exist, and fruit, beneath other trees or on permanently shaded slopes. However, what is often the limiting factor in situations of low light intensity is the availability of water and nutrients. Yew (*Taxus baccata*) is one of the few plants which can thrive in the conditions beneath a beech tree, where the competition is intense for both nutrients and water.

Some conifers are relicts from periods when the climate was different to that of today. These species often have very restricted natural ranges and usually are not very adaptable. Sometimes the restriction is due to the lack of suitable habitat within range of effective seed dispersal. Monterey pine (*Pinus radiata*) is one such. In its native region it is restricted to three sites on the mainland of California and two offshore islands, but has been planted over large areas of the world as a timber tree, including over 400,000 hectares in New Zealand alone. Another relic conifer is the Chihuahua spruce (*Picea chihuahuana*) which is only found within a few metres of permanent streams in three rather dry and mainly streamless states in northern Mexico; the number of stream-side sides available at the required altitude of around 2,500-3,000 m is rather few, about two dozen! In the wild, this species cannot compete against other conifers away from its riverine sites.

·CHAPTER 3·
Conifers
in the Garden

There are several ways in which conifers can be used in the garden. These are discussed under various 'headings', but it must be remembered that one tree can fill several roles. The uses include providing specimen or character plants; shelter or backcloth planting; seasonal or coloured foliage; bark, flower or fruit features; and habitats for wildlife. Having said this, though, probably the most frequent individual use of conifers is as hedging plants, or as Christmas trees.

Different sizes of conifers are of value in the garden setting. In this chapter the discussion will centre on the taller-growing sorts and their uses; dwarf conifers and the special uses to which they can be put will feature in the next chapter.

Specimen and Character Conifers

The purpose of a specimen or character plant is to have a shape which will be attractive to look at at all times of the year. This requires a plant which will flourish in the setting in your garden, which does not have an 'off' season visually and which has a growth habit you find pleasing. Fortunately, we all have different views on the last phrase, so there is not one tree for all situations.

Specimen plants can be used in a variety of different situations, but most will be either set at the end, or possibly the side, of a vista, or to mark a particular space, e.g. to make a feature in the front garden. It is necessary, then, to work out the size of the space in which the tree must relate, as this is an essential starting point in the choice of which plant.

The scale of the specimen tree must match the surroundings. If the space available is very tall and narrow, such as with a tree planted to mark the end of an avenue or narrow vista, it is necessary to choose a tree which has a spire-like crown, like Serbian spruce or some of the cypresses. A broad-crowned tree, like an Atlas cedar, will look entirely wrong in the above situation and, as it grows, will completely fill the end view. The situation is easier if more space is available, as either a wide-spreading tree can be chosen, or else width can be created by using a group of narrower trees to make a grove. Beware, however, of over-using trees with distinct habits, or foliage. Too much of a good thing soon tires.

As the scale of any planting is a combination of the height and the width of both the tree and the space, this relationship will change with time. The tree will grow in both height and spread, whilst the growth of other trees or peripheral plantings may crowd in from the sides. Consideration needs to be given at the design and planting stage to how the situation will alter with time.

At the early stage in any scheme the main constraint is likely to be lack of size of the trees. Planting larger plants rarely makes up for a bit of patience, as bigger sizes of planting stock usually sit around for several years before starting to make significant height growth; during this time they tend to look rather dismal and unthrifty. There are ways of getting young trees to grow quickly, and these are well worth adopting; they are discussed in Chapter 6. In some situations, it may be possible to plant a larger specimen in addition to the permanent plant, so that an initial impression of height is given, but the problem remains to keep this bigger plant looking attractive and healthy until its replacement has grown. Another possibility, where such space and flexibility exists, is to plant a faster-growing specimen, e.g. Grand fir

(*Abies grandis*) or Leyland cypress (× *Cupresso-cyparis leylandii*), which will make a tree quickly but can then be removed when the choice tree has grown to 3m or more. A major snag with this approach is actually to remove the extra tree, and not leave it there for 'just one more year'. Generally, it is more appropriate to provide a good standard of husbandry and to wait three or so years for the plant to start to look something. In this context, it is well to remember that a tree of any size will only look big provided there is not a larger one standing beside it; this alone is one of the major constraints on removing a fast-growing specimen, the slower-growing permanent tree will always look small in comparison.

More often, the problem of scale is at the other end of the time spectrum, when the tree or trees have outgrown the space. There are several ways in which either management or choice at the design stage can reduce this problem.

The most useful thing is to judge the timespan for which the tree is wanted. In a large garden or park, this will probably be for as long as the tree is fit and healthy; here it is practical to consider the full natural lifespan of the tree. Such situations often require some planning — looking forward for as much as a century. Most people, though, are planting for very much shorter timespans.

During recent years, the average time any British family stays in one house is under ten years and in the USA it is about seven years, and this has two consequences for the design of any planting. First, it needs to make an impact within a short space of time, as the person who designs the planting will wish to remain around to see at least some of the benefits and not just leave them for the next people who buy the house, after all, they may have entirely different ideas. Secondly, the planting wants to enhance the value or attractiveness of the house when it comes to be sold. In practice, the design will want to pay close attention to how the planting will appear between five and 25 years ahead.

The growth rate of the tree will need to be considered in this context. The ideal tree which grows quickly to a given height and then ceases is rarely available. Some grow very fast, but they generally continue to make height growth for many years, often at the same rate! Leyland cypress can be relied on to grow at approximately 1m a year, which is very useful if you want a quick tree but rarely convenient when it continues to do so for 30 years, until it is about 34m tall, when it seems to

stop! At the other end of the growth rate spectrum, Bristlecone pine may only make growth of 15-20cm per year and is unlikely to make more than 9m, even after 50 years. Most conifers come between these extremes of growth rate, with averages of around 45cm per annum.

It is worthwhile choosing a tree with a growth rate appropriate to the timespan you are considering, i.e. one which will make a feature within a reasonable period but which will not grow too large in the time you can expect to be there to enjoy it.

The other way in which future management can be made easier at the design stage is to plan for the removal and replacement of trees. Many trees which will ultimately grow too large can make very attractive specimens when young. Examples include the Western hemlock (*Tsuga heterophylla*) and Deodar cedar (*Cedrus deodara*), both of which eventually will make trees 20m or more tall on most sites. The pleasure of growing these specimens need not be reserved for parks and the largest gardens only; in fact, as fully mature trees they are much less attractive than when young specimens 6-9m tall. To enjoy them in the average garden demands a commitment to remove them before they become a nuisance. Obviously if the design includes space for only one such tree, a gap will be created when they are felled; however, except in the smallest gardens, it is often possible to plant a tree to one side a few years before the overgrown specimen has to be removed, giving time for the replacement to make some size.

In practice, this can take two forms. A fast-growing species can be used to make the initial tree, with a slower one beside for the long-term specimen. Alternatively, if a tree like the Deodar is the desired specimen, the first tree can be allowed to grow for, say, 15 years, with a replacement being planted after ten.

The choice of species to use as a specimen conifer is quite wide and depends in part on the individual site and on personal preference. Broadly, as noted in Chapter 2, conifers divide into two main groups, with *Ginkgo* as an odd deciduous exception. The groups are the scale-leaved species, such as cypresses, and those with longer needle leaves. The appearance of the two types is quite different.

Scale-leaved conifers make specimen trees with very tight, often rather formal and dense outlines. Many of the forms of Lawson cypress will retain a very precise habit, even when quite old, and the

Wellingtonia is similar, although slightly more open. All of these trees are useful where the space is limited or narrow, or to make a grove in a larger area. Only occasionally will these trees develop broader crowns, although obviously the degree of 'tightness' of the crown will vary between individual species or cultivar. Species of *Chamaecyparis, Cupressus, Thuja, Calocedrus* and a few of the taller-growing *Juniperus* in the cypress family and *Sequoiadendron* in the Swamp cypress or Redwood family will make specimen trees with neat upright appearances.

More variety is offered by the needle-leaved conifers. The appearance of these species differs from that produced by the scale-leaved conifers in two main ways. The foliage is much longer, ranging from 1.5 cm to 50 cm in some pines and therefore usually gives a more open and softer texture to the crown. Most of the species have the branches, or the main ones, carried in pronounced whorls. This latter trait is more evident in young trees and in those with a quicker growth rate; it tends to get blurred as the tree's growth rate slows down with age. The most pronounced whorling of the branches is exhibited by the Monkey puzzle and Silver firs, such as Grand fir. It can be a feature of interest, but is not liked by all.

There is also a greater range available in the spread of the crown. Some Silver firs and spruces have very narrow crowns, particularly Serbian spruce (*Picea omorika*). Pines, yew and the Monkey puzzle have much wider-spreading crowns, although as young plants they may be narrow. Needle-leaved conifers suitable for use as specimen trees include all the members of the pine and yew families, most of the Redwood family and a few species in *Araucaria* and *Podocarpus*. The needle-leaved conifers have much more potential for use as character plants.

As a young tree, *Ginkgo* has a narrow upright habit, similar to larch, although the broad leaves give a quite different appearance. As the tree ages, usually after the first hundred years, a broader crown with much more character develops.

The shape of mature plants of wild species varies quite a lot. As noted above, with *Ginkgo* there is a marked change with age. Some pine species also broaden considerably with maturity, such as Monterey pine (*Pinus radiata*), whilst Serbian spruce (*Picea omorika*) naturally has a very narrow crown. Other plants have features, like the nodding leaders of *Chamaecyparis* and *Tsuga*, which are only displayed by small proportions of the plants, in these examples by the stronger shoots.

Variants of some conifers have been selected in which the crown shape is very different from normal. Some of these are curiosities but others can be useful in garden design.

Narrow-crowned forms exist of several species and older ones are often called 'Fastigiata'. *Pinus sylvestris* 'Fastigiata' is a small-growing, very tight-crowned form of Scots pine, whilst *Juniperus scopulorum* 'Skyrocket' is a similarly shaped clone of the Rocky Mountains juniper. These plants are valuable for making punctuation marks in schemes, or can be used to give formality by introducing a series of columns into the landscape.

The other extreme is offered by cultivars which have an artificially pendulous habit. The main feature of these is that the branches, and in some the leader as well, hang down, rather than grow out and up. Some of the plants make wide-spreading trees as a result, e.g. *Cedrus atlantica* 'Pendula' or *Cupressus macrocarpa* 'Pendula', and can be used to create a broad low feature. Other pendulous selections retain an erect leader but have the lateral branches hanging down. Several spruces do this naturally with the weakest branchlets, such as Brewer spruce (*Picea breweriana*) in which the branches are level but the next and subsequent orders of branching hang vertically down like curtains. *Picea omorika* 'Pendula' is a selection in which the side branches hang down even more than usual for the species, giving a very narrow-crowned plant. Some selections may give inconsistent results; some plants of *Larix kaempferi* 'Pendula' just give more grace to the normal width of crown but others fail to make a leader after grafting and develop as graceful wide-spreading bushes. The pendulous form of Wellingtonia, *Sequoiadendron giganteum* 'Pendulum', is a remarkable plant; it has an erect leader and weeping branches but often does not grow vertically, instead being inclined to snake across a space in a most bizarre fashion.

A third type of crown selection is where the development of lateral buds is inhibited. This is mainly found in some cultivars of Norway spruce (*Picea abies*) and leads to some odd character plants with very open crowns; 'Virgata' is one such clone.

Shelter, Screening and Backcloth Planting

These three functions can be discussed together. Although they are not identical, the factors to consider are similar, and a well-placed shelter planting can also give valuable support as a backcloth to other plants.

Shelter plantings are usually designed to protect the adjoining areas from the effects of wind or frost. The subjects protected may range from other plants to structures such as glasshouses. The protection can take two different forms, either overhead protection, such as given to understorey plants in a woodland setting, or side protection. Although it is possible to grow many plants under the canopy of a thinned conifer wood, deep-rooting and sparse-foliaged broadleaved trees, such as Oak, are more suitable for overhead shelter, whereas conifers are very suitable for providing side shelter.

Protection from frost comes from preventing heat loss from the site by radiation. Radiation frosts occur when the soil surface gives off long wavelength infra-red radiation. If the sky above the ground is clear, there is nothing to intercept this radiation and reflect or radiate it down towards the ground. There is, therefore, a one-way passage of radiation. With an overstorey of trees, the branches will absorb some of the heat radiated from the soil; they will also be radiating themselves and a proportion of the heat they radiate will be returned to the soil. There will still be a loss of heat overnight, but not as great a loss as if there were no overstorey. On cloudy nights, frosts are rare as the clouds reduce the amount of heat lost by radiation. The situation in a glasshouse is similar, as the glass lets in solar radiation, i.e. day light, through the panes but is not so clear to the infra-red light radiated from the soil, which does not pass through.

Most frost damage occurs in late spring or early autumn and it is not the actual temperature which causes most of the damage. When soft plant tissues, such as expanding buds or new growth, are subjected to below freezing temperatures, water comes out of the cells and freezes between them. Only if the frost is very severe do the actual cell contents freeze. Most of the damage occurs not from the freezing but from the sudden thawing of the frozen water. Damage is, therefore, more severe on plants exposed to the east and south-east, where early morning sun quickly warms up the tissues. Winter cold damage is different, and relates to the absolute temperature the plant can tolerate. In the autumn, plants change their cell contents so that they can withstand the winter cold.

Side shelter gives some protection against radiation frosts and can give further protection, if on the right side, against too quick a thawing of the plant tissues.

Wind causes damage in several ways. The most obvious is physical damage, either by the abrasion of parts rubbing against each other or by breakage of limbs. Fruit orchards are often surrounded by windbreaks to give protection to the petals at flowering time. However, except for this specialised crop, breakage is not the most devastating form of damage, although occasionally very serious in its impact.

The most damaging impact of wind is in its ability to dry the plant foliage. If this is coupled with below freezing temperatures, the effect is very much more pronounced — washing will dry more quickly on a windy day, and the best instant coffees are freeze dried. The damage is caused by the wind removing moisture from the leaves and shoots; to prevent wilting, this causes the plant either to have to replace the water with further water from the soil or to cut down on the rate of loss. The breathing pores or *stomata* in the leaves are the main surface through which water is lost. Their prime function, however, is to allow the exchange of gases with the air, particularly to let carbon dioxide (which is an essential ingredient in photosynthesis) enter the leaf. If the tree has to shut the *stomata* to reduce water loss, photosynthesis is curtailed and growth reduced. Even if the *stomata* are not closed, replacing the water lost probably requires energy and therefore reduces that which is available for growth.

Providing suitable shelter can be beneficial to both amenity and culinary plants. With some shrubs or trees, e.g. *Catalpa bignonioides* 'Aurea' which has large fragile leaves, it can make growing them possible; with vegetable crops in windy situations, increases in yield following the provision of shelter can range from no change at all for peas to 20 per cent or more for potatoes.

The ideal shelter is not provided by a solid barrier such as a wall. The wind velocity may be substantially reduced immediately beside the wall but the wind is only deflected. It will swirl back on itself at a distance of around eight times the height of the barrier, creating an area of turbulence between four and eight times the height of the

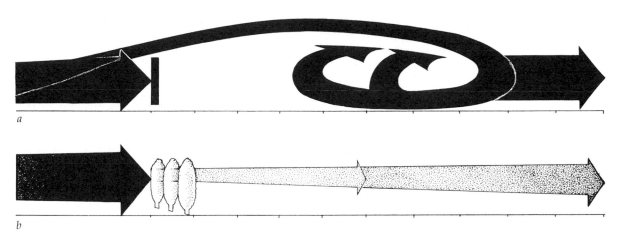

Figure 3.1 *Effect of Solid and Permeable Shelterbelts on Wind Speed.*
a Solid barrier causes back eddies and shelter of limited duration.
b Permeable shelter reduces wind speed for up to 20 × shelter height downwind of shelter and a shorter distance upwind.

barrier on the downwind side; in some circumstances, the vortex created may reach back to the barrier and can even give an *increased* wind speed.

The ideal shelter allows a proportion of the wind to pass through it. This gives a steady airflow and as it is without turbulence, the effect lasts for much longer. The best proportion is for the windbreak to have a permeability of 50 per cent, i.e. let around half the air through. With such a windbreak, the wind will be reduced to 35 per cent of its full force at five times the height, rising to only 75 per cent at ten times and even at 20 times the height of the barrier distance will only have returned to 90 per cent of its original force. Measurable reductions in wind velocity will occur for shorter distances on the upwind side.

The plants chosen to make a windbreak should not make too dense a belt. The commonly planted cypresses, particularly Leyland, are rather too dense, although they will be effective for short distances. Western red cedar (*Thuja plicata*, but not the clone 'Fastigiata') and the Lawson cypress clone 'Intertexta' have more open foliage and will be nearer the ideal 50 per cent porosity. Seedling Lawson cypresses are often suitable as they are not as dense as most of the selected forms, and add a degree of variability for those who do not like too formal a screen. Yew and various species of pine and spruce can make effective shelters. Spruces in particular tend to be very open at the top, so that the uppermost 3m or so may not contribute significantly to the shelter. Some pines, such as Monterey pine (*Pinus radiata*), can be very dense, particularly when young. Larch (*Larix* spp.) have

just about the right foliage density when in leaf but although the habit is fairly twiggy, they will present rather too thin a profile during the winter period from late November until early April for an optimum shelter. They may, however, be very suitable if the shelter is only required during the summer months, such as for the *Catalpa bignonioides* 'Aurea' mentioned above. Alternatively, they can be used to increase the porosity of a shelter composed of denser species; if this is tried, care must be taken to use species which will mix and avoid a formal arrangement, e.g. alternation of species.

Screening is similar to providing shelter, except that the objective is to shut out some intrusion, be it the neighbours or an electricity pylon. Plants are most effective at shutting out a visual intrusion, but can also be used to trap dust and debris, largely by acting as shelter. They are not particularly successful at reducing the number of decibels heard, but they can reduce the number perceived as heard, as 'out of sight is out of mind'.

Because screening is largely a matter of creating the right visual environment, thought needs to be put into deciding what form of screen is necessary. Too often, large forest-style trees are used to screen an object for which a screen need only be 3m or 4.5m high. If the objective is to screen your lounge window from one of your neighbour's downstairs windows, the screen only needs to be taller than 3m if you are on sloping ground; even for upstairs to upstairs windows, it is unlikely to need to be as much as 6m. Planting trees which will naturally grow to 20m in 25 years, e.g.

Leyland cypress, will result in one of two things: either they will cause unnecessary shading, or frequent, time-consuming and expensive pruning will be needed. Another disadvantage of many taller-growing trees is that they tend to lose the lower branches, and in the circumstances where only a low screen is needed actually to provide no screen at all. Pines and spruces are the worst here, at least the cypresses usually remain clothed to the ground, even when overgrown.

Low screens are probably better achieved using broadleaved and even evergreen shrubs, rather than conifers. Few conifers will grow fast enough to be suitable to plant to block out an unsightly view without continuing to grow too tall. However, species which will fit into this situation include some of the true cypresses, such as Smooth cypress (*Cupressus glabra*), which normally makes a tree 6-9 m tall.

Conifers are very suitable where a tall screen is needed. Here their ability to grow fast on a wide range of sites can be very useful. Beware, however, with any screen of creating an eyesore almost as unsightly as the object to be screened.

A screen does not need to be either evergreen or solid to achieve its purpose. If the planting is used to draw the eye away from the screened item, it will be far more attractive than a planting which presents a solid phalanx of dismal green. Any planting to hide a large object, e.g. a factory building, must not simply follow the outline of the building, but must soften the edges. To be effective, it must be attractive to look at in its own right.

Deciduous trees have their place in many screens. They will introduce an element of variation, coming into leaf at different times from the evergreen species; equally in most landscapes a proportion of evergreen trees are needed to give a well-rounded appearance. The only deciduous conifers which are at all likely to be used in screen plantings are the larches, although Dawn redwood (*Metasequoia glyptostroboides*) and Swamp cypress (*Taxodium distichum*) could be useful on especially wet sites.

The purpose in backcloth planting is to display a plant, or other item, such as a statue, to best effect. Many attractive garden plants need either to be seen from above or to be seen against a dark background; if placed against a bright sky they may appear dark or not be seen.

The first essential is to know what you are intending to display, and when. Just because a single plant will be enhanced by having a sombre background in, say, June, does not mean that the background planting has to be dull at all times of the year. If just helps if it is then. The golden form of Scots pine, *Pinus sylvestris* 'Aurea', only turns gold from December till early April, for the rest of the year it is a fairly normal Scots pine colour and would set off many summer flowers or foliages; it would not do, though, for winter-flowering items.

Generally, for backcloth planting, various greens are best. Normally, avoid plants with strong colours to their foliage, such as bright blues or golds. However, there are, as always, exceptions. For example, purple foliage can be very effectively shown against gold or yellow foliage, such as a purple Japanese maple or even Pissard's plum set against the golden foliage of *Cupressus macrocarpa* 'Goldcrest'.

Shelter, screening and backcloth belts are like any other plantings in that the trees used will compete with the other plants in the general area for soil moisture and nutrients. Some species are more demanding than others; for instance, the larches generally take more out of the soil than would be expected from the light canopy they have. Cypresses also tend to be demanding of moisture and nutrients, whereas Silver firs are often deeper rooting by nature and not so competitive, although some cast a denser shade. Thought must be given to the effect of moisture and nutrient competition on the surrounding plants. If the shelter or screen is the most important element, choose species which will tolerate the conditions, but if the backcloth is to set off a chosen plant, care should be exercised in choosing one, or so placing it, so that it does not interfere with the item it is intended to show off.

When establishing a shelter or screening belt, the spacing of the plants needs to be suitable. If the intention is to form a screen very quickly, a closer spacing, down to 45-60 cm is suitable. Such a spacing will, however, give a very dense screen which will be less efficient as a windbreak, unless it is thinned at an early stage. It will not produce a satisfactory tall screen. If a windbreak is the objective, wider spacing of the initial planting, up to 1.8-2.4 m will produce a better long-term belt but may look very sparse for a few years. Such spacings are very good where tall or large-scale belts are desired, or where there is space for two or more staggered rows to be planted. In the garden setting, though, something closer, around 1 m is usually better.

When a close-planted belt grows together, it is worth thinning out the number of trees, so that the remaining ones can grow stronger, rather than let them all fight it out. Instead of removing every alternate tree, and thereby creating a gap, the trees to be removed can be clipped to let the adjoining trees grow over them from the sides.

Foliage Effect

Conifers are very useful for the varied foliage effects they have to offer. These range from different hues of green, grey or blue to exotic golds or silvers. The deciduous species add a further dimension, whilst some 'evergreen' species also change colour in the winter. These different colours will be discussed with reference to their garden uses.

The purpose of different colours of foliage in the garden is to create interest and variety. This will not be achieved if a hotchpotch of different colours and textures of foliage are indiscriminately mingled together. Most plants are green and this colour is the most restful to the eye. Too much green, however, tires, even if the threshold is higher than for other colours.

Green foliage, however, is needed, if only to make the contrast with other coloured foliages. It is the colour most suitable for mass uses, such as for shelter or backcloth planting. Even green foliage, though, comes in many different shades.

The same foliage may appear to alter considerably depending upon from where it is viewed. The needles of Monterey pine (*Pinus radiata*) are very grassy green when seen close-to, but in a tree on the skyline they appear dark, almost black.

The time of year also alters the perception of the colour. Evergreen conifers which appear bright and green in winter when all the surrounding deciduous trees are bare suddenly seem to become drab with the first flush of spring, when the deciduous trees deck themselves with vivid new leaves; many of these 'drab' trees, however, will in turn become brighter in late spring or early summer when they make their new growth, at a time when the leaves of the broadleaved species have themselves turned duller. Come autumn, they again provide a contrast to set off the autumnal colours. Different types of light alter the perception of a colour; many plants look very different between bright sunlight and when a thunderstorm is imminent.

The brightest greens are provided by the new foliage. Larches are very good as early harbingers of spring, when the new leaves open before those of many other trees. Some of the larch species from continental climates, such as *Larix gmelini*, may be in leaf in January in Britain, although severe frosts can damage the plants. Bright green mature foliage is distributed amongst several groups of conifers: Wilson spruce (*Picea wilsonii*) is a small spruce which has grassy green needles; Incense cedar (*Calocedrus decurrens*) combines fresh foliage with a narrow upright habit; and the Lawson cypress clone 'Erecta' (*Chamaecyparis lawsoniana* 'Erecta') is a very bright, although darker, green.

Darker greens are shown by species of Yew (*Taxus*), many Podocarps (Podocarpaceae) and a host of other species.

The dullest colours are often the grey-greens. As attractive foliages, they are the also-rans, needing some aspect of habit or texture to make them desirable; as contrasts they can be useful. Ponderosa pine (*Pinus ponderosa*) has a foliage colour which would be dismally dull if the needles weren't so long and bold. The commonly grown clone of Leyland cypress (× *Cupressocyparis leylandii* 'Haggerston Grey') also belongs here, without the redeeming features! Good grey foliage is rare, being offered by only a few species and usually as a dwarf. As a taller tree, some plants of White fir (*Abies concolor*) can make desirable greys.

Blue foliage is one of the more unique colours offered by conifers and unmatched by other plants, except for just a few *Rhododendron* species. The blue coloration comes from the waxy layer which covers the leaves. Many species develop this in response to an alpine habitat, probably as a protection against high levels of ultra-violet radiation. Some species, though, may show considerable variation between plants growing side by side. In north-east Mexico, adjacent plants of Vejar fir (*Abies vejari*) may be grey-green or distinctly blue.

Most of the blues grown in gardens are selections from within naturally-occurring blue populations. They are essentially plants to be used as specimen trees, or to make a bold feature and, like any strong or unusual colour, should not be used too often.

The best blues are found either in several of the cypresses or in some members of the pine family. The most sought after blues are provided by various selections of the Colorado blue spruce (*Picea pungens glauca*), such as 'Kosteri' or

'Hoopsii'. Growing at their best, these are fine plants, although the contrast between such a strong blue and the brown of older shoots can be off-putting in older trees. Some plants of White fir (*Abies concolor*), such as 'Candicans' and 'Violacea', can be equally blue but not have such as strong and discordant contrast with the older foliage and twigs. Several pines exhibit blue foliage, especially the Blue pine (*Pinus wallichiana*) and some forms of the Japanese white pine (*P. parviflora*).

The blue foliage of many cypresses can be very appealing after rain, especially when the sun catches the drops of moisture hanging on the branches; it seems to add an extra dimension, particularly in a wet summer. The best blue of the cypress type is *Chamaecyparis lawsoniana* 'Pembury Blue', although 'Naylors Blue', a cultivar of Leyland cypress, is most impressive after rain.

Gold foliage is another colour conifers do very well. Most gold plants are variegated but many conifer golds are 'self' colours, i.e. all the foliage is the same colour. Again, most gold foliage is offered by cypresses, but many other species also have cultivars or forms with gold needles, particularly the yews and some members of the pine family.

Gold foliage is not found in wild populations, although the genes for it are obviously well distributed, and all gold-leafed conifers are garden selections of the occasional golden plant. Many of the older ones have the cultivar name 'Aurea' or 'Aureus'.

Golden plants are very much a garden feature; they are rarely at all suited to use in more natural environments. In the garden, they are especially good as specimen trees, to brighten up a view or vista, to complete a contrast, or as the 'permanent' feature in a shrub bed.

As such a bright and strong colour, the over-use of golden foliage plants is to be avoided. They may look excellent as single specimens, in larger settings a group of three or five may be appropriate, but unless the scale of planting is vast, more will quickly tire. This is especially true of screening where a line of most gold conifers will need its own amenity planting to mitigate the visual effect. Often, as the plants are selected on the base of their colour, the habit and other features of the plant are not of the first order. Few of the gold foliage plants available would be considered as really first rate garden plants if it were not for the colour of the foliage, which is not to deny their value.

Generally, different golds do not mix well. The several plants will all have slightly varying degrees of yellow and green in their appearance; put together, these lose the element of surprise which the colour offers.

The best golden cypress is *Chamaecyparis obtusa* 'Crippsii', a medium-growing form of Hinoki cypress. This keeps the foliage a good colour, even in some shade, where many other cypresses become somewhat greener. Good Lawson cypress cultivars include 'Lane' and 'Stewartii', although with both the inner foliage may only be a slightly brighter yellow-green than normal. Two cultivars of Leyland cypress have come to prominence recently: 'Castlewellan', which has rather dismal yellow-green foliage and a coarse appearance, and 'Robinson's Gold', which looks from young specimens to be a much more attractive plant. *Juniperus chinensis* 'Aurea' is an excellent small tree with a conical habit, enlivened in the autumn when it carries masses of yellow male cones.

Yellow foliage is offered by a few cultivars. As a colour it lies between green and gold, and many of the less intense golds verge on being yellow, especially in their shaded foliage. Some of the yellow foliage plants, though, have a more reddish or bronzy hue. The main use of yellow foliages is to enliven a dull corner.

Variegated foliage is not very common, except in some of the cultivars of Yew and in *Thuja plicata* 'Zebrina'. Usually, the two colours are green and a form of yellow or gold, although cultivars exist where white or cream colour patches of foliage occur on a normal background. As a colour variant, variegated foliage does not often work very well in conifers. Usually, the contrasts between the two different foliages are not that appealing when seen close-to. At a distance, due to the small size of most conifer leaves, the two colours merge into one, which is rarely an improvement on what can be obtained with some of the better self-coloured cultivars. An exception to this is in the Dragon Eye cultivars of two Japanese pines, *Pinus densiflora* 'Occulus-Draconis' and *P. thunbergii* 'Occulus-Draconis'. Both of these have yellow bands running across the needles and can look interesting on close examination.

Dual-coloured foliages are very different from variegated ones and are much more attractive. In these the leaves have distinct areas which are differently coloured from the rest of the leaves. These areas are usually associated with the control of water loss from the stomata and the second colour comes from the thick layer of wax which covers the bands of stomata. The wax is similar to the overall glaucous coating on blue conifers but in this group of plants is more restricted in its distribution. Unlike variegated or gold foliage, dual foliage is an entirely natural phenomenon and serves a useful function for the plant.

In most conifers the bands of stomata are concentrated on the sheltered undersides of the needles, where desiccating winds and heating by sunlight are less of a problem. The upper surface, which is exposed to the light, is a normal green, or occasionally blue, colour. This surface is where the cells carrying out photosynthesis are concentrated and is protected by a thick protective layer or cuticle. The manufacture by the plant of the wax to protect the stomata must require quite a lot of energy, and one reason why the stomata are concentrated in most species on the underside of the needle may be to reduce the amount of protective wax needed, as well as restrict water loss. By contrast, species like Subalpine fir (*Abies lasiocarpa*) which come from exposed and alpine areas, where all surfaces may need protecting, often have stomatal bands on both the upper and lower leaf surfaces.

In species with dual-coloured foliages, the stomata are usually silver-coloured, with a thick layer of glaucous wax. Many species have this feature but in most the silver areas are only visible when closely inspected, e.g. in Lawson cypress. The feature becomes of garden value when the silvery effect covers sufficient of the leaves to be seen at a distance.

Silver firs, or *Abies* species, are so called because many of them are vividly silver on the undersides of the foliage sprays. Undoubtedly the best are some of the Asiatic species, particularly Forrest fir (*A. forrestii*) and Korean fir (*A. koreana*). In these species, the upper foliage is a medium green and does not carry any stomata. The lower surface, however, has two broad bands of stomata which are copiously protected by wax. Not all Silver firs are good for this feature. Several other members of the pine family, such as some of the spruces, e.g. *Picea brachytyla*, and Western hemlock (*Tsuga heterophylla*), share the same character. A few rare members of the Yew family also exhibit this feature.

Some pines have dual-tone foliage. Basically, the situation is similar, but because the needles are much longer than in the Silver firs, and less rigid, the effect is different. In these species, which are all species of soft pines (see page 159), the stomata are restricted to the inner two sides of the triangular needles, which are thus silvery, whilst the more exposed surface is green or bluish. Examples are selected forms of the Japanese white pine (*Pinus parviflora*) and good plants of Blue pine (*P. wallichiana*) and Armand pine (*P. armandii*) show this.

Dual foliage conifers can be particularly attractive when the wind blows the foliage about, intermittently displaying the attractive undersides. They are also useful where the foliage will be displayed above the head of the viewer, such as above paths. In many, the new foliage will be more brightly coloured.

The new foliage of many conifers can be an attractive feature. As mentioned above, it is often more brilliantly coloured, whether green, blue or silver, but some species have produced individuals in which the expanding shoots bear very distinctly coloured leaves. The value of these plants is in creating an extra, often short-term, attraction, as the foliage will mature to more staid colours. Because the effect is limited in its duration, siting does not have to be so strictly thought out.

The plants displaying this foliage are mostly cultivars of spruce. The best one is a form of Oriental spruce, *Picea orientalis* 'Aurea', which was awarded a First Class Certificate by the Royal Horticultural Society as long ago as 1887. In this plant, the new foliage is an attractive golden green for around six weeks in June, after which it is scarcely to be distinguished from any other Oriental spruce. A number of cultivars of Norway spruce (*P. abies*) exist in which the new foliage is reddish purple (almost the nearest a conifer gets to purple foliage), such as 'Rubra Spicata'. Some forms of Eastern hemlock (*Tsuga canadensis*), such as the cultivar 'Dwarf White Tip', have very pale new foliage.

Autumn and winter colour is provided by several conifers. The five deciduous genera all have good autumn foliages. Ginkgo leaves turn a particularly good gold colour, although not as rich a colour as that offered by the rare Golden larch (*Pseudolarix amabilis*). True larches (*Larix* spp.) are also good for yellow-gold colours. Dawn redwood (*Metasequoia glyptostroboides*) turns a reasonable russet colour whilst Swamp cypress (*Taxodium distichum*) turns a remarkable brick red, somewhat later than almost everything else in the second half of November.

Unusual winter colour, though, is not only

offered by the deciduous species or those with odd or variegated foliage. A number of plants actually change the colour of the leaves during the winter. Two of the best are the golden form of Scots pine (*Pinus sylvestris* 'Aurea'), which only assumes a bright golden foliage with the onset of cold weather in December and turns back to a normal Scots pine blue-green in April, and the cultivar 'Elegans' of Japanese cedar (*Cryptomeria japonica*), which turns a bronze colour over the winter period. The setting for these plants is where the changed foliage will most brighten the winter scene, such as when viewed from the kitchen window.

Bark, Flower and Fruit

All conifers, like all other plants, have bark, flowers and produce fruits. However, not all give desirable or useful features for the garden.

Bark

The bark of many conifers is an attractive feature but usually only becomes so as the plant matures. In the larches, though, the one-year twigs are brightly coloured and can make a vivid display when seen *en masse*. Apart from this special group of plants, the features provided by bark will be in either the colour or the texture of the mature bark.

Distinct colours can be used to draw the eye towards a tree or a vista. However, colour is only going to be a draw either with the largest-growing species, such as Redwoods, where the rich reddish brown bark on a stout bole can act as a magnet, or with exotically coloured barks as shown by the Lacebark pine (*Pinus bungeana*) or several Pinyon pines, where the olive green bark flakes to reveal creamy white patches. Another bark which may create a feature by its colour is the orange bark of the upper crown on a Scots pine.

The beauty of most barks, though, is not so much in the coloration as in the texture. This is a feature which cannot usually be enjoyed at a distance. Such barks need to be located where they can be seen and felt, such as beside a path or sitting area.

Many conifer barks are deeply fissured and ridged. These include most pine species, and trees like the Redwoods. Some have stringy fibrous ones, like Japanese cedar (*Cryptomeria japonica*). Other barks are composed of small plates which crack into squares or oblongs, such as Greek fir (*Abies cephalonica*) or Cedar of Lebanon (*Cedrus libani*). Many species have smooth barks when young but this character is retained in few older trees. Smooth cypress (*Cupressus glabra*) has a very smooth bark, as does Yew, although in Yew as the bole is fluted it often does not appear quite so smooth. In a choice few conifers the bark is flaky, exfoliating in small thin scales like a birch. Best of these is the very rare Flaky fir (*Abies squamata*) although on a smaller scale some of the junipers, such as *Juniperus squamata*, share this feature. Monkey puzzle (*Araucaria araucana*) has grey bark, wrinkled like an elephant's hide.

Most barks are hard to the touch but some of the Redwood family have much softer barks. Coastal redwood (*Sequoia sempervirens*) has the softest and thickest bark of any species, with Wellingtonia (*Sequoiadendron giganteum*) not much harder. In both of these trees the bark will absorb a punch without hurting the hand. In nature, the role of these barks is to protect the trees against forest fires. Because these barks are soft, they can be rubbed away by too much attention, leading to the death of the tree.

Be cautious if planning to remove lower branches so that the bark can be more clearly seen. The beauty of many conifers is enhanced by their being clothed with foliage to the ground and the over-zealous removal of lower branches can detract from this.

Flowers

Conifer flowers are either male (pollen bearing) or female (ovule bearing), as discussed in Chapter 2. The two types of flower may be carried on separate trees, although more usually they are found in different parts of the same tree.

The male flowers are much the more numerous, and therefore capable of making more of a display. They are also produced more freely on the lower and weaker branches, thereby making them more easily seen from the ground. The display can range from the massed erect yellow 'cones' produced by the true Cedars (*Cedrus*) in the autumn (see if you can find a female flower on a cedar!), to the small brick red ones found on Lawson cypress in April. Pines cluster the male cones at the base of the new shoots, whereas other species develop them from side buds on last year's branchlets or at the ends of shoots. The pollen is usually yellow and can make its own display. After the male cones have shed their pollen they usually turn brown and soon drop off.

Most male cones are small, those of cypresses

being much less than 6 mm whilst cedars and other members of the pine family have cones up to 5 or 7.5 cm long. The most remarkable male cones are provided by the Monkey puzzle. This has male cones larger than the mature female cones of all but a few conifers, up to 15 cm long, and carried at the ends of the branches of male trees in clusters of up to half a dozen; they also persist for up to a year.

Female flowers are often only borne on the uppermost branches, making them largely invisible from the ground. Also, as they are wind pollinated, they do not need to attract attention. The most insignificant ones belong to the cypress family but they are interesting in detail and worthy of study, as the naked ovules can be seen between the cone scales.

Only two genera of conifers have species with female flowers which can be considered beautiful in the flamboyant sense of the word. These are some of the Silver firs and spruces. In these two groups of plants, the female flowers are large enough to be seen as separate entities. The best spruce is Likiang spruce (*Picea likiangensis*), which has bright reddish purple flowers 7.5 cm long, although several other species are almost as strongly coloured, albeit with smaller flowers. In the Silver firs, the most colourful ones belong to a group of species from the Sino-Himalayas which includes Forrest fir (*Abies forrestii*), Delavay fir (*A. delavayi*) and the Himalayan fir (*A. spectabilis*). In these the flowers are violet-purple candles up to 10 cm long.

Fruit

More conifers are attractive in fruit. The Sino-Himalayan firs retain the violet-purple colour for several months as the cones ripen, whilst Likiang spruce assumes a darker purple for its cones. Some pine species have strongly coloured ones; in Ponderosa pine (*Pinus ponderosa*) they can be shiny dark purplish brown, whilst in the Bosnian pine (*P. leucodermis*) they are a rich cobalt blue. Most conifers, though, have mature cones of various hues of brown, which can be attractive *en masse*.

The other way mature cones can create a visual display is by their size or shape. Species in this grouping are mainly pines. Coulter pine (*P. coulteri*), also called 'Bigcone pine', has the heaviest cones of any species, weighing up to 2.2 kg; these are bright brown and armed with vicious spines. Some of the soft pines have larger, though lighter cones. In Sugar pine (*P. lambertiana*) they

may be 45 cm long, and only slightly shorter in the Mexican white pine (*P. ayacahuite*).

Flower and fruit characters should be sited where they can be seen. The ideal location for the showy cones of Silver firs is where they can be viewed from above or from the side. If only looked at from below, they are inevitably lost against the sky and behind the foliage. The cones of pines and spruces are carried at the ends of the branches and are more visible from below, especially the larger ones. However, only the largest cones of some species of soft pine will look good silhouetted against a bright sky. Beyond this, it is a case of appreciating that they are there, and consequently will add another dimension to the display you are planning to create.

Habitats for Wildlife

Conifers provide very useful habitats for wildlife in the garden, as shelter, as a source of food and as lookout points.

Probably the most important in urban situations is in providing shelter for birds and other wild animals. In Britain there is a dearth of native evergreen plants and, apart from ivy, introduced conifers are often the only source of protection for birds in the winter and for nesting sites during the early part of the season. The presence of sufficient suitable shelter can assist the overwintering of songbirds, and also hide their early nests from prying eyes. The shelter element is not confined to the foliage. If you look at the trunk of a Wellingtonia you will often see a number of small neat cavities hollowed out of the soft bark. These are made by Tree Creepers seeking shelter during cold nights. The general effects of shelter offered by trees and woods, as discussed above, is useful to many wild animals.

Species which provide the best winter shelter for birds are the cypresses, with their dense foliage carried on many twiggy branches. In other species the foliage is not so dense and, therefore, gives a lower degree of protection. For Tree Creepers, the soft-barked Redwoods, either Wellingtonia or Coastal Redwood, are best, although other species in the Redwood family may be used.

Food is provided in two ways: as food which can be eaten directly off the tree, and in supporting smaller animals which in turn can be eaten.

Conifers are eaten by a wide range of organisms, from humble fungi which may digest or 'decay' the timber to larger herbivores such as deer, which will eat the foliage. Between these two extremes are a large number of insects, from aphids to sawflies and moths, which feed on the needles, or some feed inside the needles. Species of bark beetle live out their early stages as grubs under the bark. It is sometimes suggested that conifers are not good for wildlife but in Britain Scots pine has over 50 species of invertebrate animals associated with it and spruces over 40. Although these figures do not compare with the mammoth 300 or so for English oak (*Quercus robur*), they are very respectable when compared to most British broadleaved trees.

Some conifers provide special sources of food. The seeds of many species are eaten by a wide range of birds and small mammals. Squirrels in particular eat the seeds by gnawing away at the cone scales. The red fleshy aril around the Yew's berry is reported as a choice food of Badgers. In a few species the seeds are large enough to be an item of human food. The Romans imported seeds of the Mediterranean Stone pine (*Pinus pinea*) to Britain, whilst the seeds of other pines are eaten by people in Mexico and South-west USA and in parts of Asia and are used in confectionery. The Monkey puzzle (*Araucaria araucana*) has large very choice seeds which are delightful raw or roasted.

Providing a home for small organisms inevitably makes food for others higher up the food chain. Many birds for instance eat the aphids and other insects, whilst Woodpeckers will extricate grubs from under the bark. Raptors and mammals will feed on the birds, or their eggs, and so on up the food chain. This recycling of food does not always involve predations. Particularly in spruces, sap-sucking aphids excrete a sugary solution called 'honey-dew' which is collected by bees and turned into honey.

The final way in which conifers are beneficial for wildlife is in providing tall trees which can be used as either lookout points, for raptors, or for display purposes for songbirds.

Conifers for Difficult Sites

Most plants will grow very nicely thank you on good soils but often the need is for effective plants to use in the less desirable situations. Not all conifers will grow on these sites but within the group as a whole there is a sizeable number of species which tolerate or thrive on these problem sites.

Dry Sandy Sites

The main constraint on plant growth on these soils is the availability of moisture during the growing season, although on many the soil is also extremely acid. Nutrients are almost always in short supply on these soils as any dissolved chemicals are soon washed out by periodic heavy rainfall. The plants which thrive here need to be capable either of rooting very deeply, or of controlling moisture use. The two groups of plants which on a world-wide scale flourish on these sites are conifers and oaks. In the conifers, it is cypresses and pines which provide the bulk of the species, although other genera in these two families contain useful species.

Pines are undoubtedly the best conifers for these soils. In the wild they are very successful in regions with dry summer climates. The many pine species in Mexico and south-east USA are found in such climates and pines are also characteristic of the Mediterranean basin. They can grow fast on low nutrient levels, can root extensively and have tough needles designed to restrict moisture loss.

Virtually all species of pine are suited to these sites and the genus, therefore, gives the greatest opportunity to select plants for different uses, whether the requirement is for large trees or for smaller more shrubby ones like Pinyons (e.g. *Pinus edulis*) or the Lacebark pine (*P. bungeana*).

Cypresses of the genus *Cupressus* are also very tolerant of drought conditions. The Saharan cypress (*Cupressus dupreziana*) grows in a part of Algeria where rainfall is minimal; several other species are native to the dry south-west of the USA. The range of plant types available from the cypresses is less extensive than in the pines but they include a few choice small trees as well as useful hedging plants.

Junipers are also drought-tolerant and provide a number of plants of smaller size than found in either the pines or the cypresses. They are useful for offering ground cover and small bush forms, as discussed in Chapter 4 on dwarf conifers, but do include a few arborescent species from very dry regions. Some other genera in the cypress family, such as *Tetraclinis*, are restricted in the wild to dry conditions but most are too tender for widespread use in temperate parts of the world.

In the pine family, Western hemlock (*Tsuga heterophylla*), some species of spruce, particularly Likiang spruce (*Picea likiangensis*) and its close allies, and a small number of Silver firs, e.g. White fir (*Abies concolor*) and Vejar fir (*A. vejari*), do very well on these sites. Likiang spruce will naturally make a smaller tree than normal on such soils but will provide a much better display of flowers and fruits from an earlier age. The true cedars (*Cedrus*) are also adapted to dry sites, although preferring a higher nutrient supply than is often available on many sandy ones.

Clay and Waterlogged Soils

These two are not the same, although many characteristics are similar. Both soil types are poorly drained with low levels of oxygen available to the roots. However, they usually have adequate supplies of nutrients, due in clay soils to the structure of the soil particles and in waterlogged ones from the inflowing of water containing dissolved salts.

The low level of oxygen available to the roots is the main constraint to plant growth on both soil types. In normal soils, the roots obtain the oxygen essential to life and growth from the air present in the soil but to thrive in conditions where there is no air in the soil, or where such air as there is contains no oxygen, the trees need to be able to supply the oxygen by some other means. In Lodgepole pine (*Pinus contorta*), which can tolerate waterlogged soils to a certain extent, the new roots have been found to grow with air spaces running through them. How common this phenomenon is is not known, although it is likely that many species which grow in these soils have a similar mechanism. A unique approach is adopted by the Swamp cypress (*Taxodium distichum*) which produces special aerial roots, variously known as 'pneumatophores' or 'knees' when growing on waterlogged or swampy sites. These structures are used for 'breathing' in the widest sense, as they may be involved in venting harmful gases rather than simply in absorbing oxygen. In practice, poorly aerated soils have an excess of harmful chemicals, largely because there is not the oxygen to allow bacteria present in the soil to break them down.

One other problem for many trees on these sites is drought. As the soil dries out during the summer the lower levels become aerated and available for rooting but unless the tree's roots can grow down fast enough to follow the water table, they may quickly exhaust the water held in the upper soil horizons. During the winter when rain raises the level of the water table, the lower roots may be killed, leaving the tree with an inadequate surface root system. Some species, such as several spruces, are capable of growing well with a shallow plate-like root system but the most appropriate species for these soils are ones which can root deeply despite the conditions.

Most conifers are capable of growing on clay soils, although trees will take longer to get established. Their establishment can be speeded-up by planting the young tree on a small mound *and* keeping an area around the plant 3m or more free from all competing vegetation.

Some of the Silver firs, such as European silver fir (*Abies alba*), and Lawson cypress and other species of *Chamaecyparis* will flourish in these conditions once established, appreciating the generally high nutrient status. Amongst the pines, Coulter pine (*Pinus coulteri*) and Ponderosa pine (*P. ponderosa*) both do very well. Swamp cypress and Dawn redwood also thrive.

On really waterlogged sites the choice is more restricted. The deciduous conifers do disproportionately well. Swamp cypress and more especially the rare Chinese swamp cypress (*Glyptostrobus pensilis*) will both grow in water permanently several centimetres deep. In fact, it is the only reliable way to grow the Chinese swamp cypress, as on drier sites it is distinctly tender. Dawn redwood will thrive in very wet conditions and the Olga Bay larch (*Larix gmelini olgensis*) occurs in bogs in the wild.

With evergreen species the choice is more limited. Lodgepole pine will tolerate wetter conditions better than many other species but probably the best two are Western red cedar (*Thuja plicata*), which will grow more or less anywhere!, and White cedar (*Chamaecyparis thyoides*). Growth will be slower and the time taken to establish longer than on more favourable sites for these evergreen species.

Chalk and Other Very Alkaline Soils

These soils present special problems for many plants because of the way in which the preponderance of calcium ions in the soil affects the uptake of other nutrients, such as iron and because the high pH level restricts the chemical availability of most nutrients. The amount of calcium absorbed by the roots is toxic to many plants and Rhododendrons cannot be grown on most of these soils for that reason.

Very often there is a small depth of less alkaline, or even acidic, soil above the chalk or limestone bedrock. Many species can grow for a number of years on this, either until the roots reach the bedrock, or until the tree exhausts or locks up all the available nutrients; but when this stage is reached the trees will turn yellow or chlorotic and begin to fail. A number of species, though, can fully tolerate these conditions, without becoming chlorotic.

Another factor which affects the survival of plants on alkaline soils is the actual elements making the alkalinity. Magnesium ions are generally more benign than calcium ones. Limestone has a chemical structure which makes it less severe to most plants than chalk.

The cypress family is generally well adapted to these soils and all species seem to thrive on them. Yew and other species in its family are also well suited, chalk downland being one of the main places where Yew woods occur naturally in Britain.

In the pine family, the situation is more varied. Some species in each major genus thrive on these soils but others may become chlorotic after a few years.

Of the pines, Scots (*Pinus sylvestris*) and Corsican (*P. nigra laricio*) pines may survive in the long term but can often be seen to fail after 20 or so years. Species which should do well are ones which are found on limestone in the wild, like the Bosnian pine (*P. leucodermis*) and several of the pines from northern Mexico and south-west USA. Most of the soft pines also grow well, at least on limestone.

In the spruces, Serbian spruce (*Picea omorika*) grows on more or less any soil, at a surprisingly steady rate whatever the nutrient status, and Likiang spruce is also good. Dragon (*P. asperata*) and Morinda (*P. smithiana*) spruces also grow well in some situations on these soils. In the wild in Japan *P. glehnii* occurs on the very alkaline and more restrictive serpentine rocks.

In the firs, most species do not like chalk soils but a few such as Spanish or Hedgehog fir (*Abies pinsapo*) and some other Mediterranean species, can be relied on. Forrest (*A. forrestii*) and Vejar (*A. vejari*) firs are also found on limestone sites in the wild and should do well; Forrest fir, though, may require more moisture than the others.

All the species of true cedar (*Cedrus*) thrive on these sites.

Seaside Planting

The difficulties in planting near the sea are largely two-fold, consisting of damage by salt spray and exposure.

Salt spray is damaging due to the toxic effects of sodium ions. Similar damage can occur beside roads where salt is used for de-icing in winter. The salt can cause damage both on absorption through the roots and also by direct scorching of the foliage. Salt spray may be carried several kilometres inland during severe gales.

Exposure is also more severe at coastal sites as there is no sheltering topography or planting on the seaward side to abate the full force of the wind.

The best species for seaside plantings include cypresses of the genus *Cupressus* and some pines. Monterey cypress (*C. macrocarpa*) is very tolerant of coastal conditions and can make a large tree. The clone 'Lutea' is even more tolerant than the parent species. Some of the other American species are equally tolerant and Monterey cypress has passed this character on to its hybrid, Leyland cypress. Also, some junipers are adapted to coastal conditions and Land's End is one of the few natural locations of Common juniper (*Juniperus communis*) in south-west Britain.

In the pine family, suited species are largely restricted to several pines. The best adapted is the Japanese black pine (*Pinus thunbergii*) which grows along the seashore in Japan. Tests on the effects of de-icing salts have shown it to be highly tolerant of common salt in the soil, unlike Weymouth pine (*P. strobus*). The Maritime pine (*P. pinaster*) is also good for coastal sites. In north-west Scotland, Scots pine grows close to the sea. In the Araucariaceae, Monkey puzzle is capable of growing in exposed coastal situations.

A number of other conifers would probably tolerate these conditions but may not have been tried sufficiently often. Who would have expected Bristlecone pine (*P. aristata*), coming from 3,000-4,000m up in inland south-west USA, to flourish in north-east Iceland! Other drought-tolerant species might be expected to survive, as part of the problem for the plant may be lack of moisture due to the drying effects of exposure or the unavailability to the roots of the soil moisture due to the high concentration of salt ions in solution.

Occurring naturally near the sea is not a guarantee of suitability for coastal planting, though. Sitka spruce is only found in a narrow band in western North America, never more than 80 km from the Pacific coast, yet can be scorched by salt spray. The high moisture availability in its native habitat and the vigour of the species may explain its ability to survive.

Exposed Sites

Survival on exposed sites requires trees which can tolerate both the drying and the buffeting effects of the wind. Species with soft floppy leaves are not suited but other than this many conifers will tolerate some exposure, the number decreasing as the exposure becomes more severe.

Moderate exposure is tolerated by several cypresses, particularly Leyland cypress and species like Noble fir (*Abies procera*), Western hemlock and many pines like Scots pine.

The most exposure-tolerant species are some of the spruces, especially Sitka spruce (*Picea sitchensis*) and several pines, including Lodgepole, Mountain (*P. mugo*) and Macedonian (*P. peuce*) pines.

Conifers in the Landscape

Landscapes can be attractive whether consisting of conifers only, broadleaved trees only or a mixture of the two; equally, they can be unattractive, although in most lowland situations any trees are likely to improve the view over that found in treeless landscapes. The purpose of any landscape is to look pleasing to the eye; the nature of plants is that they are continually changing, either with the seasons or in the way the wind blows the foliage about. In the sections 'Specimen and Character Conifers' and 'Shelter, Screening and Backcloth Planting' the point that what appears dull today may be the bright and cheerful item next week was discussed. These points are as valid when considering a country landscape as a garden one.

Nearly all landscapes will have a greater year-round appeal if they include a proportion of evergreen or coniferous trees. Unless the purpose of a vista is to beautify the bleakness of winter, an evergreen element will enhance the winter scene, without detracting from the summer beauty. Wildlife provision is also increased, by raising the number of different forms of food and by increasing the shelter given.

What percentage of evergreen conifers are included should vary with the circumstances. Generally, a figure of between 10 and 40 per cent is appropriate, with an average of 25 per cent. Less than 10 per cent and the benefits to wildlife and the winter scene are negligible, more than 40 per cent and some of the element of seasonal change is lost. All of the evergreen element does not have to be coniferous, although conifers grow faster and usually support a wider range of wildlife than evergreen broadleaved trees.

The evergreen element in the landscape should not be spread out too diffusely; clumping the different elements is much more pleasing to the eye than a regular (and monotonous) scattering.

Conifers for Hedging

Conifers can make very useful hedges as they fulfil many of the properties required of a good hedging plant, particularly when compared with the preferred plants of earlier generations. This is not to say that a conifer is always the right choice of species for a hedge, as there are some styles of hedge which are better filled by other plants.

Hedges can be either informal barriers or neatly clipped structures. Conifers are promising as clipped hedges, while some of the dwarf cultivars can make effective informal hedges. Some of the larger-growing sorts can be used to make taller, informal hedges but these are really screens and have been discussed on pages 28-30.

The ideal requirements of a perfect hedge are that it will grow on a wide range of soils, be easily trimmed to the right size, be evergreen or make an effective barrier throughout the year, not need too much trimming, be fully hardy and disease resistant. By choosing the right species, conifers can fit all the above requirements. In addition, though, the hedge should be quick to establish, which in practice competes with the need for not too much trimming.

Ideally, a clipped hedge should be broader at the base than at the top, so that light can reach the lower foliage and prevent it being shaded out. As the plants make more vigorous growth from the top, the natural tendency is for the hedge to become wider at the top than at the bottom. With many hedging plants, this leads to the bottom becoming bare, but most conifers are more shade-tolerant than other plants and are better able to retain the lower foliage.

With only a few notable exceptions conifers cannot make new growth from branches which are not carrying live foliage. If all the leaves are removed from a conifer it will die. The exceptions are a few species in the Redwood family and the Yew family and of these only Yew is at all commonly used as a hedging plant.

It is, therefore, vital that conifer hedges are regularly trimmed and only cut back to the extent that there is live foliage below. In the cypresses, if the bark is brown the plant will not make new growth from that shoot, although it can, and will, make new growth from a green side branch nearer the trunk, if one is present. If the cut is made into tissues which still have green leaves or bark (in cypresses the leaves are decurrent and the bark only shows after the scale leaves have died), new growth will be made from buds close to the position of the cut. In Yew new growth can be made from brown bark, although it will take longer to reclothe the hedge than if clipping takes place only into live foliage. Except for Yew, conifer hedges are not tolerant of neglect and are harder to reshape than some other hedges.

Clipping should be carried out at least twice a year, although with a very large hedge or screen it is possible, with extra care, to leave it to only once a year or even every other year; the top will then look untidy after clipping but is unlikely to be visible from below. However, the more frequently clipping is carried out, the neater will be the finished job, the less time it will take and the less material will need to be cleared away. With normal hedging plants, there is no special time of the year for clipping. However, if the effect of the clipping is going to make the hedge look somewhat untidy until new growth is made, late spring or early summer will shorten this period.

Hedging plants want to be spaced at around 75-90 cm apart. If they are much more than 90 cm apart, the hedge will take longer to form a full barrier. If closer, extra plants are needed which will not add anything but cost. The only exception to this is where a low hedge, under 1.2 m is required, for which dwarf or slow-growing conifers should be chosen; the vigorous species normally used for hedging are not suited to such small hedges.

The best plants to use are those 45-60 cm tall. These will establish quickly, without losses, and will make the best hedge. The temptation is to plant larger trees, which rarely cuts down the time taken to form the hedge, and just puts up the cost. If you insist on buying larger plants, Western red cedar transplants better than most other species, and 1.8-2.4 m tall plants can be bought. However, with good care in the planting and establishment, as discussed in Chapter 6, smaller plants will give at least as good a result in the same time.

The species mainly used for hedging are several of the cypress family and Yew. Three are widely used and the other two were more widely planted in the past. Other species can make excellent hedges, sometimes only needing a little extra care to produce a much more interesting effect.

The most commonly planted conifer hedging plant is Leyland cypress. This is very quick to establish and is soon growing at the rate of 1 m a year, which is probably its main drawback, as after it has reached the allotted size, there is still 1 m of growth to remove annually. It withstands clipping very well and can be brought back from a degree of neglect better than some other species. It is the most popular individual hedging plant, mainly due to the very quick initial growth, but suffers from being rather formless and dull. It is not very good in shade, only tolerating light shading before it starts to become very thin and sparsely foliaged. The yellow-gold form 'Castlewellan' offers a different colour option, but is slower and no more attractive.

Lawson cypress is slower-growing than Leyland cypress, which means it takes longer to reach the full size required for the hedge but does not require so much clipping when it gets there. Also, as a species it requires a slightly richer soil for optimum growth, although tolerating clays and chalk very well; a hedge, whatever the species, needs to be growing vigorously to look good. The Lawson cypress used for hedging are usually seedling plants, as opposed to the single clone of Leyland cypress generally available which is raised by cuttings; they therefore show some degree of variation. This can be an attribute except in the most formal situations. A very wide range of Lawson cypress cultivars are available and a hedge of almost any plant colour except purple can be made. Some of the cultivars, such as 'Fletcheri' and 'Ellwoodii' are small trees, making no more than 6 m or so, and relatively slow-growing. They can be used as less formal hedges whilst growing and will require much less clipping when full height is attained. On the denser foliaged cultivars, though, the surface veneer of live foliage is shallow and only a small amount can be removed before exposing the dead and brown old material inside. Generally, compared to Leyland cypress, Lawson cypress does not have the same capacity to grow after a severe cutting back.

The third commonly planted conifer hedge is

Western red cedar. This has two features not shared with Lawson and Leyland cypresses. The foliage is delightfully fragrant, with the scent best described as 'pineapple'. The foliage does not need to be cut or crushed to give the scent, except in winter, although this makes it much stronger. The other point is that Western red cedar will grow on any soil, and therefore is suited to the wet and boggy sites upon which the above cypresses do not thrive. It is also better at withstanding transplanting at a larger size than the others, and therefore has attractions for the impatient. Western red cedar has a growth rate faster than Lawson cypress but not quite as fast as that of Leyland cypress. The foliage is somewhat sparser than with either of them. Although it will make just as dense a screen, initially this is more by depth of foliage, rather than by the density on the outside. With repeated clipping to one shape the inner foliage eventually will be lost, but it does give more freedom periodically to reshape the dimensions of the hedge. A few different colour cultivars are available, as is a narrow-crowned one, 'Fastigiata', which will naturally make a narrower hedge.

The oldest conifer hedges were made from Yew. This is slow-growing and, therefore, takes much longer to establish; it is very long-lived and the obvious choice for long-term hedges. Yew is very disease-resistant, much more so than the above or most other species. It is one of the few conifers which will coppice, that is make growth from the stump if cut down; this means that Yew hedges can be reshaped much more freely than other conifer hedges. Several colour forms are available. Yew is also very suitable for topiary work. Its only practical drawback is the long time taken to make a given size of hedge, and even if larger plants are used, which transplant well, they still take several years to thicken.

Monterey cypress has been used in the past and is especially good for maritime situations. Generally, though, it is less effective than its hybrid Leyland cypress and does not make such a controllable hedge, tending to lose the lowest foliage to give a bare bottom. Recently it has proved very susceptible to a fungal disease, *Seiridium* (= *Coryneum*) *cardinale*, and it also is not as reliably hardy as the other cypress species throughout Britain.

Many other members of the cypress family could be tried in hedges. Forms of Chinese juniper (*Juniperus chinensis*), such as 'Japonica', could be used where a slightly prickly effect was required or Smooth cypress (*Cupressus glabra*) could be used to give a better blue-grey-coloured hedge than is available from Lawson cypress.

Few species in the pine family are really suitable for hedges, the notable exception being Western hemlock (*Tsuga heterophylla*). This can make a very neat hedge and with the needle-shaped leaves silvery below is quite different in appearance from any of the above; it is particularly good on very acidic sandy soils. Other pine family species can be used but require much more attention to how they are clipped and trained.

Conifers for Topiary

Topiary is the creation of sculpture out of a living, growing plant. Those used as the basis of this art-form need to be capable of withstanding repeated clipping. Ideally they are evergreen, tough and fully hardy. Several conifers can fit these requirements; they are broadly the most suitable species for hedging, as discussed in the above section. One species stands out above all others and that is Yew (*Taxus baccata*). Yew has the double-edged advantage that it is also slow-growing — making for less trimming but taking longer to achieve the intended representation.

The plants can be trimmed to make a variety of forms, ranging from pocket battleships to regular cones suitable for very formal settings.

In making and caring for a topiary, the guiding principle is to clip it regularly and often. This will keep the plant evergreen and neat. If trimming is only carried out once or twice a year, the inner foliage will soon be shaded out and after clipping the plant will look ragged and bare. Plenty of patience is also a requisite.

Christmas Trees

Conifers are the traditional Christmas trees because, in the northern hemisphere, Christmas comes during the mid-winter and most other trees are leafless.

The species of tree used, however, varies widely from country to country, being dependent upon such things as availability, tradition and the effect of central heating on the cut tree! Many conifers are suitable, with what could be considered one of the least suitable being widely used. This is the Norway spruce (*Picea abies*) which in Britain is the usual species, but on the continent, from whence the tradition was introduced to Britain, the tree is more likely to be Silver fir (*Abies alba*). In North America pine species, particularly Scots pine (*Pinus sylvestris*) and Douglas fir (*Pseudotsuga menziesii*), are widely employed, giving bluish trees.

Silver firs have distinct advantages over spruces in that they are less ready to drop their needles; they do have more widely spaced tiers of branches, which were utilised in the past to display candles relatively safely, but with the advent of electricity this is not such an advantage. Spruces are widely used in Britain because Silver firs have not been planted recently on a large scale and Norway spruce has as a consequence become 'traditional', despite its appalling ability to drop needles everywhere and, unless carefully treated, to become bare before Twelfth Night.

Scots pine is used in the USA because it does not drop needles, even when neglected in centrally-heated houses. However, because of the very open and sparse branching habit, the trees have to be sheared annually during the summer to develop a denser tree.

Other conifers, such as Grand fir (*Abies grandis*) or Noble fir (*A. procera*), can be used. Cypresses are not often chosen, because the branches are too weak to hold any decorations and the growth habit is somewhat too dense and formal.

Christmas trees are simple to grow, although keeping one alive after it has been used for Christmas is much harder.

Small transplants should be planted at around 60 cm spacing each way. The transplants will be three- or four-year-old seedlings which have been transplanted once in the nursery and will be 30-45 cm tall. The trees will only grow about 15 cm during the first year, when it is vital to control the weeds and competing grass but without scorching the foliage. Afterwards, growth will be faster, and an average 2 m tree will have been growing about five years from planting.

Purchased trees are difficult to keep alive because they are ripped out of the ground with few roots. Amongst the millions of trees used every Christmas a small proportion survive, but to have a reasonable chance, smaller and preferably potgrown trees should be chosen. Although it is just possible to keep one tree going for several Christmases, the effect of repeated annual uprootings will cause the tree to deteriorate steadily in condition unless it is grown in a pot. The condition of a cut tree can be enhanced by not letting it dry out, either when it is inside, or when dug up and purchased. Also avoid siting it near to a heat source like a radiator.

Some trees have a need for a specific number of cold days during the winter before they will break dormancy in the spring. Bringing such a tree into a warm environment can lead it to behave as if it has not experienced sufficient cold days because after the warm period it restarts the count; if this happens it may not make any new growth until after the next winter.

Conifer Litter

Conifer litter can be a very useful source of mulching material. Normally, it can be left to break down where it falls, but it needs to be removed from grass and some other areas. Burning it, however, is an utter waste — it should be used as a mulch.

The litter is slow to break down and is quite acidic in its pH, making it suitable for mulching species like Rhododendrons; it will be low in nutrients and therefore not suitable for plants which require a high nitrogen level. It looks attractive as a mulch and will be efficient at controlling the growth of most weed species, except a few like Sheeps sorrel (*Rumex acetosella*).

The bark is also a very good mulch and is used in soil-less composts, providing good drainage. Fresh bark in large quantities will release phenolic compounds which can be damaging to other plants and therefore the commercial conifer bark preparations are stacked and allowed to heat up for a few weeks before being hammered into small pieces. However, in shallow layers, these should not be a problem, and neither does the material need breaking down into small fragments to be useful. Coarser chunks are good at controlling weeds, as well as making an excellent material for paths.

Conifers for Cut Foliage

Many species can prove useful for indoor floral displays. The material can range from foliage for flower vases to cones for painting or Christmas decoration.

Western hemlock foliage is frequently used in floristry. The various colour forms of cypresses and junipers are also very useful, whilst the bold foliage of some of the pines is only suitable for the largest displays. Spruce foliage can be used, but will drop its needles if allowed to dry out, whereas cypresses, some Silver firs and pines will retain their foliage and can be used to create 'everlasting' displays.

If planting conifers to provide material for flower arranging, beware of choosing those species whose leaves are not pleasantly fragrant. For instance, Savin (*Juniperus sabina*) emits a disagreeable odour, especially when bruised or dried.

Conifers in Tubs

Conifers can be used as patio plants or in similar situations in small tubs or large pots. In this way they can be used to improve the appearance of areas either unfit or inappropriate for regular planting.

Plants used in this way will need to be ones naturally adapted to hot dry sites, as with the best will in the world, watering during the summer will not be as regular as the tree would like and high soil temperatures will develop in the containers. Except in mild areas, the pots will also freeze during the winter.

The plants chosen will usually need to be the smaller-growing sorts. Large, fast-growing species like Grand fir are unlikely to be a success. Cypresses (*Cupressus*) and junipers are best suited, both in scale and colour of foliage and also tolerance of hot dry conditions. Some other conifers can also be tried and the Bristlecone pine (*Pinus aristata*) might be an attractive alternative to cypresses.

The containers used should be as large as possible, as this will give a more even temperature to the compost and leave a reserve of water against drying out. They should also be heavy and flat bottomed to prevent the plant and pot being blown over during strong winds. Good drainage of the pot and rooting medium is essential. The soil should contain both a good percentage of sand and gravel, for drainage, and peat or other organic material, for water-holding capacity, aeration and to retain a good soil structure. An organic or pebble mulch will keep the compost structure open, preventing the top of the compost being compacted by watering. Feeding will also be necessary, although it is important not to overfeed.

Conifers as House Plants

Conifers can be used as houseplants, with some species surviving the demanding conditions very well. It can be the only practical way to grow some of the more tropical species in temperate parts of the world, although not all species will tolerate this treatment.

The species chosen have to be able to grow in relatively low light intensities, not need a pronounced winter break or 'cold period' and tolerate alternate wetting and drying of the soil, as well as a dry atmosphere and diurnal temperature variations. The plants should be positioned where they receive the maximum amount of sunlight as, except in the sunniest house or conservatory, this will almost always be lower than they would receive outside.

Norfolk Island pine (*Araucaria heterophylla*) is very suitable for indoor culture, as are other members of the genus *Araucaria* and also species of *Agathis*. The cultivar 'Goldcrest' of Monterey cypress is often sold as a houseplant, as are the juvenile forms of some pines, e.g. *Pinus canariensis* or *P. pinea*.

Bonsai

Bonsai is a technique for retaining the essential growth form of a tree but reducing it to pocket size. It started as a way of emulating the rugged dwarf plants found on the tops of mountains and which have been shaped by the wind and weather. Originally a Chinese tradition, it was introduced into Japan many centuries ago. Bonsai is not restricted to reproducing montane dwarfs but can be used to make whole miniature forests.

The basis of the art is to control the root and top growth of the plant by judicious pruning and training. It is not achieved by starving the plant, as this will lead to a moth-eaten specimen, not a neat bonsai, but the feeding does not want to be rich. Conifers can be used very effectively for this purpose. Although dwarf conifers can be used, normal seedlings of the tall-growing sorts can with skill be turned into good bonsai. Many books have been written on bonsai and there are several national bonsai societies which should be consulted for more information.

·CHAPTER 4·
Dwarf Conifers

Dwarf conifers can give all the elements of colour, scale, texture and seasonal variation provided in the garden by their larger-growing cousins, but they offer these features within a small-growing plant more fitting to the average pocket handkerchief of a modern garden or as one of several elements of a larger garden. In addition, dwarf conifers can be used as ground cover, whereas the taller-growing relatives make sky cover!

Dwarf conifers can be used as island features in the lawn or in a sea of gravel; as permanent plants on the rockery, associated with small plants such as heathers; to provide a contrast in other plant groupings; or as a feature in their own right. As a group, they are very useful plants in the garden, providing many characters not available from other plants.

In this chapter the origin of and uses to which dwarf conifers can be put are considered. Details of individual plants are given in the gazetteer section. Propagation, planting and moving dwarf conifers, if they have grown too large, are dealt with in Chapters 5 and 6.

What are Dwarf Conifers?

Dwarf conifers range from some of the smallest woody plants recognisable, growing perhaps 5 cm in ten years (e.g. *Chamaecyparis obtusa* 'Pixie'), through to larger-growing sorts which merge into normal conifers. The larger-growing forms are often termed 'slow-growing conifers' but the discussion here accepts them all as dwarf conifers, with the proviso that for any individual use or planting, selection of suitable plants must be made from the range of forms available. Many of the tree conifers can very effectively be used as 'temporarily' dwarfs whilst they are young, and provided they are moved or removed in due course!

Dwarf conifers have originated in one of several ways. Most exist solely because they have been spotted by man, but a few are naturally-occurring with a definitive niche or place in nature.

Naturally-occurring Dwarfs

Conifers are generally large shrubs or trees but a few are found in the wild as prostrate or dwarf species. They occur in areas where the climate or soil conditions are particularly severe and where plants with the normal upright habit of growth would be too susceptible to being blown over (such as on rocky sites or sandy seashores), where the nutrients available for growth are insufficient for larger forms or where the plants would be liable to dieback caused by winter cold; many plants from the high mountain ranges can only grow as tall as the winter snowfall will cover them, and any growth protruding beyond this protection will be killed. In most of these species the selection for the dwarf habit has led to genetically stable populations; these plants will retain their slow growth rates and dwarf habit in cultivation, although, in the richer soils and sheltered climates of our gardens, they tend to grow larger and faster than in the wild. Most of the dwarf junipers (*Juniperus*) fit into this group. Within these species, there will be variation in the colour and texture of the individuals; very often blueness of foliage goes with harshness of climate.

Genetically, the individuals from the top end of the natural range of many treeline species are slower-growing than those from lower altitudes for the above reasons. Similarly, where the species has a long north-south range, such as Sitka spruce

(*Picea sitchensis*), the individuals from the polar end of the range are slower in growth, but tougher, than those from the other extreme. These plants are not necessarily dwarfs, although they can be useful where an intermediate or slow-growing plant is needed.

Small plants of treeline species may be found in the wild above the treeline. Usually, if they are brought down the mountainside, their dwarfness will be found to be largely environmental in origin, and therefore transient. However, because the extreme conditions favour dwarf growth forms, sometimes a naturally dwarf mutation which would not survive lower down can find an ecological niche and such plants will retain their dwarfism. Examples of such plants which have been found in the wild are *Abies balsamea* 'Hudsonia' and *Picea glauca albertiana* 'Conica'. Such plants, though, very rarely fruit, in contrast to the naturally prostrate-growing species.

Seedling Mutations

The seed is formed from the union of genetic material from both the pollen and seed-bearing parents and occasionally the resultant new individual has genes which make it either very slow-growing or with some other characteristic feature. In the wild such forms are rarely observed, as the selection pressures on the seeds are very great and only a small number survive even to make young plants; normally such slow-growing forms may be expected to be swamped by faster-growing siblings, or other competing vegetation. The situation is very different in nurseries, where the seeds are sown spaced out and without any competing weeds. Here, any distinctive individuals have a chance to grow and may be spotted and grown-on, although most will probably get discarded as runts! Lawson cypress (*Chamaecyparis lawsoniana*) illustrates this very well; in the wild it is a very uniform species but in cultivation it has given rise to many hundreds of different forms, the first ('Erecta') being named in 1855 only a year after the species was discovered.

Seedling mutations may be fixed and reliable in their growth but are not invariably so. Some plants which fail to form an erect leader as a seedling may do so later, possibly by activating the genes for the production of the appropriate hormone. *Picea omorika* 'Expansa' was selected as a prostrate individual from a nursery row but is inclined to make a leader in cultivation. Also, there is a tendency for the features shown by seedling mutants to become less pronounced with age.

The genes which make seedling mutations probably occur as recessive genes in a proportion of the population, so it is quite likely that sooner or later another individual will turn up with the same unusual characters. With some forms, this has happened quite frequently, so that the various entities can be considered as a group of cultivars; very often the various forms only differ in minute details one from another and a confusing number of names can be created, or else confusion can exist where one name is applied to several different cultivars; such has happened with *Tsuga canadensis* 'Pendula', where several similar seedlings were found at one time and confusion exists as to which individuals have been propagated and distributed as cultivars.

Seedling mutations are usually sterile but some forms every now and then may produce cones. Where seeds have been collected from these cones a range of different forms have arisen.

Juvenile Fixations

The juvenile foliage of many conifers is markedly different from that of the adult plant. This is mainly a feature of the cypress family, where the juvenile leaves are acicular (needle-shaped) and often carried in threes, whereas the adult leaves are scale-like and usually in pairs. It also happens in other families, especially in some species of pines (*Pinus*) where the juvenile leaves are single and linear and the adult leaves are short shoots with fascicles of 2-5 needles (the juvenile leaves are retained in the adult shoots, but become brown and scale-like structures situated at the base of each short shoot); in a species like Stone pine (*P. pinea*), juvenile leaves are carried by the tree for several seasons. Normally, seedling trees soon lose the juvenile foliage as it matures (under changes in hormone level) but sometimes this does not happen.

Juvenile forms generally have longer, softer and more spaced foliage than displayed by the adult plant; this gives them a more feathery texture. The degree to which the foliage retains the juvenile characters can vary. In Sawara cypress (*Chamaecyparis pisifera*) the fully juvenile forms are assigned to the 'Squarrosa' group of cultivars, whilst in the 'Plumosa' group of cultivars the foliage is still recognisably juvenile but is shorter and halfway to the adult form. This situation is further confused as both the juvenile forms are fertile and seedlings can be raised showing a range of foliage characters. In the past, juvenile foliage forms were thought to resemble heathers (*Erica*) and the cultivar name 'Ericoides' was often used.

The fertility of juvenile forms has in the past also caused some confusion. At one time the juvenile selections, mainly of *Chamaecyparis* species, made in Japan over many centuries were considered to belong to a separate genus (*Retinospora*), and it was only as the occasional plant produced some normal adult foliage that the identity of many cultivars was sorted out.

Bud Mutations

Bud mutations or 'sports' give rise to many forms. Something appears to go wrong in the bud which causes the foliage developing from it to be different in some way — more juvenile, or golden or some other colour. Forms arising from bud mutations are rather unstable; for instance, from the original seedling-raised plant of *Chamaecyparis lawsoniana* 'Ellwoodii' have been raised the following forms as bud mutations: 'Bleu Nantais', 'Blue Gem', 'Blue Surprise', 'Chilworth Silver', 'Ellwoods Gold', 'Ellwoods Pygmy' and 'Ellwoods White'.

Bud mutations are also unstable in that many of them will revert and throw out shoots with the normal foliage type. Where reversion occurs, it should be removed as the reverted form will almost always be more vigorous and faster-growing than the mutant form, and therefore liable to swamp it.

Witches Brooms

Witches brooms are the local proliferation of side buds on a shoot making a cluster of short erect shoots, usually with small leaves. They occur on many species of trees, not just on conifers. The causal agent is not known, although mycoplasma-like organisms (related to viruses) are implicated in their occurrence on broadleaved trees. However, there is little substantive evidence of either viruses or mycoplasma-like organisms on conifers.

Cuttings taken from these growths (which can form large masses of foliage) will develop into small-growing plants with a distinctive habit. Examples are some of the Norway spruce (*Picea abies*), e.g. 'Pygmea', or Scots pine (*Pinus sylvestris*), e.g. 'Doone Valley', which have arisen this way.

In normal circumstances witches brooms do not produce cones or male flowers. However, on a number of occasions, they have been formed and seed collected. About half the resulting seedlings have made normal plants but the others have shown varying degrees of dwarfism. This suggests that either the genetic content of the witches broom has been altered in favour of producing dwarfs or that the causal agent can be transmitted by seed.

Cultivariants

This term is used to describe plants which differ one from another not because of any genetic factors but as a consequence of where the cutting or scion was removed from the mother plant. Two groups of cultivariants exist!

In many genera, especially in the pine family but not in *Pinus*, the foliage on the lateral shoots is arranged more or less spreading either side of the twig which grows out more or less horizontally, whilst that of the erect leading shoots is perfectly radial. If a scion is taken from a side branch it can be difficult to encourage it to make a normal erect leading shoot; several prostrate plants have arisen as grafts of side branches, e.g. *Abies amabilis* 'Spreading Star' and *A. procera* 'Glauca Prostrata'. These plants can be useful, although are entirely artificial in origin; they may eventually make a leader, but if this is removed, they can be kept as prostrate forms.

The second group is more interesting and is especially a feature of some cypress cultivars. The variation again is due to the position of the cutting on the mother plant. If the cutting is taken from one of the shoots near or including the leading shoot at the top of the plant, it will develop into a comparatively narrow and fast-growing individual; if the cutting is taken from the lower, outer crown where the foliage is shaded, the result will be a slower-growing and more rounded plant. A possible explanation for this behaviour is that in the stronger growths, hormone levels are higher than in weaker shoots; when a new plant is raised from the latter type of cutting, it has lost or has only a limited ability to make new hormone and, therefore, makes less growth. As the two plants mature, they may become indistinguishable.

Dwarf Conifers in the Garden

Dwarf conifers can be put to a number of different uses in the garden and the following subheadings are by no means exhaustive. In addition, the points made about scale, colour, etc. in Chapter 3 apply equally to the dwarf kinds.

As a Dwarf Conifer Collection

Dwarf conifers can be used to make an interesting collection of plants which will give variety throughout the year but with a minimal maintenance requirement. The interest from a collection can range from simple enjoyment offered by the judicious siting of plants of different form, colour and texture to the indefinable fascination that comes from any hobby.

Careful siting of a collection is important if the assemblage of plants is to have general appeal and if the variety of different shapes and textures offered by dwarf conifers are to be fully utilised.

Dwarf conifers can be categorised into a number of different habit forms: these include prostrate forms, rounded buns or mounds, vase or table shapes which grow out and slightly up from a central point, cones, obelisks and those showing 'erratic' or 'character' growth habits. When colour, size and texture are added, it is apparent that there is considerable scope for variation.

Simply planting a hotch-potch of individuals of these different plants is unlikely to look good. It is important, therefore, to consider what you want from the collection. For example, if you wish to compare the growth habits of two plants, you would need to locate them together for comparison but aesthetically this would not be the best way, as pairs of plants only look good in certain very limited circumstances (such as when a path passes between two trees). Groupings of similar items need to be either in large numbers or in odd numbers, i.e. 3, 5, 7, or a dozen or more; if they are planted in low even numbers, such as 2, 4, 6 or 8 the eye automatically pairs them off and the formality that results is not pleasing.

When establishing a collection of dwarf conifers, the layout needs to lead the eye. With an island bed, this means that a taller plant (or plants in a large bed) needs to be positioned approximately in the centre, with smaller items towards the edges. The smaller-growing cultivars need not be uniform in stature, but only in special circumstances can an outer plant be as tall or taller than the core plant. The design is helped if the bed is slightly raised but a path or stepping stones should let access be gained to each plant, both for close inspection and for maintenance. If the bed is formed adjacent to an end wall, the tallest item can be near or beside the wall, leading the eye outwards to the edge of the bed. Where paths cross the area, the same considerations apply, with the generally smaller items kept nearer the path (where they can be seen) and taller ones further back. However, these principles should not be followed precisely, or else the layout will lack any spontaneity and become dully formal.

Dwarf conifers cannot be intimately mixed with larger-growing plants; as scale is important to the beauty and dignity of any tree, even dwarf ones, too abrupt a contrast of sizes will make the smaller plant look insignificant. They can, however, be associated with a number of plants, in the context of a collection of dwarf conifers; these need to be plants of similar appearance and comparable growth rate. Items such as *Daphne* spp. can be very successful, adding an element of flower and floral fragrance. Some of the smaller-growing brooms (*Cytisus* and *Genista*) or Rock roses (*Cistus*) can also be successful.

The ground under a dwarf conifer collection can be kept as bare earth but some form of mulching is much better. It will keep the soil cool, moist and help control weeds; with a mulch, such weeds as do germinate are easily pulled or can be treated chemically. Mulches also do not show footprints as clearly as does bare earth, so access for maintenance is easier. Bark, peat or other organic mulches are very good. Gravel also makes a good mulch, using stones about 1 cm in diameter; when new it can appear rather harsh but is soon weathered and mellows to a more subtle colour. All mulches need laying down in a layer at least 5 cm, and preferably 10 cm thick; this will need to be topped up on a regular basis, either as the organic matter is broken down or the gravel is incorporated into the soil by worms. Of the materials mentioned above, conifer bark and gravel are the longer-lasting.

On no account should strong competitor plants like grasses be tolerated around the roots, as the dwarf conifers will look dismal and sickly from the reduced supply of nutrients and water.

With Other Plants

The role of dwarf conifers when grown with other plants is to add a degree of scale or charm otherwise lacking in the scene. The situation is very different from the above association, where the objective is a collection of interest in itself.

Dwarf conifers will associate very effectively with attractive but rather flat and formless plants, such as heathers. Here the conifers need to be well dispersed, or the floral beauty of the heathers will be diluted and the conifers will not form the intended landmarks or features of scale. The conifers also need to have a distinctive shape complementary to that of the heathers. Prostrate or low bun-shaped plants will not add to the display; rather the plants need either to have a bold shape, such as obelisk, conical or 'character' forms, or else to offer a colour not found amongst the heathers, such as a good blue foliage.

On a Rockery

An effective rockery is intended to represent the moorland conditions at the top of high mountains. Alpines are the major plants used, set amongst large rock outcrops. Selected dwarf conifers fit into a rockery very well, providing a degree of permanence (remembering that most of the alpine perennial plants and small bulbs are transient in their flowers and foliage) as well as a sense of scale. The rockery can also be the place where the very smallest of dwarf conifers can be grown, although some of these are so slow that they are best left to the alpine house or a connoisseur.

Unless the rockery is very large, the dwarf conifers used on it will need to be carefully chosen, so that they marry with the rocks whilst giving scale and contrast to the association. Small obelisk forms, such as *Juniperus communis* cultivars 'Suecica Nana' or 'Compressa', or plants with a 'character' miniature tree habit, such as *Chamaecyparis obtusa* cultivars 'Kosteri' or 'Nana', will make interesting feature plants. Some of the smaller *Tsuga canadensis* forms, such as 'Fantana', 'Gables Weeping' or 'Hussu' can also look very attractive and give year-long beauty and background.

Prostrate forms can be used to creep down over rocks but the more rampant forms should be avoided, as they will quickly become a nuisance here. *Juniperus conferta* and *J. procumbens* 'Nana' are suitable plants, and will creep over only a small area. These dwarfs can provide protection for early bulbs, whilst not making a thick layer of foliage over the ground to damage the new shoots as they emerge. Other dwarf conifers, such as *J. squamata* 'Blue Star' can be effectively placed on the rockery.

As an Isolated Specimen

An isolated dwarf conifer set in a vast sea of green grass can be a very effective plant. It gives that essential element of the unexpected to the otherwise uniform medium, in a way similar to the use of rocks set in a sea of gravel in some styles of Japanese gardening. It is essential that the plants are not over-used, or the surprise will be lost. This means that in most lawns, there is space for no more than one plant.

Suitable plants will include the larger-growing sorts, such as some of the stronger forms of Norway spruce (*Picea abies*), such as 'Clanbrassiliana' or 'Tabuliformis', or *Tsuga canadensis* 'Pendula'. These will make plants with gently rounded or billowing habits; plants with erratic or angular outlines rarely look well placed in this situation.

As Ground Cover

The more rampant prostrate dwarf conifers can make efficient forms of ground cover. Plants such as the many cultivars of *Juniperus horizontalis* can cover and control the weeds over a sizeable area of ground, yet not be so thick as to preclude the planting of smaller growing sorts of bulbs, such as miniature daffodils. Totally prostrate forms of other conifers will also spread over the ground, such as *Picea abies* 'Repens' or *Abies amabilis* 'Spreading Star', giving good control but some other plants may be too open to be effective (although still remaining attractive), e.g. *A. procera* 'Glavea Prostrata'. As with other forms of ground-cover, dwarf conifers used this way should be planted into clean ground, although they are more tolerant of herbicides, such as Simazine, than many ground cover plants.

The taller-growing low conifers can also be used to fill vacant or unwanted space. Junipers like *Juniperus chinensis* 'Pfitzeriana' or *J. virginiana* 'Hetzii' are very suitable. These will cast a dense low shade, preventing the establishment of rampant weed growth. With these plants, growth is by a succession of arching horizontal layers, eventually leading to a plant 1m or 2m high. Mountain pine (*Pinus mugo*) is also attractive for this purpose, but more open and requiring more weed control. These plants are very useful for covering banks, especially dry ones in full sun.

Manhole covers and other unsightly structures are often very difficult to hide, let alone make attractive. The difficulty is that most suitable ground cover plants are ones which sucker or root as they cover the ground, something they cannot do over a metal manhole cover. *Juniperus chinensis* 'Pfitzeriana' is very suitable for 'beautifying' such edifices. The advantage is that as miniature trees, they root from one point only and spread over the monstrosity. They are also well suited to growing on dry or poor soils.

As a Hedge/Screen

Informal screens or barriers can be made from dwarf conifers. Generally, they are useful where the screen is needed to mark a boundary, rather than physically to separate two areas. Therefore a complete hedge is not required, a series of pillars or flat bushes serving the purpose.

Dwarf conifers are not really suited to more formal hedges, except possibly those with a naturally neat growth form which does not need trimming. For a good formal hedge, the plants used need to make sufficient annual growth for some of it to be removed in clipping, and few dwarf conifers will do this.

Suitable plants are either the upright slow-growing forms, such as *Chamaecyparis lawsoniana* 'Ellwoodii', or the stronger-spreading forms, like *Juniperus chinensis* 'Pfitzeriana'. Weaker-growing plants can be used in areas where a small hedge is needed but will require more effective control of weed competition than with other hedging plants.

Other Situations

Dwarf conifers can be used in a variety of other situations. They are especially useful for dry sites, either in full sun (where junipers are very good) or dense shade (cultivars of *Taxus* or *Tsuga*). These might include dry beds adjacent to the walls of the house or in pots on the patio.

There are a few situations for which they should only be used with careful thought, such as mixed with strong-growing shrubs or vigorous herbaceous plants. They can fit neatly into these situations but, without careful management, the surrounding plants can swamp the dwarf conifers; this may not matter during the summer when all the plants are fully clothed with foliage, but could lead to the conifers losing their lower foliage and becoming unsightly in winter. In plantings like these, if an evergreen coniferous element is wanted, the use of stronger-growing forms should be considered, even though this may mean removing and replacing the plant after a few years.

·CHAPTER 5·
Propagation

Conifers respond to nearly all the traditional methods of plant propagation and most can be raised in a variety of ways. The principal methods used are seeds, cuttings and grafting. Layering can be used and is an important natural method for Black spruce (*Picea mariana*) but root cuttings are not successful. Micropropagation using cell culture can be used, particularly when portions of seedlings are used as the starting material, but this method requires specialist conditions and is not discussed in this book.

Seed

Seed is the best method for the species and used on the largest scale for forestry plants or for rootstocks. It requires the availability of viable seed, a commodity which is not always on offer for some species. It is the cheapest way to produce a large number of plants but the seedlings of some species may be slow to germinate or grow. Plants raised from seed will all be different from each other and from their parents as all conifer seed originates from the union of egg cell and pollen cell. Apomixis, whereby all the genetic material comes from the mother, does not occur in conifers.

Seed should be collected as soon as it is ripe, to prevent natural dispersal or predation. Very often the seed is fully mature before the cone appears ripe and seed collected from under-ripe cones may still be viable if the cone is allowed to ripen before the seed is extracted. Such seed will require more careful handling than normal seed. Some pines are adapted to regions where forest fires are an occasional, if infrequent, certainty and these species have cones which do not open unless heated by a fire. With Monterey pine (*Pinus radiata*) ripe unopened cones may remain on the tree for 25 years or more and viable seed can be collected from those over 20 years old. Seed in cones can be extracted by drying the cones in gentle heat, but avoid over-heating as this will kill the seeds. With some, if the cones only partly open, wetting and redrying them may assist.

Seed can be stored for periods of several years in airtight containers at or around freezing point. If stored at room temperature, viability is much shorter.

The seed of many conifers will germinate once it receives suitable conditions. Some, however, will only germinate after certain dormancy requirements have been fulfilled, and others will germinate more evenly if given similar pre-treatments.

Dormancy confers several advantages to the plant. If the seeds are distributed in early autumn, when the soil conditions are suitable for initial growth, the seedling may not be large enough to survive the ensuing winter. A requirement for a definite cold period, shown by some Arctic pines such as *Pinus pumila* or *P. sibirica*, postpones germination until the next spring. Some species are intended to be eaten as part of the dispersal mechanism; these are mainly yew (*Taxus* spp.) and junipers (*Juniperus* spp.). These require a seedcoat which can withstand the stomach acids of the birds and mammals which eat them. If passed through a bird's stomach, or treated with sulphuric acid, these seeds will germinate (normally after a cold period). If seeds of this type fall to the ground and are not eaten, they can only germinate after a warm period has allowed the soil bacteria to break down the tough seedcoat to let the seed absorb water. Many species produce a proportion of the seeds in any one cone requiring slightly different dormancy treatments for optimum germination. Treating these seeds with a cool moist period of six weeks or so in the bottom of the refrigerator (i.e. at around 2-4°C) will give more uniform germination and at this temperature seeds which can otherwise germinate immediately will not do so.

Seeds should be sown either into a prepared seedbed or, more probably, into small pots or trays. The trays should be fairly deep, preferably at least 10 cm. The compost needs to be light, moist and acidic with pH of around 5. The seed should be covered with its own depth of material. The covering material must be one that does not form a solid layer above the seed, but which remains open for the seedlings to push through as they germinate. Burying the seeds under a surface which 'cakes' may mean that the germinating seedling cannot reach the surface and fails to emerge. Insufficient covering may lead to the seeds drying out as they germinate.

The density of sowing should not be too high, as this is likely to lead to trouble from damping-off fungi and Grey mould (*Botrytis*). These and other fungal problems can be controlled by spraying with fungicides such as Captan, Thiram or Benomyl, but wider spacing of seedlings assists. The desirable density of seedlings is affected by how long they will remain before being transplanted or potted up. Generally, most conifers respond better if they are not potted up until the beginning of their second or third year; potting up as soon as germination is complete is not a good idea as the young plants are very brittle until the tissues have lignified, and seem to take a long while to recover from the ensuing check to growth. However, if more seeds germinate than anticipated, it is better to prick out the seedlings rather than grow them in cramped conditions. With plants raised in outdoor beds, where they will remain for two years, a density of 50-100 plants per 30 cm² is suitable for most species.

One method of raising conifer seedlings which is effective is to use Dunemann seedbeds. In these, conifer needles from the forest floor are used as the substrate and a layer at least 15 cm deep is needed. The original prescription included 2 cm of leafmould from a beech wood on top of the conifer needles, but this is not essential for success. The seeds are sown on the surface and covered with a layer of sand, grit or needles. The seedlings are left in the seedbed for at least one year and will produce sturdy little plants with good root systems which are innoculated with mycorrhizal fungi. Nutrients need not be added but attention must be given to watering.

The seedlings can be transplanted into a prepared bed outside for growing on for one or two years, until large enough for final planting out; if more time is needed, they must be transplanted again or they will produce diffuse, sparse root systems unsuited to moving.

Alternatively the seedlings can be potted up into small containers. The size of pot used must relate to the characters of the plant, e.g. how large it is and how quickly it will grow. Personally, I see little point in too small a pot and would prefer to keep small seedlings in the tray in which they germinated until they are large enough for a litre (9-10 cm) pot. Plants grown in containers will usually grow faster than those in the soil, as the water and nutrient supply is more closely controlled, and most items will need repotting after a year.

The potting medium used should be one which remains open. Too much soil in the compost is not advisable, as this tends to cake with repeated wetting and drying. I use pure peat composts, but with these it is important to get the nutrient supply right, as peat has no natural nutrients. Slow-release fertilisers such as Osmocote or Ficote should be used for all soil-less composts.

Cuttings

Propagation by cuttings is an effective way to produce many genetically identical plants. It is used for the production of cultivars of some species, and for bulking up the numbers of genetically superior seedlings in forestry research. It is also a way to obtain identical plants for an avenue or hedge where formality is required.

Although the plants produced from cuttings will all be genetically the same, there may be an influence on the resulting plant depending upon from where on the original plant the cutting was taken. With some cultivars, cuttings from the upper portions will give fast and more upright growing individuals than those raised from cuttings taken from the shaded lower parts, which may make slower growth and more bushy specimens.

Cuttings taken off seedlings of almost all species will root relatively easily, but with many species cuttings taken from older plants do not have the same capacity to root. This is called the juvenility factor and if more than the occasional cutting is required, it is worth keeping the stock plant in a juvenile state. This can be done by clipping it regularly. Juvenility is particularly important with members of the pine family, and much less significant in the cypress family. In spruces the capability to root readily is progressively lost after the young plant is over six years old. Difficult to root plants can be treated to make them root more readily. The idea is to increase the reserves of sugars in the cutting, so any treatment which does this should be beneficial. One method which has been reported as successful is to remove the bark from the base of the cutting whilst it is still attached to the tree, brush hormone rooting powder over the exposed wood and wrap the barked area in aluminium foil. The foil both protects the exposed wood and, by excluding light, etiolates the base of the shoot, a not fully understood process which enhances rooting. This procedure is carried out about a month before the cuttings are taken. Another method is to encourage the production of juvenile shoots by removing the normal shoots or buds. Both these methods have been recommended for pine species (*Pinus*).

Also important is only to make cuttings out of healthy shoots, otherwise they will usually rot rather than root.

Cuttings can be taken at several times of the year. The best periods are in the early summer, autumn and late winter. Early summer cuttings can be either softwood or semi-hardwood cuttings, depending upon how firm the base is. This can be a very useful time to take cuttings of old spruces (*Picea*), when partially grown shoots will root, albeit extremely slowly (hence mist is not appropriate). Autumn cuttings are suitable for readily rooted species and should not need any artificial heating. Cuttings after Christmas, preferably with bottom heat, are suitable for other species.

The cuttings should be around 8 cm long and for items which root readily can be two or three times longer. They can be taken either with or without a heel but the use of a hormone rooting treatment is beneficial; this is most easily administered as a powder. All of the generally available hormones seem to work, although different species respond better to some than to others.

Cuttings can be wounded to increase absorption of water and rooting powder and also to encourage the natural production of the plant rooting hormone, indole acetic acid. Wounding is carried out either by running a knife blade down through the bottom 2 cm of the bark or removing a similar sliver of bark only. Removing the lower leaves is occasionally recommended, but for spruces it is thought better to leave them on as this increases aeration to the base of the cutting.

Mist, warm bench and plastic, cold bench and plastic and cold frames with close fitting lids can all be used to root the cuttings. With mist, it is important to avoid getting the compost too wet, otherwise the cuttings will rot. Also mist is not suitable for plants which are slow to root (except where it has the extra effect of speeding rooting), as the repeated watering inherent with mist will leach nutrients from the leaves over a period of time. The difference between warm bench and cold bench is that the former has the compost heated by some means, usually electric soil warming cables. This gives the ideal of warm bottoms and cold tops and will hasten rooting; the thin plastic or polythene film prevents desiccation, but the cuttings must not be exposed to full sun. Rotting is less of a problem with the plastic-based methods, and the cuttings will often look healthier than comparable ones under mist, although take slightly longer to root. Cold frames are most useful for autumn cuttings and for the growing on of the rooted plants.

The rooting compost used should allow both for aeration and moisture retention. Pure peat can be used, as this retains an open structure, but peat/sand mixtures are more common and essential for mist. Perlite and vermiculite are also useful. The cuttings should not be firmed in too hard, as this may destroy the aeration to the base of the cutting and hinder rooting.

The time taken to root will vary from a few weeks to several months. Cuttings taken from young plants in early summer may root within four weeks or so, particularly under mist. Those taken in a cold frame in September should not be expected to be ready for potting on until May or June. Cuttings made with additional heating in January to April can also be ready for potting on in June or July.

After the cuttings have rooted, they will need to be potted on. Before this, they will need to be weaned off the closed humid conditions by gradually increasing the ventilation. Weaning is particularly critical with cuttings rooted under mist, as they produce coarser and more brittle roots. The compost used can be similar to those described above, but avoid too strong a fertiliser base.

Root cuttings cannot be used on conifers, as they do not have the capability to make new top growth from the roots.

Grafting

Grafting is necessary for those species which will not root from cuttings and where seed is not available or appropriate. The plant obtained will be genetically identical to the original, and grafting is therefore particularly useful for reproducing superior genetic trees, trees of scientific interest and selected cultivars. The practice is also used to make saleable plants of some dwarf conifers more quickly and economically than produced by cuttings, e.g. in the genus *Tsuga*; this practice is to be deplored as the rootstock will confer additional vigour on the resulting plant which will not have the same growth habit as the original dwarf plant on its own roots.

Grafting involves taking a scion, a piece of shoot, from one plant and attaching it to the root system of another. Success requires that the cambium tissue of both rootstock and scion are correctly aligned and able to complete the union. The conditions and timing of the operation must be directed to ensuring a successful union.

Graft incompatibility can occur in two forms. The growth rate of the two parts can be at different rates, leading to a large diameter root system and base of the stem and a smaller diameter top (or vice versa) which can look unsightly; whichever element grows faster is termed 'soft' and the other element 'hard'. Whether a proposed union with a specific rootstock will give a hard scion can be predicted to some extent from the relative growth rates; dwarf cypress cultivars will make hard scions onto seedling cypresses. Less predictable but potentially more serious is a form of incompatibility in which the union fails, leading either to the death or blow out of the top. This can occur after many years of apparently healthy growth and appears to be due to the failure, despite outward appearances, of the two tissues to join together in a strong and effective bond; it can be a problem with Douglas firs (*Pseudotsuga* spp.), more than with other conifers.

The rootstock should wherever possible be closely related to the scion. In the pines, soft pines will not take on hard pine stocks, or vice versa, and within the hard pines, the number of needles on both stock and scion should if possible be the same. In other genera of the pine family closely related species will make better unions, although *in extremis* all species in a given genus seem to be compatible. In the cypress and redwood families, grafts using different genera within the family appear to work satisfactorily.

The two main periods when grafting of conifers takes place are the late winter and mid- to late summer, with the former period being the most widely used.

Although grafting is possible using bareroot rootstocks, especially with Lawson cypress (*Chamaecyparis lawsoniana*), the usual practice is to have the rootstock potted for several months in advance. The pots used should be deep, rather than shallow, and the rootstock should not be kept in them for so long that the roots get constricted and potbound. The stock should be making root-growth at the time of grafting but not growing actively; with spruces and some other plants, the rootstock needs to be slightly dry, otherwise it will bleed and prevent a union forming.

The grafting technique normally used is a side-veneer graft, but top grafting techniques can be used, especially on deciduous species. In the side-veneer method, a sliver of rootstock is removed by two downward cuts of a (very sharp) knife, as shown in Figure 5.1. Matching cuts are made on the scion, taking care not to cut into the pith but only to remove a slither of bark and wood. The scion is placed against the stock and held in place with either latex ties (which are self-rotting) or material like raffia or thin strips of polythene (which must be removed after several weeks — this can be done by gently running the knife down the rootstock on the side away from the scion). Tying needs to be firm but not too tight, else the bark tissues of the scion will be constricted. The diameters of the stock and scion need to be approximately equal, with that of the stock the larger; if one is much larger than the other, though, it will not be possible to align both sides of the cambium together and care must be taken to ensure that on one side at least they are aligned.

To prevent the union drying out, it can be either plunged in damp peat or covered with a grafting wax or similar material — the tree paint 'Lac Balsam' is very effective and much more convenient to use than traditional waxes which had to be applied melted. Plunging the grafts in damp peat will keep the humidity high and also encourage the scion to make roots from the lower corners; such roots should be encouraged as they

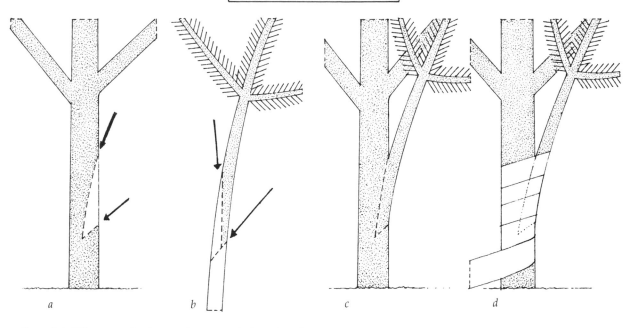

Figure 5.1 Side-veneer Grafting Technique. a Slither of wood cut from rootstock. b Matching cuts on scion. c Cambium layers of scion and rootstock put together. d Scion held in place with latex or other tie.

give an insurance against incompatibility.

The scion must also be protected from desiccation and polythene sheeting is normally used to cover the grafts; shading will be necessary to prevent overheating. A temperature of around 16°C at the union will hasten the bond; in late winter this means that additional heating will be desirable.

After a few weeks, the grafts are gradually hardened off by increasing the ventilation and reducing any extra heat. When fully hardened, they can be repotted to promote active growth of the new top. In the side-veneer method the top of the rootstock is left at the time of grafting to draw the sap, although it may be reduced slightly. As the hardening off process is completed, between half and two-thirds of the remaining top is removed, including the stronger shoots and buds; the rest of the stock topgrowth can be removed in one or more stages before the next spring. Beware of both overhasty removal of the rootstock foliage and of buds developing from the rootstock as both can cause failure of the scion.

Top grafting is similar to the side-veneer method, except that the rootstock is cut off where the cuts are made. This and other aspects of grafting are fully discussed in Garner, *The Grafter's Handbook* (see Bibliography).

The scions chosen should be from the strongest growths on the tree, without being pithy. With pines and cypresses, the origin of the shoot used as the scion is not critical. However, with many other species in the pine family, especially with Silver firs and spruces, the shoots used must be from spare leading shoots or epicormic ones with the radial leaf arrangement or from the strongest terminal shoots of the upper crown. Lateral and weak terminal shoots will not easily adopt the erect growth pattern with radially-arranged leaves needed from a leader, but will grow horizontally with the leaf arrangement relevant to the position on the tree from which the branch came; this is one way to make 'new' ground cover dwarf conifers, but can produce weird specimen trees!

The young grafted plant will need to be trained to make the shoot grow in the required direction. With most this is upwards, but with plants such as the weeping form of Japanese larch (*Larix kaempferi* 'Pendula') the main branches should be trained horizontally or the attractive habit will be lost. Staking, using a bamboo cane, and encouraging quick growth are the best ways to get the tree growing erect. If this does not work, the new growth can be nipped out about 2cm from the bud, preferably before the shoot has fully extended. This will cause normally dormant buds at the base of the shoot to develop and these are often plastic and more easily trained.

Finally, the graft union will be a point of weakness for the first few years, particularly until the scar from the complete removal of the rootstock has callused over; take care not to knock it!

Layering

Layering can be used to propagate conifers and often occurs naturally with several species. These are mainly species like Western red cedar (*Thuja plicata*) or Wellingtonia (*Sequoiadendron giganteum*) which will easily adopt the erect growth habit. Black spruce (*Picea mariana*) layers extensively in its native habitat where layering forms a significant method of reproduction. Most other members of the pine family, though, are reluctant to form an erect leading shoot from the lowest branches which inevitably are the ones most easily layered, and this limits the application of the technique.

The branch to be layered must be one which can both be bent down to touch the ground and which can then be held down whilst the roots form, a period of up to two years. The soil or compost around the branch should be rich in organic matter and preferably be kept moist. The base of the layered branch can be treated, either by damaging the bark or by applying a hormone rooting powder.

After the layer has rooted, it should be cut off from the parent plant and moved to a nursery bed for a further year. The layer can be left *in situ* for a while after severing from the parent, to form further roots.

Air-layering can be tried and will allow more vigorous material to be rooted. It is similar to the techniques used to encourage rootability in difficult to root plants; the main difference is that the exposed wood is covered with sphagnum moss or some other material into which rooting can occur. The rooting medium must be kept moist, not sodden, for the time taken for roots to form. Getting air-layers to establish after severing from the tree can be difficult, as the roots formed are thick, fleshy and extremely brittle.

·CHAPTER 6·
Planting
and Replanting

Planting and Establishing Conifers

The basic essentials in planting any tree are to start with a healthy live specimen, which is planted — not buried! — into a prepared piece of ground and then maintained until it is established. This chapter looks at soil preparation, obtaining healthy plants, the act of planting, and subsequent maintenance to ensure survival and quick establishment. The replanting of trees, such as the larger 'dwarfs' which may have outgrown their allotted space, is also discussed.

Soil Preparation

With plants which can thrive on the most barren or intractable of soils, preparation of the site prior to planting may seem superfluous. It can, however, make all the difference between success and failure. After all, although a species can grow on a particular site, the plant which survives in the wild is one out of several hundred seeds which started out together from the cone; in gardening the object is to shorten the odds, to around 99-1 on!

The first part of site preparation is to rid the planting area of weeds. Grass is the most devastating weed as it is very effective at competing for both soil moisture and nitrogen (and other nutrients) against woody plants. Clover is as bad but other broadleaved weeds are more benign. Still, an established weed will grow more quickly than a newly-planted tree and may cause damage by shading the plant during the summer season, even if it does not compete for water or nutrients.

The best way to rid the site of unwanted vegetation is by the use of herbicides such as Glyphosate (Roundup or Tumbleweed), which is a foliage-acting contact herbicide which is not persistent in the soil. Several other herbicides are available and should be used in accordance with the instructions on the label. These are discussed further on pages 60-1. A method to remove weeds which does not involve herbicides is repeatedly to cultivate the soil, e.g. by hoeing.

The next stage is to tackle the soil itself. If the site is compacted, it is worth loosening the soil over the whole affected area. On a large scale this can be done by machinery and a ripping blade; in the garden it involves double-digging. Incorporating organic matter in the soil can be carried out at this stage and will be beneficial, except on poorly drained heavy clay soils. If feasible, any appropriate drainage should be put in, as although many conifers will thrive in poor drainage, virtually all of them will do better with good drainage. The act of ripping or double-digging will improve the drainage but it may be necessary or worthwhile to put in a series of land drains, especially to take the drained water away.

Unless the soil is deficient in nutrients, there is usually little to be gained by adding them at this stage; far better to wait until the tree is beginning to get established when it will be able to utilize them. If fertiliser is added, it is imperative to control the weed growth, otherwise the grasses, etc., will gain at the expense of the tree, and the growth made can be *less* than it would have been without the addition of nutrients.

Obtaining and Handling Plants

A healthy plant is the key to success, as no amount of care and attention will revive a dying one. Too often, plants are not healthy at the time of planting. Conifer material will come in three different types: bare-root, potgrown and rootballed.

Bare-root stock is satisfactory for small items, and also where large numbers are being planted, where a 90 per cent survival rate is adequate. The plants should not be more than 75 cm tall, and preferably be no more than 45 cm.

Bare-rooted stock may be seedlings, but more usually the plants will be 'transplants'; these are seedlings which have been transplanted once, or occasionally twice, in the nursery to develop a sturdier plant with a compact, fibrous root system and a relatively broad stem diameter at the root collar. In catalogues, seedlings and transplants are described as 1 + 0, 2 + 0 or 2 + 1, where the first number relates to the time spent in the seedbed and the number after the '+' is the time spent lined out in the nursery after transplanting. Seedlings or transplants may have the roots trimmed or undercut by machine without being moved, in which case the '+' is replaced by a 'u' and the time after the 'u' refers to the period spent in the bed after undercutting, e.g. a 1 u 1 + 1 plant is three years old, was undercut in the seedbed, was transplanted one year later and has spent a further year in the nursery.

Transplants or seedlings should be supplied with the entire plant enclosed in a polythene bag to prevent the plants drying out. However, equally fatal can be to let them heat up, either by wet foliage starting to ferment, or by leaving a bundle in the sun, even for a few minutes. Should it not be possible to plant them straight away, the plants should be taken out of the bags, the bundles opened out and watered if dry and the roots either heeled in the soil, or put in moist but not sodden peat or similar organic matter; almost whatever the weather, the plants will need watering weekly. Bare-rooted stock will usually come in bundles of 50 plants.

Bare-rooted stock can only be planted during the dormant season. This restricts planting to the period November to April. Planting during mid-winter is better avoided, because cold dry winds during the winter can desiccate the young plants before the roots have been able to make new growth. Planting after April is only feasible if the plants have been held dormant in a cold store.

Potgrown or container-grown stock is suitable where high value or difficult trees are being planted, where larger stock is required or where planting must take place during the growing season. It increases the percentage survival and, therefore, is especially useful where all the plants need to survive.

The main danger with container-grown stock is that the root system may be potbound, i.e. with the roots circling around the inside of the container. If this happens, the plant may appear to take very well, only to blow over after a few years as the roots never get properly spread. With bare-root stock this is less of a risk, as the plants usually make an entirely new root system, using the old one only to keep the plant alive *pro tem*. If the roots appear to be circling the pot, they can be either straightened out on planting (if possible) or cut at several points; it is better for the tree to have to make new roots, rather than fail later due to some roots strangling the remainder, or the tree blowing down.

Container-grown stock can be planted at more or less any size but make sure that the plant has not spent longer than two growing seasons, and much better only one, in the pot, and that the size of the pot is suitable for the size of the tree. A ratio of pot diameter to plant height of 1:4 is about right, but the diameter safely can be slightly smaller if the pot is extra deep. Unless in specially large pots, I would not recommend trees more than 2 m tall are used; better still to use ones in the 45-90 cm range, where establishment will be quicker.

Container-grown stock can be planted out during most of the year, although the period of maximum growth from late May to early August is better avoided unless watering is no problem. A check should be kept on whether winter-planted stock needs watering; it is very easy for the compost to dry out during dry periods in the winter.

Balling or rootballing is the process whereby a tree is dug up with soil attached to the roots and wrapped in hessian or polythene netting to retain the soil. It is useful for moving larger items, but ideally these should be prepared by digging around the outline of the ball in the autumn one year in advance. Trees less than 1.2 m tall are unlikely to be able to keep the rootball intact and unless it remains integral, a bare-rooted plant may as well be used!

Although rootballed trees can be planted throughout the year, early autumn and late spring are better times, provided water is available, as at these periods the soil should be relatively warm and the tree capable of making new root growth but not shoot growth.

With container-grown stock reasonable care should suffice, with special attention as always to not letting the plant dry out or stand in water.

With rootballed plants, though, extra care is needed to ensure that the rootball is not damaged. In frosty weather, unplanted trees of both types should be protected from drying winds and have the rootballs/pots covered with straw or sacking.

Planting

The act of planting is usually a once only operation, not to be repeated; it is therefore worth getting it right first time. In the garden setting, pit planting will be the main, or only, method, but in forestry bare-root stock is usually notch planted.

Pit planting is carried out by excavating a hole or pit. The dimensions of the planting hole will vary with the size of the tree and its existing roots: 45 cm square and 30 cm deep should be considered the minimum, but it must always be larger and deeper than the pot or rootball of the plant. Once excavated, the sides and bottom of the pit should be lightly forked over, so that they are not glazed smooth and uninviting for root growth.

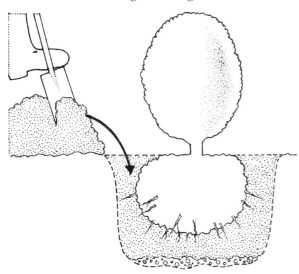

Figure 6.1 Pit Planting. Backfilling of soil around rootball. Ensure that final level of the tree is at nursery soil level.

The turf or weedy soil from the surface should be placed at the bottom of the pit and chopped up. Under no circumstances should this soil be replaced around the tree at surface level after planting. At this stage check that the pit is the correct depth to take the plant and its roots. Generally, as the soil beneath the rootball or pot will settle, it is better to have the surface of the plant 2.5 cm or so higher than the original soil level, especially on heavy ground. Usually at this stage

some more soil will have to be put into the bottom of the pit, but occasionally some of the turf has to be removed. Planting on a slight mound, however, is much better than burying the tree.

The tree is then placed in the hole, the roots spread out and soil firmed in around the sides of the pit. The soil must be properly firmed but take care not to compact the soil. With rootballed trees, the tree should be placed in the pit with the hessian or polythene netting still tied up. Cut or untie it but do not attempt to remove it from beneath the tree; rather, cut it away around the outside of the ball. Pulling it away from under the tree is likely to damage the rootball and the hessian will soon rot away.

The final level of the soil should be at or just above the surface of the surrounding ground, to allow for settlement, and the soil should come to within 2.5 cm or so of the nursery soil mark on the stem; this is the level that the tree was in the ground in the nursery and shows as a dark line or mark. With container-grown stock, the top of the compost should be used.

Amendments, such as peat or bark, or fertiliser can be added to the soil to be used for backfilling the planting pit. Opinions differ as to whether these are beneficial or do more harm than good. On heavy waterlogged soils, organic matter can remove what little available oxygen there is in the soil as it breaks down, exacerbating the situation. On other soils, though, adding peat or some other form of organic matter will do no harm and generally is beneficial. Peat can be added both to the soil and incorporated in the bottom of the pit. Putting the turves in the bottom of the pit adds both organic matter, as the grass decays, and nutrient rich topsoil.

Adding fertilisers is less certain, especially if weeds are not effectively controlled. Most ordinary chemical fertilisers may be washed out of the soil before the tree has made sufficient roots to find them. Slow-release formulations are expensive, but prevent this problem. Generally, the time to fertilise is at the start of the second year, provided there are no weeds.

Staking should not be necessary for most plants, and what is needed can be provided by a bamboo cane. This should be loosely tied into the stem so that the tie will not cut into the bark, or the cane rub against it. Larger plants, though, will need staking. Ideally, the stake should hold the roots firm in the soil but let the stem bend with the wind, as this is the mechanism by which the tree knows whether to make the stem thicker. A rigid stake extending up into the crown with the plant tightly attached is useless and often positively harmful.

It can be difficult to position a stake so that it is close to the base of the tree, without damaging the roots or rootball. A solution is to make a triangle of short stakes outside the rootball and attach the tree to them with either long rubber or plastic ties or guy ropes. Whatever method is used, ensure that the tree cannot rub against the stake and that the tie does not constrict the stem.

Any form of staking or guying should not be needed after the first season if the tree is growing well. Leaving stakes on too long can create problems, such as the tree depending on the extra support, or the ties constricting the stem, and lead to failure later. It is better, however, to remove supports in the late spring, after the winter storms but before growth starts.

Where very large numbers of bare-root trees are being planted, such as in forestry, the need for speed and economy in planting and the acceptability of a small level of losses allows notch planting to be used. By this method, several hundred trees can be planted by one man in a day. Notch planting involves using a spade to make a vertical notch in the ground. The spade is rocked back and forth to create a small opening below ground level which is deep enough to accommodate the tree's roots. The roots are pushed into this hole and the tree pulled up slightly so that they are straightened out and not bent and the tree set at the right level. The spade is inserted to one side of the notch to fill the hole and the tree firmed in by using the heel. It is important to firm the tree in properly, else if an airspace is left, failure may result from the roots drying out, or the tree may be blown over.

Notch planting is only suitable for large numbers of trees and not advisable on sticky soils, at least not when wet, or the soil around the tree will be compacted.

Establishing Trees

Weed control of newly-planted trees is vital on all sites. It is beneficial in two ways. Weeds compete for soil moisture and as the tree does not have a proper root system when planted, it is at a disadvantage relative to established or quick-growing weeds. Weeds also compete for nutrients. Adding nutrients to a weedy site will usually result in less growth to the newly-planted tree as the weeds seize the opportunity and grow faster, making the

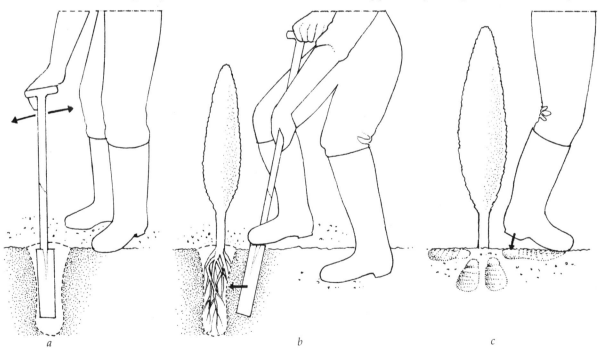

Figure 6.2 Notch Planting. a The notch is opened by the spade. b The tree is put into the notch, which is closed by the spade. c The tree is firmed by using the heel.

competitive situation for the tree worse.

Weed control can be achieved by three methods: herbicides, mulches and mechanical means.

The area kept weedfree wants to be as large as possible. One less than 60 cm diameter is not of any benefit and the ideal practical size is around 90 cm-1.2 m in diameter. Above this the area will start to look unsightly, although growth, certainly in the second year after planting, will benefit. A newly-planted tree can be expected to make roots up to 90 cm long in the first season, and continue to expand the radius of its rootspread at that rate for several years. A weedfree area 90 cm in diameter will give the newly-planted tree a zone 60 cm across in which it will be the only plant.

Herbicides can be harmful if not properly used but are extremely effective if correctly applied. Some herbicides are soil-acting and have a season-long persistence; others are taken in through the leaves and only kill the foliage treated. Care must be taken with the latter category not to get the herbicide on the foliage of the tree.

Persistent herbicides are ones such as Simazine and Propyzamide and they largely control germinating weeds. Propyzamide is very safe to use even on newly-planted stock. It will control grasses and some broadleaved weeds, including existing grasses. Its drawbacks are that it is fairly expensive and must be applied from October to January (December in southern England) to give season long control as it is volatile and will disappear before being bound into the soil if this is warm. Simazine must be used with more care, as it can damage plants if applied at too strong a dose. The soil must also be wet but it can be applied at any season. It will only control new germinating weeds and will have no effect on established ones. Use it at a rate of no more than 1 kg per hectare of product for newly-planted stock.

Foliage-acting herbicides like paraquat (Weedol) and glyphosate (Tumbleweed) will control existing weeds. Glyphosate is generally to be preferred as it is not poisonous to man and is moved around in the plant so that if applied to the leaves, it also kills the roots. Usually the herbicide is sprayed onto the foliage but glyphosate can also be applied by means of a 'Weed Wiper'. This is a wick which is fed by a reservoir of diluted glyphosate and wiped across the weeds. Foliage-acting herbicides are only useful when there is sufficient weed foliage to spray and are less useful over the winter period.

Mulches not only control competition but can also prevent water loss due to the natural drying of the soil. Either organic matter or black polythene sheeting can be used.

Mulches made of organic matter are more aesthetic. The material used needs to be one which will last for a reasonable time and not encourage weeds. Pine needles and conifer bark are excellent mulches, but grass cuttings should only be used with care as they can heat up and cause damage to the plant. Peat, whilst good, only lasts for a year or so. The mulch needs to be used in a layer deep enough to be effective and not to get scattered by birds searching for food; 10-15 cm is usually appropriate. Organic mulches can lead to a temporary loss of available nitrogen from the soil as the soil bacteria break it down. On most soils, conifers tolerate this without showing any ill effects, but on sandy ones, adding a nitrogen fertiliser may be beneficial.

Black polythene can make a very effective mulch. It is less aesthetic than other mulches but is more efficient; it prevents water loss from the soil surface and also leads to higher soil temperatures which tend to make nutrients more available to the tree's roots. Another great attribute is that polythene can be applied at planting on a relatively weedy site and give full protection for the first three years, without additional work. This makes it especially useful on farms or in countryside planting schemes, where labour is not available for weeding in the early summer.

The polythene must be black and at least 500 gauge, otherwise it will not last and a rich crop of weeds will grow beneath it. A slit is made halfway to the middle in one side of a square piece of polythene. This is placed around the tree. The polythene can be fixed by placing stones or clods on the corners but it is much better to dig it in; this is done by making a slit around the outline of the polythene and 7.5 cm in from the edge. Using the blade of the spade, the polythene is pushed into the slit and a tight fit can be attained. Voles and other mammals can be a nuisance with any mulch and I know of one arboretum where badgers caused the cessation of polythene as a mulch by forever digging it up!

Shelters and Protection

Growth can be enhanced and protection against rabbits, deer and other herbivores given by the use of shelters. The old-fashioned spiral rabbit guards are rarely worth considering, providing little effective protection and often causing the new tree to blow over.

Shelters are made out of tubes of rigid polythene sheeting and several brands are available. They act as mini-greenhouses which give enhanced growth with many species; they also prevent browsing. The shelters are approximately 7.5-15 cm in diameter and are placed over the tree at the time of planting; they need to be held up by a small stake. Further information on this technique can be obtained from the Silviculture Branch, Forestry Commission Forest Research Station, Alice Holt Lodge, Farnham, Surrey GU10 4LH, England.

The older method of protecting against rabbits was to use chicken wire. This is effective, but must be supported. It is untidy and will not give any enhanced growth.

Post Planting Maintenance

This includes weed control, pruning and getting a grafted plant to make a leader. Removing a stake or guy is discussed above (see page 60).

Keeping an area around each tree permanently weedfree is beneficial to the plant. It is especially useful where mown grass covers the site. A buffer of grass-free soil (or mulch) will prevent the machinery coming close to the stem of the tree and greatly reduce damage caused to the bole by mowers hitting it.

Pruning is occasionally necessary to remove dead, damaged or competing branches or to clear the bole so that the bark can be seen.

Branches or forked leaders should be removed flush with the stem when they are as small as possible. The cut should be made so that the bark of the stem is not damaged, but neither should long snags or stubs be left.

Conifers differ from other trees in that they do not appear to heal wounds by making growth from the sides, over the wound. Rather, they seem to occlude a stem wound by making diameter growth, which will at first leave the wound in its own dimple and only later grow over it. Most conifers produce resin which covers wounds and treatment with tree paints is not needed. There is no particular time of the year at which pruning should be carried out.

Grafted conifers, especially of spruces and Silver firs (select blue forms of *Picea pungens* are one example) can be reluctant to make a true lead-

ing shoot which grows upwards and has the leaves arranged radially around it; rather, they may be inclined to grow horizontally like the side branch from which the scion was taken.

There are two ways in which these plants can be encouraged to make leaders. The safest way is to control the weeds and feed and mulch the plants so that they are growing vigorously. The strongest shoot can then be tied in to a cane and will usually make a proper leading shoot after a year or two.

If this doesn't work, the tree can be encouraged to make epicormic growth, that is to develop dormant buds from the bark. Many Silver firs will produce these naturally, complete with radial leading shoot from the stem and main branches. They can be encouraged by snipping off the terminal shoot about 2.5 cm from the bud. This is best carried out when the shoot is partly grown and not ripened, although it will work, albeit more slowly, if carried out later. Around the base of the shoot, often in the portion which remains enclosed in the old bud scales, there are one or more latent buds. The growth made from these buds will be more 'plastic' and more amenable to training to make a leading shoot; occasionally, though, just removing the terminal shoot will cause a side shoot to become a leading shoot.

Moving an Established Plant

Occasionally it is desirable to move a plant. Possibly it was planted in the wrong place, or it is one of the slow-growing conifers which has eventually grown too large for the dwarf conifer bed but which you are reluctant to give the chop. With a considerable amount of heaving, it is possible to move trees up to 3 m tall; larger ones can be moved, but machinery will be needed as the necessary rootball will weigh a tonne, or more!, and growth thereafter is unlikely to be satisfactory, at least not for some years.

If you have decided to move a plant, reconsider and check that it will really be worth moving. This is especially important with dwarf conifers where the one to be moved may be growing cheek by jowl with others. The size of the area which will have to be disturbed to give a good chance of success is considerable, and much larger than the eventual rootball; the remaining trees may suffer.

The plant must be moved with a rootball to have more than a faint chance of surviving. The diameter of the rootball will depend upon the size

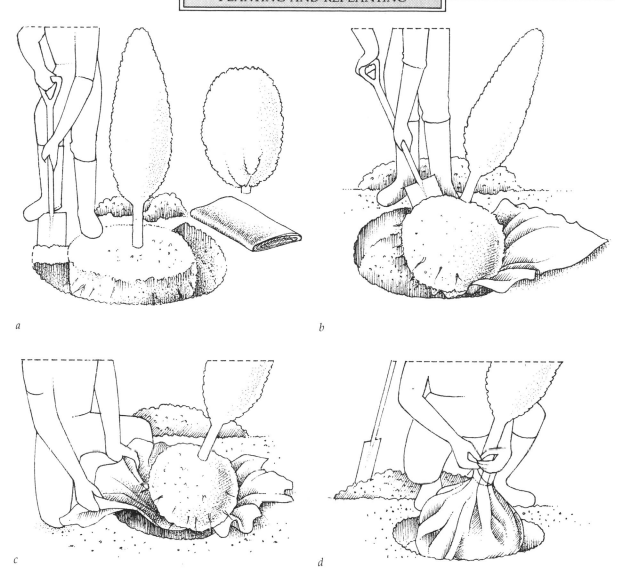

Figure 6.3 Lifting and Moving an Established Plant. a A trench is excavated around the outline of the rootball. b The plant is undercut and rolled over onto a sheet of hessian. c The hessian is moved under the rootball. d The rootball is tied round with string to prevent it falling apart.

of the tree. A tree 1.8m tall should have a rootball 45-60 cm in diameter and a tree 3m tall, a rootball 75 cm in diameter. The plant can be prepared by digging around the proposed rootball one year in advance — autumn is the best time for this — so that new roots are made within the soil to be moved with the plant; this results in more of the roots being kept and the extra roots in this soil will help to hold the ball together.

The best times to move a plant within a garden are early autumn and late spring: times when the tree will be making new roots but not shoot growth and the soil will be relatively dry. Late August or early September is best provided irrigation is available if needed. Generally, mid-winter should be avoided.

The mechanics of moving a plant are that a circular trench is dug on the outside of the rootball and down to around 45 cm. The trench will need to be at least another 30 cm wide, probably more, to allow for working space. When the required depth is reached, the soil beneath the ball is removed and the roots severed. The tree is carefully leant over on its side and hessian placed underneath it;

it is leant back so that the hessian can be brought out the other side. The tree can then be lifted out of the hole, but if it needs to be rolled to the new site, or roughly handled, the hessian should be sewn together to protect the rootball. Planting should be as described above for rootballed trees.

·CHAPTER 7·
Pests and Diseases

Damage to conifers can be categorised under three headings: damage by infectious agents (fungi, bacteria, etc.), damage by animals (including insects) and damage by non-living agents. It is not possible in the space available to give more than an outline of the most pertinent examples in each category. Damage by fungal and non-living agents is comprehensively covered in *Diseases of Forest and Ornamental Trees* by Phillips & Burdekin (Macmillan). In Britain, advice about all forms of damage to conifers can be obtained from the Forestry Commission Forest Research Station, Alice Holt Lodge, Farnham, Surrey GU10 4LH or the Forestry Commission Northern Research Station, Roslin, Midlothian. In other countries, the national forest authority will doubtless be willing to advise. The pathogens and insect pests briefly outlined below relate to Britain and different agents may be significant in other countries.

Non-living Agents

When damage occurs to plants, it is important to question whether a non-living agent could be involved. These include climatic factors, aspects of the soil and chemical factors.

Climatic factors include extremes of heat and cold, especially unseasonable frosts and hail, as well as drought and lightning.

Some aspects of climatic damage can be avoided by careful siting, e.g. trees known to flush early in the season can either be planted on a cold north aspect or where the early morning sun will not quickly thaw frozen tissues. Other factors of climate are less certain, e.g. hail or lightning.

Winter cold can kill plant tissues or the entire plant but in a number of species it causes the foliage to change colour without suffering any harm. *Cryptomeria japonica* 'Elegans' turns bronze over winter, while *Pinus sylvestris* 'Aurea' becomes a bright golden yellow, only resuming the normal coloration in late spring. Western red cedar (*Thuja plicata*) will turn bronze in cold spells which is quite normal; however, if leaves are killed by winter cold they will become a deep glossy black.

Wet snow can cause havoc with trees such as Cedar of Lebanon (*Cedrus libani*) which have tiers of horizontal branches. Protection can be given by using cables to brace the branches into the main stem but should only be attempted with the assistance of a professional arboriculturist.

Damage by lightning varies from the death of the top few whorls of branches, which can be observed in many Wellingtonia (*Sequoiadendron giganteum*), to gouging out or merely killing a strip of bark and wood (which occurs on all sorts of trees), to killing whole trees or (fortunately rare) instances where the tree is completely shattered. It is possible to protect individual trees with a lightning conductor but the cost is substantial.

Drought due either to excess use (or transpiration) of moisture (such as on windy sites) or lack of available moisture can retard plant growth and kill leaves and whole plants. In addition, on a number of conifers, cracks may open in the bark during dry summer periods. These drought cracks may be a metre or two in length and follow the grain of the wood, which is generally set at a slightly spiral angle to the bole. They are frequently observed on Noble (*Abies procera*) and Grand (*A. grandis*) firs and also on Sitka (*Picea sitchensis*) and occasionally Norway (*P. abies*) spruces. Although they degrade the timber value, they do not appear structurally to weaken the tree and heal over in the following seasons.

Soil Factors

The main nutrients (nitrogen, phosphorus and potassium, as well as magnesium, sulphur and calcium) are needed in quantity for good growth of plants. Other elements are also essential, albeit in much smaller amounts, and these are termed trace elements. Insufficient of any of these nutrients may have characteristic effects on growth, e.g. plants with insufficient nitrogen are generally yellow. Nutrient deficiencies can be caused by the absence of a nutrient or by its non-availability due to soil pH or site factors. On many soils derived from chalk or limestone, iron and manganese are not available to the plant due to the excess of calcium and lime-induced chlorosis occurs; the affected trees turn yellow, appear unhealthy and may eventually die. Nutrient deficiencies can be corrected by the application of the appropriate fertiliser but, especially on sandy soils, the possibility that the symptoms are caused by the absence of a trace element rather than by one of the main nutrients should be considered.

Inadequate soil aeration (due to poor drainage, compaction or the soil surface being impervious) can also lead to diminished growth or death of trees. The basic cause is insufficient oxygen available for healthy root growth. Most trees require the soil atmosphere to contain more than 10 per cent oxygen and will die if this figure drops below 3 per cent. Exceptions are trees like the Swamp cypress (*Taxodium distichum*) and the Chinese swamp cypress (*Glyptostrobus pensilis*) which can grow in water or waterlogged soils.

Chemical Factors

Chemical factors include air pollution, salt and herbicide damage.

Air pollutants are derived from the burning of fossil fuels or from chemical processes, either in industry or in vehicles. Sulphur dioxide is released by burning coal or oil, but other pollutants (such as ozone and peroxyacetyl nitrate) are formed from exhaust gases of cars, particularly in hot sunny periods. Above certain concentrations all of these chemicals can kill leaves or entire plants. The damage is often more severe to evergreen trees due to the higher concentrations of pollutants released during the winter but larches (*Larix*) are susceptible to several pollutants. Where sulphur dioxide pollution is a known risk (which is only likely to occur when high doses are released by nearby factories during periods of temperature inversion), the following species are relatively tolerant: *Chamaecyparis lawsoniana*, *Juniperus* spp., *Pinus nigra*, *Thuja plicata* and *Ginkgo biloba*.

Salt damage can be caused by spray from the sea or by de-icing salt applied to roads during cold periods. This is discussed further in Chapter 3, page 38.

Herbicide damage can result from the misuse of a particular herbicide or from its use on a susceptible species. Herbicide damage should always be suspected if damage follows after herbicide use. The label recommendations should always be followed to reduce the risk of damage by these otherwise useful tools to management.

Infectious Agents

These include fungi, bacteria and similar non-photosynthesising members of the plant kingdom. The most important are the fungi and the most serious damaging species under British conditions are discussed below. However, some plants can be damaging infectious agents; these are the Dwarf mistletoes (*Arceuthobium*). Fortunately they are not found in Britain. However, one species (*A. oxycedri*) causes minor damage on *Juniperus* in central and southern Europe and a number of species in western North America are serious pests on certain conifers.

Some fungi are beneficial to trees, such as those which form mycorrhizal associations discussed in Chapter 2, page 21 or break down organic matter to release nutrients into the soil. A number, however, are pathogens and some are extremely damaging. Some fungi affect a wide range of plant species, but others may only be serious on a small number of species, or only occasionally. Apart from causing the death of trees, fungi can lead to instability due to the destruction of roots, to the breakage of stems or limbs as a result of wood decay, cause unsightliness due to the death of many small areas of foliage and also cause shoot and branch dieback. Only a very few of the more general and important damaging fungi are discussed here.

Honey Fungus

This disease is almost certainly responsible for the death of more trees than any other fungus and is caused by species in the genus *Armillaria*. The disease usually kills trees in ones and twos over a period of time, rather than causing wholesale devastation at one time. The fungus kills and decays the roots and decay may extend for 50 cm or so up the bole. The disease can be recognised by the development of a thin layer of white fungal tissue (mycelium) beneath the killed bark, and also by the rhizomorphs which grow through the soil from infected roots and stumps. Rhizomorphs are black rootlike strands of fungal tissue and can grow for several metres through the soil, causing new infections on any suitable substrate encountered. Their similarity to bootlaces has led to the alternative name of Bootlace fungus. Spores are produced by the honey-coloured fruitbodies but are only thought to be involved in long-distance dissemination of the fungus. Apart from killing trees, the decay of roots will make trees less stable and susceptible to being blown over in strong winds.

Control measures against Honey fungus consist mainly of removing stumps and all dead woody matter which the fungus could use as a food source. The site should preferably then be left without woody plants for one or two years to let any remaining woody material be consumed. No effective chemical treatment has yet been developed. Physical barriers such as walls or sheets of pvc buried in the soil may prevent the spread of rhizomorphs. It is unwise to move a plant from an area infected with the disease to elsewhere in the garden. Where a broadleaved tree is felled and the stump cannot be removed, it should be killed by the use of a herbicide, preferably Ammonium sulphamate, which encourages the invasion of the stump by competing non-pathogenic fungi which thus tend to exclude Honey fungus.

Conifers vary in the degree of tolerance or susceptibility to the disease. Most can be killed when young, but the following are susceptible and are frequently killed at any age: Monkey puzzle (*Araucaria araucana*), Cedars (*Cedrus*), Cypresses (*Chamaecyparis*, × *Cupressocyparis* and *Cupressus*), Japanese cedar (*Cryptomeria*), spruces (*Picea*), pines (*Pinus*), Wellingtonia (*Sequoiadendron giganteum*), Western red cedar (*Thuja plicata*) and Western hemlock (*Tsuga heterophylla*). The following are more resistant and are likely to succeed where the disease is present: Silver firs (*Abies*), Incense cedar (*Calocedrus decurrens*), Larches (*Larix*), Douglas fir (*Pseudotsuga menziesii*) and, especially, Yew (*Taxus baccata*). More information can be found in the Department of the Environment (DoE) Arboricultural Leaflet 2 'Honey Fungus'.

Phytophthora Root Rot

This is a disease caused by several species of *Phytophthora*. These are microscopic fungi which thrive in wet soils and kill the root tissues of a number of trees. The fungus may soon be succeeded by other fungi, such as Honey fungus, in the killed portion of the roots and because of this, and the microscopic nature of the fungus, it can be difficult to know whether it or some other agent may be the cause of the damage observed. The disease is spread by contaminated water or soil or by moving infected plants. In the garden it is best prevented and controlled by providing good drainage and by not allowing water to lie around the base of plants. Of conifers, Lawson cypress (*Chamaecyparis lawsoniana*) and yew (*Taxus baccata*) are notably susceptible, and severe damage occasionally occurs on young nursery plants of Silver fir (*Abies*) and Douglas fir (*Pseudotsuga menziesii*). The disease is significant because of the widespread planting of the first two species and the devastation the disease can cause in a nursery. More information is given in DoE Arboricultural Leaflet 8 'Phytophthora Diseases of Trees and Shrubs'.

Heterbasidion (Fomes) annosum

This fungus affects a wide range of plants. Economically it is very significant, causing the decay of more coniferous timber in Britain than any other species, but in the garden is less common. It decays the roots of trees and will also decay the bole to a height of several metres. Infected trees may die and are liable to blow down. The fruit body is a perennial bracket fungus; it is found on infected tree stumps at or just below ground level. Pines (*Pinus*) may be killed by the disease (especially on alkaline sites) and many conifers are susceptible to root decay, especially Western hemlock (*Tsuga heterophylla*); Silver firs (*Abies*) are generally resistant. However, many conifers may be killed in the first few years after planting.

Freshly cut conifer stumps are liable to be infected from airborne spores which alight on the cut surface, and the fungus almost always gains entry to a healthy tree through contact between its roots and those of an infected stump or tree.

In conifers, control can be achieved in three ways. The removal of stumps prevents the build up of the disease and deprives the fungus of food; this is the most effective method where the fungus is already established. Where removal of stumps is not practical or economic, the stumps of newly felled trees should be painted with a urea solution; this encourages competing but non-pathogenic fungi to colonise the stump and exclude *Heterobasidion annosum*. The third method is available on pine stumps only, where, instead of urea, a competing fungus (*Peniophora gigantea*) can be applied to the freshly felled stump to prevent the growth of the fungus. Forestry Commission Leaflet 5 gives more information.

Twig Blights

A number of diseases enter the twigs or branches of trees through the needles. They may girdle the shoot and lead to the death of the distal portions. Where the shoot affected is the main stem, death of the entire tree may result. Also, where extensive small areas of the crown are killed, the tree may be made too unsightly to be worth keeping or possibly so weakened as to make it susceptible to infection by a general pathogen such as Honey fungus.

White pine blister rust, caused by *Cronartium ribicola*, can affect some of the soft pines (*Pinus* subgenus *strobus*). It has prevented the widespread forestry planting of Weymouth pine (*Pinus strobus*) in Great Britain and can with time kill large trees; Sugar (*P. lambertiana*), Mexican white (*P. ayacahuite*) and Western white (*P. monticola*) pines are also seriously affected by it. It is a rust fungus with an alternate host (i.e. successive generations of the fungus occur on different host plants), in this case Blackcurrants and other species of *Ribes*. Blackcurrants are infected by the stage on the pines but little damage is caused; the stage of the fungus which develops on the Blackcurrants infects the pine. The fungus enters the tree through the needles, spreads into the shoot, killing the bark and eventually reaches and girdles the stem; the dead bark exudes resin. Effective control is only by removal of Blackcurrants.

Resin top disease caused by *Peridermium pini* is another rust fungus. It can cause the death of Scots pine (*Pinus sylvestris*) and related species, and is quite common in eastern Scotland and East Anglia. Symptoms closely resemble those caused by the White pine blister rust but the fungus passes from pine to pine without passing through an alternate host. Infected trees should be removed.

Phomopsis juniperovora affects *Juniperus sabina* and some other species. It causes the death of small portions of the crowns by girdling the shoots and ultimately makes the plants unattractive. In shrubs and small trees, spraying with Benomyl will give control.

Death of scattered shoots and twigs on Deodar (*Cedrus deodara*) is common and caused by *Potebniamyces coniferarum* (syn. *Phomopsis pseudotsugae*) but is not serious.

Seiridium cardinale is a fungus causing a serious and common disease of Monterey pine (*Cupressus macrocarpa*) and has been found causing severe damage on Leyland cypress (× *Cupressocyparis leylandii*) and may possibly affect some other *Cupressus* species. It can cause considerable death of twigs, leading to the death of the tree and no practicable control measures are yet available.

Animal Pests

Animal pests include both insect pests and other animals. Of these the insect pests are potentially the more serious. Larger mammals such as rabbits and deer can cause damage to conifers by browsing either bark or foliage and voles may also girdle the stems of small trees; these forms of damage are only occasionally serious in the garden context and, where necessary, appropriate fencing can be used to prevent damage.

Insect Pests

A small number of the several hundreds of species of insects which may be found feeding on conifers can cause serious damage but only a few are sufficiently general to warrant mention here. Apart from the Conifer spinning mite, all the species discussed below are aphids but certain species of weevil can also cause intermittent damage, girdling newly-planted trees, and bark beetles (*Scolytidae*) take advantage of older trees (especially *Picea* and *Pinus*) suffering from water stress.

Aphids feed by sucking the sap of plants, from which they obtain amino-acids and sugars. However, sap does not have both sugars and amino-acids in the correct proportions for aphid development and the surplus sugars are secreted as a sugary solution known as 'honeydew'. Honeydew is collected by ants and bees (it makes a good honey!) and is colonised by some fungi, especially 'Sooty moulds', which turn it black. The presence of many aphids on a plant will remove much of the products of photosynthesis; it will often cause the death of the affected parts and may kill or seriously disfigure the whole plant.

Green Spruce Aphid

This tiny aphid (*Elatobium abietinum*) sucks the sap from the undersides of the older needles of many species of spruce (*Picea*). The attacked needles turn a mottled yellow, then go brown and fall. Feeding can occur throughout the year, except for a short period in summer, but damage is most severe from the autumn to late spring; mild winters increase the risk of damage. Death of the entire plant does not usually occur, as the current year's needles are rarely affected. However, a severe attack can remove all the older foliage and destroy the amenity value of a plant for several years. It is particularly a problem on selected blue forms of Colorado spruce (*P. pungens glauca*) and on *P. glauca* 'Conica'. Control on small trees is possible by spraying with an aphicide, such as malathion or pirimicarb, either when a problem is detected or in August as a precautionary measure. This insect is discussed in more detail in Forestry Commission Research & Development Paper 116.

Conifer Woolly Aphids

Several species of Conifer woolly aphid (*Adelges*) can cause problems on conifers, and are collectively known as Adelgids. They are discussed more fully in Forestry Commission Bulletin 42.

The Pineapple gall woolly aphid (*A. abietis*) is unusual amongst the pest species of aphid in that it has only one host; most species have alternate generations on, usually, different genera of trees. It causes distinctive pineapple-shaped galls on the new shoots of several species of spruce (*Picea*). It may disfigure Christmas trees by spoiling the symmetry of the branching. The eggs overwinter near the buds and infect the new shoots in May; control can be brought about by a single high-volume spraying of the foliage with gamma-HCH during a mild spell over the winter.

Two Conifer woolly aphids on Silver firs (*Abies*) are *Adelges nordmannianae* and *A. piceae*. The former species feeds on the underside of the foliage of several mainly European species of Silver fir where the insects secrete a white woolly wax for protection; it originated on Caucasian fir (*Abies nordmanniana*) but can be very serious on European silver fir (*A. alba*). The second species feeds on the bark of several species, occasionally being serious on Grand (*A. grandis*), Subalpine (*A. lasiocarpa*) and Pacific (*A. amabilis*) firs but Balsam fir (*A. balsamea*), in particular, suffers from a twig attack causing gouty stunted shoots. The insect forms waxy white patches on the stem. Both aphids can be controlled by spraying during mild periods from November to late February with gamma-HCH.

Other frequently found aphids are the Spruce shoot aphid (*Cinara pilicornis*), Black spruce bark aphid (*Cinara piceae*), both on spruces (*Picea*), the Cedar aphid (*Cinara cedri*) on foliage of *Cedrus* species, and two leaf-sucking pine aphids, *Schizolachnus pineti* and *Eulachnus agilis*. More information on these species can be found in Forestry Commission Bulletin 58 'Conifer Lachnids'.

Conifer Spinning or Spider Mite

The mite (*Oligonychus ununguis*) is scarcely visible in either the adult or egg stages but may be seen under a hand lens. The young and adult stages are a pale yellowish colour and are found under the silk webs on the needles and young shoots during the summer. The affected foliage appears as a dirty yellow, becoming bronze before the needles fall. The brown circular eggs are laid on the older shoots. The mite can cause quite severe defoliation, especially on dry sites or in dry seasons; species affected include spruces (*Picea*), some Silver firs (*Abies*) and sometimes Scots pine (*Pinus sylvestris*). Control can be achieved by spraying with dicofol in late May after the eggs have hatched. Affected trees treated in late summer may require a second back-up spray to give good control. The mite is often called Red spider mite, but should not be confused with the horticultural pest of that name.

·CHAPTER 8·
Gazetteer of Conifers

The layout of this section of the book is alphabetically by the botanical or Latin name of the genus. This makes it easier to locate a given genus but less easy to follow a family or group of related genera; to do this, use the synopis of Conifers on page 15. In the larger genera, the species are treated in groups of related species and not alphabetically; this permits their relative characteristics to be considered and the page number of any individual species can be found from the index under both its Latin name and principal common name. Within each genus discussion an indication of the general character of the genus, how it relates to the other members of the family and its ecology and distribution is given, followed by brief descriptions and observations on the garden value of the species. In the descriptions, where a single measurement is given, it is the maximum common figure but where two figures are given, they represent the range of sizes. Measurements are given in centimetres (cm) and metres (m), but a table of comparable imperial units is given on page 220.

Some species have much greater garden value and more useful cultivars than other species, and therefore warrant more space but the objective is at least to mention less common species so that the section is relevant as a reference of all genera and of all species likely to be hardy in temperate regions of the world. With cultivars, though, only a selection of those which are commonly available or worth searching for is included. Some of the reference books in the bibliography give brief details about complete ranges of cultivars.

Information is given on the hardiness of conifers, using the zone system based on the average minimum temperature. The climate is divided into a number of zones, and maps showing the zones for Europe and America are to be found on pages 219-20. The coldest zone in which a species is hardy is given after the descriptive paragraph. When using hardiness zones, it is important to remember that (a) winter temperature is not the only factor which influences a plant's hardiness, (b) all species will have hardier and more tender forms, (c) for rare or newly introduced taxa, the zone given is based on a subjective assessment and not on hard experience, (d) the zone given is the probable minimum or coldest zone; most conifers will be hardy in all warmer zones as well.

Abies Miller **Silver firs Pinaceae**

The Silver firs are the second largest genus in the pine family. Some 55 species are found in the northern hemisphere. The most southerly species is *A. guatemalensis* which occurs in the mountains of southern Mexico, Guatemala and Honduras, to just south of 15°N. In Asia, species are found straddling the Tropic of Cancer in Taiwan and southern China, whilst the most northerly-growing species, *A. sibirica*, grows beyond the Arctic Circle to 67°40′N. Several species are found in Europe, particularly around the Mediterranean, and three are found in North Africa.

Ecologically, Silver firs are found growing in subalpine, cold and warm temperate zones. Most species grow where rainfall is reliable and abundant but some of the northern and montane species survive on relatively dry sites where moisture is limited. These species can be very useful where the soil is dry, at least for part of the year. Most other species, however, prefer a rich and moisture-retentive soil. In Britain all the species except a couple from southern Mexico are hardy but some species, especially those from cold continental climates, are liable to start into growth too soon in the spring and then be damaged by late spring frosts. Shelter from spring frosts is worth giving to most species. Silver firs are generally very tolerant of shading and most will make steady, if slow, growth under quite dense shade.

Silver firs are evergreen conifers. They are distinguished from other species in the pine family by the single and relatively long needles arranged helically on the shoot but usually twisted so that the lower and shaded foliage is 'pectinate', i.e. arranged so as to spread on both sides of the shoot like a comb, or with a V-shaped groove. The needles are set on small circular depressions on the usually smooth shoots; they are generally flat with the stomata restricted to two bands on the lower surface but in some species they are more quadrangular and stomatiferous on all four sides. The cones are carried erect and ripen in the one year. They break up in the autumn or over winter releasing the winged seeds and the bract scales which are scattered by the wind, whilst the central axis or rachis remains on the tree. The male cones are carried on the undersides of the weaker shoots of the previous year.

When identifying Silver firs, choose sterile foliage from the outer crown and not weak shaded material or very strong growths. The shoot colour is best displayed on last year's growth but any pubescence shows up more clearly on the current year's shoots, although you may need a hand lens to see it clearly.

In the garden, Silver firs have several uses. Most will be used to make large bold evergreen trees either for effect or as screening. Most species have a rather whorled and open habit. The species in which the foliage is blue or silver, especially on the stomatal bands, can make very interesting colour variants. The cones of others are violet-blue and have a long season of attractive display. Several good dwarf forms are available. Silver firs make good Christmas trees as they do not readily drop their needles. The growth rates of the species range from very fast for Grand fir (*A. grandis*) to slow and small in Korean fir (*A. koreana*).

No satisfactory classification scheme has been produced for the genus, and in the absence of one, the species will be discussed in the following groupings:

Group 1   *bracteata.*
Group 2   *alba, cephalonica, nordmanniana,*
borisii-regis, bornmuelleriana, nebrodensis, equi-trojani.

Group 3   *pinsapo, numidica, cilicica, tazaotana, marocana.*
Group 4   *firma, homolepis, recurvata, pindrow, gamblei, chensiensis, holophylla, beshanzuensis.*
Group 5   *amabilis, mariesii.*
Group 6   *spectabilis, densa, delavayi, forrestii, fabri, fargesii, squamata, chengii.*
Group 7   *sibirica, semenovii, nephrolepis, sachalinensis, veitchii, koreana, sikokiana, kawakamii, lasiocarpa, balsamea, fraseri.*
Group 8   *grandis, concolor, durangensis, coahuilensis, mexicana, guatemalensis.*
Group 9   *procera, magnifica.*
Group 10   *religiosa, vejari, hickelii, oaxacana.*

Group 1

Contains but a single species which has been placed in a separate subgenus but warrants only its own section.

A. bracteata D. Don
Santa Lucia fir

Tree to 25 m. Crown upright, dense, with short branches. Bark black-grey, smooth, becoming fissured at base into scales. Shoot smooth, stout, glabrous, purplish green or reddish brown. Buds spindle-shaped or fusiform, acute 1.5-2.5 cm, pale brown. Leaves parted into 2 ranks either side of shoot, dark or greyish green above, 2 silvery bands of stomata below, apex sharply pointed, 5 cm. Fruit golden brown, ripening brown, ovoid, 8 cm by 5 cm, only at top of mature trees, bract scale with long pointed and exserted cusp, with blobs of resin, to 3 cm. Zone 7.

Santa Lucia fir has unique buds like those of a Beech tree and also is distinctive in the extent to which the cusp of the bract scale is drawn out and in the long hard bony point to the leaves. It is restricted in the wild to the Santa Lucia Mountains of coastal California and is found in canyon bottoms in an area where the sparse amount of rain falls during the winter. It is hardy in Britain as far north as Aberdeen. In the garden, its value lies in the bold foliage and curious buds; the beautiful cones are only produced on mature trees.

Group 2

This is a group of species from Europe and Asia Minor. They are all restricted in distribution and considered relict species from the Tertiary Period. It is helpful to understand them as having arisen by past segregation from a single species or gene pool. They have narrow cylindrical cones 10-15 cm long with exserted bracts which leave a very narrow rachis on the tree when the cone disintegrates. Most occur in regions with winter rainfall. They are also found in the wild on soils derived from limestone but tolerate acidic ones very well.

A. alba Miller
Silver fir or European Silver fir

Tree to 40 m. Crown regular when young, in old trees restricted to the upper part of the bole with dead broken branches. Bark grey, smooth, becoming progressively cracked into small squares. Shoot pale brown or grey, with a scattered covering of short brown hairs. Buds ovoid, red-brown, with none or some resin flecks. Leaves lax, spreading below the shoot and widely parted above or rising and pointing forwards, dark glossy green with 2 silver or pale bands of stomata below, apex notched, 2.5 cm, up to 3.5 cm on young trees. Fruit cylindrical, 10-15 cm by 3.5 cm wide, green, ripening to brown in September, bract scales exserted and reflexed. Zone 6.

Silver fir was once the tallest tree in Britain but has been displaced by other species and is little planted due to damage by a leaf-sucking aphid (*Adelges nordmannianae*). In Europe it makes an important timber tree but is susceptible to atmospheric pollution and does not tolerate exposure well. It is native to much of Europe from the Pyrenees to the Balkans and is naturalised in the western parts of Britain. By comparison with most other species it is a second-rate tree but was the original Christmas tree popularised by Prince Albert. This tree is the type species of the genus.

Several cultivars are recorded but none are of particular merit.

'Fastigiata' has crowded erect branches making a narrow-crowned tree.

'Pendula' makes an erect tree with hanging side branches.

A. cephalonica Loudon
Greek fir

Tree to 30 m. Crown in old trees massive, with large low spreading branches, in young trees broadly conic and bushy. Bark grey, becoming fissured into small plates in old trees. Shoot glabrous, shiny red-brown. Buds ovoid, resinous. Leaves somewhat radial around shoot, with more above, no or scarcely a groove in foliage arrangement, stiff, deep glossy green, stomata bands white below, apex acute, leaf base a large rounded sucker-like pad, 2-3 cm. Fruit cylindrical, tapers at both ends and nipple-tipped at apex, 10-16 cm by 3.5-4.5 cm, bracts exserted, reflexed. Zone 6.

Greek fir is recorded from the mountains of southern Greece and was first described from the island of Cephalonia. It will make a large tree with time but is one of the first into leaf in the spring and is liable to be frosted. It is rather a coarse tree. The shoot is very distinctive in the shiny red-brown colour and bearing the round and yellowish bases of the needles.

var. *apollinis* (Link) Beissner is a form with more densely set and blunter leaves which lie above and to the side of the shoot; it was originally described from Mount Parnassus in southern Greece. It may be the same as var. *graeca* (Fraas) Liu (which would then be the correct name).

'Meyer's Dwarf' is a mound-forming cultivar with shorter needles 0.8-1.5 cm and without a leader.

A. nordmanniana (Steven) Spach
Caucasian fir

Tree to 35 m. Crown a dense column. Bark grey, smoothly cracked into small squares on older trees. Shoot matures from olive-brown to pink-brown over three years, with scattered brown hairs on weaker shoots. Buds ovoid, light brown, not resinous. Leaves dense and luxuriant, parted below the shoot, spreading forwards at the side and pointing along the shoot above or with a weak groove in the arrangement, rich shiny green above, dull whitish green below, apex bluntly notched, 2-3 cm, to 3.5 cm. Fruit to 15 cm. Zone 5.

Caucasian fir is the best member of this group for normal planting; it has an attractive dense crown and makes a better tree than European silver fir. It is native to the Caucasus Mountains and adjoining north-east Turkey. Recently it has been used to a greater degree as a Christmas tree which does not shed its foliage. It can retain the leaves for an inordinate length of time; usually Silver firs will keep them for four or five years and occasionally up to ten, but I have counted live needles 26 years old on Caucasian fir.

Amongst the several cultivars named are:

'Golden Spreader', an outstanding dwarf form eventually making a metre or so, with foliage a bright golden yellow;

'Pendula' with hanging side branches;

'Tortifolia' with twisted falcate needles.

A. borisii-regis Mattfeld
King Boris fir

Tree to 25 m. Crown heavily branched. Shoot densely covered with black hairs. Buds ovoid, with some yellow resin. Leaves dense, parted either side of shoot and pointing forwards, dark glossy green, 2 narrow bright silver stomatal bands below and a few in a spot near tip above, apex acute or rounded, rarely notched, to 3 cm. Fruit cylindric-conic, to 15 cm, bracts exserted. Zone 6.

Native to the central part of the Balkan peninsula (southern Bulgaria, south Yugoslavia and Macedonia) and the Greek island of Thasos, it is intermediate between European silver fir and Greek fir. It has been considered a natural hybrid between them but has a separate natural distribution and is better understood as part of the group from which all these species have separated to become distinct. It is a better plant than *A. alba* and was named after the King of Bulgaria.

A. bornmuelleriana Mattfeld
Bornmueller fir

Tree to 25 cm. Crown similar to Caucasian fir. Bark black or dark grey. Shoot olive-green, becoming red- or orange-brown, glabrous, smooth. Buds ovoid conic, resinous, with prominently ridged scales free at tip on strongest shoots. Leaves spreading below, foward and rising but with distinct V groove above, mid to dark shiny green with scattered white bands of stomata above, and silvery white stomatal bands below, apex rounded, occasionally notched especially in young plants, 2.5-4 cm. Fruit ovate-oblong or cylindrical, 12-15 cm by 4-6 cm. Zone 5.

Bornmueller fir occurs in northern Turkey in the mountains south of the Black Sea and to the west of the distribution of Caucasian fir. Hybrid origin from Greek and Caucasian firs has been postulated but does not accord with the distinctive features and geographical distribution. It does not have the very distinct rounded sucker-like leaf base of Greek fir; from Caucasian fir it differs in the resinous buds, longer leaves with distinct lines of stomata on the upper surface and the broader cone. In the garden it makes as good a plant but is less readily available.

A. nebrodensis (Lojacono-Pojero) Mattei
Sicilian fir

Small tree to 15 m. Bark orange, finely shredding, in old trees irregularly flaked. Shoot shiny whitish grey, with pink or yellow tinge, glabrous except on weaker growths. Buds resinous. Leaves dense, on stronger shoots all assurgent, more spreading on weaker ones, dark glossy green above, stomata in 2 white bands below, apex rounded or often acute, 1.5-2 cm. Fruit to 10 cm. Zone 5.

Very distinct in foliage from Euopean silver fir with which it has been allied, Sicilian fir is native to the mountains of northern Sicily. Due to deforestation, only a score of old wild plants exist. In cultivation it makes a vigorous tree with a dense leafy crown and is a smaller-growing tree than others in this group.

A. equi-trojani Aschers & Sintensis
Trojan fir

Shoot yellow-brown, glabrous. Buds broadly ovoid, pointed, chestnut brown, slightly resinous. Leaves spreading below the shoot, those above forwards with a V groove or as for Bornmueller fir, apex blunt, notched at least in young trees, 1.5-2.5 cm, to 3 cm. Fruit 10 cm, similar to Bornmueller fir. Zone 5.

Trojan fir is restricted to the Ida range of mountains in north-west Asiatic Turkey and lies between the ranges of Greek and Bornmueller firs. Liu (Monograph of the Genus *Abies*, Taipei, 1971) equates it with his *A. cephalonica* var. *graeca* and other authorities treat it as a subspecies of Caucasian fir; however, it seems to be better placed as a separate entity within the group. It does not have the distinct leaf base of Greek fir. It is rare in cultivation but should make a tree comparable to Caucasian fir.

Group 3

This group is closely related to the above species and is found with a more southerly distribution, in Spain, North Africa and in Asia Minor from southern Turkey through to the Lebanon. It differs in the more cylindrical cones which end in a pronounced nipple tip and have the bract scales hidden between the ovuliferous scales. These species are more tolerant than most other firs of limestone and chalk soils.

A. pinsapo Boissier
Spanish or Hedgehog fir

Tree 20 m. Crown neat when young but becoming ragged. Bark dark grey, smooth when young, later fissured and rugged. Shoot orange-brown, glabrous. Buds very resinous. Leaves arranged perpendicularly around shoot, with only a few more above, on broad sucker-like bases, stiff and straight, dull grey-green or glaucous blue with stomata on both surfaces, apex rounded, blunt, 1-1.8 cm. Fruit 10-15 cm, pale green, ripening brown. Zone 7.

Spanish fir is restricted to three sites around Ronda in southern Spain. It is unique in the way the needles stick out all around the shoot. Young trees make interesting specimens but older plants lose some of their appeal. It is the best Silver fir for sites on chalk. Despite its southerly origins, Spanish fir (and the others in the group) is fully hardy throughout the British Isles, although slow-growing.

'Glauca' is the commonest cultivar but really only represents part of the natural variation of the species; at one of the three sites, trees are particularly variable in the blueness of the foliage.

'Aurea' is a weak-growing form with yellow-gold foliage; it is better on a dry sunny site.

A. numidica De Lannoy
Algerian fir

Tree to 20 m. Crown dense, conical. Bark purplish grey, smooth, becoming scaly. Shoot orange-brown, glabrous. Buds ovoid conic, with adpressed scales, not resinous. Leaves arranged with a parting above and below the shoot, perpendicular, stiff, blue-green or grey-green with stomata in a broad band above and 2 below, apex rounded, 1-2 cm. Fruit cylindrical, apex mucronate, 12-18 cm by 4-6 cm, bracts hidden. Zone 6.

Algerian fir is native to the mountains around Mount Barbor near the coast of Algeria. It makes an attractive slow-growing tree but is variable in the colour of the foliage. 'Glauca' is a form with more bluish foliage.

A. cilicica (Antoine & Kotschy) Carriere
Cilician fir

Tree to 30 m. Crown narrow conic. Bark smooth, dark grey. Shoot yellow or brownish green, with scattered brown hairs. Buds resinous or not resinous, ovoid conic, with free tips to the bud scales. Leaves lax, spreading below with a V groove above, on strong growths, the upper leaves more forwards as in Caucasian fir, shiny dark green with stomata below only, apex rounded, 2.5-4 cm. Fruit 16-20 cm, rarely 30 cm long by 4-6 cm. Zone 6.

Cilician fir is rare in cultivation. It is native to the Taurus Mountains of southern Turkey and to north-west Syria and Lebanon. The cones are the longest in the genus and at once place it in this grouping, but the foliage is more similar to Caucasian and Bornmueller firs, from which it can be distinguished by the thinner and narrower leaves and the buds with free tips to the scales.

Subsp. *isaurica* Coode & Cullen is recorded from the Isaurian Taurus and said to differ in the glabrous branchlets and resinous buds. It is doubtful whether it is worth recognising.

A. tazaotana S. Cozar
Tazaotan fir

Shoot brown, glabrous. Buds non resinous, with scales free at the tip. Leaves spreading both above and below, lanceolate, apex acute or acuminate, stomata below, with very few above. Fruit 16-20 cm, bract scales to half length of ovuliferous scale. Zone 7.

A rare tree recorded only from one mountain in Spanish Morocco. It is often referred to Spanish fir as a variety or subspecies but seems to share some characters in common with the firs from Turkey. It is not in cultivation.

A. marocana Trabut
Moroccan fir

Shoot shiny purplish red, glabrous. Buds ovoid, resinous. Leaves spreading above and below, stomata mainly below but some in 1-2 lines above, apex acute, 1-1.5 cm. Fruit 10-18 cm. Zone 7.

Closely related to Spanish fir, of which it may be a form, it differs in the pectinate foliage, the leaves having marginal resin canals (median except in juvenile plants in *pinsapo* and other characters). It may not be in cultivation, as plants so called are of unknown origin and do not fit the description. It is restricted in the wild to the mountains south of Tetuan in Morocco.

Group 4

This group is characterised by species with a conical rachis to the cone which usually has included bract scales. Some of the species have violet-blue cones and some have very long needles; all tend to have white or ash grey shoots. The species fit into a clear series from the Himalayas across China to Japan. They mirror the distribution of group 6 species, but occur at lower altitude, in association with pines and oaks.

A. firma Siebold & Zuccarini
Momi fir

Tree to 25 m. Crown broad conic. Bark pink-grey, becoming corky. Shoot grey- or yellow-brown. Buds conic. Leaves spread widely either side of shoot, yellow-green with stomata in 2 bands below of the same colour, leaf abruptly contracts to narrow stalk with large basal pad, tapers to rounded deeply notched apex in old plants and to two bony divergent spines (bifid) in young trees, 2.5-5 cm, to 0.3 cm in width. Fruit cylindric-conic, greenish yellow, ripening brown, 10-14 cm by 5 cm, bracts exserted, erect, rachis conical. Zone 7.

Momi fir is native to the southern Japanese islands of Honshu, Kyushu and Shikoku, where it occurs in the warm temperate zone. In cultivation it tends to make new growth early in the spring and the buds get frosted. It is interesting for the yellow-green colour and more so for the strong and curiously bifid needles of young trees.

A. homolepis Siebold & Zuccarini
Nikko fir

Tree to 25m. Crown open, conical until in mature trees it is columnar. Bark pink-grey, finely flaky. Shoot deeply ridged and grooved, glabrous, white or pale brown. Buds ovoid or ovoid conic, blunt, resinous. Leaves parted above and below shoot, stiff, greyish bloom to upper surface, later shiny green, 2 silver bands of stomata below, apex bluntly notched, 1.5-3cm. Fruit oblong-cylindrical, rounded at both ends, 7-12cm, violet-blue, bracts hidden. Zone 5.

Nikko fir comes from southern Japan, from Honshu and Shikoku. It is distinctive in the glabrous ridged and grooved shoot and makes an attractive tree with a medium growth rate. In good seasons the beautiful cones can be carried all over the tree and not as in most other species only on the top few whorls of branches. Nikko fir is the species most tolerant of urban conditions and atmospheric pollution.

'Tomomi' is a cultivar with more open branching and shorter needles.

var. *umbellata* (Mayr) Wilson is a form with the apex of the cones umbilicate, or dimpled, and the bracts just exserted; it shows characters of *A. firma* and is the result of introgression of *A. firma* into *A. homolepis*.

A. recurvata Masters
Min fir

Tree to 15m. Crown conical. Bark finely flaky, pink-brown or orange-brown. Shoot pink-brown, becoming ash grey in older wood, glabrous. Buds ovoid conic, slightly resinous. Leaves parted below the shoot, rising above, on very vigorous shoots. The leaves can be recurved, glossy green above with green stomatal bands below, apex acute, 2cm to 2.5cm. Fruit ovoid-oblong, often mucronate, 6-8cm by 3-3.5cm, violet-blue, bract scale just may be exserted at tips. Zone 6.

Min fir comes from north-west Sichuan in China. Only very strong foliage has the leaves recurved back down the shoot as implied by the Latin name. It is an interesting tree for its habit, bark and foliage. It is naturally slow-growing and is extremely shade-tolerant, able to survive under dense shade.

var. *ernestii* (Rehder) Rushforth is a form with longer needles to 3.5cm, which are frequently bloomed and notched or bifid at the apex, straw-brown first-year shoots and the more cylindrical cones with a dimpled apex. It comes from west Sichuan.

A. pindrow Royle
Pindrow or West Himalayan fir

Tree to 30m. Crown columnar. Bark dark grey, becoming shallowly fissured. Shoot smooth, ash-grey, stout, glabrous. Buds rounded, resinous. Leaves spreading forwards above and below the shoot, those at the side droop down, deep green above, 2 greenish stomatal bands below, apex bifid, narrow, 5cm, up to 7 or even 9cm by 0.2cm. Fruit cylindrical, 10-14cm by 5.5-7cm, violet-blue, ripening brown. Zone 7.

Pindrow fir is found in the western Himalayas from west Nepal through to Afghanistan and forms forests at between 2,000-3,000m. It is interesting in the long needles arranged so they droop at the sides of the shoot and when flourishing makes an attractive luxuriant tree. It is liable to damage by spring frosts and is slow to get established. The best specimens tend to be in the cooler and wetter parts of Britain, and it is unsatisfactory in the south-east.

var. *intermedia* Henry, at least as now cultivated, appears to be *A. spectabilis* and not a form of *A. pindrow*.

A. gamblei Hickel
Gamble fir

Tree to 15m. Crown conical, becoming more columnar with age. Bark grey. Shoot shiny pink or orange-brown, glabrous, stout. Buds ovoid, blunt, strongly resinous. Leaves perpendicular to and more or less radial around shoot, with many more above, mid-green above, paler green below, stomata in 2 lines below and 1 or 2 scattered lines above, apex rounded, blunt, faintly notched, base a sucker-like pad, 2-2.5cm above shoot, to 4cm below and to sides. Fruit conical, 8-12cm, violet-blue, bracts included. Zone 7.

Gamble fir is a bit of an enigma. The species is founded on a specimen collected from the Indian region of Garwhal, in the state of Himachal Pradesh, but this is a region where considerable deforestation has occured and it may now be extinct. It has also been called *A. pindrow* var. *brevifolia* Dallimore & Jackson but is quite distinct from Pindrow fir. It shows some affinity to species in groups 2 and 3 and is very similar to *A. × vasconcellosiana* Franco, which is believed to be a hybrid between Pindrow and Spanish firs. Gamble fir may be better placed with groups 2 and 3 and represent an eastern outlier of these groups. Morphologically it is not likely to be a hybrid of Pindrow fir with *A. spectabilis* which is the only other species present in the western Himalayas. In cultivation it makes an interesting tree with lush shiny foliage but is not suited to hot dry sites.

A. chensiensis van Tieghem
Shensi fir

Tree to 15 m. Crown columnar. Bark dark grey or light brown, smooth, becoming fissured at the base into scaly plates. Shoot fawn brown to ash grey, shiny, stout, finely hairy or glabrous. Buds ovoid-conic, resinous, brown. Leaves widely parted on both sides of the shoot, yellow-green above with stomata in 2 pale or whitish green bands below, apex bifid into 2 bony sharp points, broad and flat, to 4.5 cm by 0.3-0.35 cm. Fruit cylindrical or conical, 8-10 cm, green, ripening brown with the bracts included. Zone 6.

Shensi fir is native to northern China. It is closely allied to Momi and Manchurian firs but is very rare in cultivation.

subsp. *salouenensis* (Bordéres-Rey & Gaussen) Rushforth **Salween fir** is also rare but is more widely grown. It differs in having much longer and broader needles, regularly to 7 cm and rarely up to 11 cm, which can droop down at the sides of the shoot a bit like in Pindrow fir, and more conical buds. It is native to Yunnan, south-east Tibet and the extreme east of India. It is a very interesting plant but must have a sheltered damp site to develop to its best.

subsp. *yulongxueshanensis* Rushforth differs in the longer cones, 10-14 cm, the narrower glossy green needles to 4 cm by 0.25 cm and, from the typical subspecies, in the marginal resin canals. It is recorded from the Yulongxue shan, which is the main mountain massif in the Lijiang or Likiang range in Yunnan, China, and is in cultivation from seeds collected by T.T. Yu under his 15050.

A. holophylla Maximowicz
Manchurian fir

Tree to 15 m. Crown columnar conic. Bark grey or grey-brown, becoming platy; in some trees it exfoliates in thin papery buff-coloured scales. Shoot shiny pink-brown or buff-brown, slightly ridged, soon glabrous. Buds ovoid-conic, pointed, not or only slightly resinous. Leaves widely parted on shaded shoots but on those in full light all the leaves are assurgent above the shoot, without any V groove, yellow-green, stomata in 2 pale bands below, apex acute, or obtuse, entire, neither notched nor bifid, 2-4.5 cm. Fruit cylindrical, 9-14 cm green, ripening brown. Zone 5.

Manchurian fir is native to Korea and north-east China. It makes an unusual tree and in some plants in cultivation the bark is interestingly flaky, although not as attractively as in Flaky fir (*A. squamata*).

A. beshanzuensis M.H. Wu
Beshan fir

Tree to 10 m. Shoot ridged, glabrous. Buds broad conical. Leaves spreading below shoot, assurgent above, stomata below only, apex deeply notched, 1-4 cm by 0.3 cm. Fruit cylindric-conical, 7-8 cm by 3-4 cm, bracts exserted, reflexed. Zone 7.

A recently described species from southern Zhejiang province of China, it has not been introduced. It shows alliegance to both Momi and Nikko firs. Recently a further species, *A. ziyuanensis* Fu & Mo has been described from north-east Guangxi province in southern China, but also has yet to be introduced.

Group 5

The two species in this group come from opposite sides of the Pacific. They are united by the similar violet-blue cones with included bracts, the cylindric-conical rachis, and the foliage. They are also related to the species in group 6.

A. amabilis (Douglas) Forbes
Pacific fir

Tree to 20 m. Crown conical. Bark grey, becoming corky. Shoot obliterated by dense short pale hairs. Buds globular, thickly encrusted with white resin. Leaves dense, spreading below the shoot, upper rows progressively more forwards above the shoot, shining dark green, 2 wide white bands of stomata below, apex notched, square, 2-3 cm. Fruit oblong or ovoid-cylindrical, 9-15 cm. by 5-6.5 cm. Zone 6.

Pacific fir is found along the north-west seaboard of North America from the Californian border to southern Alaska. The luxuriant foliage is similar to Caucasian fir on casual examination but it is easily distinguished by the cones, the resinous buds, the hairy shoots and the strong odour of tangerines from crushed foliage. Pacific fir does very well on glacial moraines in Scotland, being better suited to a cool damp climate than to the south-east of Britain.

'Spreading Star' is a ground-hugging form produced by grafting a side branch; it makes an interesting ground cover, eventually forming a mound a metre high, but may revert in time.

A. mariesii Masters
Maries fir

Tree 15 m. Crown narrowly conic. Bark smooth silvery grey. Shoot covered by rusty-brown, pink-brown or orange hairs, darkening in second year. Buds globular and thickly encrusted with white resin. Leaves as for amabilis but with more of a parting above and shorter, to 2 cm. Fruit ovoid, 5-10 cm by 4 cm. Zone 6.

Maries fir is a subalpine species from northern and central Honshu, Japan. It makes a very neat but slow-growing tree, with an attractive habit.

Group 6

This group ranges from the Himalayas to north-west China and includes the most attractive of all firs. The species are found in the cold temperate and subalpine zones up to the treeline. Occasionally they are mixed with species in group 4 at the lower end of their ranges, but they generally occur at greater altitude. They are characterised by the violet-blue, usually dimple-tipped cone with a spindle-shaped rachis, strongly resinous buds, and by the bract scales usually being exserted. The crown can be somewhat gaunt and is composed of slightly ascending spaced branches which grow up at the tips and has a pagoda-like appearance. The branches are oval in cross-section.

A. spectabilis (D. Don) Spach
Himalayan or Webb fir

Tree to 15-20m. Bark smooth grey in young trees, becoming rough, cracked and scaly in older ones. Shoot strongly ridged behind the needles, with linear tufts of coarse reddish brown hairs in the grooves, ash grey or pale brown, stout. Buds ovoid conic, reddish brown or reddish purple. Leaves irregularly parted below with a wide V groove above, often pointing slightly forwards, deep glossy green above, stomata in 2 greenish white or silvery bands below, apex deeply notched or bifid, 2-4.5cm, up to 6cm on some plants. Fruit oblong or ovoid-oblong, 8-15cm, bract scales included. Zone 6.

Webb fir is found in the Himalayas from Nepal west to the Hindu Kush in Afganistan; it also occurs in the Chumbi valley in Tibet. It normally only cones on old trees and is slow to get going, although once established it will grow reasonably fast. Despite its Latin name, it is not the most beautiful fir. In its native habitat the cone scales have been used to make purple dye.

Plants are occasionally encountered under the varietal names *intermedia* Henry and *brevifolia* (Henry) Rehder; the former is also attached to Pindrow fir but represents only a longer-needled form whilst the latter is the high altitude form which includes the type of the species.

A. densa Griffiths
Sikkim fir

Tree to 15-20m. Bark smooth, fissuring at the base into large platy scales. Shoot less ridged and hairy than in Webb fir, yellow-brown or fawn brown. Buds rounded conic, orange. Leaves more or less radial around shoot but with a narrow V groove above, mid-green above with 2 silver stomatal bands below, apex rounded, notched, margins distinctly curved down at sides, 2-4cm by 0.15cm. Fruit cylindrical, 8-10cm by 4.5cm, bract scales exserted at tip. Zone 7.

Sikkim fir is found from east Nepal through Sikkim and Bhutan to Arunachal Pradesh state on north-east India. It has been confused with Webb fir, from which the more radial arrangement of the leaves, different shoot and bud characters, smaller cones with exserted bract scales and the leaves with revolute or down-curved margins amply distinguish it. The whereabouts of the exact geographical boundary between Sikkim and Webb firs is unknown but Sikkim fir comes from a generally wetter area than Webb fir; it is more closely related to Delavay fir. It is not common in cultivation but has recently been introduced from Nepal, Sikkim and Bhutan; the leaves are a better silver below than in Webb fir.

A. delavayi Franchet
Delavay fir

Tree 10-15m. Bark grey, smooth, fissuring at base. Shoot matt, maroon, less often reddish brown or orange-brown, usually glabrous. Buds globular, orangey green-brown or reddish brown. Leaves lax, radial in arrangement but denser above the shoot, on shaded material with a narrow V groove, much longer below shoot and shorter above, fresh to mid-glossy green, stomata in bright silver bands below, apex squarish, notched, margins strongly revolute, needles usually curved in an S shape along their length, narrow, 1.5-3cm, rarely 4cm, by 0.1-0.2cm. Fruit narrow cylindric, 6-10cm, rarely to 14cm by 3-3.5cm, bracts exserted. Zone 8.

Delavay fir is recorded from west Yunnan across Upper Burma to the Mishmi Hills of north-east India. The revolute margins of the leaves appear to be a response which keeps the stomata dry in the very wet summer rainfall it experiences. It makes a better tree in the cooler and wetter parts of the country and is especially effective when the blue cones are seen from above against the backcloth of the grass green foliage. Several years are required before the tree will start to make annual growths of around 25cm. In parts of Upper Burma an infusion of the leaves is used to cure headaches!

'Major Neishe' ('Nana') is a delightful miniature form with smaller and denser foliage; it makes a small plant but may eventually start to make normal growth and represents a high altitude form. The name 'Nana' was used for this plant by Hillier but is invalid. In fact, there are three similar but indistinguishable plants in cultivation, probably seed raised from a Kingdon-Ward collection in the 1930s.

A. nukiangensis Cheng & Fu is a closely related species which perhaps should be treated as subspecies; its main difference is that the bract scales are hidden within the cone scales; it is reported from the upper Nukiang or Salween river valley in north-west Yunnan. Some of the plants from Upper Burma appear intermediate between *delavayi* and *nukiangensis*.

A. forrestii C.C. Rodgers
Forrest fir

Tree to 20m. Crown conical. Bark grey, smooth, fissuring at base, in a few trees becoming very cracked and scaly. Shoot reddish brown, glabrous or hairy. Buds globose, encrusted with white resin. Leaves parted below and with a V groove above, point slightly forwards, very dark dull green above with 2 brilliant silver bands of stomata below, apex rounded, notched, flat on lower surface, 3.5cm by 0.25cm. Fruit ovoid oblong or short cylindrical, 8-15cm by 4-7cm. Zone 6.

Forrest fir, named after George Forrest, comes from north-west Yunnan and south-east Tibet, from areas considerably drier than those of Delavay fir. It is still treated as a variety of Delavay fir by some authorities but is very distinct in the cone, foliage and bud characters given above. Forrest fir is the most vigorous species in this group and can also tolerate chalky soils. The silver underside to the foliage can be very attractive, especially when the new growth is floppy and caught by the wind, and the dull upper surface of the leaves makes a good foil.

var. *smithii* Viguie & Gaussen is a form with stout and densely hairy shoots; all trees labelled *A. georgei* belong here; the true *A. georgei* Orr differs only in the much longer exserted bract scales and may not be in cultivation.

Plants from north-west Yunnan and south-east Tibet which resemble Forrest fir but differ in having generally smaller cones, densely hairy shoots (as in var. *smithii*) and with the resin canals in the leaves placed within the leaf tissue (not adjacent to the lower leaf margin) have been given a variety of names, including *A. ferreana*, *A. yuana* and *A. rolii* by Bordéres-Rey & Gaussen and *A. chayuensis* Cheng & Fu; they have also been erroneously referred to as *A. fargesii*. These plants appear to represent a northerly subspecies of Forrest fir. They were introduced by Frank Kingdon-Ward and by Forrest but are rare in cultivation.

A. yuanbaoshanensis Lu & Fu is a recently described species from the Yuanbao shan of northern Guangxi province, China. It is related to Forrest fir but I have not seen specimens and it is not in cultivation.

A. fabri (Master) Craib
Faber fir

Tree to 15m. Bark grey, fissured in older trees. Shoot fawn brown or yellow-brown, shiny. Buds conical or rounded, greenish purple. Leaves spreading beneath the shoot with a narrow V groove above, mid-green above, 2 narrow silver bands of stomata below, apex rounded, notched, margins slightly revolute, 1.5-2.5cm by 0.25cm. Fruit ovoid, 5-9cm by 4-4.5cm, bracts exserted. Zone 6.

Faber fir is restricted to a small area in west Sichuan province of China. It is rare in cultivation but quite hardy. Sometimes included with Delavay fir, it shows more similarity to Sikkim fir, and like both comes from a region with a high summer rainfall.

subsp. *minensis* (Bordéres-Rey & Gaussen) Rushforth comes from a drier area to the north-west. At the two extremes they are very distinct but intermediates make treating it as a subspecies more appropriate. It differs in the very shiny honey-coloured shoots, the longer and more pectinate foliage and in the conical purple buds; the needles are flat below without revolute margins. This subspecies is more vigorous than the type and in cultivation has the aspect of Grand fir (*A. grandis*)

A. fargesii Franchet
Farges fir

Tree to 15m. Crown columnar, dense. Bark buff-brown, finely flaky. Shoot shiny rich purple, glabrous or with reddish brown hairs. Buds purple, conical. Leaves spreading below shoot and parted above, sometimes forwards as in Caucasian fir, dark glossy green above with 2 vivid bands of stomata below, apex rounded, notched, on strong shoots can be acute or acuminate, broad, 1-2.5cm by 0.25cm. Fruit ovoid oblong, rich purple, 4-7cm by 2.5-3.5cm. Zone 5.

Farges fir comes from a wide area of north China and shows some variation. At its best it is the choicest species with the branch ends turning erect and displaying the silvery undersides of the needles. It thrives better in the cooler and damper parts of the country. The needles on strong shoots can be notched, acute or acuminate on the same branch; this is found on other species in the group but is more noticeable in Farges fir. *A. sutchuenensis* (Franchet) Rehder & Wilson and the type specimen of *A. faxoniana* Rehder & Wilson are synonymous with Farges fir.

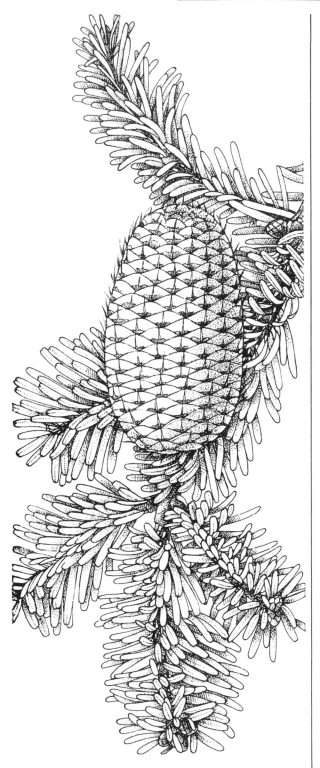

Figure 8.1 Abies fargesii. *Foliage and mature cone.*

A. fanjinshanensis Huang, Tu & Fu is a recently described species from the Fanjing shan of east Guizhou. I have not seen specimens (and it is not in cultivation) but from a drawing it is clearly related to either *A. fargesii* or *A. forrestii*.

A. squamata Masters
Flaky fir

Tree 10-15m. Crown columnar. Bark mahogany or reddish brown, flaky, exfoliating in thin papery scales. Shoot shiny, maroon, usually glabrous. Buds globular, white with thick resin encrustation. Leaves spreading below shoot, assurgent above, without V groove, stiff, grey-green with 2 pale bands of stomata below and a broad irregular band above, apex acute, rarely notched, 1-2.5cm. Fruit purple, ovoid, 5-6cm, bracts exserted. Zone 5.

Flaky fir comes from a very dry region of China on the border with Tibet. It holds the arboreal altitude record, having been found at 4,700m. It is a very interesting species with the remarkable flaky bark; this character develops after the shoot or truck is four to six years old and resembles a birch or Paperbark maple (*Acer griseum*). It is very rare in cultivation and slow to make a tree. As might be expected from its natural habitat, it tolerates both the hot dry south of Britain and the cooler north. The new foliage, in June, is a very fresh green.

A. chengii Rushforth
Cheng fir

Tree to 15m. Crown broad conical. Bark grey, smooth, fissuring at the base. Shoot mahogany, becoming orange-brown, shiny. Buds conical or ovoid conical. Leaves adpressed below shoot, spreading at sides, with V groove above, dark glossy green with 2 pale or whitish green stomatal bands below, apex rounded, bifid, 1.5-4cm, up to 6cm, by 0.25-0.3cm. Fruit ovoid cylindrical, 6-9cm, pale violet, tips of bract scales just emerging between cone scales. Zone 6.

Cheng fir is presumed to have come from somewhere in Yunnan and to have been raised from seed collected by George Forrest in 1931. It is closely related to Forrest fir, differing in the longer foliage, pointed pale brown buds and the cones, but also shows some similarities to Salween fir and could possibly be a hybrid between them. It makes a vigorous tree and is better suited to drier conditions than Forrest fir, but is not so colourful a garden tree.

Group 7

The group comprises species with relatively small, narrow cylindrical cones with narrow conical rachis, generally thin and narrow needles which are notched at the apex and small very resinous buds. The crowns tend to be narrow conic or even spire-like. The smooth young bark of these species tends to be rich in blisters of resin, although similar resin blisters are a feature of some other species, especially those in group 8. The species often have a few scattered lines of stomata in the groove running along the upper surface of the needle. The cones are primarily a violet-blue colour during the growing season but several of the species have occasional plants with green cones; they ripen brown. The constituent species occur across the northern parts of Eurasia and North America, with outlying species running south down the mountain chains in central Asia, Japan/Taiwan, and in the USA along the Rockies and Appalachians. The species are all adapted to harsh conditions and form extensive forests up to the treeline.

A. sibirica Ledebour
Siberian fir

Tree 10-15m. Crown narrow. Bark smooth, grey. Shoot shiny silvery grey or fawn brown, becoming matt later, with scattered dark hairs. Bud globose or ovoid conic. Leaves rather radial with a parting above and usually one below, lower side leaves droop, reminiscent of Pindrow fir, soft, shiny fresh green above, stomata in 2 green-white bands below, 3cm by 0.1cm. Fruit cylindrical, 5-7.5cm by 2.5-3.5cm, violet-blue, ripening brown, bract scales hidden. Zone 2.

Siberian fir is native to a vast region from west of the Urals to the western part of Manchuria. Largely situated south of the Arctic Circle, it extends to 67°40'N. It grows in regions where the temperature may drop to below −50°C and with only a short summer growing season. As with Balsam fir, Siberian fir will be growing on permafrost over much of its range. Coming from such a continental climate, it can be started into growth too early in Britain and therefore needs careful siting to avoid damage by spring frosts.

A. semenovii Fedschenko
Tienshan fir

Tienshan fir is closely related to Siberian fir but differs in the following characters: branchlets yellow-brown with prominent ridges, less resinous buds, leaves with more lines of stomata in the 2 bands below, and marginal (not median) resin canals, and yellow-brown cones with much broader bract scales. It is restricted to the Tienshan of central Asia. Often included as a synonym or variety of Siberian fir, it may be better treated as a subspecies. Zone 2.

A. nephrolepis (Trautvetter) Maximowicz
Khinghan fir

Tree to 15m. Bark grey, smooth, becoming shallowly fissured. Shoot shiny fawn, slightly ridged, with scattered dark hairs. Bud ovoid conic, red-brown or brown. Leaves spreading below, widely parted and slightly forwards above, fresh or yellow-green, with 2 white bands of stomata below, apex squarish, notched, 2-3cm by 0.15cm. Fruit cylindrical or ovate-oblong, 4.5-7.5cm by 2-3cm, bracts exserted. Zone 3.

Khinghan fir is native to the Greater and Lesser Khinghan ranges in Manchuria, or north-east China, south to the Wutai shan west of Beijing (Peking) and also to adjoining areas in maritime Russia and Korea. It is sometimes called East Siberian fir, which is slightly misleading! The Latin name refers to the kidney-shaped ovuliferous scales. Khinghan fir makes a small tree in cultivation but needs careful siting to avoid damage by late spring frosts.

forma *chlorocarpa* Wilson has cones green during the growing season.

A. sachalinensis (Schmidt) Masters
Sakhalin fir

Tree 15m. Bark greyish white, smooth, becoming shallowly fissured and slightly scaly. Shoot grey-brown, with scattered hairs. Bud ovoid, shiny red. Leaves somewhat radial and forward pointing, slightly parted above and below, dense and soft, fresh green above, stomata in 2 greenish-white bands below, apex squarish, notched, 3.5cm by 0.1cm. Fruit cylindrical or ellipsoidal, 5-8cm by 2-2.5cm, bracts hidden or exserted, erect. Zone 5.

Sakhalin fir is found in the northern Japanese island of Hokkaido, and along the Sakhalin and Kurile archipelagos. It makes an interesting soft-leaved tree with its bright foliage but like the preceding species it can be tender to spring frosts.

var. *mayriana* Miyabe & Kudo **Mayr fir** differs in the thinner smooth bark which does not fissure on old trees and the yellowish green immature cones, which have exserted and reflexed bracts. It is recorded mainly from south-western Hokkaido. A form of the species with smaller cones with included bracts and resembling Veitch fir has been named var. *nemorensis* Mayr but is normally included in the species.

A. veitchii Lindley
Veitch fir

Tree 15-20m. Crown conic. Bark grey, corky, smooth, bole fluted on old trees. Shoot pink-brown or grey, hairy. Bud ovoid, purple. Leaves all point forwards, those below shoot parted, sometimes narrow V groove above, somewhat shiny dark green above, stomata in 2 silver bands beneath, apex truncate, notched, to 3 cm. Fruit cylindrical, apex flat with short mucro, 6-8 cm, bracts about the same length as scale and just exserted or just hidden. Zone 3.

Veitch fir is native to the central Japanese island of Honshu. It can look similar to both Pacific fir and Caucasian fir but is quickly separated by the characters of the shoot and cone. It is a fast-growing species but relatively short-lived. The silvery undersides to the needles make an interesting feature; the cones are more attractive than with the other species in the group, being a brighter blue and are often carried on young trees. Veitch fir is very hardy and specimens survive near the Spital of Glenshee in the Highlands of Scotland but it is less affected by spring frosts than the previous species.

var. *olivacea* Shirasawa is a form with green cones.

var. *nikkoensis* Mayr is an indistinct form with smaller cones to 5 cm and included bracts.

'Glauca' has the needles somewhat grey-blue.

A. koreana Wilson
Korean fir

Tree to 10 m. Crown broad conic. Bark dark brown to black, shiny. Shoot fawn, slightly hairy. Bud globular. Leaves rather radial and perpendicular to the shoot, often rather spaced, dark green above, contrasting with the vividly silver stomatal band beneath, apex rounded, notched, leaf broader towards apex, 1-2 cm by 0.2-0.25 cm. Fruit cylindrical, apex rounded, pointed, 5-7 cm by 2.5-3 cm, bracts exserted, reflexed or hidden. Zone 6.

Korean fir is native to the peninsula of Korea and a few offshore islands. The original introduction in the early part of the century was from one of the island sites and produced many very small-growing trees which coned at an early age, often when less than a metre tall; recent introductions are from the mainland and may make better trees. The small nature of the tree, coupled with the brilliant silver undersides to the leaves, make it a desirable garden plant, although often the colour of the cones is not as brilliant as in Veitch fir.

var. *flava* Browicz is a form with green cones, which makes the plant much less attractive.

'Aurea' has light golden yellow leaves.

'Compact Dwarf' and 'Piccolo' are dwarf forms with shorter leaves and which make squat flat-topped bushes.

'Prostrate Beauty' is a side graft which forms a spreading plant but may revert.

'Horstmann's Silver' has the leaves twisted and curling upwards, thereby showing off the brilliant undersides; it is slow to form a leading shoot but when it does, growth will be as for a normal Korean fir. The foliage is less twisted in older plants.

A. sikokiana Nakai
Shikoku fir

Tree 10-15 m. Bark grey, smooth. Shoot fawn brown, with lines of blackish hairs. Buds rounded conic, reddish, with a thin coating of resin. Leaves widely parted below and narrowly above, spaced, shiny mid-green above with stomata in 2 white, not silver, bands below, apex rounded, notched, leaf slightly broadened towards apex, 1-2 cm by 0.15-0.20 cm. Fruit cylindric-elliptic, apex rounded, 3-4 cm by 1.5-2 cm. Zone 7.

Shikoku fir is restricted to the Japanese island of that name where it forms a small tree. It is closely related to Veitch and Korean firs and lies midway between them both geographically and in botanical characters; treating all three as subspecies of Veitch fir would seem appropriate. Shikoku fir has only recently been introduced to cultivation and promises quickly to make a neat small tree; it will cone at an early age.

A. kawakamii (Hayata) Ito
Taiwan fir

Tree 15 m. Crown broad conical, with open branching. Bark bright grey, becoming corky and buff-grey. Shoot yellow- or orange-brown, ridged with reddish hairs in grooves. Bud rounded conic, purple. Leaves parted above and below shoot, slightly forwards, shiny dark green with 2 pale green bands to stomata beneath, apex rounded, faintly notched, narrow, to 2.5 cm by 0.15 cm. Fruit ovoid-cylindric, pointed or rounded at apex, 7-9 cm by 4 cm, bracts included. Zone 6.

Taiwan fir is restricted to the higher parts of the island of Taiwan, which straddles the Tropic of Cancer off the coast of China. It has slightly larger cones than the other species in this group and has been aligned with Maries fir but seems better placed here, sharing characters with a wide range of group members. It is fully hardy and interesting for the open crown and corky bark.

A. lasiocarpa (Hooker) Nuttall
Subalpine fir

Tree to 25 m. Crown very narrow spire. Bark grey, thin. Shoot grey-brown, hairy. Bud globose. Leaves spreading beneath, crowded, forwards and erect above with a narrow V groove, grey-green or blue-green with 2 bands of stomata on both surfaces, apex rounded, notched, 2.5-4 cm. Fruit oblong-cylindric, 6-10 cm, bracts included. Zone 2.

Subalpine fir occurs along the Rocky Mountains from north of the Mexican border to Alaska. In the north it is found at sea level but at the southern end of its range it is forced high into the mountains, at over 3,000 m to find suitable conditions. It has a very narrow spire habit but, in the wild, the lowest branches tend to spread out as a skirt at ground level. The Latin name refers to the very hairy cone scales, more noticeably hairy in this species than in most others. In cultivation it can be damaged by spring frosts.

var. *arizonica* (Merriam) Lemmon **Corkbark fir** differs in the much bluer foliage, smaller cones generally 7-8 cm, and in the thick corky bark. It is found in the south-east part of the range, in southern Colorado, Arizona and New Mexico, where the main rainfall occurs in late summer.

'Compacta' is an attractive slow-growing form of Corkbark fir which makes a blue ovoid conical tree.

'Green Globe' is a cultivar which makes a globular bush with light green foliage, growing about 60 cm in ten years.

'Roger Watson' has a broadly conical crown with level branches bearing silvery grey-green foliage. It will make 75-90 cm in ten years.

A. balsamea (Linnaeus) Miller
Balsam fir

Tree 15 m. Crown conic. Bark dark grey, smooth, becoming cracked. Shoot dull grey, hairy. Bud ovate or globose. Leaves spreading above and below the shoot, dark green with a patch of stomata near apex above, 2 grey or white bands below, apex notched, 1.5-2.5 cm. Fruit oblong-cylindrical, 5-8 cm by 2-3 cm, bracts included. Zone 3.

Balsam fir is found across the northern part of North America from Maine to Alberta and south to West Virginia. The resin blisters in the bark are the source of Canada Balsam. It makes a short-lived tree of limited value in cultivation.

var. *phanerolepis* Fernald is a form found growing with the typical form from West Virginia to Labrador and west to Ontario; it has the long cusp of the bract scales exserted.

'Nana' and 'Hudsonia' are two dwarf forms.

A. fraseri (Pursh) Poiret
Fraser fir

Tree 15 m. Crown narrow conic. Bark brown, becoming grey with age. Shoot yellow-brown, later reddish brown, hairy. Bud ovoid, chocolate brown. Leaves spreading below, upwards and forwards above, spaced, dark shining green above with a few scattered lines of stomata and 2 white bands below, apex notched, leaf usually broader above the middle, 1.5-2 cm. Fruit oblong ovoid, yellowish green, 3.5-6 cm, bract scales exserted and reflexed. Zone 4.

Fraser fir is limited to a few mountain tops in south-west Virginia, western North Carolina and eastern Tennessee at the southern end of the Appalachian Mountains. It is closely related to Balsam fir, also having fragrant foliage and many blisters of resin in the bark of young trees. It is usually short-lived in cultivation, although bearing its interesting cones whilst still young.

'Prostrata' is a ground-hugging form which probably originated as a side-graft; it will revert.

Group 8

This group forms a very natural alliance which runs down the length of western North America from British Columbia to Guatemala and Honduras. The cylindrical cone with a narrow conic rachis and the usually included bract scales are the main unifying feature, but the foliage, especially on young plants (and shaded parts of older ones), is invariably rather long and very pectinate in arrangement. This group may be considered the American version of group 4; the constituent species rarely occur right up to the treeline but form forests at lower levels.

A. grandis (Douglas) Lindley
Grand fir

Tree 30-60 m. Crown narrow conic. Bark brownish grey, smooth, but in old trees fissured into small plates. Shoot olive green, later becoming browner, finely hairy. Bud globose or globose-conic, small, becoming purplish with resin. Leaves spreading flat in several ranks of different lengths either side of the shoot on lower foliage and seedlings, the upper ranks of needles more assurgent and forwards above on stronger foliage from the upper crown, shiny mid to dark green above, stomata in 2 white or greenish white bands, apex rounded, notched, orangey aroma from broken needles, 2-5 cm. Fruit cylindrical or cylindric-elliptic, green, ripening brown, 7-12 cm, bracts hidden. Zones 2-5.

Grand fir is native to western North America from Vancouver Island south to northern California along the coast and east of the Rockies in a separate disjunct distribution from inland British Columbia to Idaho. It is the tallest growing fir, frequently in the wild to 75 m, possibly to over 90 m, whilst it is one of three species breaking the 60 m barrier in Britain. The coastal origins from west of Cascade Mountains in Oregon make the fastest-growing plants in Britain, capable of sustaining a rate of a metre a year for many years. The inland forms are much slower; in Idaho they tolerate temperatures down to −55°C. Grand fir is useful for the fast growth rate quickly making a tree of substance and emerging above the head of surrounding trees. It does not take kindly to exposure and emergent trees often become ragged; this is the time to fell them, as they have fulfilled their purpose.

A. concolor (Gordon) Lindley
White fir

Tree 25-40 m. Crown conic, in larger trees columnar. Bark dark grey, smooth, becoming finely cracked and corky. Shoot yellow-green, maturing to grey-brown, with patches of red and scattered hairs, later glabrous. Bud globose, conical on strong branches, resinous. Leaves rather sparse, spreading below, above the shoot assurgent or erect, without a V groove except on shaded material, stomata on both surfaces, which are a uniform glaucous grey or bluish green colour, apex rounded, bluntly pointed or finely notched, 4-6 cm. Fruit cylindrical or cylindric-conic, variously coloured from green, olive green, yellow to pale blue, 7-12 cm, bracts hidden. Zone 3.

White fir is native from southern California, across to Colorado and south into north-west Mexico. The foliage is attractively coloured and may be a very bright glaucous blue on some plants. These forms do not suffer the aphid problems which blight the Blue cultivars of Colorado spruce, and retain a more subtle and pleasant contrast between the vividly coloured young foliage and the dull green of the leaves on older shoots; also the leafless twigs do not present the harsh brown found in Colorado spruce. White fir does better in the drier eastern parts of the country. It is a very attractive young tree but can become unsightly when older if in an exposed position, where it will lose the lower branches.

'Compacta' is a dwarf form with steel blue foliage; it makes a small irregular-shaped plant to 2 m, with slightly outward arching branches.

'Candicans' and 'Argentea' are two selections with the leaves more silvery white; such plants are occasionally found amongst seedlings.

'Pigglemee' is a very dwarf form whose annual growth rate is scarely more than 1 cm. It makes a tight bun and has blue-grey foliage.

'Violacea' is a beautiful form with bright bluish white leaves; again, wild origin seed often produces some such plants.

'Wattezii' is a slow-growing form with yellow new foliage which turns grey-white.

var. *lowiana* (Gordon) Lemmon **Low fir** differs from the typical form of White fir in the foliage and bark. The leaves are arranged so that there is at least a wide V or U groove above the shoot, if they are not fully pectinate. There are also less stomata on the upper surface and hence the needles are not concolorous, i.e. the same above and below; rather, they tend to be green-grey or blue-grey above and dull white beneath. The bark varies from black and shallowly fissured to brown with deep fissures which are pale or reddish brown.

Low fir is recorded from southern Oregon down the Sierra Nevada to central southern California. It is a distinct geographical variety, and probably should be treated as a subspecies or even as a species. From Grand fir it differs in having stomata on the upper surface of the needles, which are some shade of grey, not green, and the more cracked and fissured bark. In effect it is intermediate between White and Grand firs, but this is not to suggest it is a hybrid; rather, this whole group of species represents a 'cline', i.e. shows steady variation along the length of the group from north to south. Along the variation different constituent species have been formed. In cultivation, Low fir makes a fine tree, to 50 m tall although usually much shorter. The bark is quite distinctive and, unlike Grand fir and Noble fir, it never shows 'drought cracks', which are caused by the bark and wood beneath splitting in dry summers.

A. durangensis Martinez
Durango fir

Crown narrowly conical. Bark greyish red, deeply fissured. Shoot purple-brown, glabrous. Bud oblong-ovoid, resinous, yellowish. Leaves spreading either side of the shoot, upper surface light green with a few rows of stomata in groove along needle, 2 broader white bands below, apex rounded, 2.5-3.5 cm, to 5 cm. Fruit cylindrical, yellow, 5-10 cm, bracts included. Zone 7.

Durango fir is recorded from the north-west Mexican states of Chihuahua, Durango and the extreme north of Jalisco. It clearly fits into the cline, and may be considered a southerly extension of Low fir.

A. coahuilensis Johnston
Coahuilan fir

Crown said to emulate a Douglas fir. Bark thick and rugose at base in old trees. Shoot olive green, later brown, covered with short brown hairs visible under hand lens. Bud globose, slightly resinous, with a ring of free scales at base. Leaves widely parted above and below, mid-shiny green, stomata in 2 greenish white bands below and a few scattered along groove above, apex rounded or acute, twisted stalk at base, 2.5 cm, to 3.5 cm on young trees. Fruit cylindrical, 10 cm by 4 cm, bracts included. Zone 7.

Coahuilan fir is restricted to the extreme north-west of the Mexican state of Coahuila, where it is an uncommon plant of damp canyon floor sites. It is closely related to Durango and Mexican firs, and often treated as *A. durangensis* var. *coahuilensis* (Johnston) Martinez.

A. mexicana Martinez
Mexican fir

Tree to 20 m. Crown broad conic, in old trees columnar. Bark grey-brown, cracked into small squares. Shoot reddish brown, glabrous or initially hairy. Bud globose, resinous. Leaves on shaded shoots spreading above and below the shoot, on those open to the light, the leaves are more assurgent and forwards, mid-green above with scattered rows of stomata, with 2 bands of whitish stomata below, apex acute or rounded, 1.5-2.5 cm. Fruit cylindrical, brown or violet when young, 6-10 cm, bract included. Zone 7.

Mexican fir is restricted to the region of the Sierra Madre Oriental on the borders of the Mexican states of Coahuila and Nuevo Leon. It is found to the east across the Coahuilan desert from Coahuila fir, to which it is allied. It has erroneously been treated as *A. vejari* var. *mexicana* (Martinez) Liu, which occurs in the same area but differs in foliage arrangement, cones and bark and also in ecology.

A. guatemalensis Rehder
Guatemalan fir

Tree to 30 cm. Crown conical. Shoot purplish red, with brown hairs. Bud ovate or ovoid, resinous. Leaves on shaded shoots spreading, on shoots in light, more crowded and assurgent above, covering the shoot, shining green with perhaps a few stomata above, and in 2 white bands below, apex obtuse or bifid, 1.2-5.5 cm by 0.13 cm. Fruit oblong-cylindric, purplish brown, 8-12 cm by 4-5.5 cm, bracts hidden or exserted. Zone 9.

Guatemalan fir is the most southerly-occurring species, coming from southern Mexico, and the high mountains of Guatemala and Honduras. It is variable in the length of the needles and in the degree of exsertion of the bracts; a form from the Volcan de Tacana in Chiapas, Mexico, which has short dense leaves and smaller cones with slightly exserted bracts was named *A. tacanensis* by Lundell and is treated as a variety by Martinez. Guatemalan fir may not be very hardy, but as it has a great altitudinal range from 1,800 m up to over 3,600 m, plants from the top of the range should be suited to cultivation.

Group 9

This group consists of two very similar and very beautiful firs from north-west North America. They have rather 4 sided leaves and produce enormous cones. The group may be closely allied to group 10.

A. procera Rehder
Noble fir

Tree to 40 m. Crown very narrow conic with open whorled branches when young, broad columnar when old. Bark bright silver-grey, duller in some older trees, lightly fissured. Shoot only visible through the foliage from below, orange with dense fine hairs, later dark red-brown. Bud small and hidden, acute, red-brown. Leaves widely parted below the shoot, side and upper ranks adpressed at base before turning forwards or erect, variously grey-green or bright blue-grey, with stomata on all surfaces, leaves with a distinct groove running along all or part of the length, in cross-section flat on shaded shoots but 4-sided on those in light, apex rounded, notched, only to 1 cm above shoot but up to 3.5 cm at side. Fruit cylindrical with a rounded pointed apex, 15-25 cm by 5-6.5 cm, bracts exserted, reflexed and covering 95 per cent of cone surface. Zone 5.

From Oregon and Washington, Noble fir is a truly magnificent plant when flourishing. The large cones are freely borne even at the top of young trees, whilst the bright blue foliage on the silver bark makes it always attractive. It does not tolerate dry conditions and will not make a particularly large tree in the south-east of England. Where subjected to drought, it too freely produces 'drought cracks' in the bark and wood, which degrades the timber. These show for many years afterwards as strips of silver bark extending spirally upwards for a metre or so and about 5 cm wide. The frequency of occurrence of drought cracks severely limits the role of this tree in forestry.

forma *glauca* (Ravenscroft) Rehder covers the forms with good blue foliage and comes true from seed. 'Glauca Prostrata' is the result of grafting a weak branch of *glauca* and forms a prostrate mat form but will revert. Selection of nursery plants for the blueness of foliage is better than grafting to obtain good foliage forms.

'Sherwoodii' has the foliage golden yellow. Similar is 'Aurea' with sulphur yellow foliage.

A. magnifica Murray
Red fir

Tree to 30 m. Crown narrowly spire-like with short branches. Bark purple and grey, rough. Shoot covered with purple-brown hairs, only visible from below. Bud hidden by foliage, chestnut brown. Leaves less crowded than in Noble fir, adpressed at base, spreading below the shoot, upper ones erect, shorter, grey-green with stomatal bands on each surface, apex acute, needle 4-sided, nearly round, without a groove running along the upper surface, 1.5-3.5 cm. Fruit barrel-shaped, golden green, 18-25 cm by 7-10 cm, bracts hidden. Zone 6.

Red fir comes from southern Oregon and central and northern California. It is very similar to Noble fir, which it replaces to the south, but differs in the foliage which is laxer and does not have a narrow groove running along the needles, and the cone, which is broader with included bracts. Red fir makes a stout bole more quickly than other species.

var. *shastensis* Lemmon **Mount Shasta fir** is found at the northern end of Red fir's range, from the mountain of that name. It is intermediate between Red and Noble firs, having the foliage of Red, but grey bark, and cones in which the bracts are exserted and cover approximately half the cone surface; the cones are smaller than in either species, only some 14 or so cm long.

forma *xanthocarpa* Lemmon has even smaller golden cones.

forma *glauca* Beissner covers the plants with bright blue foliage.

Group 10

This group consists of a small number of Mexican species, which share a violet cone with a cylindric-conic rachis, acute needles, olive-coloured shoots becoming red-brown in the second or third year and small resinous ovoid buds which have rather lumpy scales. They probably are most closely related to species in groups 8 and 9. Ecologically, they occur higher up the mountains than species in group 8, but do not extend right up to the tree-line, having a species of pine growing above them.

A. religiosa (Humboldt, Bonpland & Kunth) Schlechtendal & Chamisso
Sacred fir

Tree to 30 m. Crown narrow conical. Bark grey, smooth, becoming cracked. Shoot olive green, later red-brown, slightly ridged, glabrous or hairy in small grooves. Bud ovate or rounded, resinous. Leaves parted below shoot, those at the side droop down, upper leaves forwards and parted with narrow V groove, dark glossy green above, stomata only in 2 silvery grey bands below, apex acute, bony, 2-3.5 cm. Fruit conical, apex pointed, violet, ripens brown, 8-15 cm by 4-6 cm, bracts exserted, erect or reflexed. Zone 8.

Sacred fir is found across the central part of Mexico, from the states of Mexico to Veracruz. The name comes from its use as decoration in religious festivals. It is found over quite an altitudinal range and some forms have not proved as hardy as others. It makes a rather conical tree which appears glaucous in the distance.

A. vejari Martinez
Vejar fir

Tree to 20 m. Crown columnar-conic. Bark grey, smooth, becoming cracked into small squares. Shoot olive brown, turning medium brown, red-brown in third year, glabrous. Bud globular, resinous. Leaves parted below the shoot, spreading forwards and upwards above it, with an irregular V groove, greyish green to vivid glaucous above, with scattered rows of stomata, also 2 bands of pale greenish or bluish white bands below, apex acute, bony, leaves not twisted at base, but bent along length to make leaf arrangement, 2-2.5 cm. Fruit cylindrical or ovoid, violet-purple, 6-15 cm long, bracts exserted. Zone 6.

Vejar fir is native to north-east Mexico, in the states of Nuevo Leon, Coahuila and Tamaulipas. It is very variable in the colour of the foliage; adjacent trees may be grey-green or bright glaucous blue. Also the size of the cones is variable. The plants in the northern part of its range, which have more strongly blue foliage and larger cones, have been separated as var. *macrocarpa* Martinez, but really form part of the natural variation. Vejar fir is native to an area where the rainfall is low and it will tolerate drought conditions; it also grows naturally on limestone. It has proved a very hardy species in cultivation, making an admirable small tree.

A. hickelii Flous & Gaussen
Hickel fir

Tree to 30 m. Crown columnar-conic. Bark grey, becoming thick and scaly. Shoot olive green, later purplish red or reddish brown, slightly ridged with dark hairs in grooves. Bud ovoid, resinous. Leaves widely parted, mid-green to grey-green above with a few lines of stomata, and in 2 whitish or steel blue bands beneath, apex acute, 2.5-3.5 cm. Fruit cylindrical, 6-8 cm by 2.5-3.5 cm, bracts exserted, erect. Zone 8.

Hickel fir is found in southern Mexico. It is similar to Sacred and Vejar firs but differs in the number of resin canals in the leaves. Most firs have only two such canals, although occasionally four are found in Momi fir and exceptionally in other species; Hickel fir has 4-12 scattered about in the needle tissues. The resin canals are only clearly visible under a microscope.

A. oaxacana Martinez
Oaxaca fir

This species appears close to Hickel fir, with which it shares the proliferation of resin canals in the leaves. It is said to differ in the glabrous branches, broader and often notched leaves and the larger cones with hidden bract scales. The trees in cultivation under this name have not coned but native herbarium material I have seen does look quite different in the cone, which is 9-12cm and about 5cm in diameter. Despite its southerly distribution (Oaxaca, Mexico), it appears hardy. Zone 8.

Hybrid firs

A number of hybrid firs are recorded. They generally take up more pages in books than there are trees in gardens! However, they are of some interest in showing or confirming affinities within the genus and are briefly described.

A. × arnoldiana Nitzelius (A. veitchii × A. koreana) This occurs whenever seed is collected from the parents growing together in cultivation. The plants are intermediate between the parents and equally garden worthy.

A. × insignis Carriere ex Bailly (A. nordmanniana × A. pinsapo) was artificially raised in France around 1850. Six cultivars are recorded, 'Andreana', 'Beissneriana', 'Kentiana', 'Masteriana', 'Pendula' and 'Speciosa'.

A. × pardei Gaussen (A. numidica × A. ?) Spotted in cultivation in France where it was labelled A. numidica. Speculation has suggested that it is a form of A. alba from Calabria, without any firm basis.

A. × vasconcellosiana Franco (A. pindrow × A. pinsapo) was found in Portugal; it bears a close similarity to A. gamblei but appears to be of independent origin.

A. × vilmorinii Masters (A. cephalonica × A. pinsapo) was raised artificially in France in 1868. Similar hybrids are recorded wherever seed is collected from the two parents growing together. Hybrids often occur when seed is collected from arboretum trees of other European species growing together.

Acmopyle Pilger Podocarpaceae

A small evergreen genus now restricted to the islands of New Caledonia and Fiji but from fossils known to have been more widely spread in southeast Asia, South America and Australasia. It differs from Podocarpus and Dacrydium in the apical micropyle; the micropyle is the small pore through which the pollen reaches the ovary and the name of the genus comes from two Greek words, akme apex and pule entrance. The aril is much shorter

than the seed, only surrounding it at the base. The species have yew-like foliage 1-4cm long and make small trees. They are not hardy outside but may be grown in a conservatory.

A. alba Buchholz New Caledonia This species may be synonymous with the following one. Zone 9.

A. pancheri (Brongniart & Griesbach) Pilger New Caledonia Zone 9.

A. sahniana Buchholz & Gray Fiji Zone 9.

Actinostrobus Miguel Cupressaceae

A genus of three species from western Australia, it is related to Callitris but differs in the triangular-pointed cone scales and by the cones being subtended at the base by closely pressed ray-like bracts. The derivation of the name is from actin ray and strobus fruit or cone. The leaves are set in 3s; on juvenile plants they are around a centimetre in length whilst the adult leaves are scale-like and 0.3cm. The cones have 6 fertile woody scales, each carrying 1 or 2 3-winged seeds. In the wild the species are low bushes 2-3m in height. They make small, slow-growing plants suitable only for the mildest parts of the country.

A. acuminatus Parlatore has more slender shoots. The cones are contracted at the apex into a neck and each scale has a spreading hooked tip. Zone 9.

A. pyramidalis Miguel has slender erect sprays of shoots and ovoid cones 1.5cm. Zone 9.

A. arenarius Gardner is close to A. pyramidalis but has the leaf tips more spreading, green and triangular-ovate, and blue-green cones. Zone 9.

Agathis Salisbury Kauri pines
Araucariaceae

The Kauri pines are one of two genera in the Araucariaceae; they differ from Araucaria in the seed not being fused to the ovuliferous scale and in the broad and flat leaves arranged either spirally or in opposite pairs. The genus consists of 13 species restricted to tropical and subtropical climates without a pronounced dry season in Malaysia, Indonesia, New Guinea, the Philippines, New Caledonia, Fiji and Queensland with a southern outlier in the warm temperate climate on the northern portion of the North Island of New Zealand. The genus is considered to be a relict from the old southern hemisphere continent of Gondwanaland, from which Africa, South

America, Australia, New Caledonia, New Zealand and Antarctica originated; eight of the 13 species are restricted to two small fragments of this super-continent — in New Caledonia and Queensland. In tropical climates they make fast-growing trees with a very valuable timber, but the only species which can be grown outdoors in Britain, and then only in the mildest parts, is the New Zealand species. The genus was reviewed by T.C. Whitmore (1980) in *Plant Systematics and Evolution*, vol. 135, pp. 41-69, which should be consulted for information on the other species.

Agathis australis Salisbury
Kauri pine

In the wild a tree to 40m developing a massive branch-free trunk but in cultivation outdoors restricted to a small tree. Shoot green, later purplish brown. Leaves in opposite pairs, lanceolate, dull grey-green above, pale bluish grey beneath, to 8cm, less on older plants. Cones only produced under glass in Britain, male cones 3-4cm, cylindric, female cones subglobose, woody, 7-8cm, breaking up to release the winged seeds. Zone 9.

Kauri pine is borderline hardy. In Cornwall it may survive for a few years in the mildest parts but not long enough to cone. It is interesting in that the tree is monoecious, that is the male and female flowers are carried on the one plant, but only after a period prior to full maturity when flowers of only one sex are produced. It has smaller and narrower leaves than the other species.

Amentotaxus Pilger Catkin yew
Cephalotaxaceae

A group of four species from China, Taiwan and north-east India. They are yew-like in general appearance but have much larger leaves which are set in opposite pairs on the shoot (not spirally as in yew). The main botanical difference is in the male catkins, or *aments* (*taxus* being the Latin for yew), which are set in clusters of 2-6 (rarely singly) racemose spikes arising from 1 bud; these are pendulous and 3.5-15cm in length. The fruit is set on a stalk to 1.5cm and is a reddish yellow bony seed enclosed in a fleshy aril. They are often placed in the Taxaceae but seem to be closer to *Cephalotaxus* and if the Cephalotaxaceae are put in the order Taxales, they would appear to fit better here.

A. argotaenia (Hance) Pilger
Catkin yew

Shrub or small tree to 4m. Leaves yew-like, with white bands below, usually falcate or may be straight, apex acuminate, 4-7cm by 0.6cm. Male catkins 1-3, 3.5-6.5cm, stamens with 2-4 pollen sacs. Zone 8.

This species is found from Hong Kong across central China to Sichuan province. It has been introduced from Hong Kong and should be hardy in mild areas.

A. formosana Li
Taiwan Catkin yew

Tree to 10m. Leaves silver-white below in 2 bands, 5-8cm by 0.6-1cm. Male catkins 2-4, 3-5cm, stamens bearing 5-8 pollen sacs. Zone 9.

A rare small tree from Taiwan, it is in cultivation but may only be suitable for conservatory culture.

A. yunnanensis Li
Yunnan Catkin yew

Small tree. Leaves brownish or yellow-white below, straight, 4-7cm by 1cm. Male catkins 4-6, 10-15cm, stamens with 4-6(-8) pollen sacs. Zone 9.

A rare tree from Yunnan province, China, remarkable for the length of the male catkins, but not in cultivation.

A. assamica Ferguson
Assam Catkin yew

Tree to 20m. Leaves white or silvery grey below, falcate or S shaped, 7-11.5(-15)cm. Male catkins 4, 4-5.5cm, stamens with 2-4 pollen sacs. Zone 9.

Only recently described although first collected in Assam (the area is now in Arunachal Pradesh) in 1874. It has not been introduced into cultivation.

Araucaria Jussieu Monkey puzzle
Araucariaceae

Araucaria is a genus of around 18 species confined to the southern hemisphere. Most of the species are found in the same parts of Oceania as are the Kauri pines but two species occur in South America; the genus is absent from New Zealand and Malaya. The cones consist of many scales each with a single seed; they ripen over two or three years before disintegrating to release the seeds, which are fused to the ovuliferous scale. The trees are usually dioecious, i.e. the male and female flowers are on different plants.

The genus is divided into three sections as follows:

Section *Araucaria* has broad flat leaves with many parallel veins; the cones are large (15-25 cm) and the seedlings have hypogeal germination, i.e. the two cotyledons remain below ground and the first shoot consists only of true leaves. The section includes the two South American species, *A. araucana* and *A. angustifolia*, and one species from Queensland, Australia, *A. bidwillii*.

Section *Eutacta* Endlicher has awl-shaped leaves, smaller cones (to 15 cm, usually 10 cm or less) and the germination is epigeal, i.e. the 2-4 cotyledons are raised above the soil and function as the first leaves. This section includes most species but is confined to Papua New Guinea, eastern Australia, New Caledonia, New Hebrides and Norfolk Island. In cultivation only the Norfolk Island pine (*A. heterophylla*) is of any importance.

Section *Intermedia* White consists of one species — the Klinki pine (*A. hunsteinii*) from Papua New Guinea and differs in the leaves of seedling trees being awl-like but those on mature ones broad and flat as in the first section, whilst the germination is epigeal.

Only the following species are frequently found in cultivation. Others might be hardier than supposed but have not been sufficiently widely tried. The Pirana pine (*A. angustifolia*) in particular may be worthy of trial, whilst a plant of Klinki pine I have has withstood a small amount of frost and might be suitable for mild areas. Information on the other species can be found in Krussmann, *Manual of Cultivated Conifers*.

A. araucana (Molina) K. Koch
Monkey puzzle

Tree to 20 or 25 m. Crown open with very distinct whorls of branches, in young trees narrow conic, rounded dome in mature trees. Bark grey, wrinkled, best described as like an elephant's hide. Leaves radial around the shoot, triangular, firm and very sharp-pointed, 3-5 cm by 1-2 cm in width. Male cones ovoid or cylindrical, 1-6 together just behind the branch tips, green when shedding the pollen in June but turning brown, persist for several months, 8-15 cm. Female cones terminal on the outer branches, globose ripening over two years, golden green, 15 cm. Seed brown, 4 cm long. Zone 7.

Monkey puzzle is native to the Andes in Chile and south-west Argentina from around 37-39°S. It was introduced by Menzies when on Captain Vancouver's expedition in 1795; the seeds are edible and very tasty either raw or if roasted like chestnuts and some were served at an official

Figure 8.2 Araucaria araucana. *Foliage.*

89

banquet and five plants raised on board ship. One of these survived at Kew until 1892. The colloquial name 'Monkey puzzle' was given at a planting ceremony at Pencarrow in Cornwall in 1834 when a guest observed that to climb the tree with its prickly foliage 'would be a puzzle for a monkey'. The Latin name comes from the Araucano Indians, for whom the seeds are an important food, and the main stands of the species are in Arauco province, Chile.

Monkey puzzle is totally different from other hardy trees and does not associate with them. It needs either to be planted as a single specimen or in a group of its own kind, where the tasty seeds would be an extra attraction. It flourishes throughout Britain, although preferring a moist site for best development. A well-grown plant with the foliage retained to the ground makes a very attractive specimen. The tree retains the leaves for many years, during which time the shoot or branch will have increased in girth; the leaves tolerate this by becoming broader at the base. Dead brown leaves are kept on the shoots for a further long period, finally dropping off in bunches with the bark to leave thin, bleached white shoots. The tree has the ability to coppice, or make new growth from the stump if cut down; this is rare in conifers. Plants should always be raised from seeds, although cuttings of epicormic shoots will root. Side shoots cannot be used, as they will only grow out laterally and never develop into erect growing shoots — in this character the whole family is firmly fixed. The timber has the longest fibres of any tree, with tracheids up to 11 mm. It makes a good yellow wood but is very resinous.

A number of cultivars have been described but are not important.

A. heterophylla (Salisbury) Franco
Norfolk Island pine

Tree to 30 m or more, but usually grown as a pot plant. Crown regularly whorled, plumose with the branchlets rising above the main branches. Bark exfoliating in thin layers. Leaves awl-like, fresh green, soft, incurved, 1.5 cm long on young trees but only 0.6 cm on mature plants. Zone 10.

Norfolk Island pine makes a very distinctive and attractive whorled tree for mild climates. It will survive for a number of years in selected sites in Cornwall and has made a tree 30 m high in the Scilly Isles. It is much planted around the Mediterranean and in similar climates. However, it is mainly encountered as a houseplant.

A. bidwillii Hooker
Bunya-bunya

Potentially a large tree, it differs from A. araucana in the laxer, longer (to 10 cm) and more pectinate foliage on sterile shoots and in the larger cones. Zone 9.

It is native to coastal Queensland where the seeds are an important foodsource for the Aborigines. It has been planted widely in warm temperate and subtropical regions, both for amenity and for the very fine timber. In Britain, only a single tree is recorded from Cornwall but, like some other species, it might prove hardier if a range of seed origins was tried in mild areas.

A. columnaris (Forster) Hooker
Cook pine

Very similar to Norfolk Island pine, from which it differs in the narrower habit and less feathery foliage. The habit is narrower, because the older branches are lost and new epicormic ones develop on the stem and replace them. It is native to New Caledonia and planted for ornament in warm temperate or subtropical regions. Zone 9.

Athrotaxis Don **Taxodiaceae cedars**
Taxodiaceae

This genus consists of three closely-related species from Tasmania, where they are restricted to the western mountains. The genus is closely related to *Cryptomeria*, from which it differs in the cone scales ending in a single point and lacking the half dozen or so pointed appendages; the 3-6 ovules are inverted on the scales. As in *Cryptomeria*, the ultimate branchlets are deciduous. The cones are composed of 10-16 radially-arranged scales which are partly fused to the bract scales, which have a free exserted tip. They ripen a golden brown in the first year and are carried terminal on the lateral shoots.

A. cupressoides D. Don
Smooth Tasmanian cedar

Tree to 10 m or so. Crown broadly columnar, open. Bark thin, brownish grey, slightly shredding. Leaves adpressed, scale-like, making the shoots smooth and rounded, margins translucent, finely toothed, dark green, 0.3 cm. Cone globular, 1 cm. Zone 8.

It is easily recognised by the terete shoots carrying adpressed shiny foliage but is slow-growing and rather uncommon in cultivation.

A. laxiflora Hooker
Tasmanian cedar

Tree to 20 m. Crown open, broadly conic, rounded. Bark red-brown, fissured and shaggy. Leaves awl-shaped, loosely adpressed, tip free, margins translucent, not toothed, 0.4-0.6 cm. Cone freely borne, 1.8 cm, opening to 2 cm across. Zone 7.

In many respects this species is intermediate between the other two taxa. It is usually found as scattered trees near one or other species; this suggests it may have arisen by hybridisation but the cytological evidence does not appear to support this interpretation. It is the commonest species in cultivation, thriving as far north as Aberdeen, and makes an interesting small but slow-growing tree.

A. selaginoides D. Don
King William pine

Tree to 15 m but up to 30 m in the wild. Crown rounded conic. Bark thick, furrowed, peeling in long slivers, red-brown. Leaves awl-shaped, incurved but held away from the shoot, acute, thick, bright green on the outer surface, stomata on all surfaces but in 2 broad bright white bands on the inner (adaxial) one, margins neither translucent or toothed, 0.8-1.2 cm. Cone globular, to 2.5 cm. Zone 8.

King William pine occurs in the temperate rain forests of Tasmania and its predilection for moister conditions is shown by the increased growth rate it shows in wetter parts of Britain. It is uncommon and appears, in the forms introduced, to be less hardy than the other two species. Although nothing like the thickness of Wellingtonia bark, it is sufficiently thick in mature trees to be hollowed out by Tree Creepers and used as shelter on cold winter nights.

Austrocedrus Florin & Boutelje **Chilean incense cedar Cupressaceae**

This is a monotypic genus and has been included in *Libocedrus* in the past, and from which it is distinguished by the cone scales ending in a short mucro (not a long curved appendage). It is also related to the Incense cedar genus, *Calocedrus*, but this genus has 6 fertile cone scales, each bearing 2 seeds (1 or 2 in *Austrocedrus*).

A. chilensis (D. Don) Florin & Boutelje
Chilean incense cedar

Tree to 15 m. Crown narrow, columnar conic. Bark grey, slightly scaly. Leaves fresh to yellow-green in flat sprays, set in dimorphic pairs at right angles; the larger lateral pairs flat, spreading, curved forwards, bluntly pointed at the apex,

dimpled in the centre wherein usually is a white stomatal zone, to 0.5 cm; facial pairs small, scale-like, acute, 0.1-0.2 cm. Cones terminal, ovoid, to 1.5 cm, with 4 valvate scales, only the upper pair of which are fertile. Zone 8.

This small tree comes from Chile between Valparaiso and Valdivia and also from adjoining western Argentina; in the wild it occurs in a transition zone between the temperate rain forest and the arid interior. It is hardy throughout Britain and makes an unusual small tree.

Forms which lack the glaucous stomatal bands have been identified as var. *viridis* Gordon; this is sometimes treated as a cultivar but appears to occur in the wild in at least part of the range, as a plant I have raised from Chilean seed of indeterminate provenance clearly belongs here.

Austrotaxus Compton **New Caledonia yew Taxaceae**

This genus contains only the following species.

A. spicata Compton
New Caledonia yew

It resembles species of Podocarpus in the long foliage and habit but has a fruit which places it in the yew family. The leaves are spirally arranged, 8-12 cm by 0.4 cm. The male cones are carried in axillary spikes 1.5 cm long. The female cone is 3 cm long and enclosed by a fleshy aril which is open at the apex. The seed is drupe-like and 1.5 cm in length. Zone 10.

Unlikely to be hardy, it shows some similarity to *Amentotaxus*, but differs in the spirally-arranged leaves. It is native to moist forests in New Caledonia.

Callistris Ventenat **Cypress pines Cupressaceae**

The Cypress pines are a group of 14 species confined to Australia and New Caledonia. The genus is characterised by the very fine shoots with scale foliage arranged in whorls of 3 and by the cones. These have a single whorl of 6 scales except in one species, *C. macleayana*, which is placed in a separate section (*octoclinis* Bentham) as it has 2 whorls of 4 scales. The cone scales are united and hinged at the base, with 2-9 seeds per scale. Zones 8-10.

The genus is very drought-tolerant but only hardy in mild areas. A few species have been successfully tried in Cornwall and Ireland and probably others would be found to have hardy forms if tried using a range of origins. The species from Tasmania and higher altitudes in Victoria and

New South Wales are more likely to yield hardy forms. The very slender foliage with the scale leaves in whorls of 3 will serve to distinguish the genus; information on the constituent species can be found in Krussmann's *Manual of Cultivated Conifers*.

Calocedrus Kurz **Incense cedars** **Cupressaceae**

This genus contains only three taxa which are found in western North America, Taiwan, and Yunnan, China. The genus has been included within *Libocedrus* in the past but differs in the more flatter sprays in which the leaves are in pseudowhorls of two pairs with the facial leaves only slightly smaller than the lateral pair, and in the seeds having only one wing.

C. decurrens (Torrey) Florin
Incense cedar

Tree to 30 m. Bark purple and grey, fissured into longitudinal plates. Leaves in flat sprays, in 2 pairs, coming together at one point, facial leaves broad, with acute triangular apex, lateral pairs somewhat falcate, narrow, keeled, tip incurved, acute, uniform shiny mid-green, all leaves decurrent on the shoot but not joined, 0.5-1 cm long with free tip to 0.2 cm. Cones erect or pendulous under their own weight, with 6 scales but only the middle pair are fertile and bear 2 seeds each, scales with small spine at tip, yellow-brown, ripening red-brown, 2-2.5 cm. Zone 5.

Incense cedar is native to the Pacific coast of western North America from Oregon south to northern Baja California in Mexico. It is extraordinary in its crown habit. In the wild this is broad columnar, with irregular rather horizontal branches; in cultivation, particularly in eastern Britain, it is very tight fastigiate, with very short branches, although the further west and near the south coast it tends to become broader. The tree is very valuable in gardens for this narrow habit but also because of its considerable resistance to the ubiquitous Honey fungus (see Chapter 7). For these reasons, and for the greater resistance to *Phytophthora* root rot, it deserves wide planting in preference to Lawson cypress (*Chamaecyparis lawsoniana*). The timber of Incense cedar is much used in the manufacture of pencils.

'Aureovariegata' is a tree form with golden yellow branches splashed over the plant, without having any beneficial effect upon the plant's appearance.

'Berrima Gold' is a newly introduced form with

Figure 8.3 Calocedrus decurrens *(above). Foliage; Microbiota decussata (below). Foliage and ripe cones.*

foliage a pale yellow gold. It originated in Australia and should make a small columnar tree.

'Depressa' is a dense compact form which develops a globose crown as broad as high.

'Intricata' is similar to 'Depressa' when young but makes a small dense column with time and turns bronze over winter.

C. macrolepis Kurz
Chinese incense cedar

Small tree, although up to 30 m in the wild. Crown broadly conical. Bark scaly, white. Leaves larger, thinner and more flattened than with C. decurrens, decurrent bases to 1.2 cm on strong shoots, 0.6 cm on side ones and 0.15 cm wide, tips of sterile lateral leaves more spreading, free, sharp. Cones 0.6-1.2 cm, set on 4-sided shoots up to 3 cm long, with obtuse scales. Seeds usually only 1 per fertile scale. Zone 8.

A rare tree native to Yunnan, Hainan and along the Burmese border. Discovered in 1868, it is in cultivation but is very rare.

C. formosana (Florin) Florin
Taiwan incense cedar

Small tree. Bark smooth. Leaves scale-like, obtuse, 0.15-0.25 cm wide. Cones 1-1.5 cm. Seeds 1 or 2 per fertile scale. Zone 8.

Native to the island of Taiwan, it is very closely related to the mainland form and is sometimes treated as a variety (*C. macrolepis* var. *formosana* Florin). It is in cultivation but is rare.

Cathaya Chun & Kuang **Pinaceae**

A monotypic genus only discovered in the mid-1950s in central and southern China. It has both long and short shoots, as in *Larix* and *Cedrus*, but differs from them in the cones being carried on the long shoots; in both these other genera, the male and female flowers develop from the short shoots. In other characters, *Cathaya* is closer to *Abies*, *Picea*, *Pseudotsuga* and *Tsuga*. Two botanists have placed the single species in *Tsuga*, but it does not fit well there and is better kept in a separate genus. Although restricted to China, a fossil species has been found in Germany.

C. argyrophylla Chun & Kuang
Cathaya

Tree to 20 m in the wild. Leading shoots erect as in Abies. Leaves linear, dark glossy green above, silvery beneath, 4-6 cm long; juvenile leaves unique in bearing ciliate hairs on the margins and on the upper surface. Cone 3-5 cm, persisting on the tree for several years. Zone 7.

This very interesting tree has a scattered distribution in the Chinese provinces of Guangxi and Sichuan. It has yet to be introduced but comes from sufficiently great an altitude to suggest that it will be hardy. The one young plant I have seen in cultivation in China suggests it will make an attractive addition to our garden flora. The Latin name *argyrophylla* translates as 'silvery leaves' and refers to the silvery undersides of the needles.

Cedrus Trew **Cedars Pinaceae**

The true Cedars are a group of four taxa from the eastern Mediterranean, the Atlas Mountains of North Africa and the western Himalayas. They are allied to the larches in their possession of short and long shoots, and in the flowers being formed on the short shoots, but the cones break up at maturity as in Silver firs. Cedars are unusual in the Pine family in flowering in early autumn, with the cones fully mature in the autumn of the second or third year. The leaves are carried singly on the long shoots, but in false whorls on the short shoots which develop from buds in the axils of the needles of long shoots. The leaves are set on the shoots on a small peg or pulvinus, although smaller than in the Spruces. Four taxa of Cedars are universally accepted but sometimes the Mediterranean species are treated as subspecies or varieties of *C. libani*.

Although there are a few dwarf forms, all the Cedars are basically large forest trees; however, to restrict their use where they can be allowed to grow to full maturity would be to deny the enjoyment of their beauty. Majestic as full grown trees, they rank as amongst the most beautiful of young trees, and can be very effectively used in all gardens, with the proviso that they may outgrow the situation after 20 or so years and need replacing.

C. atlantica (Endlicher) Manetti ex Carriere
Atlas cedar

Tree ultimately to 40 m. Crown spiky when young, conical, in old trees denser, broader, branches ascending, but lower ones in old trees become more horizontal. Bark pale grey, smooth in young trees, becoming eventually fissured into small flaky plates, which reveal red-brown beneath. Shoot grey-brown with short black hairs, short shoots only developed above the twig. Bud ovoid 0.2-0.3 cm, on long shoots surrounded by a few extra short leaves. Leaves on long shoots radial, quadrangular, acute with a bony point, 1-2.5 cm, on short shoots in whorls of 30-45, with 0.3-0.4 cm between successive annual whorls, 1.5-2 cm, stomata in 4 bands. Male cones terminal on

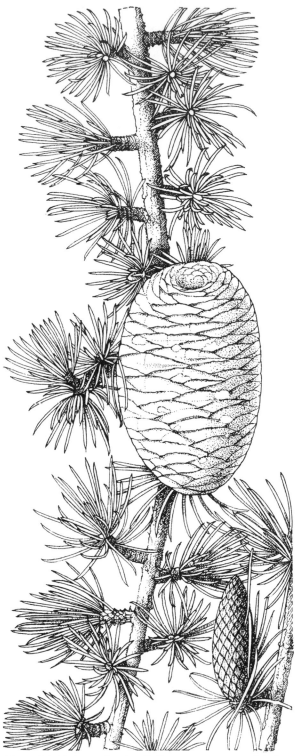

short shoots, massed particularly on the lower half of the tree, cylindrical, erect, pale brown, 5 cm, falling over and soon lost after shedding yellow pollen in September. Female flowers difficult to spot, 1-1.5 cm, green, generally carried in greater numbers in the upper parts of the tree. Cones pale green, ripen brown, break up over the second or third winter, 8 cm by 4 cm. Scales to 3.5 cm broad, bracts small, hidden. Zone 6.

Atlas cedar is native to the Atlas Mountains of Morocco and Algeria. In the wild the trees are variable in the development of the wax associated with the stomatal bands, giving both very blue trees and less attractive grey-green ones. The plants in cultivation are mainly derived from the glaucous blue form, forma *glauca* Beissner. Atlas cedar thrives on a variety of soils, being very tolerant of chalk and dry sites. It is very closely related to Cedar of Lebanon and is best distinguished by the crown which is usually on a single bole, the more pointed habit, the shorter and more numerous needles on the short shoots and the smaller cones.

'Aurea' is a slow-growing conical form with golden yellow needles; they become greener as they age.

forma *fastigiata* (Carriere) Rehder covers those plants with a narrow crown composed of branches ascending at an acute angle to the stem; several clones have been named, such as 'Columnaris'.

forma *glauca* covers the plants with silvery blue foliage. This is probably the most commonly planted specimen conifer. It is very attractive when young and spectacular when old, particularly in late spring when the new growth is made and is a brilliant silver. Usually grafted, seedlings will come fairly true.

forma *pendula* (Carriere) Rehder covers the plants with pendulous branching. The original plant, 'Pendula', has green foliage and is not particularly attractive. A better garden plant is 'Glauca Pendula' which has the foliage colour of *glauca*; as a mature specimen, it is attractive but suffers somewhat when young due to the initially rather sparse branching.

C. *libani* A. Richard
Cedar of Lebanon

Tree to 40 m. Crown usually composed of a number of separate boles, less often with a single bole, branches spreading horizontally in tiers, making extensive flat areas of dense foliage. Bark brown or blackish, cracked into small scaly ridges, smooth in young trees. Shoot coffee brown, finely pubescent. Buds small, 0.2-0.3 cm, ovoid. Leaves on long shoots to 3 cm, on short shoots to 2.5 cm, in whorls of 10-20, apex acute,

Figure 8.4 Cedrus atlantica. *Foliage, mature cone and male cone (below).*

shorter and greener than in atlantica, *dark green, grey-green or bluish depending upon the number of lines of stomata. Male cones shed pollen in late autumn (November). Cones barrel-shaped, broadest at one-third and taper to apex, grey-green, lumpy, somewhat resinous, 8-12 cm by 4-6 cm. Scales to 5 cm wide. Zone 7.*

Cedar of Lebanon comes from the Lebanon around Mount Lebanon, where due to exploitation over the centuries it is scarce, and from south-west Turkey. It is probably the Cedar of Lebanon which Solomon used for building the Temple in Jerusalem (although that could have been a juniper) and has a fragrant, durable and hard timber. In cultivation it makes a majestic tree with a wide-spreading crown. It adorns many country houses and nearly all the old cedars are this species. It is long-lived but nowadays less frequently planted and young trees are not as attractive as either Atlas or Deodar. The large horizontal branches with the foliage massed at the ends are not designed for wet snow, which can wreak havoc. Also, it does not tolerate atmospheric pollution.

The plants from the Cilician Taurus of south-west Turkey are sometimes treated as subspecies *stenocoma* (Schwarz) Davis. They differ in the columnar habit usually on a single bole, the more silvery grey leaves and the branches horizontal, with slightly nodding tips. The cones are intermediate between those of the type and *C. atlantica*. It is hardier than the type, to Zone 5.

'Aurea' has needles golden yellow with a green undertone but shows some variation over the year. It forms a conical, slow-growing tree, to 15 m. 'Golden Dwarf' ('Aurea Prostrata') is a prostrate form, possibly originating from a sidegraft.

'Comte de Dijon' is a dwarf form with shorter and thinner foliage, to 2 cm. It makes a slow-growing small tree with a densely branched habit, growing about 5 cm per year. 'Nana' is a name applied to possibly a number of different dwarf clones over the ages.

'Pendula' has weeping branches but will make a tree if trained.

'Sargentii' also has pendulous branches but is a much smaller-growing form; it can be trained to make a rounded bush with long sweeping branches but left to its own devices it will spread erratically over the soil surface.

C. brevifolia (Hooker f.) Henry
Cyprus cedar

Tree to 15-20 m. Crown narrowly conical, open. Bark dark grey, with spaced fissures. Shoot yellow-brown to grey, with fine hairs. Bud 0.3 cm. Leaves on long shoots to 2.5 cm, on short shoots in whorls of up to 20, 1.5-2 cm, acute, in mature trees the needles are shorter, rarely more than 1.2 cm. Cone more cylindrical than in C. libani. *Zone 7.*

Restricted to two forests on Mount Paphos on Cyprus, this species is closely allied to Cedar of Lebanon but differs in the more open habit, much shorter foliage and generally in the single stem. The foliage is green or grey-green and the habit is usually too sparse to make an attractive tree.

C. deodara (Roxburgh) G. Don
Deodar or Deodar cedar

Tree 35 m. Crown usually with a single bole, conic, broader in old trees with horizontal spreading branches, the shoot tips hang down vertically, especially when the plant is growing vigorously, making young plants dense and extremely shapely. Bark becomes thick and separated into narrow fissures and vertical ridges, dark brown or black, in young trees smooth and grey. Shoot fawn brown, hairy, becoming dark grey or grey-brown. Bud rounded, 0.1-0.3 cm. Leaves grey-green, quadrangular, with lines of stomata on all faces, abruptly tapered to a pointed apex, on long shoots the needles are up to 5 cm, those on short shoots to 4 cm. Male cones 6-7 cm, shedding pollen in mid-autumn (October). Cones barrel-shaped, glaucous when young, ripening brown, 8-12 cm by 5-6 cm. Scales 5-6 cm wide. Zone 6.

Deodar is native to the drier western Himalayas from west Nepal to eastern Afghanistan. It makes a large tree with a good timber similar to Cedar of Lebanon. It is commonly grown even in small gardens for the very shapely habit of young trees, with the weeping branch tips and leader. Deodar is tolerant of dry sites and is very hardy, although the needles may be damaged at the tips in some winters. Deodar comes from a range of habitats in the Himalayas and shows some variation in ability to withstand winter cold. The plants from the west of the range in Paktia province, Afghanistan are generally more hardy and a number of these have been named as clones for use in very cold districts.

Deodar is the most distinct of the cedars, in the strongly weeping habit of the shoots less than one year old, the longer needles and the broader cones with wider scales. It is much more attractive as a young tree, never having the open spikiness of Atlas cedar, but when mature tends to lose the lower branches and be reduced to a tree with a high crown at the end of a fat bole.

'Albospica' makes new growth which is whitish, changing through yellow to green. It is a rare tree form.

'Argentea' has the new foliage more glaucous green than usual.

'Aurea' flushes golden yellow, greening in the autumn to adopt a waxy yellowish hue over winter. It makes a slow-growing miniature of the type, eventually to 5 m.

'Golden Horizon' is a plant with yellow-green leaves, although more blue-green when not grown in full sun. It makes a horizontally spreading bush, with slightly shorter needles.

'Pygmy' is a very dwarf blue-green glaucous plant, annual growths of 0.5 cm being usual. It forms a bun-shaped bush suitable for a rockery. The original plant made only 30 cm high by 40 cm in 17 years.

'Robusta' is the name applied to a plant with much longer needles, to 6 or even 8 cm. It is a strong-growing form and probably represents the normal plant in a part of the species range.

Cephalotaxus Siebold & Zuccarini
Plum yews Cephalotaxaceae

The Plum yews are a group now restricted to eastern Asia but of which fossils are known from North America and Europe. The foliage is rather similar to that of Yew, with the leaves decurrent onto the green shoot and with a ridge running along the upper surface of the needle. The fruit is large and drupe-like, with a fleshy shell on the outside of the bony seed (hence plum yew) but is derived from a cone in which only one of the ovules matures; this distinguishes the genus from the Taxaceae. It is often placed as a family in with the true conifers, but may be more closely allied to members of the Taxales; here it is aligned with *Amentotaxus* and *Torreya* in its own family, but these other two genera have previously been placed in the Taxaceae.

The Latin name means 'head yew' and comes from the male catkins, which are arranged in clusters of small globose heads. The male and female cones usually are carried on separate trees, although there have been reliable reports of trees changing sex after a period of time! The female cones are carried at the base of last year's shoots and ripen in the autumn of the first year. The bud scales are persistent as a rosette around the shoot.

Plum yews make evergreen small trees or large shrubs. They are very tolerant of shade and will grow better there than in full sun. In the garden their main use is as interesting evergreens for shady spots, although length of the leaves of Fortune plum yew is sufficient to make it interesting as a plant in its own right, rather than just good for a dank corner.

C. fortuni Hooker f.
Fortune plum yew

Tree to 10 or 15 m. Crown a slender single-stemmed tree or a large bush. Bark red-brown, shredding or with coarse scales. Buds to 0.5 cm. Leaves pectinate in 2 ranks, 1 either side of the shoot, falcate, regular, tapering to a hard point, mid-to yellow-green above, with 2 matt white or silvery bands below, 4-9 cm, occasionally to 13 cm, by 0.4-0.5 cm. Male catkins shortly pedunculate. Fruit ovoid or elliptic ovoid, 2.5 cm, on a peduncle 2 cm. Zone 7.

Native to eastern and central China, it makes a small tree notable for the length of the foliage. It is very tolerant of shade. The branches are arranged in whorls, which is especially noticeable on young plants.

var. *alpina* Li is a form from north-west Yunnan, west Sichuan and south Gansu with sub-sessile male catkins and narrower leaves, 0.3-0.35 cm wide.

var. *concolor* Franchet from east Sichuan, Guizhou and Jiangxi has generally shorter needles (to 5 cm) which are light green on the underside, with the stomatal bands bluish.

'Prostrate Spreader' is a vigorous ground cover form.

Several plants with leaves at the longer end of the spectrum have been named, including 'Grandis' (which is a female clone) and 'Longifolia'.

C. harringtonia (Forbes) Koch
Plum yew

Shrub or rarely a small tree, to 10 m. Shoot green for three years, later red-brown. Buds ovoid conic, green with loose acute scales, 0.2-0.3 cm. Leaves spirally set but twisted at the petiole to make 2 ranks spreading irregularly either side of the shoot, or with the 2 ranks rising in a wide V or nearly vertical above the shoot, straight or falcate, apex acute, often spine-tipped, glossy pale green above, grayish beneath, 4-6 cm by 0.3-0.4 cm. Male catkins on short stalks 0.1-0.4 cm, or rarely on peduncles to 2.5 cm. Fruit ovoid or obovoid, apex rounded, depressed, green, striped dark green, ripening brown, 3 cm. Zone 6.

Plum yew or Cowtail pine is native to Japan, with forms or related species in Korea and China. The above description includes var. *drupacea* (Siebold &

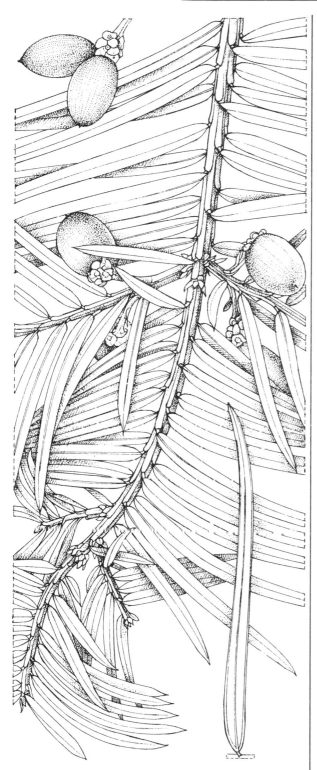

Figure 8.5 Cephalotaxus fortuni. *Foliage and fruit.*

Zuccarini) Koidzumi, which is said to differ in the shortly pedunculate male catkins (0.1-0.4 cm, as given above, restricting var. *harringtonia* to the plants with long peduncles to the male flowers) and in the generally shorter leaves to 3.5 cm. It represents the wild Japanese plant from Honshu, Shikoku and Kyushu, whereas the name *harringtonia* is based on the cultivar 'Fastigiata' discussed below.

'Fastigiata' makes a small bush, to a maximum of 5 m, in which the foliage is set radially on vertical shoots. The leaves are longer, to 8 cm, but reduce in length along each annual growth, so that the foliage appears in a series of tufts on branchless erect shoots. On the lower outer side of the plant, a few shoots with the pectinate leaf arrangement may be found. The plant is known only in cultivation and is vaguely similar to Irish yew (*Taxus baccata* 'Fastigiata'), but with much longer foliage on unbranched shoots.

var. *nana* (Nakai) Rehder is a form from the Japan Sea side of Honshu and Hokkaido islands. It makes only a small spreading shrub to 2 m with ascending branches. It is reported as spreading by suckers in the wild, although fruiting, and the seed is edible.

var. *koreana* (Nakai) Rehder (*C. koreana* Nakai) is a form from Korea which makes only a small tufted bush to 1.5 m.

'Prostrata' is a plant with ground-hugging capabilities. It probably originated from a cutting which failed to make a leading shoot.

C. sinensis (Rehder & Wilson) Li
Chinese plum yew

Shrub to 5 m, although a tree to 15 m in the wild. Crown spreading, arching out. Shoot yellow-green for three or four years, later red-brown. Buds ovoid, acute. Leaves linear, set in 2 ranks, those on shaded shoots pectinate, those on shoots in the light with the ranks semi-erect with a narrow V groove or erect, dense with 4 leaves per cm of shoot, shiny mid-green above, yellow-green beneath or with 2 faint pale stomatal bands, apex tapers to acuminate bony tip, 4-5 cm by 0.4 cm. Male catkins subsessile, to 0.3 cm in diameter. Fruit obovoid, mucronate at the rounded apex, 2.5 cm. Zone 7.

Native to east and central China south to Yunnan, it is closely related to *C. harringtonia* but is most clearly differentiated by the acuminate tips of the leaves.

var. *latifolia* Cheng & L.K. Fu is a form from east Sichuan, Hubei, Guizhou, Guangxi and Guangdong in which the leaves are noticeably broader, to 0.5 or 0.6 cm.

C. wilsoniana Hayata
Taiwan plum yew

Tree to 10m. Bark smooth, fibrous. Shoots green for three or four years, becoming dark red-brown. Bud ovoid, acute, small, less than 0.2 cm. Leaves spreading pectinately, curved down at sides lax, 2-3 per cm of shoot, shiny dark green above, whitish or pale silvery below on stomatal bands, tip tapers to acute apex, length variable up to 6 cm by 0.5 cm. Fruit ellipsoidal, 2.5 cm on a 1 cm peduncle. Zone 8.

Native to the island of Taiwan, this species is similar to *C. fortuni* but differs in the much laxer foliage. It is rare in cultivation but appears hardy in southern Britain.

C. hainanensis Li
Hainan plum yew

Tree to 20m in the wild. Leaves shorter than in C. sinensis and abruptly mucronate, 2.5-4 cm by 0.25-0.35 cm. Fruit obovoid, mucronate, 3 cm. Zone 9.

Originally described from the Island of Hainan in Guangdong province, it is now known to occur in Guangxi and south-east Yunnan. It is closely related to *C. sinensis* but differs in the taller habit and in the leaves; these are thinner and in dried specimens remain flat, whereas in *sinensis* they become revolute on drying.

C. mannii Hooker f.
Assam plum yew

Shrub to 8m. Leaves linear, straight or slightly falcate, gradually tapering to the acute apex, glossy green above, pale green below, 3-4 cm by 0.25-0.4 cm. Male catkins on a peduncle 0.6 cm. Fruit often 3 or 4 together on a common stalk, obovoid, mucronate, with a narrowed base, 4 cm. Zone 9.

Recorded from the Khasia hills of Assam, northern Burma and from southern Yunnan, this tree is not in cultivation. It is allied to *C. fortuni*.

C. oliveri Masters
Oliver plum yew

Shrub to 4m. Crown flat, spreading. Buds large, globose or conical, 0.3-0.5 cm. Leaves densely set so as to touch, widely parted and slightly rising, base square on very short petiole, apex abruptly pointed, dark green with 2 glaucous stomatal bands beneath, 1.5-2.5, rarely 3.5 cm, by 0.3-0.45 cm. Male catkins on 0.3 cm peduncle. Fruit ellipsoidal, 2.5-3 cm by 1.5 cm, on peduncle 1-1.2 cm. Zone 9.

This species is restricted to Sichuan and Hubei provinces of China. It is very distinct in the closely set leaves which are truncate or almost heart-shaped at the base.

C. griffithii Hooker f.
Griffith plum yew

Tree to 15m. Bark brown, polished. Leaves falcate, glossy green above, white below, apex abruptly tapered to a point, base broad, rounded, 4 cm by 0.3 cm. Fruit oblong, in clusters of 3 or 4, 4 cm. Zone 9.

From the Indian border state of Arunachal Pradesh, this small tree remains to be tried in cultivation.

C. lanceolata K.M. Feng
Yunnan plum yew

Tree to 20m. Leaves widely spreading in 2 ranks, lanceolate, tapering gradually from broad rounded base to acute apex, 4.5-10 cm by 0.4-0.7 cm. Fruit obovoid, 3.5-4.5 cm by 1.5-2 cm. Zone 9.

Described from north-west Yunnan, but yet to be introduced, this tree is allied to *C. fortuni* but differs in the lanceolate leaves and much larger fruits.

Chamaecyparis Spach **Cypresses or False Cypresses Cupressaceae**

Chamaecyparis is a genus closely related to the true cypresses (*Cupressus*) and both share the colloquial name 'Cypress'. Indeed, in many older books and some nurserymen's catalogues, they are all included in the latter genus and three hybrids between the two genera (× *Cupressocyparis*) have occurred in cultivation. The genus is characterised by the flattened arrangement of the foliage sprays, the small cones with 2 (rarely 3-5) seeds per scale, ripening in the first year (except one species) and, in horticultural terms, an amazing propensity to throw up different cultivars! The cone scales are peltate, as in *Cupressus*, but the germinating seedlings only have 2 cotyledons (cf. 2-4). The adult leaves are scale-like, set in decussate pairs of facial and lateral leaves. The tips of the shoots are nodding, unlike *Cupressus* where they are always erect, and the foliage sprays are flattened and fern-like.

The genus is found in North America and in Japan and Taiwan.

C. lawsoniana (Murray) Parlatore
Lawson cypress

Tree to 40m. Crown columnar, in old trees with erratic branches breaking the formality, a feature absent in many cultivated plants, usually dense except for the top couple of metres. Bark dark purple-brown or red-brown, ridged, slightly fibrous, in young trees smooth, grey-green, somewhat shiny.

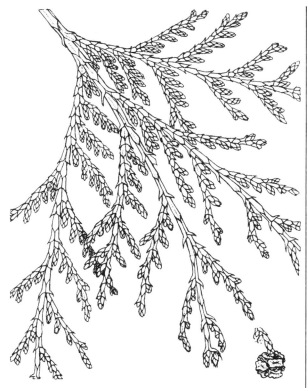

Figure 8.6 Chamaecyparis lawsoniana. *Foliage and open cone.*

Shoot green and covered by the decurrent leaf bases for the first year or so, later smooth shiny brown. Leaves in opposite pairs, facial leaves smaller, all leaves with a translucent gland in the middle (visible when held against the light) and free, usually incurved, acute tips, normal wild plant dark shiny green with lines of stomata showing on the underside between the lateral and facial leaves as a series of white Xs. Male cones terminal on weakest shoots, bluish black in bud, bright brick red when releasing pollen in April, to 0.4 cm. Female flowers terminal on shoots close to the base of the spray near the main axis of the shoot, composed of acute greyish blue scales. Cones globular, wrinkled, with 8 scales, ripening in first autumn, to 0.8 cm. Scales with a transverse hooked boss. Seed with 2 lateral wings. Zone 6.

Native to a restricted region of western North America, from south-west Oregon and north-west California, Lawson cypress is, in one or other of its forms, the most frequently-planted garden conifer. It is moderate in its growth rate, averaging only 30 cm a year over a protracted timespan. Extremely hardy, it will tolerate poor conditions but prefers a rich loamy soil with a high nutrient status for optimum development. Much planted for hedging, it withstands clipping reasonably well. It can also make very effective tall screens if left unclipped,

with the foliage of seed-raised plants introducing an element of variation in habit, colour and texture of foilage. It is moderately shade-tolerant and will make a suitable screen or hedge in these conditions, something which Leyland cypress will not successfully do.

In the wild, the trees are very uniform, growing up to 50 m tall, but it has produced a vast range of cultivars since its discovery and introduction in 1854. Over 200 cultivars are now named, including variations of habit, colour and foliage. A full account of all these cultivars is given in Krussmann's *Manual of Cultivated Conifers*, whilst the following is a selection of the more valuable or interesting.

The cultivars discussed below are treated under the following headings: upright tall tree forms, conical dwarf or slow-growing forms, spreading dwarfs and foliage variants, including juvenile, filamentous and crispate or clustered foliage forms. The first three groups are further divided into green, blue, gold and variegated foliage forms.

Tall-growing Forms — Green Foliage

'Erecta' was the first cultivar named in 1855, a year after the species was introduced. The branches are fastigiate and carry the dark green foliage in erect plates. The crown is fusiform, frequently lacking foliage at the base where the bark and bases of the branches are exposed. The lower branches often have small conical lumps near the base. It will make 25 m with time.

'Green Hedger' and 'Green Pillar' are two upright plants with bright green foliage; they have been recommended for hedging as the narrow habit will reduce the need to clip. Using many plants of one clone for hedging will increase the uniformity and is advisable where formality is essential or desirable; elsewhere, the informality of a mixture of clones may look more attractive.

'Intertexta' is a full-size tree. The foliage is grey-green, hard and rather stouter than usual and is carried in lax pendulous sprays. Old trees develop a tall columnar habit with some of the branches splaying out to give character and distinction to the plant. It is a hardy selection.

'Kilmacarrugh' is a bright green very narrow-crowned tree, making 10-15 m. It makes a very good narrow specimen, or 'exclamation' mark.

'Pottenii' has a fusiform crown with a conical apex. The foliage is soft, feathery and yellow- or grey-green. It is excellent when young but in old trees the branches are displaced during storms or periods of wet snow and reveal the dismal brown inside; if this happens, it may be possible to tie them in, but a new tree should be planted to be brought on as a replacement.

'Youngii' makes a slender conical tree to 20 m which retains a single bole. The foliage is in wide sprays.

Tall-growing Forms — Blue Foliage

'Allumii' is a narrow conical plant with blue-grey foliage in erect sprays; however, with time the lower branches billow out at the base and may form a competing circle of leaders. It will eventually make 15 m.

'Columnaris' has a crown of pale blue-grey foliage as columnar as a classical Grecian pillar, to 10 m.

'Fraseri' is similar to 'Allumii' but does not develop the skirt of billowing branches at the base.

'Pembury Blue' is a magnificent cultivar. The foliage is a bright shade of blue-grey and it makes a broadly conical plant with the pendulous sprays. It can be particularly fetching after rain when drops of water reflect the light. It is likely to make a tree to 20 m.

'Triomf van Boskoop' is an old cultivar with a broad columnar open crown and pale blue-grey foliage. It grows to 25 m but is inferior to the more recent 'Pembury Blue'.

Tall-growing Forms — Gold Foliage

'Hillieri' makes a columnar tree with dense feathery yellow new foliage, becoming greener later in the season. It makes 10 m or more.

'Lane' is a columnar tree with foliage golden yellow above and green-yellow beneath.

'Lutea' is an old clone with golden yellow foliage set in pendulous sprays on a narrow columnar or conic tree. It is rather slow-growing but will eventually make 15 or 20 m. It is quite attractive for its hanging sprays, even though they become somewhat bare and brown at the base.

'Moerheimii' makes a conical medium-sized tree. The foliage is yellow at the exposed ends and yellow-green where in less light.

'Stewartii' has a conic crown on which are set long arching sprays of fern-like foliage, golden on the outside and greener within. To 15 m.

'Winston Churchill' is a narrow conic tree which has gold foliage. It is a seedling of 'Lutea' but does not have the pendulous branch sprays of that form. To 10-15 m, although slow to establish.

Tall-growing Forms — Variegated Foliage

'Albospica' has a narrow conic habit and foliage which is white at the tips.

'Silver Queen' has new growths which are creamy white but which are later yellowish grey. It has an open conical habit. To 15 m.

Conical Small Forms — Green Foliage

'Minima' is a dwarf cultivar in which there is no (or only a very short) main stem. The branches, which are upswept and erect, arise from the base and carry the green foliage in usually erect sprays. The crown is globose, although broadly conical in young plants. The leaf sprays are neatly rounded in outline.

'Nana' differs from 'Minima' in the presence of a central leader with the short branches arising horizontally from this. Thus it has a more conical habit, although the foliage sprays are less neat, with the terminal shoots being longer than the laterals. The leaves are small and glossy green. It will eventually make a bush to 2 m. Both 'Nana' and 'Minima' have produced a number of colour forms.

Conical Small Forms — Blue Foliage

'Forstekensis' is a very dwarf form which makes a globose bush, usually to 60 cm but to 1.5 m by 2 m in very old plants. The foliage is in dense fern-like sprays of greyish blue. The plant makes extension growth by making stronger shoots with more normal foliage which thicken up, but if a really small plant is wanted these should be removed. It is possible that there are two or more clones in cultivation under the same name, and that the taller-growing form is a different cultivar. 'Tilgate' fits the latter plant.

'Gimbornii' makes a globose or oval form with a conical apex. It will grow to 2 m. The foliage is glaucous blue-green with the new foliage of a purplish blue hue for the first season.

Conical Small Forms — Gold Foliage

'Stardust' is a vigorous-growing dwarf form which is broadly conical. The foliage is fern-like and sulphur yellow.

Conical Small Forms — Variegated Foliage

'Albovariegata' has dark green foliage liberally spotted with white specks and patches. It makes an ovate or conical bush, ultimately 2-3 m tall.

Spreading Small Forms — Green Foliage

'Knowefieldensis' makes a spreading plant in which the branches arch out, as if the central leader had been removed. The foliage is dark green or bluish green above, in fern-like sprays which are pendulous at the tips. The sprays are conical in outline and the leaves only free at the tips. It makes a plant 1 m or so high.

'Tamariscifolia' is similar to the above in habit. The leaves have longer free tips and the foliage is lighter in colour. It can make a plant 3 m high and 4 m across. 'Nidiformis' is similar, with more rounded sprays and blue-green leaves with more spreading tips.

Spreading Small Forms — Blue Foliage

'Duncanii' makes a spreading plant to 2 m high and 5 m across. The foliage is threadlike, with few lateral shoots, and gracefully arches over the plant.

'Gnome' is a very small bun-shaped plant, becoming more conical with age. The leaves are juvenile with free tips. It is apt to make stronger growths, which should be removed to retain the diminutive habit.

'Rogersii' makes a globose spreading plant to 2 m high. The foliage is in threadlike sprays and a soft glaucous blue.

Foliage Variants — Juvenile

'Ellwoodii' has leaves which are awl-like, i.e. juvenile, and blue-grey. The habit is narrow conical and the branches erect, except at the tips. It makes a small dense tree to 3 m. It has given rise to a number of different sports, and will also give cultivariants depending upon the position on the plant of the original cutting (see page 47).

'Fletcheri' is similar but makes a larger plant, 5-12 m tall. The foliage is greyer, taking on a purplish hue at the tips over winter. It makes a more spreading plant, with a number of dense erect stems. It originated as a branch sport on a normal plant and has given rise to a number of colour and habit variants.

Foliage Variants — Filamentous

'Filiformis' is an open crowned tree to 10 m in which the branchlets are whip-like, or filamentous, with few side branchlets. The twigs bend down under their own weight and the plant has a pleasant open appearance. The foliage is green. Similar filamentous forms are 'Rogersii' and 'Duncanii' described above.

Foliage Variants — Crispate

'Wisselii' has dense bunches of foliage which are arranged in three-dimensional sprays. The bunches are spaced out on branches which are erect at the tips. The plant looks as if a dwarf, but can make a tree to 25 m in 50 years. The foliage is dark blue-green or blue-grey. Apart from the curiosity value of its radial foliage and the narrow conical habit, the tree can be spectacular in April, when the brick red male cones are set massed against the blue-grey foliage.

C. obtusa (Siebold & Zuccarini) Endlicher
Hinoki cypress

Tree to 20 m. Crown broad conic, not dense. Bark red-brown, sometimes grey-brown, soft, stringy, fissured into long parallel ridges. Shoot dull orange-brown. Leaves in 2 unequal pairs, without glands, facial pair small, obtuse, lateral pair thick, incurved, blunt, coming together below facial leaves, dark green with stomata in bright silver lines at margins of leaves, especially below. Male cones small. Cones rounded, with 8 or 10 fertile scales each with 1-5 seeds and a small central ridge, 1-1.2 cm. Seed 0.3 cm. Zone 4.

Hinoki cypress is native to southern Honshu, Shikoku and Kyushu islands of Japan, where it is an important forestry and ornamental species. In cultivation it makes an interesting tree and provides some very useful colour or dwarf forms. It thrives in good soils in cool moist settings.

var. *formosana* (Hayata) Rehder is restricted to the island of Taiwan. It is also treated as a separate species, *C. taiwanensis* Masamune & Suzuki, which may be a more logical treatment. It differs in the small cones and seeds and in the richer shiny green foliage. In Taiwan it makes a very large and long-lived tree but in cultivation it has only made small specimens to date and is rare.

Cultivars have been selected over several centuries, starting in Japan and continued in other countries. They can be considered under the following headings and a brief selection are described below.

Dwarf-growing forms

'Nana' is a very slow-growing form which makes a flat-topped bush with densely packed tiers of dark green foliage. The sprays are rounded and often cupped. Plants may make 1 m high and across in 100 years. Frequently one of the faster-growing 'Nana' cultivars below is offered for sale as this plant.

'Nana Aurea' makes a larger plant, to 2 m, with

golden yellow foliage, greener in the shade.

'Nana Compacta' makes an open rounded plant with bright green leaves, glaucous beneath. It is intermediate in growth rate between 'Nana' and 'Nana Gracilis'.

'Nana Gracilis' forms a dense conical plant to 2 m, with glossy foliage and a rugged 'character' habit. It is very useful as a specimen dwarf or character plant.

'Templehof' makes an ovoid or conical plant to 2.5 m but has foliage which is yellow green with a brownish tint, especially in winter.

'Kosteri' has twisted, somewhat lustrous mid-green foliage. It makes a sprawling bush but if trained to a stake, the branches will spread out in layers.

Minute-growing Forms

'Minima' makes a very small plant to 10 or 15 cm after 20 years. The foliage light green and composed of leaves in 4 rows (i.e. tetragonal). A number of even smaller-growing plants have been raised, with growth rates as slow as 0.6 cm per annum, such as 'Pixie'. These plants are too tender for outside cultivation and must be grown in an alpine house. They are discussed in Welch's *Manual of Dwarf Conifers*.

Abnormal Foliage Forms

'Coralliformis' makes a dwarf plant to 50 cm. The foliage is threadlike and twisted, 'resembling coral in its contortions'.

'Filicoides' has the shoot ends crowded with hanging clusters of bright green sprays. The habit is narrow with level branches. It can make a tree to 15 m but is usually much less.

Gold Foliage

'Aurea' has golden yellow foliage but is inferior to the more recent 'Crippsii', although having a faster growth rate. The leaves in the shade are greener.

'Crippsii' makes a small tree to 15 m with a broadly conical crown composed of dense sprays of bright golden foliage. It has a moderate growth rate and is a most excellent golden-foliaged plant. It needs full sunlight to develop the best colouring.

'Tetragona Aurea' has the foliage arranged in 4-sided sprays with the leaves in 4 rows, not with identifiable facial and lateral pairs. The foliage is golden yellow or bronze-yellow, but in the shade it becomes greener. Although having the appearance of a dwarf and not growing fast, this plant is capable of making 13 m with sufficient time.

'Tetragona' is a name sometimes encountered in the literature; it probably never existed as a cultivar, being either a synonym for 'Filicoides' or else applied to plants of 'Tetragona Aurea' grown under glass, when they appear green.

Variegated Foliage

'Albospica' is a dense, slow-growing conical plant which will make 2 m or more. The new foliage is creamy white, changing later to pale green.

C. pisifera (Siebold & Zuccarini) Endlicher
Sawara cypress

Tree to 20 m, taller in the wild. Crown conical, relatively open, branches level, or sweeping down and up at tips. Bark red-brown, with regular deep narrow fissures, ridges finely peeling and sometimes greyish in old trees. Shoot bright green for 1-2 years, later red-brown. Foliage in flattened sprays, lateral and facial leaves similar, narrow, acute or acuminate, with free, often spreading tips, a small obscure gland in centre of each scale which can be seen on the upper leaves under a hand lens, fresh, slightly yellow-green, later darker green, with 2 prominent zones of white stomata at side of leaves beneath. Male cones shed pollen late April, later than in other species. Cones angular, carried level with or below the foliage, with 8-12 scales, to 0.7 cm. Scales 5 sided, dimpled with a minute central spine, only 1-2 seeds per scale. Zone 4.

Sawara cypress is native to Honshu and Kyushu islands of Japan, where it is much planted both for ornament and as one of the principal forest trees. It thrives in a moist soil but will tolerate a wide range of conditions. It is very distinct in the small, almost squarish, cones and the acute foliage but is more often represented in cultivation by one of its many cultivars. Apart from 'Aurea', these can be divided into four groups on the basis of habit and foliage.

'Aurea' has normal foliage but the new growth is a bright gold, changing during the season to green. It is slower-growing, but will make 10 m.

Filifera Cultivars

'Filifera' is a cultivar with hanging branches which are whip-like and with bunched side shoots at erratic intervals. The foliage on the long shoots is as described above but on the weaker bunched sprays the scale leaves are more similar to Hinoki cypress, except for the free acute tip to each scale, and the facial leaves are much smaller than the laterals. This clone has dark green foliage and may make a tree as tall as the normal form but often broader. It sometimes fruits.

'Filifera Aurea' is one of a number of similar cultivars which have been raised. It has similar foliage which is an attractive golden yellow and makes a slow-growing bush, with time to 12 m. It is prone to being scorched by full sun, but the cultivar 'Sungold' is hardier, although not of such an appealing hue.

'Filifera Argenteovariegata' and 'Filifera Aureovariegata' are small-growing plants with, respectively, white-yellow and yellow variegations. They will make plants 1-1.5 m tall.

'Filifera Gracilis' is a form with finer light or yellowish green foliage and a more regular habit.

'Filifera Nana' is a very dwarf form, making a dense bush 0.6 m high after a quarter of a century.

'Gold Spangle' arose as a mutation on 'Filifera Aurea'. It makes a very narrow conical plant with foliage mainly in normal flat sprays (although a proportion are whip-like) and an attractive yellow colour. It is very useful as a young plant, quite different in appearance from the plant which gave rise to it.

Nana Cultivars

This group has adult foliage but only makes dwarf bun-shaped plants.

'Compacta' makes a plant to 1 m. The habit is globose, often wider than high. The foliage is dense, although longer growths are made in which the shoots only become dense in the subsequent year. 'Compacta Variegata' is a mutation with yellow speckles at the tips of the otherwise green foliage.

'Nana' has dark bluish green foliage set in fan-shaped sprays. It makes a much lower bush than 'Compacta'.

Plumosa Cultivars

This group is characterised by the foliage which is intermediate between the fully juvenile 'Squarrosa' group and normal foliage. The leaves have free tips from 0.2-0.4 cm in length and are set forwards at about 45° to the shoot.

'Plumosa' makes a tree to 20 m with a broadly conic, ultimately broader columnar and flat-topped, crown. The foliage is yellowish grey-green, with the new shoots of a brighter colour. It frequently forks low down, as do most tree forms of Sawara cypress.

'Plumosa Aurea' is similar to 'Plumosa' but has foliage a bright golden colour. The foliage colour is stronger on young plants, old ones frequently reverting to 'Plumosa'. 'Plumosa Argentea' is a similar form with the green new shoots tipped with white.

Several forms which make dwarf conical plants 1-2 m high have been named. These include 'Plumosa Compacta' (green foliage), 'Plumosa Pygmea' (green), 'Plumosa Albopicta' (white variegated, needs to be seen close-to to be appreciated), 'Plumosa Rogersii' (yellow) and 'Plumosa Flavescens' (light yellow). Globose dwarf forms include 'Plumosa Compressa' (bluish to yellowish, foliage arose as a sport on 'Squarrosa'!), 'Plumosa Juniperoides' (yellow-gold in early summer, later green) and 'Snow' (white variegated).

Squarrosa Cultivars

This group has much longer leaves, with the free tips 0.5-0.7 cm. The leaves are soft to the touch.

'Squarrosa' makes a tree to 20 m. The crown is broad and set on a number of spaced branches which are horizontal at first, turning up at the tips. The foliage is blue-grey, but dead brown foliage persists inside the tree. 'Squarrosa Aurea' is a similar tall-growing plant, but with rather golden yellow foliage.

'Squarrosa Argentea' and 'Squarrosa Intermedia' make upright plants 2-3 m tall with silvery-grey foliage. 'Squarrosa Sulphurea' is taller, to 5 m. The foliage is sulphur yellow during the summer, silvery grey in winter.

'Boulevard' is a sport from 'Squarrosa'. It makes a very neat young plant, with silvery blue foliage; the leaf tips are incurved, not spreading. The colour is much brighter when the plant is grown in shade and it will look sick and unhealthy on soils which do not suit it, including clays and limey soils. Also, it becomes unattractive as an older plant, with dead inner foliage contrasting badly with the blue live foliage, so either should be regularly replaced, or clipped to retain a small stature. It is likely to make a tree 5 to 10 m tall if left.

'Squarrosa Dumosa' is a dwarf clone which will make a dense globose bush to a metre or so high. The foliage is grey-green but in winter it becomes attractively bronzed.

'Squarrosa Lutea' makes a dwarf globose or conical plant to 80 cm. The foliage is golden yellow.

C. formosensis Matsumura
Taiwan cypress

Tree to 15 m in cultivation but up to 60 m in Taiwan. Crown broadly conical, with spreading, slightly drooping branches. Bark red-brown, regularly shallowly fissured, ridges slightly peeling. Leaves in flat, very broad sprays, scale-like, acute, in 4 rows, laterals with incurved apex, yellow-green, slightly bronzed, white or paler below. Cones angular, ellipsoidal, with

10-12 scales, similar to C. pisifera but to 1 cm and carried above the foliage sprays. Scales dimpled with central quadrangular point, bearing 2 winged seeds. Zone 8.

Taiwan cypress is native to the island of Taiwan, where it occurs in the mountains of the central and northern part. It is reasonably hardy, but slow-growing, making an interesting and attractive medium-sized tree. Botanically it is very closely related to the Sawara cypress, differing in the larger cones held above the foliage and seeds with more prominent lateral wings.

C. nootkatensis (D. Don) Spach
Nootka cypress

Tree to 30 m. Crown remarkably conical, varying from narrow to broad, rarely at all ragged. The leader nods off to one side. Bark brown or orange-brown, shallowly fissured with low stringy ridges. Foliage in long narrow very pendulous sprays which hang down either side of the shoot, as an upturned U. Leaves acute, facial and lateral pairs separated, similar, tips free, grey-green above, paler below. Male cones yellow, to 0.7 cm, shed pollen in April. Cones ripen in late spring or early summer of the second year, dark blue and green, brown when ripe, globose, angular, with 4 or 6 fertile scales, each scale with large recurved central hook. Zone 4.

Nootka cypress is native to western North America, from Alaska south to northern Oregon. It is remarkable in the regularity of its crown — nearly all trees are perfect cones, even when forked. It is also unusual in the genus as the cones ripen during the second year and it is more closely related to *Cupressus* than are the other species. All the species in the hybrid genus × *Cupressocyparis* have this species as the *Chamaecyparis* parents.

Nootka cypress will thrive in most sites and its value is as an attractive specimen tree. The cones are also interesting, resembling small sputniks. It has only produced a small number of cultivars.

'Aurea' has leaves which are a more pronounced light yellow early in summer then normal but soon turn green. It is not as strong-growing as the normal form.

'Compacta' and 'Compacta Glauca' are two dwarf forms, making rounded bushes to 2 m.

'Nidifera' has in the past caused some confusion, being lost for many years and referred to either as *Thuja nidifera* or as a hybrid of some parentage. It makes a spreading bush which is 'nest-shaped', i.e. dimpled in the centre. It can be distinguished from similar Lawson cypress clones by the much narrower sprays of foliage.

'Pendula' is a most remarkable clone. The crown is attractively gaunt and open. The foliage vertically hangs in flat sprays, whilst the main branches arch down and up at the tips. I have overheard it described as an 'Afghan Hound tree', which sums it up. It grows to 20 m, but is much better as a young tree. There is a variegated form, 'Pendula Variegata'.

'Variegata' and 'Aureovariegata' are unpromising clones splashed with white and yellow markings, respectively.

C. thyoides (Linnaeus) B.S.P
White cypress

Tree to 15 m. Bark dull, grey-brown or red-brown. Foliage in rather erratic sprays of very fine shoots. Leaves acute, incurved, with a central gland, green or grey-green with white marginal bands of stomata. Cone globose, to 0.6 cm, glaucous blue-grey, ripening brown, with 4-6 scales, with a small central spine. Zone 3.

White cypress is native to the Atlantic coast of New England, south to Georgia. It is found in swampy sites, although thriving better in moist, normal soils.

Similar plants found along the Gulf coast from Florida to Mississippi are variously treated as a variety (var. *henryae* (Li) Little) or species (*C. henryae* Li). This taxon differs in the bark which has shallower and more spiral fissures, less flattened foliage sprays with paler green, longer and more adpressed leaves, green juvenile foliage and larger less glaucous cones.

White cypress makes a small tree of limited value and is usually represented by one of the cultivars.

'Andelyensis' is a small plant with a tight conical habit. The foliage is set in wedge-shaped tufts at the end of the shoots. It frequently cones, giving rise to normal and intermediate seedlings.

'Ericoides' is a form with persistent juvenile foliage. It is dwarf and rather tender.

'Glauca' has glaucous foliage and makes a dense small conical tree.

'Variegata' has large patches of yellow foliage.

Cryptomeria D. Don **Japanese Cedars Taxodiaceae**

A genus of two species from Japan and southern China. They are characterised by the awl-like needles with decurrent bases and the globose cones which have a number of appendages on the ovuliferous bract scales. The foliage is similar, though longer, .than that of Wellingtonia but the latter's cones and much thicker bark quickly sep-

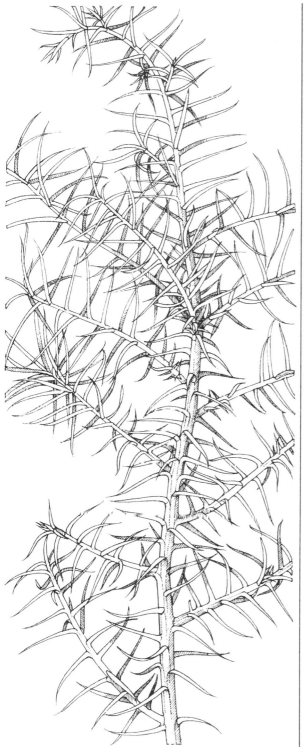

Figure 8.7 Cryptomeria japonica *'Elegans'. Foliage.*

arate them. They are closely related to *Athrotaxis* but the softer foliage and cone characters distinguish them. They make attractive, fast-growing trees and a number of dwarf and curiosity cultivars.

C. japonica (Linnaeus fil.) D. Don
Japanese cedar

Tree to 30 m. Crown conic when young, becoming more rounded with age, generally open with spaced branches but foliage on branches may be dense. Bark red-brown or orange-brown, fibrous, becoming soft and relatively thick in old trees, peeling in long strips, in young trees exfoliating in small square flakes. Shoot green, red-brown after two or three years. Buds without scales. Leaves spirally set around the shoot, more or less pointing forwards, awl-like, flattened along the line of the shoot, acute mid- to dark matt green, stomata in 4 bands, length variable from 0.5-1.5 cm, juvenile foliage laxer, usually longer and more spreading. Male cones produced in early spring, in axil of leaves, to 1 cm. Cones with 20-30 scales, terminal on 1 cm leafy shoots, globular, ripening brown in first year, remaining on tree over winter, 1.5-2 cm. Bract scale with a central pointed triangular boss, fused for the lower half to the ovuliferous scale. Ovuliferous scale shield-like, bearing 3-5 seeds, with a ring of 4-6 pointed triangular teeth, to 0.7 cm, around the margin. Zone 5.

Japanese cedar is one of the principal forest trees of Japan. It has been cultivated for many centuries as a result of which its natural distribution has been obscured but it is known to be wild on Yakushima island. It provides a very useful red timber but in cultivation it is used more as an attractive, long-lived and fairly fast-growing amenity tree. It has the ability to make regrowth from the stump if felled.

It has produced a large number of different growth forms and the following are but a small selection of the more distinctive or common.

'Araucarioides' has long spreading or nodding dark green foliage which make a cluster of shoots at the end of the branches; it forms a broad conical bush to 2 m. It originated in Japan but similar forms have occured in Europe as branch sports.

'Bandai-Sugi' makes a globose plant but will become an irregular shrub to 2 m with time; the foliage is thick and congested, varying from 1.2 down to 0.3 cm, and turns dull bronze over winter.

'Compressa' is a dwarf, dense conical form with juvenile foliage; the leaves are dark green, with those inside the plant blue-green, turning rich red-bronze in winter.

'Cristata' produces a number of fasciated or monstrous growths on the shoots; these are bright green but die off brown. It makes a small tree with short upturned branches.

'Elegans' is a very common form. The main feature is the long soft juvenile foliage to 2.5 cm, which is set spaced on the individual shoot but overall gives a dense plant. The leaves are bluish green but turn a good red-brown over winter. 'Elegans' will make a full-sized tree, to 25 m and produces cones. Large trees invariably fall partially over, only to continue growing with a pronounced lean. 'Elegans Compacta' is a dwarf form and 'Elegans Aurea' one with yellow-green leaves.

'Globosa Nana' is a dwarf broadly conical plant with dense regular ascending branches. The leaves are short and yellow-green, more bluish in winter. This form, like some of the other dwarf forms, may revert and if this happens the reverting shoot must be removed else the habit will be lost.

'Lobbii' is a large tree cultivar with an open tufted habit. The crown remains conical even in old trees and the ascending dense tufts of foliage are not pleasing; nevertheless, this was frequently planted in the past and many larger trees of Japanese cedar are of this clone.

'Lycopodioides' is characterised by the long unbranched shoots, resembling the *Lycopodium* mosses, and may make a small spreading tree.

'Nana' is a dwarf form introduced from China and probably preferable to the following species. It makes a plant to 1.5 m and has crowded upright branches. The needles are shorter and denser on the shoot than normal and remain green over winter.

'Spiralis' has very spirally-arranged, twisted and incurved leaves and makes a dense plant.

'Vilmoriniana' is a small plant, ultimately to 1 m, with a compact habit. The leading shoots may extend above the mound of the plant and the leaves inside the plant are yellow-green, which distinguishes it from 'Compacta'.

C. fortunei Hooibrenk ex Otto & Dietrich
Fortune cedar

Tree to 25 or 30 m. Crown open, with billowing branches. Leaves longer, yellow-green, more generally incurved. Cones similar but with only around 20 scales, each with 2 seeds. Bract and ovuliferous scales with shorter cusps, to 0.4 cm. Zone 7.

This tree is the Chinese form of Japanese cedar and is found across central and southern China from Sichuan to Zhejiang on the east coast. It is, however, a much more attractive tree with its more open crown and brighter foliage. It is particularly neat as a young plant and will make a satisfactory specimen tree for a small garden, if it

is removed after a number of years; like the Japanese form, it should regrow if coppiced. If left, it will make a more substantial trunk than Japanese cedar. It is often referred to as a variety of Japanese cedar, as var. *sinensis* Siebold & Zuccarini. No cultivars are recorded, although 'Nana' and some of the other forms ascribed to Japanese cedar probably belong here.

Cunninghamia R. Brown **China firs**
Taxodiaceae

This small genus of two or possibly three species is confined to China and Taiwan. The leaves are spirally arranged around the shoot and the cones are composed of around 30 or so scales. Each potentially with 3 seeds. The bark is thick and fibrous as in other members of the Redwood family but the foliage is parted, looking similar to some *Araucaria* species.

C. lanceolata (Lambert) Hooker fil
China fir

Tree 10 to 20 m. Crown columnar, usually narrow, domed, on dry sites often thin and high, with persistent brown dead branches. Bark thick, reddish brown, deeply furrowed and regularly ridged, hard compared to the similar bark of Sequoia and Sequoiadendron. Shoot green for several years. Foliage parted below the shoot, somewhat so above but with some leaves recurved. Leaves lanceolate, broadest near the base, taper to acute, occasionally sharp, apex, decurrent on the shoot, glossy green above with raised midrib and margins, 2 incomplete lines of stomata often running along the 2 grooves, silvery white beneath from two broad bands of stomata, margin finely serrate, to 7 cm by 0.5 cm. Male cones in clusters at end of shoot. Cones ovoid-conic, truncate at base, rounded at apex, 3-4 cm each way, set on a short leafy shoot. Scales ovate, with an acuminate tip. Zone 7.

China fir is found right across China from Sichuan to the east coast, as far as Hong Kong. It can make an attractive tree, with its distinctive foliage and appealing bark, but when not flourishing, particularly on sites which dry out, it can develop a high and rather sparse crown, marred by the persistent dead brown branches. China fir is hardy throughout Britain, although in Scotland it is rare and only makes a small tree.

Recently, a new species, *C. unicaniculata* Wang & Liu, has been described from Sichuan; some of the cultivated material may prove to be referable to this taxon, if held to be distinct.

'Glauca' is a form in which the 1 year old shoots bear blue-green leaves. When well grown, it makes an attractive tree, with the leaves shining out in moonlight or car headlights.

'Nana' is a form with bright green foliage; it makes only a small plant.

'Compacta' makes a small spreading dwarf plant without a leader. It is very hardy.

C. konishii Hayata
Taiwan cunninghamia

Tree to 10 m, to 50 m in the wild. Leaves on young and sterile trees similar to China fir, although tending to be shorter and more radial in arrangement; on coning shoots the leaves are much shorter, to 2.5 cm by 0.25 cm, linear-lanceolate, hard and radial in arrangement. Cones smaller, to 2.5 cm. Scales with a terminal mucro. Zone 8.

This species is native to the island of Taiwan, where *C. lanceolata* is also cultivated. Mature wild material of *C. konishii* is very distinct in the short, hard and radial foliage, but young cultivated plants are less clearly distinguished. One character often quoted, that *konishii* has stomata on both sides of the leaf, does not hold, as *lanceolata* frequently has two narrow rows in the grooves between the midrib and margins. It is hardy in southern Britain.

× *Cupressocyparis* Dallimore
Leyland Cypress Cupressaceae

This genus has originated from the hybridisation of *Chamaecyparis nootkatensis* with three different species of *Cupressus*. Although the Nootka and true cypress species involved are natives of western North America, the hybrid has only been reported as happening in Britain. The hybrids are sterile and can only be propagated vegetatively, usually by cuttings. As first generation crosses, they have 'hybrid vigour' or *heterosis*, and thereby combine the hardiness and vigour of the *Chamaecyparis* with the fast growth rate and site tolerances of the *Cupressus* species. Only two clones of one of the hybrids are in general cultivation, which is a pity as these two plants are best considered as the least graceful of the bunch.

× *C. leylandii* (Jackson & Dallimore) Dallimore
Leyland cypress

(*Chamaecyparis nootkatensis* × *Cupressus macrocarpa*)

Tree to 35 m, of considerable vigour. Crown columnar, tapering towards the top which is bent to one side. Bark smooth, brown-green, becoming shallowly ridged and slightly stringy. Foliage in more or less flat long sprays. Leaves acute, facial and laterals similar, grey-green. Cones, if produced, dark shiny brown, globular, with 8 scales each with a small central prickle, 1.5-2 cm. Seeds around 5 per scale. Zone 7.

The original hybrid occurred at Leighton Park in England in 1888 when seed was collected from a Nootka cypress and six plants raised; in 1911 the reverse cross happened when seed collected from a Monterey cypress produced two seedlings. Cuttings were distributed to several gardens before the hybrid origin of the plants was perceived in 1925. The plants stood out as extremely fast in growth and unlike the respective seed parents.

In recent years the fast growth potential has been used to provide a quick hedge, as the trees are capable of making 0.9 m a year following planting as 0.5 m plants. Unfortunately, whilst they are fast hedging plants and tolerant of a wide range of sites, they do not know when to stop and are capable of averaging 0.9 per year for upwards of 20 seasons! They also make a somewhat formless screen, as discussed in Chapter 3, pages 29-30. Although the habit is generally columnar or columnar-conic, near the coast and in the west of Britain, they develop a much more spreading, sprawling habit, becoming broad conic and rather more open. Recently, the disease caused by the fungus *Seiridium cardinale* (see Chapter 7, page 68) has caused some damage to plants of Leyland cypress; if such damage was to become more widespread, it would severely limit the planting of the tree.

The above botanical description refers to the commonest clone in cultivation, known as 'Haggerston Grey'. It is one of the original 1888 trees. It does not make as neat a young tree as some of the other plants, although filling out equally well when mature. Also, the grey-green foliage colour is rather dull. It very rarely produces either flowers or ripe cones.

The foliage of clones of Leyland cypress resembles either the Nootka parent in having flat-pinnate sprays, or are more reminiscent of the Monterey cypress parent with angular-plumose sprays, although this is independent of which species is the seed parent. 'Haggerston Grey' has angular-plumose sprays. The other named clones include:

'Green Spire' which makes a narrow columnar tree with dense foliage of a bright green. It is also an 1888 seedling and has angular-plumose sprays.

'Leighton Green' has coarser foliage which is in two flat ranks and the trees frequently carry large numbers of cones, 2-3 cm. It more resembles the Nootka cypress parent in the flat-pinnate sprays, although as a 1911 tree, the seed parent was Monterey cypress.

'Naylor's Blue' has dark grey foliage, which is blue when young and can be very attractive when covered with raindrops. It forms a more open tree and is the other 1911 seedling; it is more similar to Monterey cypress than the other clones with the angular-plumose sprays. It was nearly called 'Blue Down', as the original was blown down in 1955! It is rarely offered by nurserymen but is an attractive tree, much more so than 'Haggerston Grey'.

The 'Stapehill' clones were raised in 1940 when seed was collected from a Monterey cypress in Dorset. Two plants have survived from this raising and have flat-pinnate sprays. The more commonly distributed form ('Stapehill 20') suffers very badly in drought years, when it develops a sparse sickly crown. This tree has foliage like 'Leighton Green' but in the shade the sprays become open and rather moth-eaten. The second clone ('Stapehill 21') is more attractive, with more bluish foliage and drought-tolerant. Doubt has been cast upon the parentage of these two plants, as Nootka cypress has not been observed growing in the vicinity of the mother tree, but the resins confirm the presumed parentage.

'Castlewellan' has yellow plumose sprays of foliage, usually with an unattractive bronze hue. It grows at about two-thirds the rate of the above clones, i.e. 0.6 m per annum. It arose in Northern Ireland in 1963 and one parent is the Monterey cypress clone 'Lutea', from which it inherits the foliage colour. It is widely planted as a 'Golden Leyland' but is dismal in comparison to the next clone.

'Robinson's Gold' also occurred in northern Ireland, around 1962. It has flat-pinnate foliage sprays which are an attractive bronze-yellow in spring but becoming gold-yellow and lemon-green later during the season. It has a narrow compact conical habit and is nearly as fast in growth rate as the common green forms. It has a much better habit and shows infinitely more promise as a garden tree than 'Castlewellan'.

Several branch sports have occurred.

'Silver Dust' originated on a plant of 'Leighton Green' planted in the National Arboretum, Washington DC, USA. It has oval patches of creamy-white foliage covering approximately 20 per cent of the flat-pinnate foliage. The variegation is very erratic, somewhat bizarre and not par-ticularly pleasant. Slightly better, with more ivory-white variegated patches and plumose foliage sprays is 'Harlequin', which is a sport of 'Haggerston Grey'.

Several golden foliaged sports of 'Haggerston Grey' have been named, all with plumose foliage. 'Golden Sun' is semi-dwarf with extremely good bright gold foliage. 'Golconda' is a rapidly growing tree form with foliage which is a persistent lemony gold throughout the year, keeping a better and more consistent colour than both 'Castlewellan' and 'Robinson Gold'. To date, all the sports named from 'Haggerston Grey' have occurred in Britain.

× C. notabilis Mitchell
Alice Holt cypress

(Chamaecyparis nootkatensis × Cupressus glabra)

Crown narrowly conic, branches upswept at the tips. Bark red-brown, becoming with age more purple and slightly scaly. Foliage in sparse sprays, shoots yellow-green, later dark purple. Leaves acute, blue-grey, bloomed grey-green. Male cones prominent during summer, shedding pollen in late summer, yellow. Cones globular, blue and purple, bloomed bluish white, 1.2 cm. Zone 8.

This tree was raised when Forestry Commission geneticists collected seed at Leighton Hall in 1956 to see if further Leyland hybrids could be raised. Inadvertently, seed was collected from a *Cupressus glabra* growing some 20 m from the Nootka cypress specimen. It makes an attractive bluish tree, taking after the seed parent in a number of respects, but is uncommon.

× C. ovensii Mitchell
Ovens cypress

(Chamaecyparis nootkatensis × Cupressus lusitanica)

Crown reminiscent of Nootka cypress. Shoots green-brown, later pale red-brown. Leaves in flat sprays, deep bluish green, free with long spreading acute spiny tips, crushed foliage with a sweet lemony scent. Zone 8.

This tree was raised from seed of a *Cupressus lusitanica* which grew nearby a Nootka cypress at Westonbirt Arboretum. It is uncommon in culti-vation.

Cupressus Linnaeus **Cypresses**
Cupressaceae

Cupressus is a genus of some 20 to 25 species or taxa, most of which are very local in distribution.

The genus is closely related to *Chamaecyparis*; originally, all the species of these two genera were included in *Cupressus* and the appropriate genus for some species is still disputed by some botanists. Like *Chamaecyparis*, the cones have peltate or shield-like scales and the foliage is scale-like, but with little difference between the pairs of leaves. The cones, however, ripen at the end of the second season, whereas in *Chamaecyparis* ripening occurs at the end of the first one, except in Nootka cypress whose cones mature in late spring/early summer of the second year. In *Cupressus* the cones often remain closed on the trees after they are ripe, and there are from 5-20 seeds on each fertile cone scale. *Cupressus* is also closely allied to the junipers, but in these the cone scales do not become hard and woody.

Most cypresses have the foliage arranged in three-dimensional sprays, unlike the very flat sprays of *Chamaecyparis*, but in a number they are more or less flattened.

Cypress are very tolerant of hot dry conditions; they are intolerant of shading and require full sun. They are fast-growing trees, but not generally of great stature; they will tolerate poor sandy soils and some species are very good for seashore plantings. Most species can be grown in Britain, although several are on the tender side and suitable for the milder areas; nearly all of them will benefit from shelter from cold dry winds. Unlike the situation with *Chamaecyparis*, only relatively few cultivars have been named.

The true cypresses are found in the Old World from the Atlantic coast of north Africa to China. In the New World, they are restricted to western USA, south to Guatemala. The Old World species usually have only 2 (obtuse) cotyledons whereas the New World species have 3 or 4 (up to 6, pointed) cotyledons. The resins also vary between the two groups, but these differences are not of sufficient magnitude to warrant splitting the genus into two sections. The species are discussed in the following groupings: *C. sempervirens* alliance, other Old World species, *C. arizonica* alliance, and other New World species.

C. sempervirens alliance

This is a group of four species occurring from Morocco in the west to Yunnan in China in the east. All have been referred to as varieties of *sempervirens* at some time or other.

Figure 8.8 Cupressus sempervirens. *Foliage and mature cones.*

C. sempervirens Linnaeus
Italian cypress

Tree to 20 m, more in the wild. Crown columnar, often very narrow, less often broader. Bark brown-grey, with shallow, spiral scaly ridges. Shoot coppery brown becoming shiny red-brown or purple-brown. Leaves with blunt, abruptly mucronate tips, grooved and with indistinct, non-secreting glands on the dorsal surfaces, grey-green, ultimate shoots rounded in section, 0.1 cm, on strong shoots the scale leaves have spreading, acute tips behind side branches, scentless. Male cones shed pollen in early spring, many terminal on weakest shoots, greenish yellow, 0.3 cm. Cones globular or globose-ovoid, greyish brown, shiny, with 8-14 scales each with a small central boss, 2.5-3.5 cm. Seeds not warty. Zone 7.

This tree is recorded in the wild from the eastern Mediterranean to northern Iran. The common name 'Italian cypress' alludes to the many planted specimens in Italy, but it probably is not native there. Most cultivated trees are of the very tight fastigiate form and this probably represents the type of the species. The wild eastern plants have broader crowns with horizontal branches and are called var. *horizontalis* (Miller) Gordon. The very tight fastigiate plants are sometimes referred to as cultivar 'Stricta' but as this comes fairly true from seed and cultivated plants are variable in the tightness of the habit, it is a superfluous name. The tree is also cultivated around the western Mediterranean and may be wild in central Tunisia, from whence var. *numidica* Trabut (with the upright branches leaving the trunk at right angles) was described.

Italian cypress is hardy in Britain and useful for making a narrow upright tree; there is some variation in hardiness between origins. It is fast-growing when young but soon slows down and few trees make more than 15 m. It can be affected by *Seiridium cardinale* but, to date, this has not proved a problem in Britain.

'Swaine's Gold' is a plant with pale yellow or greenish yellow (depending to some extent on the degree of sunlight) foliage and an upright narrow habit.

C. atlantica Gaussen
Moroccan cypress

This tree is close to Italian cypress but differs in the foliage, of young trees at least, bearing actively secreting resin glands, resulting in flecks of resin on the leaves, the foliage in flatter sprays and the globose cones with usually only 8 scales. The crushed foliage is slightly scented. Zone 7. It is native to the Atlas mountains.

C. dupreziana Camus
Saharan cypress

This tree is restricted to a very dry mountain region in the Sahara desert in south east Algeria. It differs from Italian cypress in the distinctly flattened shoots and the smaller leaves which bear prominent glandular pits, secreting resin (in young trees at least), and which are faintly aromatic. The smaller and narrower cones have 10-12 scales; the seeds are flatter with wider wings, almost orbicular in outline. Zone 7.

Only a small number of old trees are still alive in the wild, with little or no natural regeneration. It appears to be a relict population from earlier times when the Sahara was not so arid. It is uncommon in cultivation, but can be separated from Italian cypress by the flecks of resin on the leaves.

C. duclouxiana Hickel
Yunnan cypress

Tree to 20 m. Crown columnar or narrow conic. Bark finely fissured. Shoots light yellow-green, later brown. Foliage in a series of short flattened sprays arranged all around the shoot. Leaves with incurved acute tips, blue-green or glaucous blue, obscurely glandular, ultimate divisions are very fine and terete, less than 0.08 cm in diameter. Cones globose, to 3.5 cm, scales 8, seeds narrowly winged, with warts. Zone 8.

Yunnan cypress is known from the Chinese province of Yunnan and is particularly common around the city of Kunming; it is also recorded from south-west Sichuan. It is possible that it is only planted in Yunnan. Plants collected in south-east Tibet have been postulated as representing a wild population of this species but I am unconvinced that they are conspecific; these trees found by the plant hunters Ludlow & Sherrif included specimens to 60 m tall but were not introduced to cultivation.

Yunnan cypress is reported as tender and only suited to cultivation in mild areas, but recent seed collected in Kunming appears much hardier and promises to make attractive blue trees. The species is similar to Italian cypress, particularly in the large cones, but easily told from it by the very fine shoots.

Other Old World Species

C. funebris Endlicher
Chinese weeping cypress

Tree to 20 m. Crown ovoid, with ascending branches. Bark grey-brown, shallowly fissured, fluted in old trees. Foliage sprays, flat, held out vertically or pendulous. Leaves in lateral and facial pairs, fairly similar but shoot slightly compressed, acute, ending in a small sharp point, spreading, mid- to fresh green and shiny on both surfaces, with an obscure but translucent gland. Cones small, globular, ripening in second year, 1-1.5 cm, to 3 cm. Scales 8, rarely to 12, with a small central boss, each bearing 3-5 narrowly winged and warty seeds. Zone 8.

Native to central China along the Yangtse valley, this tree is represented in cultivation from seeds collected by Wilson in Hupeh. It is often referred to as *Chamaecyparis funebris* (Endlicher) Franco due to the flattened foliage and small cones with few seeds per scale and which open at maturity. However, resin analysis shows that it is not closely related to any species of *Chamaecyparis* but is similar to this group of Asiatic *Cupressus*, and as the foliage is similar to the following species and the cones are recorded as taking two years to ripen, it is here retained in *Cupressus*.

The form in cultivation makes a small tree but is not suited to cold areas. Juvenile plants have very long soft foliage for a number of years. It is also recorded as cultivated in the eastern Himalayas but all these records refer to *C. corneyana*.

C. torulosa D. Don
West Himalayan cypress

Tree to 20m. Crown rounded conic, with horizontal branches upswept at the tips. Bark dull brown, with shallow curling ridges, in old trees peeling off in long strips. Shoot shiny purplish brown. Foliage in somewhat pendulous sprays. Leaves in 4 rows, acute, incurved, with a gland in groove on dorsal surface, dull green or brighter yellowish green, ultimate shoots long, unbranched, 0.12-0.15cm in width. Cones globose, bluish or pale green, ripening red-brown, loosely clustered, 1.5cm. Scales 8-10, each with a small boss and bearing 4-6 seeds. Zone 7.

This cypress is restricted to the west Himalayas from central Nepal to north-west India, and from adjoining southern and western Tibet. It can be found growing throughout Britain but is uncommon. It is not reliably hardy but as it has a large altitudinal range, from 1,800m to 3,300m, different provenances are likely to vary in hardiness. It has been called Bhutan cypress but is not the species found in that east Himalayan kingdom. Also, the name *C. torulosa* has been applied to several of the following species from Tibet and west China.

'Nana' is a dwarf-growing form with bright green foliage.

'Golden Spangle' is a form growing to 3m with foliage which is golden yellow in summer, fading to greenish yellow in winter but remaining an attractive colour.

'Corneyana' is a cultivar of uncertain application. It is not the same as the following species. At one arboretum in southern England, plants thus labelled have proved to have been received from Kenya as a deliberate cross between *C. lusitanica* and *C. macrocarpa*, whilst plants cultivated as this in France have proved to be *C. lusitanica*.

C. corneyana (Knight & Perry) Carriere
Bhutan cypress

Tree to 40m in Bhutan with a trunk to 2m in diameter. Crown columnar, with level main branches bearing hanging foliage. Bark brown, smooth, with shallow spiral furrows. Foliage in very flat pendulous sprays. Leaves in 4 rows, facial leaves smaller than laterals, often secreting flecks of resin, ovate, incurved, acute with sharp yellow tip, mid-matt green, 0.1cm but to 0.2cm with acuminate tips on strong shoots. Cones ellipsoid-globose, glaucous, ripening to pale grey, 2-2.5cm. Scales 8-10, to 1.4cm wide, wrinkled or flat, dimpled but sometimes with a blunt central boss, 10-20 seeds per scale, around 150 per cone. Seeds bright shiny brown, 0.3cm. Zone 8.

Bhutan cypress is native to central west Bhutan but is cultivated at monasteries from Sikkim to north-east India where it makes a very tall tree with an attractive weeping crown. It has only recently been introduced but appears hardy if suitably sheltered from cold winds. In the past it has been confused with the *C. funebris* and also with Kashmir cypress.

C. cashmiriana (Royle) Carriere
Kashmir cypress

Tree to 20m but in Britain only seen to 10m. Crown in old trees wide-spreading, in young trees conical. Foliage in long hanging sprays, set on ascending branches. Leaves in 4 rows, acute, tips free, spreading, to 0.2cm, glaucous blue. Cones globose, greenish yellow, ripening brown, with a leaf-like central point, 1.5cm. Scales 10, with a central depression and an acute reflexed prickle, each bearing about 10 seeds. Zone 9.

The native origin of Kashmir cypress is unknown. It could be a juvenile form of *C. torulosa*, to which it is related, or it may have originated elsewhere in the Himalayan region; the number of seeds per fertile scale is significantly higher than in *C. torulosa*. It is also related to Bhutan cypress, but differs from it in the smaller cones with a central leaf-like point, the fewer seeds per scale, the reflexed boss on the scales and in the more pendulous, glaucous blue foliage which is more juvenile with longer spreading tips to the leaves.

Kashmir cypress makes a very attractive tree but unfortunately is very tender and only survives for more than a few winters in Ireland or the mildest parts of Britain. It is an excellent plant for use in a conservatory, or for areas with a sub-tropical climate.

C. chengiana Hu
Cheng cypress

Tree to 30m in China. Crown columnar. Bark stripping vertically between fine fissures. Foliage in flattened open sprays. Leaves in 4 rows, broad-ovate, acute, incurved, 0.10-0.15cm, to 0.2cm on strong shoots, grey-green, glandular on dorsal surface. Cones globose, 1.2-2cm. Scales 8-12, with a flat boss and 4-5 seeds. Zone 6.

Cheng cypress is native to western China from north-west Sichuan and southern Gansu. It has been confused with both *C. duclouxiana* and *C. torulosa* in the past. It has recently been introduced from the Kangting region of west Sichuan and looks set to make an interesting and very hardy tree. The juvenile foliage is longer and softer than with most other species.

C. gigantea Cheng & L.K. Fu
Tsangpo cypress

This tree is similar to Cheng cypress, but differs from it (and *C. torulosa*) in the ultimate branchlets which are 0.1-0.2 cm in diameter and the rhomboidal leaves which are acute but with an expanded apex, and less glandular. The cones are 1.6-2 cm in length and the prickle in the centre of the scales points forwards. This tree is in cultivation from seeds collected in south-east Tibet by Ludlow & Sherrif (under no. 13345) but so far has only produced juvenile foliage which looks more like a juniper species. These trees are up to 15 m tall and very narrow columnar in habit; it is hardy. Zone 7.

C. arizonica alliance

This group of cypresses is found in the south-west USA and along the northern border of Mexico. They are sometimes all treated as varieties of *C. arizonica*, although as they have separate geographical distribution the level of subspecies would seem more appropriate if treated under one name. As a group, the species all make trees 10-20 m tall. Young trees are conical but they may become rounded with age. The foliage is scale-like, acute with finely toothed margins (when seen under a hand lens), set in irregularly-arranged sprays. The cones are 2-2.5 cm long and composed of 6 (rarely 8) scales, each bearing 10-20 seeds. They tolerate very dry conditions, although needing full sun and are hardy when established. The cones remain unopened on the trees for a number of years. The pollen is shed in late summer or early autumn, when the trees can be covered with showy yellow male cones.

C. arizonica Greene
Arizona cypress

Bark grey to dark brown, thick, fibrous, furrowed. Foliage blue-green or grey-green, resin glands not actively secreting resin. Zone 7.

Arizona cypress is recorded from south-east Arizona to the Chisos Mountains in south-west Texas and from neighbouring parts of northern Mexico. It is less attractive than Smooth cypress.

'Aurea' is a form with yellowish foliage and may belong to the following taxon.

C. glabra Sudworth
Smooth cypress

Tree to 15 m. Crown broad and regular conical or ovoid-conical. Bark reddish purple or deep purple, becoming blistered in the fourth or fifth season and flaking away in circular scales, leaving paler patches beneath. The foliage is blue-grey and glaucous, carried in upright sprays on orange-brown shoots. The leaves are covered with flecks of white resin from the actively-secreting dorsal glands. Zone 7.

Smooth cypress is found in central Arizona. It is very distinct from Arizona cypress in the characters of bark and the foliage and would seem to merit specific status. In cultivation, it makes a hardy and fairly fast-growing tree, very tolerant of drought and chalky conditions. The smooth bark (Latin *glabra* translates as smooth) may become more fibrous in very old trees.

'Compacta' is a dwarf form of either this species or possibly of Arizona cypress. It makes a dense rounded bush a metre or so high, with grey-green foliage.

'Pyramidalis' is the general clone in cultivation. The new foliage is blue-white. A number of other narrow forms have been named.

C. montana Wiggins
San Pedro cypress

The bark of this tree is deep red to dark brown and only partially exfoliates from the trunk; in old trees it may become furrowed and grey. The foliage has actively-secreting glands, is dark grey-green and covered in white flecks. The cones have 8-12 scales and open on maturity. Zone 8.

It is native to the San Pedro Matir range of mountains in northern Baja California del Norte and is rare in cultivation.

C. nevadensis Abrams
Piute cypress

The bark is fibrous, furrowed longitudinally, grey, whilst that of the upper crown (or young trees) is grey or reddish, smooth and not exfoliating. The foliage is grey-green and has active resin glands which secrete a clear or reddish resin. The cones are glaucous or silvery grey and the scales have inconspicuous prickles. Zone 6.

It is only found in a few localities in the Piute Mountains of northern California (the Latin name refers to the Sierra Nevada, not the state of Nevada!).

C. stephensonii Wolf
Cayamaca cypress

This has a greyish or cherry red bark which exfoliates in thin flakes. The foliage is pale grey-green and the glands are not particularly active, so that resin flecks, if present, are irregular on the sprays. Zone 8.

It is confined to a few areas in the Cayamaca Mountains in San Diego county, California.

Other New World Species

C. macrocarpa Hartweg ex Gordon
Monterey cypress

Tree to 40 m. Crown columnar in young trees, but in older ones very variable, from broad ovoid with upswept branches to

Cedar of Lebanon-like, with a flat top and tiers of level branches. Bark shallowly ridged, pinkish brown or grey, in young trees smooth, pale brown. Foliage in erect or spreading plume-like sprays, with the branchlets arranged all around the shoot, dense in old trees, with a scent of lemon verbena when crushed. Leaves in 4 similar rows, acute with incurved margins, dark green. Cones with 8-10 scales, globular, 2.5-3 cm. Scales with a flat transverse ridge. Zone 7.

Monterey cypress is restricted in the wild to two small areas at Monterey, California, although fossils indicate a much wider distribution in the recent past. As a young tree it is characterised by the spaced plumes of foliage spreading out from the stem but as it gets older, the crown becomes more dense. The cones are large in comparison to other New World cypresses, although somewhat smaller than can be found on either Italian or Yunnan cypresses.

Monterey cypress is hardy in all but the severest British winters, although young plants are much more tender. It is very useful near the coast and will tolerate salt spray; it also thrives on hot dry sites. In the past it was much used for hedging and in shelter plantings but has given way to its hybrid with Nootka cypress. Also, it is not so amenable to clipping and is much harder to bring back if a hedge is neglected. Trees can be difficult to transplant and should be put out when young; preferably this should be done when the roots are actively growing in late spring or early autumn. Recently, it has proved susceptible to disease caused by the fungus *Seiridium cardinale* (see page 68). It has been planted as a forest tree in some parts of the world, especially Kenya.

'Coneybearii' has long pendulous whip-like branches. 'Coneybearii Aurea' is similar but with yellow-gold foliage.

'Donard Gold' is a conical plant with golden yellow foliage. It makes an extremely attractive small tree and the foliage is very useful for flower arranging. 'Goldcrest', 'Golden Cone' and 'Golden Pillar' are similar attractive forms.

'Lutea' is an old cultivar. The habit is more spreading than the above forms and the foliage colour yellow at first, becoming greener. It is quite attractive and is even more tolerant of maritime exposure than the normal green form. It is the parent of the 'Castlewellan' form of Leyland cypress.

'Pendula' makes a majestic spreading tree with softly weeping branch tips. The original plant is at Glencormac in Ireland and sprawls over a ruined outhouse. The foliage is rather thicker than normal and it is not particularly hardy when young.

'Pygmaea' is one of a number of dwarf forms.

'Saligna Aurea' is a conical tree with weeping threadlike, golden yellow foliage.

C. goveniana Gordon
Gowen cypress

Tree to 20 m, but in the wild smaller. Crown columnar. Bark brown to grey, rough, exfoliating. Foliage in plumose sprays, when crushed smells of citrinella. Shoot purple-brown or paler. Leaves blunt, acute, incurved, without resin spots (except in young trees), dark green. Cones small, globose to oblong, less than 2 cm, glossy dark or grey-brown. Scales 8-10, with a small prickle. Zone 8.

Gowen cypress is restricted to two stands near Monterey, although closely allied plants are found elsewhere in California (see below). In the wild it makes an open broad conic bush less than 8 m high. It is uncommon in cultivation.

var. *pygmaea* Lemmon is a form found in Mendocino county, California. It grows on exceptionally barren soils where it makes a mature tree fruiting when only a metre high. However, on soils with some nutrients, it will grow as tall as the type. It only appears to differ from the type in the darker foliage colour, the usually shiny, warted seeds and the longer pointed leaves.

C. abramsiana Wolf
Santa Cruz cypress

Tree to 20 m. Bark grey, breaking into vertical strips. Shoots purple-red. Leaves light bright or deep green, acute, bluntly pointed, forward-spreading at the tips. Cones spherical, shiny brown, to 2.5 cm. Scales 8-10, with a small prickle. Zone 7.

This tree is restricted to the Santa Cruz Mountains to the north of Monterey county, California. It is related to Gowen cypress but differs in the fuller foliage sprays and larger cones. It is rare in cultivation, but those few trees planted have shown great vigour.

C. guadelupensis S. Watson
Guadelupe cypress

Tree to 20 m. Crown ovoid. Bark dark red-purple, cracking and flaking off. Foliage in slender sprays. Leaves long, slender, acute or blunt, grey-green or blue-green, crushed foliage with resinous scent. Cone globose, 3-4 cm. Scales 8-10, with prominent prickles. Zone 9.

This tree is restricted to the island of Guadelupe, off the coast of Baja California. The island is part of a series of ridges off the coast of California, which, in geological times, were part of the mainland. It is extremely uncommon in cultivation.

C. forbesii Jepson
Tecate cypress

Tecate cypress is related to Guadelupe cypress but differs in the sharply acute, bright green leaves which are fragrant when crushed and in the small cones, to 2.5 cm. It has open sprays of foliage and makes a neat small tree, although it is rare in cultivation. It occurs on the mainland of northern Baja California del Norte and in San Diego and Orange counties of south-west California. It is sometimes treated as *C. guadelupensis* var. *forbesii* (Jepson) Little. Zone 8.

C. bakeri Jepson
Baker cypress

Tree to 15 m. Crown conical. Bark reddish or grey, breaking into small curling plates. Foliage in sprays radiating from shoot. Leaves in 4 rows, bright or dark greyish green, acute, with a conspicuous dorsal resin gland. Cones globose, greyish brown, 1.5 cm. Scales 6-8, with prominent prickles. Zone 6.

This tree is restricted to the Siskiyou and Shasta counties of northern California and is the hardiest of the New World species. It is rare in cultivation.

 subspecies *matthewsii* Wolf was described from the northern end of the Siskiyou Mountains in Oregon. It was described as a tree to 30 m with larger and more warty cones to 2 cm, but since then intermediate populations have been found in the intervening territory and the taxon is not generally accepted as worthy of separate recognition.

C. macnabiana Murray
Macnab cypress

Tree to 15 m. Crown domed, bushy. Bark brown or grey, smooth, furrowed, becoming thick in old trees. Foliage in flattened sprays. Leaves ovate, bluntly acute, deep green and scented of citrus, with a small conspicuous dorsal resin gland. Cone brown, globose, 2 cm. Scales 6-8, with conical curved prickles. Zone 8.

Macnab cypress is confined to dry low hills in northern California. It is rare in cultivation and only suited to the milder parts.

C. sargentiana Jepson
Sargent cypress

Tree to 20 m. Crown narrow conic or more wide-spreading. Bark thick, grey-brown, fibrous and longitudinally furrowed. Leaves grey-green with a glaucous bloom, acute, blunt, glands not secreting resin. Cone globose or ellipsoidal, glossy brown, ripening dull brown or grey, 2.5 cm. Scales 6-8, with small prickles. Zone 9.

Sargent cypress is native to the coastal ranges of California but is rare in cultivation. It is allied to Gowen cypress.

C. lusitanica Miller
Mexican cypress or Cedar of Goa

Tree to 20 m or more. Crown conical, on a single bole, rarely forked. Bark brown, shallowly fissured into spiralling fibrous strips. Foliage in spreading sprays. Leaves with free spreading acute tips, grey-green or glaucous blue-green, with only a faintly resinous scent when crushed, not glandular. Cone glaucous blue when immature, ripening shiny brown, 1.5 cm. Scales 6-8, with conical dorsal prickles. Zone 8.

Mexican cypress is found through central Mexico south to Guatemala and Honduras. The Latin name refers to Portugal, where it was first noticed. For a long time the natural habitat was unknown, and it was conjectured that it might be Indian or Asiatic in origin, hence the alternate common name, Cedar of Goa (from the Portuguese colony on the west coast of India). In Mexico the origin is still not fully accepted and the alternative name, *C. lindleyi* Klotch, is used there.

Mexican cypress makes a vigorous tree but is only reliably hardy in the milder parts of Britain.

var. *benthamii* (Endlicher) Carriere **Bentham cypress** is found in the north-eastern states of Mexico. It differs from Mexican cypress in the much more flattened foliage sprays. Mature trees in Mexico of both this and the typical form are not as attractive as young plants. 'Knightiana' is a form of this variety with more glaucous foliage.

'Flagellifera' has whip-like shoots which droop, and recalls *Chamaecyparis pisifera* 'Filifera'.

'Glauca' is a form originally found in Portugal which has blue-green foliage with distinct resin glands.

'Glauca Pendula' is similar in foliage colour to 'Glauca' but is attractively pendulous. It will make a large tree in mild areas. This clone arose in England in the 1920s but such plants are commonly cultivated in central Mexico.

Dacrycarpus (Endlicher) de Laubenfels **Podocarpaceae**

The genus has only recently been raised from being a section of *Podocarpus* to a separate genus. The adult leaves are small, awl-shaped or flattened (often both types on the one shoot) and set spirally. The bract below the seed is as long as the seed and fused to the outer seed coat. The seed is terminal and usually solitary, on a fleshy receptacle.

The genus consists of nine species from southern China, Malaysia, Indonesia, Papua New Guinea and New Caledonia but only the following species from New Zealand is likely to be encountered. Information on the other taxa (and on the Podocarpaceae in general) can be found in De Laubenfels, *Journal of the Arnold Arboretum*, vol. 50, (1969), pp. 274-369.

D. dacrydioides (A. Richard) de Laubenfels
Kahikatea

Tree to 45m in New Zealand. Bark thin, greyish brown. Leaves on young trees in flat sprays, soft, bronze or bronzy green in colour, soft, 1cm, on adult trees scale-like, over-lapping, to 0.3cm, pointed, incurved, green or bronzy green. Male and female flowers on different trees. Male cones terminal, to 0.8cm. Female cones terminal on short branches. Seeds to 0.6cm, set on a red, bloomed, receptacle. Zone 9.

Kahikatea is an important native forest tree in New Zealand, where it occurs over a wide range of sites. It is in cultivation in south-west Britain and Ireland and probably could be tried elsewhere if suitable high altitude forms were obtained. It makes a small tree or bush, unusual for the bronze coloration of the foliage.

Dacrydium Solander ex Forster
Podocarpaceae

This genus has been depleted by the separation of New Zealand and Chilean species into *Halocarpus*, *Lagarostrobus* and *Lepidothamnus*, which see. With one exception, the remaining species are sub-tropical in origin, from Malaysia to the Solomon Islands and are not likely to be hardy. The genus is characterised by the foliage being scale-like, as in cypresses but spirally arranged and the male and female cones (on separate trees) being set in the axils of the upper leaves on the shoot. The female cones consist of a few scales, one or more of which bear a single ovule. The seed is subtended by a cup-shaped aril and is ovoid.

The following species is the only one likely to prove hardy.

D. cupressinum Solander ex Forster
Rimu

Tree to 50m. Crown conical, in mature trees rounded at the top, with pendulous branches. Bark brown or grey, scaly. Leaves on young trees to 0.6cm, awl-shaped, on mature trees to 0.3cm, spreading, linear, pointed, sea green or yellow-green. Male cones small, green, carried at the tips of branches. Seed ovoid, to 0.3cm, receptacle and bract fleshy, occasionally enlarged. Zone 9.

This tree is native to New Zealand, where it is an important timber tree. In cultivation it has made a small tree in mild areas, to 10m. It might be suit-able for wider cultivation if seed could be obtained from more alpine parts of its range. Young trees have attractive long pendulous foliage.

Decussocarpus de Laubenfels
Podocarpaceae

This genus used to be included as two sections (section *Nageia* Endlicher and *Arfocarpus* Bucholz & Gray) of *Podocarpus*, but is now treated as a related genus. It is characterised by the large flat leaves which are opposite (or sub-opposite) and set in decussate ranks; the leaves have several veins but lack accessory transfusion tissue, which is a feature of *Podocarpus sensu stricta*. The fruit is carried on a naked peduncle and lacks a receptacle.

It includes a dozen species from southern and central Africa and south-east Asia but only the following species is likely to be encountered.

D. nagi (Thunberg) de Laubenfels
Naki

Tree to 20m in the wild. Leaves lanceolate, broad elliptic-ovate to oblong, with many parallel veins, in opposite pairs, deep green above, pale or whitish below, 3-8cm. Fruit globose, 1.5cm. Zone 10.

This tree is native to southern Japan, the Ryuku islands, Taiwan and across central China from Zhejiang to Sichuan. Introductions to date have proved tender, although it might be hardy in mild western parts. The only time I have seen this tree in the wild was near Canton, where I first took it as a planted *Agathis!*, which the foliage resembles.

Diselma Hooker fil. **Cupressaceae**

This is a monotypic genus, characterised as below. It has been included with *Fitzroya* but is well separated by the foliage and cones.

D. archeri Hooker fil.
Diselma

Shrub or small tree to 6m. Crown compact or sprawling. Leaves in opposite pairs, short awl-like or long scale-like, lying forwards on the shoot, to 0.2cm, tapered to a blunt rounded apex, decurrent, 2 broad bands of silver stomata on the abaxial surface, none on adaxial side. Male and female cones on sep-arate plants. Male cones terminal, oblong, with 3-4 pairs of stamens. Cones small, composed of 2 pairs of scales, only the upper pair fertile, each with 2 3-winged seeds. Zone 8.

This small shrub is restricted to the western coast ranges of Tasmania. It makes an interesting plant but is somewhat tender, except in mild areas.

Falcatifolium de Laubenfels
Podocarpaceae

This is a small genus of five species which in the past have been treated in both *Podocarpus* and *Dacrydium*. It is characterised by the male and female cones being carried on specialised axillary shoots. The female cone is set on a pendulous peduncle with a receptacle which often has a thorny basal appendage. The Latin name is taken from the falcate foliage, although some *Dacrycarpus* species also show this feature.

The species are restricted to Malaysia, the Philippines, Indonesia, Papua New Guinea and New Caledonia. They are tropical in distribution, except for *F. papuanum* de Laubenfels, which occurs up to 2,400 m in New Guinea and could possibly be hardy in mild areas.

Fitzroya Hooker fil. Cupressaceae

This is a monotypic genus, characterised as given below.

F. cupressoides (Molina) Johnston
Patagonian cypress

Tree to 15 m, more usually a large overgrown sprawling shrub. Bark reddish brown, shed in long strips. Foliage in open pendulous wiry sprays. Leaves in whorls of 3, scale or awl-like, blunt, decurrent at base, tips free, spreading but slightly incurved, to 0.4 cm, dark green and keeled on abaxial side, with 2 bands of stomata on each surface. Cones ripening in the first year, composed of 3 whorls of 3 scales, only the upper 1 or 2 whorls fertile, each scale with 2-3 seeds, 1 cm. Seeds with 2 broad wings. Zone 8.

Patagonian cypress is native to southern Chile and adjoining parts of the Argentine. It is named after Captain Fitzroy of HMS *Beagle,* on whose expedition Charles Darwin sailed. It makes a tree to 50 m in Chile but is becoming rare due to over-exploitation. In cultivation, it makes an attractive plant, usually remaining clothed to the ground and growing slowly. With its whorled leaves and lax pendulous foliage it looks somewhat like a juniper.

Fokienia Henry & Thomas Cupressaceae

A monotypic genus, as discussed below.

F. hodginsii (Dunn) Henry & Thomas
Fokienia

Tree to 15 m, but in cultivation only found as a small shrub to 2 m. Shoot green for several years, becoming red-brown. Foliage in flat sprays. Leaves scale-like, in 2 whorled pairs, the facial pair are small, obovate with a small acuminate free tip, ridged with a pale band of stomata on either side of the ridge, lateral pairs spreading, broad, flat, sickle-shaped, tip free, incurved, pointed, band of stomata on each side, the successive pairs close on the pair below, yellow-green, pairs to 1.2 cm wide and 0.7 cm long, the leaves on strong shoots are more scale-like, making whip-like extension growths, on coning shoots the leaves are blunt, with incurved tips. Cones ripen in their second year, globose, 12-16 scales, 2.5 cm. Scales each bear 2-4 seeds with 2 unequal wings. Zone 7.

Fokienia was first found in the Chinese province of Fokien, now spelt Fujian; it is now known to occur across southern China from Zhejiang in the east to south-east Yunnan and along the Vietnam border. It is very rare in cultivation where it is only found as a small interesting bush with yellowish foliage. It appears to be perfectly hardy, being recorded by the Chinese as tougher than *Sequoia sempervirens;* it may be that it requires more summer heat, with copious water, for optimum growth.

Figure 8.9 Fokienia hodginsii. *Juvenile foliage.*

Ginkgo Linnaeus Ginkgoaceae

This tree is quite unlike all other 'conifers' and is placed in its own order, the Ginkgoales. The group was formerly widespread, as evinced by the fossil records from many parts of the world, but now only a single species is recorded from southern China. The foliage of this plant differs little from that found in fossils. Pollination is achieved by motile sperms, a feature unique in gymnosperms but which it shares with the ferns.

G. biloba Linnaeus
Ginkgo

Tree to 40m. Crown on young trees narrow with short branches radiating from a central bole, in older trees (after the first hundred years or so) the crown becomes much broader, with several main branches. Bark dull grey, finely shredding, with cross ridges. Shoot green, then brown, later pale grey. Bud brown, flat conic. Leaves carried on both long and short shoots, fan-shaped with many parallel veins which originate in the petiole as 2 but repeatedly fork as the leaf widens, base cuneate or wedge-shaped and tapers into the petiole, usually notched or bilobed at the ragged apex, rich green above, yellowy beneath, to 12cm in both dimensions, including petiole. Male and female flowers on separate trees, carried on short shoots. Male flowers in cylindrical, pendulous, short-stalked catkins. Fruit on a peduncle to 5cm, plum-like, yellow-green, covered by a fleshy coat which on decaying gives a rancid odour, 3cm. Seed 2cm. Zone 3.

Ginkgo has survived till modern times in two remote areas in China, one on the border between Zhejiang and Anhui provinces in the east and the other further west in Guizhou. It is very similar to the fossil species which survived in Europe until just before the last Ice age. It has been planted around Buddhist temples for a long period and was taken to Japan centuries ago with Buddhism from China. From thence, it was introduced into Europe in the early eighteenth century. An alternative common name is the Maidenhair tree, because of the similarity of the leaves to the pinnules, or leaflets, of the Maidenhair fern.

Ginkgo makes an excellent tree with an interesting habit and is quite common. The deciduous foliage turns a beautiful golden colour in autumn. Male trees are often preferred for amenity planting as they do not produce the foul-smelling fruits; however, each cloud has its silver lining and the kernel of the Ginkgo is delightful roasted. Apparently, fertilisation of the embryo only takes place at or around the time that the fruit is ripe, although pollination occurs much earlier.

Ginkgo makes a very long-lived tree. The original one introduced to Kew in 1754 still flourishes and now has a broad crown, typical of middle-aged trees. The species is hardy throughout the British Isles, although in Aberdeen it grows but weakly. It tolerates a wide range of site conditions; if not happy, it will only produce short shoots and sometimes a tree might go for several years without making a long shoot. It is also variable in the degree to which the leaf is lobed; on mature plants the lobing may be non-existent, whereas on young trees or vigorous shoots, the sinuses may extend almost to the petiole and there may be one or two pairs of other deep lobes.

Figure 8.10 Ginkgo biloba. *Foliage on short shoots.*

A number of clones of Ginkgo have been named. Most are autumn colour selections, whilst a few others have more fastigiate habits suitable for street tree planting as young trees (ultimate habits unknown!). Cultivars worthy of mention are:

'Aurea' which has leaves yellow in summer.

'Pendula' makes a small umbrella-shaped tree with nodding branches.

'Tremonia' is a fastigiate form with a very narrow crown, after 40 years the original in Germany was 12m tall and only 0.8m in crown diameter.

'Variegata' has bold streaks of whitish yellow

on the yellow-green leaves. It is curious, rather than beautiful, and slow-growing.

Glyptostrobus Endlicher **Taxodiaceae**

This is a monotypic genus of deciduous conifers.

G. pensilis (Staunton) Koch
Chinese swamp cypress

Tree to 25m, more commonly 8-10m. Crown columnar. Bark shallowly fissured, grey-brown. Shoot green due to decurrent leaf bases, becoming red-brown in second or third year. Buds very small. Foliage in 2 types. Leaves on strong shoots and coning sprays scale-like, radial and overlapping, to 0.3cm; leaves on weaker shoots linear, distichously arranged, to 1.5cm by 0.07cm, deciduous with the budless shoot on which they are borne, autumn colour red-brown. Cones on stalks to 2cm, obovoid, 2.5cm. Scales obovoid, like Cryptomeria *with a ring of teeth around the margin and a central point from the fused bract scale. Seeds winged. Zone 8.*

Chinese swamp cypress is native to south-east China. It has been much planted within that corner of China and its exact distribution is not clear. It thrives beside water and in swampy conditions and is planted to stabilise river banks; unfortunately, it is slower-growing than and is being displaced by *Taxodium distichum*. Although generally described as closely related to *Taxodium*, it shows more affinity in the cones to *Cryptomeria* and *Athrotaxis* in the ring of acute teeth on the cone scale and the fused bract scale. It is often called *G. lineatus* (Poir) Druce but apparently this name is based on a cultivated specimen of *Taxodium ascendens* 'Nutans'.

In cultivation it is rare. This is not, as is usually stated, because the tree is especially tender — for its southerly distribution it is quite hardy, but because it is rarely planted in the right place. To thrive it *must* have a very damp site and it will prove much tougher if the tree is actually standing in water; dry sites will lead to almost inevitable death after the first winter or two.

It can be raised from cuttings or seed but is often grafted onto *Taxodium*, which is quite satisfactory. Grafted plants can be planted out in 15cm of water provided the scion is below the water surface, when it will produce roots.

It is quite late in coming into leaf in the spring and late to lose its leaves in the autumn. Ideally it would like more summer heat, but is an interesting tree for the pond and it holds the glowing red autumn colour for several weeks. Krussman records that it produces 'knees' or pneumatophores (breathing roots) like *Taxodium*; I have not observed these even on plants at Canton growing in 50cm of water, and perhaps this record relates to a tree grafted onto *Taxodium*.

Halocarpus Quinn **Podocarpaceae**

This small genus of three New Zealand conifers only recently has been separated off from *Dacrydium*, from which it differs in the ovules in the female cones being inverted (not erect, i.e. they are upside down) and covered by the receptacle. The leaves of juvenile plants are linear and arranged distichously (i.e. spreading flat on either side of the shoot).

H. bidwellii (Hooker fil.) Quinn
Mountain pine or Tarwood

Shrub to 4m, often prostrate with the lower shoots rooting. Leaves on young trees and lowest branches pectinate, linear, abruptly pointed, to 1cm, on strong shoots scale-like, radial, to 0.2cm. Male cone solitary, stalkless, 0.3cm. Fruit near tips of branches, developing as one or two small 0.2cm nuts set on a fleshy white cup. Zone 8.

This plant is mainly a native of the South Island of New Zealand, where it occurs up to 1,300m, but is also found on Stewart Island and in parts of the North Island. Appropriate provenances should be hardy and it is represented in cultivation in Britain by shrubs 2m tall at Bedgebury, in Kent and Wakehurst Place, in Sussex. It would seem worthy of more widespread trial.

H. biformis (Hooker) Quinn
Alpine tarwood

Tree to 13m, although shrubby at the top of its range. Bark grey to red-brown. Foliage in 2 types. Leaves on juvenile shoots distichous, to 2cm, with a twisted base, those on adult shoots scale-like. Male cones to 0.4cm. Seed solitary or rarely in pairs set on white fleshy aril, compressed, ovoid, striated, 0.25cm. Zone 8.

This plant is native to alpine forests throughout New Zealand. It should be hardy, but does not appear to have been tried, although plants are in cultivation under the name *Dacrydium colonsoi* Hooker, with which this tree has been confused, and these may belong here. They are small shrubs to 2m.

H. kirkii (F. Mueller) Quinn
Monoao

Tree to 25m. Bark greyish brown or pale brown. Leaves on juvenile and weak shoots distichous, to 4cm in length, on fertile and strong shoots scale-like with membranaceous margins, 0.3cm. Male cones 0.3-0.9cm. Female cones in a short oblong head 0.6-1.2cm in length with 1-5 oblong compressed seeds, 0.3-0.8cm, set on an orange aril. Zone 9.

This, the largest species, is the one least likely to be hardy. It occurs in mixed forests in the northern portion of the North Island, where the climate is warm temperate. It is not recorded in cultivation, but is likely only to be suited to mild western areas.

Juniperus Linnaeus **Junipers**
Cupressaceae

Junipers are closely related to *Cupressus*, with similar juvenile and scale leaves, and in coming mainly from rather hot dry climates. Where they differ from all other members of the cypress family is in the fruit. At the time of pollination, the female cone is very similar to a cypress cone, with several pairs or whorls of scales and a number of ovules. As the cone develops, however, the scales do not become woody and open to release the seeds; instead, they are fleshy or fibrous and the seeds are released by the fallen cone rotting away. The cones or 'berries' may ripen in the first year, although in most species they ripen after two or even three summers. The berries are intended to be eaten and the seeds have a very thick woody case so they can survive the passage through the gut. The action of the stomach acids aid germination, as without this treatment the tough seedcoat may take one or two years to break down. The actual seed inside the woody case is usually no larger than the lightweight seeds of *Thuja* or other genera. Junipers are often dioecious, i.e. the male and female flowers are carried on separate trees.

The leaves are in two types; juvenile ones are in whorls of 3 and awl-shaped or acicular. Adult leaves are scale-like; they are often in pairs but can be in 3s. Some junipers only produce juvenile leaves, others mainly have adult leaves but a large number have both types on the plant throughout its life. The genus has been divided into three separate genera on this character but the distinctions do not seem worthy of more than sectional status.

Junipers are often thought of only as prostrate shrubs or small trees. Some, however, can make large trees upwards of 20m, although they are slow in growth. They are most useful as ground cover plants for hot dry sites, although having attractive shrub species. They will grow on a wide range of sites.

Taxonomically, the junipers are a difficult group; no satisfactory classification system exists for the genus. The following account uses Gaussen's system as the base but does not accept the separation of the genus into three subgenera and many sections; this seems to be a rather top-heavy treatment, so less formal groupings are used here. In the descriptions, reference is made to ultimate shoots; these are the finest final divisions of the foliage sprays.

Group 1	*drupacea.*
Group 2	*communis, conferta, rigida, oxycedrus, cedrus, brevifolia, formosana, taxifolia.*
Group 3	*recurva, squamata, pingii.*
Group 4	*phoenicia, pseudosabina, indica, wallichiana, convallium, saltuaria, przewalskii.*
Group 5	*flaccida, martinezii, deppeana, californica, osteosperma, durangensis, jaliscana, pinchotii, erythrocarpa, gamboana.*
Group 6	*monosperma, comitana, occidentalis, ashei, saltillensis, sabinioides, standleyi.*
Group 7	*excelsa, macropoda, procera, tibetica, centrasiatica, komarovii, semiglobosa, foetidissima.*
Group 8	*sabina, thurifera, chinensis, gaussenii, davurica, sargentii, procumbens, virginiana, silicicola, scopulorum, blancoi, barbadensis, bermudiana, horizontalis.*

Group 1 — Section Caryocedrus Endlicher

This group includes one species and is characterised by the berries containing 3 seeds which are fused together.

J. drupacea Labillard
Syrian juniper
(*Arceuthos drupaceae* (Labillard) Antoine)

Tree to 15m. Crown columnar, although more broadly conic in the wild. Bark orange-brown with rufous fissures. Shoot green, then grey-green. Leaves all acicular, jointed at base and not decurrent on the shoot, linear-lanceolate, spreading, acuminate, 2 white bands of stomata on the inner face, light green on the outer face, 1-2.5cm by 0.1-0.4cm. Male cones in axillary fascicles. Cone ovoid or subglobose, pruinose, brown or blackish blue, ripening in the second year, containing 3 seeds fused into 1 single stone, 2-2.5cm. Zone 8.

Syrian juniper is found in Syria, Turkey and southern Greece. For a juniper, it makes a fast-growing tree with a columnar crown of ascending branches and clothed to the ground. It is hardy and justifies further planting.

Group 2 — Section *Juniperus*

This group has juvenile leaves in whorls of 3 jointed at the base and not decurrent on the shoot. The shoot behind the leaf is ridged with narrow grooves on either side; it is green for only a short period. The male and female cones are solitary and carried axillary at the base of the leaves. The shoots carry distinct winter buds.

J. communis Linnaeus
Juniper

Spreading or prostrate shrub or occasionally a small columnar tree. Bark reddish brown with papery scales. Shoot yellow-green, grooved, soon red-brown. Leaves in whorls of 3 linear-ovoid, tapered to sharp apex, single broad glaucous band on the inner faces, shiny mid or yellow-green on outer face, 1-2 cm by 0.1-0.2 cm. Fruit ovoid or globose, green in first year, glaucous blue in second, usually ripens to black in third year, 0.6-0.9 cm; seeds usually 3, or 1-2. Zone 2.

Juniper has a very wide distribution, occurring across Europe, in north Africa, northern Asia to Japan and in North America, mainly across Canada and the northern USA but extending south along the Rocky and Appalachian Mountains. It grows on a wide range of sites; in Britain it is as much at home on alkaline chalk downland as on acid boggy peat soils.

The species has been split into innumerable varieties and cultivars. Four subspecies can be recognised as follows.

subsp. *communis* with the spreading needles open, linear and up to 2 cm by 0.1-0.15 cm. It is found throughout Europe and in northern Asia, as a shrub or tree.

subsp. *depressa* (Pursh) Franco has the leaves with the glaucous band of stomata no wider than the margins on each side but otherwise is very close to subsp. *communis*. It is usually low-growing but can make a tree and is the form found in North America from Canada and the USA except on the Pacific side of the Rocky Mountains where it is replaced by subsp. *nana*.

subsp. *hemisphaerica* (J & C Presl) Nyman has closely set linear-oblong leaves mainly less than 1.2 cm and 0.13-0.2 cm in width with a broad white stomatal band. It is found on high mountains in southern Europe, north Africa and the Near East, including the Caucasus and Crimea. It is usually a hemispherical bun as in the type from Mount Etna but may become a small tree.

subsp. *nana* Syme (*J. sibirica* Burgsdorf, *J. c.* var. *montana* Aiton, *J. c.* var. *saxatilis* Pallas) has a prostrate or procumbent habit with stout rigid branches and closely set incurved leaves which are 1-1.5 cm by 0.15 cm. The apex is obtuse or acute, mucronate with a stomatal band two to three times the width of the green margins. It is found in Britain, northern Europe, across Russia to north-east China, into Japan and along the Pacific coast of North America.

The cultivars can be divided in the following groupings.

Prostrate Habit

'Berkshire' is a very slow-growing, cushion-like spreading plant.

'Hornibrookii' makes a carpeting plant building up successive layers of branches.

'Depressed Star' makes a broad flat plant with the shoots erect; like a number of other forms, the foliage takes on a brownish tinge over winter.

'Minima' makes a very small-spreading form with short needles, less than 0.8 cm.

'Repanda' is a vigorous ground cover plant carpeting the ground with dense layers of slightly ascending arching shoots, slowly building up a mass of branches 30 cm high.

Vase Habit

'Vase' makes a bush to 1 m with the shoots arching out, leaving a nest depression in the centre. The leaves turn chocolate-coloured in winter.

Columnar Habit

'Compressa' is a very dwarf form with a fusiform crown; it grows only 2-3 cm per annum and will make no more than 80 cm. It is very useful as an exclamation plant for a rockery. 'Columnaris' ('Suecica Nana') is more vigorous, to 1.5 m by 30 cm.

'Hibernica' is a narrow columnar form, making erect growths and attaining 3-5 m with time. It grows fairly fast, around 20 cm or so per annum. 'Suecica' is similar, but with the tips of the branches nodding, not erect as in 'Hibernica'. It represents the plants from Scandinavia, Poland and western Russia and several clones may be found under the name. 'Cracovica' is intermediate between the above two forms. All of these plants will become broader with time and due to the fastigiate branching are liable to be damaged by wind or wet snow.

'Wilseder Berg' is similar to 'Hibernica' but with the leaves bright green, holding this colour into winter.

Weeping Habit

'Oblonga Pendula' makes an interesting somewhat sprawling bush with an open crown of ascending arching branches bearing pendulous shoots and distinctly long needles. It will grow to 4m. 'Horstmann' is a new introduction which sounds similar.

'Pendulina' makes a small tree with an erect stem, more or less horizontal branches and pendulous twigs, similar to Brewer spruce.

Foliage Variants

'Depressa Aurea' is a spreading plant with the new growths yellow in the spring, becoming bronze later.

'Hornibrook's Gold' is a sport of 'Hornibrookii' with the new foliage green-yellow, becoming bronze-golden yellow during the winter.

'Schneverdinger Goldmachangel' is a plant like 'Hibernica' but with the needles bright golden yellow in the summer.

'Tage Lundell' is a spreading plant with the leaves alternately golden yellow, variegated yellow or green. It has only recently been described.

J. conferta Parlatore
Shore juniper

This makes a prostrate shrub with dense leaves 0.6-1.5cm long by 0.15cm. The leaves are sharply pointed, grooved on the glaucous inner face and keeled on the glossy green outer face. The berry is globose, 0.6-1.2cm, black with a glaucous bloom. Zone 6.

It grows wild on sandy seashore sites around the Japanese islands of Honshu, Kyushu and Hokkaido, also on Sakhalin. It makes an interesting spreading plant, although on young plants the leaves are more spaced out.

'Blue Pacific' is a selection with blue-green needles.

'Emerald Sea' has emerald green leaves with a bluish stomatal band, becoming yellow-green in winter. It is very salt-tolerant.

J. rigida Siebold & Zuccarini
Temple juniper

Tree to 8m. Crown rather open with the branches nodding and carrying pendulous foliage shoots. Bark grey or brown, stripping. Leaves in whorls of 3, grooved on the inner face with a single glaucous band of stomata, otherwise bright green, very sharp, slender, 1.2-2.5cm by 0.1cm. Cone with 1-3 seeds, globose, 0.6-0.9cm, ripen in second year, purplish black, bloomed. Zone 6.

Temple juniper is native to Honshu, Kyushu and Shikoku in Japan, in Korea and across northern China from Gansu to Heilongjiang. It makes an attractive if sprawling bush with viciously sharp needles.

subsp. *nipponica* (Maximowicz) Franco is a dwarf form found at high altitudes in northern Honshu and Hokkaido. It differs in the leaves being only 0.6-1cm and the cones having but a single seed. It has been referred to *J. communis* as var. *nipponica* Maximowicz but the distinct groove on the inner face of the needles places it with Shore and Temple junipers.

J. oxycedrus Linnaeus
Prickly juniper

Tree to 15m or a shrub. Crown slender. Bark reddish grey, shredding in older trees. Leaves in whorls of 3, spreading, with the stomata on the inner face of the needles separated by a green midrib. Cone globose to pear-shaped, yellowish, ripening reddish in the second year, with 3 seeds. Zone 9.

Prickly juniper is native to southern Europe, the Caucasus and Iraq. It is hardy but needs a warm summer climate and is not well suited to cultivation in Britain. Three subspecies are recognised:

subsp. *oxycedrus* is further identified by the leaves to 2.5cm with the apex acuminate on young vigorous plant but only subobtuse on old ones, with the cones 0.8-1cm, ripening dark red to purple. It is found throughout the range of the species, often at altitude as a shrub or a tree.

subsp. *macrocarpa* (Sibth. & Smith) Ball has leaves to 2.5cm by up to 0.25cm wide, acuminate on young plants as in the typical subspecies and with cones 1.2-1.5cm across which are dull when ripe. It is confined to maritime sites throughout the range of the species. It varies from a prostrate plant to a small tree.

subsp. *transtagana* Franco has leaves 0.4-1.3cm by 0.1-0.15cm which are obtuse and mucronulate at the tip. The cones are 0.7-1cm and ripen red. It only occurs as a shrub to 2m, usually fastigiate in branching habit. It is restricted to maritime sands in south-west Portugal.

J. cedrus Webb & Berthelot
Canary Islands juniper

This species makes a broad shrub. It is similar to *J. oxycedrus* in the leaves having the stomatal bands on the inner face separated by a green midrib but differs in the strikingly white shoots and the pendulous blue-grey foliage, 1.5-2 cm long. The cones are globose, 1-1.2 cm, red-brown and pruinose. Formerly it was quite common in the Canaries, making trees to 30 m, but it is now restricted to inaccessible places. In cultivation, it needs a warm sunny site, otherwise it is tender. Zone 9.

J. brevifolia (Seub.) Antoine
Azores juniper

This species is closely related to *J. oxycedrus* and *J. cedrus* but differs in the short dense incurved leaves 0.6-0.9 cm long by 0.2 cm. It is restricted to the Azores; high altitude forms might prove hardy. Zone 9.

J. formosana Hayata
Taiwan juniper

Tree to 12 m. Crown columnar, very narrow. Bark grey-brown, fibrous, peeling in long thin strips. Shoots pendulous, triangular. Leaves in whorls of 3, spreading, sharp, with 2 bands of whitish stomata on inner face, green on outer face, 1.2-2 cm, rarely to 3.2 cm, by 0.12-0.2 cm. Cone globose, 0.6-1 cm, ripening orange to reddish brown in second year. Zone 9.

This small tree is found across southern China from Qinghai in the north to Yunnan in the south and Taiwan in the east. As seen in the wild near Kunming in Yunnan, it is very distinct in the columnar habit. It is in cultivation and should be hardy.

var. *concolor* Hayata is a form found at low altitudes in Taiwan with the leaves the same green colour on both sides; it makes a small tree or shrub. It is not in cultivation.

J. taxifolia Hooker & Arnold
Luchu juniper

This species varies from a prostrate shrub to a small tree of 12 m with pendent branch tips. The leaves are obtuse, bright green, 1-1.3 cm by 0.13-0.16 cm, with 2 stomatal bands on the inner face. The cone is globose, 0.6-1 cm, ripening light chestnut brown; the scales have prominent prickles. This tree is found in the Bonin and Ryuku (or Luchu) islands which stretch between Japan and Taiwan. It may not be in cultivation. Zone 9.

Group 3 — Section Recurvoides Gaussen

This group is intermediate between section *Juniperus* and section *Sabina*. The plants have awl-like or acicular leaves in whorls of 3 as in the typical section but they are decurrent on the shoot as in *Sabina* and the fruits are also carried on very short leafy shoots. The cones ripen black in the second year and contain only a single seed.

J. recurva Buchanan-Hamilton ex D. Don
Himalayan weeping juniper

Tree to 20 m, or sometimes a small prostrate shrub. Crown conic, branches level with weeping tips and foliage. Bark smooth, exfoliating in thin sheets, orange-brown, grey-brown and fibrous in old trees. Leaves adpressed or more open forwards pointing, long conic or ovate-lanceolate, acute or acuminate, sharp pointed, grey-green on outer face, silvery white with a partial green midrib on inner face, 0.4-0.7 cm by 0.075-0.13 cm. Cone globose or ovoid, pointed tips of the upper 3 scales remain on the fruit, 0.7-1 cm. Zone 7.

This tree is found along the Himalayas from Afghanistan to south-west China and northern Burma. It makes a very attractive small and slow-growing tree, although ultimately capable of attaining 20 m. It is particularly attractive for the soft grey-green or sometimes more bluish foliage and the weeping branchlets. Individually the foliage sprays are very open but together they make a dense display. The foliage is very dry to the touch and rustles.

var. *coxii* (Jackson) Melville **Coffin juniper** is a form in which the leaves are slightly longer and less adpressed but is effectively part of the normal variation for the species. It was originally named from plants collected in northern Burma by Cox and Farrer but plants answering the description are found throughout much or all of the range of *J. recurva*. The cultivated plants, which belong to more than one clone, have bright green foliage.

'Castlewellan' has pendulous branch tips.

J. squamata Buchanan-Hamilton ex Lambert
Flaky juniper

Shrub, often prostrate but sometimes making a sprawling bush or small tree to 5 m. Bark flaky, reddish brown, smooth. Shoots erect or spreading, not or scarcely pendulous at tips. Leaves forwards spreading, not adpressed, acute or acuminate, lanceolate-conic, sharp, fresh green or bluish green on the outer face, silvery white on the inner face, 0.4-0.8 cm. Cone ovoid, 1 cm. Zone 4.

Flaky juniper is found from Afghanistan along the Himalayas to west China and across central China, always at high altitudes. It makes a useful small conifer with the bright silvery inner faces of the needles displayed by the spreading branches. It is very variable across its range.

'Chinese Silver' is an excellent form. It was almost certainly raised from seeds collected by T.T. Yu under his number 15614, not under Yu 7881 as given in the *Hillier Manual* (see Bibliography). It makes a large sprawling bush with the leaves bluish on the outer face and vivid silver on the inner. The original clone is female but plants are cultivated at several gardens which shared in the seed collected by Yu and may include males.

Figure 8.11 Juniperus squamata *'Chinese Silver'. Foliage and mature fruit.*

'Embley Park' is a form with bright green leaves which have greenish white stomatal bands on the inner face. The leaves are spreading at right angles to the shoot whilst the branches are erect or spreading, not pendulous. It probably originated from seed collected in Yunnan by George Forrest. It is often placed under *J. recurva* but, I think, fits better here.

'Holger' makes a wide-spreading plant with sulphur yellow growing points which contrast with the steel blue older foliage.

'Meyeri' makes a plant with a steely blue aspect. The short growths have the needles densely set and widely spreading, clearly revealing the glaucous silver inner faces, whilst the extension growth shoots are arching and nodding, although less so than in *J. recurva*. The needles are usually 0.6-1cm but can be up to 1.5cm in length. It is a female clone, with ovoid-oblong cones 0.5-0.6cm. It is not known in the wild but has long been cultivated in China. It will make a small tree, to 10m or more, but is most attractive when young. More than in other forms of Flaky juniper it is inclined to keep the dead brown needles on the branches, making the plant unattractive as it loses vigour. 'Blue Carpet' and 'Blue Star' are two mutations of 'Meyeri' which make dwarf plants with the attractive blue foliage but without the long extension shoots. 'Blue Star' makes a dwarf rounded bush whilst 'Blue Carpet' is more vigorous and will cover quite a large area, although still no higher than 30cm. Both are an improvement on 'Meyeri'. 'Golden Flame' is another mutant which has gold spots on the foliage.

var. *morrisonicola* (Hayata) Li & Keng is a form native to Taiwan, where it ranges from a shrub to a tree to 10m. It has smaller more globular cones 0.6-0.8cm and is in cultivation.

'Pygmaea' is a form which makes 30cm. It is similar to many wild plants from the Himalayas, yet less attractive than most.

J. pingii Cheng ex Ferre
Ping juniper

Tree to 30m. Bark grey-brown, fissured. Leaves ovate-lanceolate, free tips incurved, 0.3-0.4cm, although to 0.7cm on extending shoots, yellow-green to mid-green on outer face, bluish silver on inner; some leaves are very broad, to over 0.2cm. Cones ovoid, 0.7-0.9cm. Zone 7.

This tree is recorded in south-west Sichuan and north-west Yunnan. It is closely allied to Flaky juniper but seems quite distinct in the 'flesh'. It ranges from a tall tree to a dwarf, almost prostrate shrub at higher elevations. There are two earlier names than *J. pingii* which have been applied to this tree, viz. *J. lemeeana* Leveille and *J. fargesii* Komarov, but according to the *Chinese Flora* (see Bibliography), they are synonyms of Flaky juniper. Ping juniper is in cultivation, normally under the name *J. squamata* var. *fargesii* (Komarov) Rehder & Wilson, and makes an interesting small tree.

var. *wilsonii* (Rehder) Silba is a small-growing form, making a shrub to 2m. It differs in the crowded broad lanceolate leaves, 0.4-0.8 cm long and the cone being 0.7 cm by 0.6 cm with the points of the upper 3 scales recurved. It is recorded from Xizang, Yunnan, Sichuan, Gansu, Shaanxi and Hubei provinces of China. 'Loderi' is a clone with a dense conical habit and 'Prostrata' one with a spreading habit. This entire group of species needs critical revision to determine the specific entities involved.

Section Sabina (Miller) Spach

Section *Sabina* has the leaves in part at least in scale form, in pairs or whorls. The flowers are carried terminally on short scaly shoots. The section can be divided into those species in which the leaf margins are finely toothed when viewed under a hand lens (Groups 4-6) and those in which the margins are entire (Groups 7-8).

Group 4 (Section Phoenicioides Gaussen)

This group includes all the Eurasian species with very finely toothed leaf margins.

J. phoenicia Linnaeus
Phoenician juniper

Tree to 8 m or a shrub. Crown conical, or a prostrate seashore shrub. Shoot slender, 0.1 cm, round. Juvenile leaves 0.5-1.4 cm by 0.05-0.1 cm, acicular, acute, mucronate, spreading, with 2 stomatal bands on both faces; adult leaves scale-like, ovate-rhombic, adpressed, blunt or somewhat acute, with a dorsal gland, bright green. Monoecious, male cones carried over winter, pale brown. Cone ripens dark red second year, globose to ovoid, 0.8-1.4 cm, containing 3-9 seeds. Zone 8.

Phoenician juniper is found throughout the Mediterranean region and in Portugal. It is distinct in this group in the cone containing several seeds, all the others have only 1, rarely 2, seeds and normally black cones. It occurs mainly near the coast. It is in cultivation and makes a small tree but from part, at least, of the range of the species is tender.

J. pseudosabina Fischer & Meyer
Xinjiang juniper

Small shrub, occasionally to 4 m. Bark ash grey. Shoots thick round, 0.2 cm in diameter. Juvenile leaves acicular, with white stomatal bands. Adult leaves convex to obtusely keeled, grey-green, with an elongated gland, grooved, apex bluntly acute, incurved, 0.15-0.2 cm. Cone globose to obovoid, dark purple-black, 0.7-1 cm by 0.6-0.7 cm, with a single seed. Zone 6.

Xinjiang juniper is recorded from the Altai shan on the border between China and Russia in central Asia. It may not be cultivation. It is the type species of a group of poorly defined taxa.

var. *turkestanica* (Komarov) Silba is recorded from the south-west of the type, again along the Sino-Russian border. It differs in tree-like habit, to 12 m, and the larger globular cones, 1.2-1.7 cm. It probably is not in cultivation.

J. indica Bertoloni
Black juniper

This plant is closely related to Sinjiang juniper. It is found along the dry inner valleys of the Himalayas as far east as north-west Yunnan. It makes a small-spreading plant, no more than 0.5 m tall, with grey-green foliage. The fruit is black, ovoid, 0.7-1 cm. Zone 4.

Black juniper occurs as high as 5,200 m and makes a dark patch on the distant hillside, hence the name. It is very confused with Wallich juniper, from which it is distinguished by the smaller cones and different flowering period, and Xinjiang juniper, with which it may be conspecific. It is treated under the name *J. wallichiana* in the *Chinese Flora* and as *J. pseudosabina* (in part) in the *Flora of Bhutan* (see Bibliography).

J. wallichiana Hooker f. & Thomas ex Parlatore
Wallich juniper

Tree to 20 m. Crown varies from single stemmed trees with horizontally-spreading branches to more shrubby plants with erect branches arching out at the tips (young plants and those at the highest elevation). Bark fibrous, stripping, fissured with orange. Leaves adpressed, of two types, on strong shoots in 3s, needle-like, 0.4-0.5 cm by 0.1-0.13 cm, on short shoots scale-like, ovate, in decussate similar pairs, 0.2-0.25 cm by 0.13 cm. Cone ovoid, 1-1.3 cm, enclosed in 2 pairs of fleshy scales. Zone 6.

This tree is found in the Himalayas. It has been thoroughly confused with *J. indica*. In the herbarium it is very similar to that species but in the field the two are quite distinct, although often found growing together. Apart from the habit differences, this species flowers in the spring, whereas *J. indica* is autumn-flowering.

Wallich juniper makes a tall but slow-growing tree, desirable for the upright habit and attractive fibrous bark.

J. convallium Rehder & Wilson
Mekong juniper

(*J. mekongensis* Komarov, *J. ramulosa* Florin)

Tree to 20 m. Bark grey-brown, smooth, stripping. Leaves scale-like, adpressed, in 4 rows, overlapping, ovate, blunt or acute, convex with a depressed dorsal gland, 0.1-0.15 cm, pale green or glaucous. Fruit subglobose or ovoid, 0.6-0.8 cm, rarely to 1 cm, by 0.5-0.8 cm. Zone 6.

This species is recorded from the Min and Mekong river valleys in west Sichuan and east Xizang, China, in a dry zone. It is rare in cultivation.

var. *microsperma* (Cheng & Fu) Silba is a form with generally finer leaves and smaller ovoid glaucous cones, to 0.5 cm. It is recorded from south-east Xizang (Tibet).

J. saltuaria Rehder & Wilson
Sichuan juniper

Tree to 15 m. Shoots nearly 4-angled. Leaves scale-like, obscurely glandular on the back, adpressed, dark green, 0.1-0.2 cm long. Monoecious. Cone erect, subglobose or ovoid, 0.5-0.8 cm, ripening black, with 1 whorl of scales. Zone 6.

This species is found in Gansu, west Sichuan and north-west Yunnan. It is rare in cultivation.

J. przewalskii Komarov
Przewalski juniper
(*J. zaidamensis* Komarov)

This species makes a tree to 12 m with a dense crown. It is allied to Mekong and Sichuan junipers but differs in the grey-green more loosely imbricate scale leaves obscurely glandular on the back and 0.12-0.3 cm long. The cone is broadly acuminate, dark green ripening to a dark bright red, 0.8-1.3 cm, with a single seed 0.7-0.95 cm with a diameter of 0.7-1 cm. Zone 7.

Przewalski juniper is native to Qinghai, Gansu and north Sichuan. It is rare in cultivation.

Group 5 (Section Pachyphlaeoides Gaussen)

This group includes the North American species with finely toothed leaves but which do not have blue fruits. *J. flaccida, J. deppeana, J. californica* and *J. osteosperma* have very distinct cones which are dry and fibrous, not shrinking on drying and probably justify separate group or subsectional status.

J. flaccida Schlechtendal
Mexican weeping juniper

Tree to 12 m. Crown broad conic. Bark fibrous, red-brown with interlacing fissures. Adult foliage in flat drooping sprays, scale leaves opposite, narrowly ovate, 0.15-0.2 cm, apex adpressed, margins with few irregular teeth, juvenile leaves in pairs or 3s, soft, fresh green, 0.8 cm. Cone fibrous, resinous, subglobose, umbos of scales often visible in mature cone, tan to reddish brown with a light white bloom, 1.3-2 cm; seeds 6-13, rarely only 4. Zone 8.

Mexican weeping juniper is found throughout most of northern and central Mexico and also in the Big Bend National Park in Texas. It makes a very attractive tree which is more *Chamaecyparis* in appearance than juniper; the first specimens I collected in north-east Mexico I took for a cypress until I opened a cone! It probably is not in cultivation as the plants examined bearing this name appear to be *J. monosperma*.

var. *poblana* Martinez differs in the scale leaves on the ultimate twigs being acute with spreading tips and the female cones showing suture lines between the scales 'like a soccer ball'. It is recorded from Jalisco to Oaxaca.

J. martinezii Perez de la Rosa is a newly described species related to *J. flaccida* but which has much smaller globose or ovoid cones, only 0.5-0.8 cm by 0.5-0.9 cm with only 1 to 3 seeds. It is recorded from north-east Jalisco, south Aguacaslientes, southern San Luis Potosi and northern Puebla.

J. deppeana Steudel
Alligator juniper
(*J. pachyphlaea* Torrey, *J. deppeana* var. *pachyphlaea* (Torrey) Martinez)

Tree to 10 m or an arborescent shrub. Crown open conic or dense and globular. Branch tips spreading to erect. Bark usually strongly divided into small quadrangular plates, ash grey with the fissures deep chocolate brown, peeling on branches. Scale leaves opposite, in 4 rows, obtuse to acute, yellowish green to blue-green, 0.1-0.3 cm. Cone subglobose to broadly ellipsoid, with dry fibrous pulp, reddish tan to dark reddish brown, with a thick or thin glaucous white bloom, 0.8-1.5 cm; seeds 2-4, rarely 1-6, irregular and angular, 0.6-0.7 cm by 0.4-0.6 cm. Zone 8.

Alligator juniper is found in its typical state from south-west Texas, New Mexico and Arizona across the Mexican border south down the Sierra Madre Oriental to Puebla. If damaged by fire or cutting, it will sprout from the base. It makes a small tree with generally blue-green foliage but it is most attractive for the bark; this is cracked into small squares as in the hide of an alligator. It is very tolerant of hot and dry situations; it is hardy in cultivation but ideally needs more sunlight than available in Britain.

forma *sperryi* (Correll) Adams differs in the weeping terminal whip-like branches and the longitudinally furrowed bark. It has been found in the Davis Mountains of Texas and in north-east Sonora.

var. *robusta* Martinez makes a tree to 25 m with a single bole. The bark is often more rectangular but the main difference from the type is in the seeds; these are usually 2-3 per cone and 0.7-1 cm by 0.6-0.8cm. This plant is found along the Sierra Madre Occidental in Durango state, Mexico.

var. *patoniana* (Martinez) Zanoni makes a very open, sparse branched tree with an irregular crown and a bark composed of longitudinal strips. It occurs as scattered trees with var. *robusta* in Durango state, northern Mexico.

var. *zacatecensis* Martinez is a shrubby form with cones 1.3-2cm which are heavily overlaid with glaucous white wax and contain 1-4, rarely to 7, seeds. It is recorded from western Zacatecas and adjoining Durango.

J. californica Carriere
California juniper

This tree or large shrub differs from Alligator juniper in the cones having only one or two broadly triangular and often bilobed seeds, the scale leaves usually being in whorls of 3, broadly ovate, acuminate and with an obtuse apex, and in the bark having long interconnecting ridges. It is found throughout California and in south Nevada, western Arizona, in scattered localities in Baja California and on Cedros and Guadelupe islands off Baja California. The origins introduced to date have proved tender and only suited to hot dry climates. Zone 9.

J. osteosperma (Torrey) Little
Utah juniper

Tree to 12m. Crown spreading, bushy. Bark grey, furrowed, shredding. Ultimate shoots slightly quadrangular, stiff, 0.2cm. Scale leaves in pairs, rarely in 3s, tightly adpressed, acute, dorsal gland usually present and secreting resin but sometimes absent, pale yellow-green, 0.3cm. Cone globular or broadly ellipsoid, glaucous, maturing in second year to red-brown, flesh dry, thin, 0.7-1.5cm; seeds 1-2. Zone 6.

Utah juniper is found from the mountains around the Great Basin in western USA, with Utah in the centre. It is allied to California juniper but is most easily distinguished by the scale leaves being in pairs, not ternate or in whorls of 3. It is uncommon in cultivation.

J. durangensis Martinez
Durango juniper

Shrub or small tree to 5m. Bark thin, ash grey, in long fibrous strips, on branches smooth and peeling, reddish brown. Whip shoots pendulous at tips. Scales leaves opposite, on finest twigs appear like a string of beads, grey-green, 0.1-0.2cm. Cone with a soft pulp, globose, unequally convex on both sides, 0.6-0.7cm by 0.4-0.6cm; seeds 1-3, rarely 4. Zone 8.

This small tree is found in north-west Mexico mainly in Sonora, Durango and Chihuahua but also from adjoining portions of Jalisco, Zacatecas and Aguacaslientes. At the top end of its altitude range, if not generally, it ought to be hardy.

J. jaliscana Martinez
Jalisco juniper

This tree differs from Durango juniper in the grey-brown bark, the scale leaves being only 0.075-0.1cm long and not appearing like a string of beads, the erect whip shoots, and the reddish brown lightly bloomed cone containing 4-9, rarely 2-11, seeds. Zone 9.

Jalisco juniper is recorded from a restricted region of north-west Jalisco and southern Durango. It is not in cultivation and might not be hardy.

J. pinchotii Sudworth
Pinchot juniper

Shrub or shrubby tree to 6m. Bark thin, ash grey, in long interconnecting strips. Leaves on whip shoots elongated, often with ruptured glands, scale leaves opposite or ternate, yellowish green, adpressed, triangular-ovate, acute, 0.15-0.25cm. Cone ovoid to globose, pulp resinous and juicy, bronze to dark reddish brown, not bloomed, 0.6-0.8cm, rarely to 1cm; seeds 1, rarely 2. Zone 8.

Pinchot juniper is found in west Oklahoma, west central and western Texas, south-east New Mexico and in scattered localities in Coahuila. It is often, but not invariably, found on limestone, gypsum or gravel soil. It is rare in cultivation but should be hardy, although requiring an open site.

J. erythrocarpa Cory
Cory juniper

This species is allied to Pinchot juniper but differs in the scaly bark; the yellowish orange, orange or dark red cones which are overlaid with a white bloom and appear pink or rose; and in the inner face of the scale leaves on whip-like extension shoots having a glaucous band of stomata. Zone 8.

Cory juniper is found in southern Arizona, southern New Mexico, Trans-Pecos Texas, northern Sonora, Chihuahua, Durango, Coahuila, eastern Nuevo Leon, Tamaulipas and northern Zacatecas. It is hardy, at least in plants I collected in northern Nuevo Leon.

J. gamboana Martinez
Gamboa juniper

This tree differs from Pinchot juniper in the bark being in quadrangular plates, not longitudinal strips, the reddish brown cones, straight, not curved, terminal whip branches and the sub-globose or broadly ovoid seeds. The cones are covered with a light bloom. Zone 9.

Gamboa juniper is found in the southern Mexican state of Chiapas and in Huehuetenango province of Guatemala. It is recorded from an altitude at which it could, but probably would not, be hardy.

Group 6 (Section Occidentalis Gaussen)
This group differs from group 5 in the cones ripening to blue.

J. monosperma (Engelmann) Sargent
One-seed juniper

Tree to 18 m or often a shrub. Crown often branched from base. Bark thin, light grey, with ridged fibrous flat strips, reddish to brown in the fissures, often fluted, branches with ash white peeling bark. Leaves on whip shoots with a gland for three-quarters of the length, inner face glaucous, scale leaves ovate, acute to acuminate, deep green, 0.1-0.3 cm. Cone globose or ovoid, with soft juicy pulp, dark reddish purple with thick white bloom giving a pale blue effect overall, ripening in the first year, 0.4-0.8 cm; seeds 1, rarely 2-3, chocolate coloured. Zone 7.

One-seed juniper is found in south central Colorado, northern Arizona, New Mexico and north and west Texas. It is rare in cultivation but should be hardy.

var. *gracilis* Martinez has longer ultimate twigs (0.6-1.2 cm, instead of 0.6-0.8 cm, rarely to 1.2 cm) which are finer (less than 0.13 cm in section) making a greater angle to the central axis of the twig and smaller oval cones. It is found in the Sierra Madre Oriental in eastern Coahuila, Nuevo Leon, south-east Tamaulipas, northern Hidalgo and north-east Queretero. It may be in cultivation from seeds I collected in Nuevo Leon and should prove hardy.

J. comitana Martinez
Comitan juniper

This tree differs from One-seed juniper in the very slender ultimate branchlets to no more than 0.1 cm in cross-section, the ragged fibrous bark, the globose cones 0.5-0.8 cm long and the scarcely scented foliage. It is recorded from Chiapas in southern Mexico and northern Guatemala. It has not been introduced. Zone 8.

J. occidentalis Hooker f.
Western juniper

Shrub on several stems or a tree to 20 m. Crown broad, spreading. Bark red-brown, fissured into long thin strips. Leaves almost entirely adult scale leaves, in pairs or 3s in 6 ranks, bluntly acute, with a prominent dorsal gland, grey-green, 0.15-0.3 cm. Monoecious or sometimes dioecious. Cone ovoid, blue-black with a glaucous bloom, ripening in the first year, scales 6-9, 0.6-0.9 cm; seeds 2-3. Zone 7.

Western juniper is found along the mountains of the Pacific coast of the USA from Washington through Oregon to southern California, just entering Idaho and Nevada. It makes an interesting small tree juniper but the clone 'Sierra Silver' is more desirable for the garden. This plant has conspicuous silvery grey foliage.

J. ashei Buchholz
Ashe juniper

Shrub or tree to 6 m. Crown globose or irregular. Bark light ash grey, shredding in strips, on branches peeling reddish grey. Whip shoots often pendent. Scale leaves triangular ovate, in pairs or 3s, adpressed, older leaves often with an oval brownish red resin gland protruding like a bead on the dorsal grey-green surface, 0.1-0.2 cm. Cone globose to ovoid, pulp juicy, soft, resinous, bluish black but appearing light blue due to waxy bloom, 0.7-0.85 cm by 0.6-0.75 cm; seeds 1, rarely 2. Zone 8.

Ashe juniper is found from the Ozark Mountains of Missouri, Arkansas and Oklahoma across central Texas to north west Coahuila in Mexico. It is hardy in cultivation, in mild areas with shelter, but needs full sun. The juvenile foliage is glaucous blue-grey.

J. saltillensis Hall
Saltillo juniper

This tree or large shrub differs from Ashe juniper in the bead-like resin gland on the scale leaves being the same light grey-green as the mature leaf, the bark of the smaller branches being greyish brown and the leaves on the ultimate shoots appearing like a string of beads. It is recorded from Coahuila, Chihuahua, Zacatecas and Nuevo Leon. It has not been introduced but should prove hardy, at least from the higher parts of its range. Zone 8.

J. sabinioides (H.B.K) Nees
Mountain juniper
(J. monticola Martinez)

Prostrate or low shrub, rarely a tree to 10 m. Bark thick, grey to greyish brown, fibrous in longitudinal strips. Shoots with ultimate divisions distichous or subdistichous. Scale leaves usually opposite, thick, like a string of beads, rounded or obtuse, adpressed, grey-green or green, sometimes with an obvious dorsal resin gland, 0.1-0.2 cm. Cone globose or unequally convex, flesh soft, pulpy, bluish black with a thin bloom, 0.5-0.9 cm; seeds 3-7, rarely 2-9. Zone 6.

Mountain juniper is found on the high mountains of Mexico from Cerro Potosi in Nuevo Leon state to Pico de Orizaba on the border of Veracruz and Puebla states and Nevado de Colima in Jalisco. It is not in cultivation. On Cerro Potosi I saw it as a dwarf shrub under an elfin forest of *Pinus culminicola*.

J. standleyi Steyermak
Standley juniper

Prostrate shrub or tree to 15 m. Bark with interwoven longitudinal strips. Shoots spreading or ascending, tips of whip shoots straight, reddish brown. Scale leaves opposite or in 3s, ovate or broadly ovate, apex adpressed, rounded or obtuse, yellowish to dark green, 0.15-0.2 cm. Cone ovoid-conic, with soft fleshy pulp, dark blue, lightly bloomed, 0.7-0.9 cm, on short curved peduncles; seeds 3-5, rarely 6. Zone 8.

Standley juniper occurs above the treeline on Volcan Tacana on the border of Mexico and Guatemala and on other high altitude sites in Guatemala. It has not been introduced but should prove hardy, coming from upwards of 3,000 m.

Group 7 (Section Excelsioides Gaussen)

This group includes the Eurasian and East African species with entire margins to the scale leaves and cones red, black or blue-black with 1 to 3 seeds.

J. excelsa Bieb.
Grecian juniper

Tree to 20 m. Crown conical, broadening and opening out with age. Bark purple-brown, irregularly scaly. Ultimate shoots very slender, 0.06-0.08 cm. Juvenile leaves 0.5-0.6 cm, borne for only a short period. Scale leaves in pairs, ovate rhombic, closely adpressed, acute, linear or ovate gland central on the dorsal face, dark green, 0.1-0.15 cm. Monoecious or dioecious. Cone globose, dark purplish brown, slightly bloomed, ripens second year, 0.8 cm; seeds 4-6. Zone 7.

Grecian juniper is native from the Balkan peninsula across Turkey to southern Russia, Iran and the Lebanon. It is hardy in cultivation but rare. Cultivated trees in Britain tend to have the scale leaves with longer and more spreading tips. This could be due to the origin of the plants or due to local climatic factors.

'Stricta' is a narrow conic form with glaucous and more juvenile foliage.

J. macropoda Boissier
Persian juniper
(J. seravshanica Komarov)

This tree is closely related to Grecian juniper and sometimes treated as a variety of it (*J. excelsa* var. *polycarpos* (Koch) Silba) but is well distinguished by the light open foliage with spreading sharp-pointed juvenile needles to 0.8 cm on the lower foliage, with the dark green scale leaves on the upper crown foliage being very closely pressed to the stem, with an ovate inflated resinous gland, 0.15 cm. The cone is globose, bluish black, resinous and bloomed, with 2-5 seeds. Zone 7.

Persian juniper is found from Iran through Afghanistan to Uttar Pradesh in north-west India, and also in parts of Turkey and southern Russia. It may not be in cultivation but should be hardy, coming from altitudes of up to 4,300 m in the dry inner valleys of the western Himalayas.

J. procera Hochst. ex Endlicher
East African juniper

Tree to 40 m. Bark red-brown, exfoliating in the thin sheets. Ultimate shoots fine, less than 0.1 cm, quadrangular. Juvenile leaves in 3s, rarely found on old trees, 1 cm. Adult leaves ovate-lanceolate, acuminate to an acute tip, grooved with a linear dorsal gland, yellowish green, 0.1 cm but longer on extension shoots. Cone globose, violet-brown, conspicuously bloomed, 0.6-0.8 cm by 0.5 cm; seeds 2-3, ovoid. Zone 10.

East African juniper is native to Kenya, the equatorial montane forests of East Africa and to parts of Ethiopia. It has a useful durable but brittle timber. It is closely allied to *J. excelsa* but differs most in the smaller fruit. It is tender in cultivation, but as it is recorded as occasionally occurring at altitudes of up to 3,000 m, hardier forms might be awaiting introduction.

J. tibetica Komarov
Tibetan juniper
(J. potanini Komarov, J. distans Florin)

Tree to 30 m but also occurring as a shrub. Crown ovoid, dense. Bark pale brown, exfoliating in papery sheets. Juvenile leaves in pairs or 3s, lanceolate, sharp, light green with 2 bright glaucous-white stomatal bands on inner face, 0.4-0.8 cm. Adult leaves scale-like, in pairs, acute, incurved, with a linear dorsal gland, dark green, 0.15-0.3 cm. Cone ovoid,

1. *Abies forrestii* – young female cones

2. *Abies procera* – mature cone

3. *Cedrus atlantica glauca* – male cones

4. *X Cupressocyparis leylandii* 'Haggerston Grey'

5. *Cupressus corneyana* – NW Bhutan

6. *Glyptostrobus pensilis*

7. *Juniperus chinensis* 'Aurea'

8. *Juniperus squamata* – NW Bhutan

9. *Juniperus wallichiana* – NW Bhutan

10. *Keteleeria fortunei* – Hong Kong

11. *Metasequoia glyptostroboides*

12. *Picea omorika*

13. *Picea likiangensis* – male cones

14. *Picea asperata* – female cone

15. *Pinus bungeana*

16. *Pinus culminicola* – NE Mexico

17. *Pinus engelmannii* – NE Mexico

18. *Pinus hartwegii* – W Mexico

19. *Taxodium distichum* – 'knees'

20. *Thuja plicata* 'Zebrina'

variously dark brown, reddish brown, ash or grey-brown to blackish, shiny, 0.9-1.6 cm by 0.7-1.3 cm; seed 1, globose, 0.8-1 cm. Zone 6.

Tibetan juniper comes from southern Gansu, northern and western Sichuan, southern Qinghai and south Tibet. The form in cultivation as *J. distans* makes an interesting rather columnar tree with light green foliage and was raised from seeds collected in Gansu by Joseph Rock in the 1920s.

J. centrasiatica Komarov
Kunlun shan juniper

This small tree to 12 m is allied to Tibetan juniper but differs in the more clearly quadrangular branchlets, the obtuse keeled scale leaves usually without a prominent dorsal gland and the globular or oblong cones, 0.9-1.1 cm, with the single seed being more oval. Zone 5.

Kunlun shan juniper (also spelt Kuenlun) is native to the Kunlun shan of southern Xinjiang province of China. It has not been introduced but should be very hardy.

J. komarovii Florin
Komarov juniper
(*J. glaucescens* Florin)

This small tree of 3-10 m differs from Tibetan juniper in the nearly round ultimate twigs and the ovate-triangular juvenile leaves 0.6 cm long which, like the scale leaves, are set in whorls of 3; the adult leaves are grey-green, bluntly acute, incurved, triangular-ovate or lanceolate, with a prominent round gland at the base of the scale, 0.1-0.15 cm; the cones are ovoid to subglobose, blue-black with a pruinose bloom, 0.6-0.9 cm, rarely to 1.2 cm; seed 1, obovoid, 0.6-0.8 cm. Zone 5.

Komarov juniper is native to the Min shan of northern Sichuan and southern Gansu provinces, China. It is not in cultivation but should be hardy.

J. semiglobosa Regel
Russian juniper

Tree to 12 m. Crown open, narrow, sometimes with pendent or weeping branch tips. Leaves scale-like, glossy green, acute, rhombic, tightly adpressed, with an oblong dorsal gland, 0.1-0.15 cm. Cone semi-globose with a truncate apex, dark brown to black, slightly waxy bloomed, scales 4, 0.5-0.8 cm; seeds 4. Zone 4.

Russian juniper is native to Soviet Central Asia and probably also to adjoining Afghanistan and Xinjiang province of China. It is in cultivation but is rare.

J. foetidissima Willdenow
Stinking juniper

Tree to 17 m. Crown narrow conical. Bark brownish red, becoming grey. Ultimate shoots quadrangular, 0.1 cm thick, irregularly arranged. Leaves in decussate pairs, giving off a foetid smell when crushed, ovate-rhombic, tip free, acuminate, usually glandless, greyish green, 0.15 cm. Cone globose, bloomed when young, ripening to red-brown or nearly black, 0.7-1.2 cm; seeds 1-2, rarely 3. Zone 9.

Stinking juniper is found in the Balkan peninsula from Albania and Macedonia southwards and also in Asia Minor and the Crimea. It is uncommon in cultivation but should be hardy.

Group 8 (Sections Virginioides Gaussen & Chinensioides Gaussen)

This group of species consists of the Eurasian and North American species which combine entire leaves with blue or brown cones.

J. sabina Linnaeus
Savin
(*Sabina vulgaris* Antoine)

Low and spreading shrub, occasionally to 4 m. Bark red-brown, exfoliating. Ultimate shoots slender, 0.06-0.08 cm, quadrangular. Juvenile leaves spreading, in pairs, acuminate, sharp, blue-green with a distinct raised midrib, glaucous stomatal bands on inner face, 0.4 cm. Scale leaves in pairs, ovate, adpressed, subacute or obtuse, with an elliptic dorsal gland, dark green, 0.1-0.13 cm; all leaves have a foetid smell when crushed. Dioecious or monoecious. Cone depressed globose, bluish black, bloomed, ripening in autumn of first year or early in second season, 0.4-0.6 cm, set on a recurved scaly peduncle; seeds usually 2. Zone 4.

Savin is found from southern and central Europe across Russia into China from Xinjiang to Gansu provinces. It makes a useful ground cover shrub, particularly for alkaline sites. The plant is strongly aromatic when bruised, giving off a strong foetid smell.

'Blue Danube' is a low-spreading plant with the branch tips bowed upwards. It carries mainly scale leaves, which are a light grey-blue.

'Cupressifolia' makes a low compact and horizontally-spreading plant with the leaves scale-like and blue-green. It is a female clone and fruits freely. 'Aureovariegata' is a similar mutation with yellow branch tips.

'Musgrave' is a prostrate ground-hugging plant which only grows a few centimetres tall. It has blue-green foliage, with juvenile leaves at both ends of the one season's shoots.

'Tamariscifolia' is a spreading bush which

slowly builds up tiers of horizontal foliage. The leaves are mainly short, spreading, sharp and juvenile, carried in pairs or 3s, and bright green or light bluish green. 'Arcadia' is a similar selection which is lower, with light green leaves; 'Broadmoor' has grey-green leaves on upward directed shoots. Several other similar clones have been named.

'Variegata' makes a slow-growing plant, eventually to 1.5m, which has horizontal nodding branches bearing white variegated foliage.

'Von Ehren' makes a rather open vase-shaped plant with light green, mainly juvenile, leaves.

J. thurifera Linnaeus
Spanish juniper

Tree to 20m. Crown conical. Bark dark brown, scaly and stripping. Ultimate shoots 0.1cm, quadrangular, arranged in flat or distichous sprays. Juvenile leaves in pairs, 0.3-0.6cm, inner face with 2 glaucous stomatal bands separated by a green midrib. Scale leaves in pairs, apex acuminate or acute, incurved but free, dorsal oblong furrowed gland, dark green, margins entire or slightly toothed, 0.15-0.2cm. Cone globose, pruinose, ripening dark purple in second year, 0.7-0.8cm; seeds 2-4. Zone 9.

Spanish juniper grows in the mountains of central, southern and eastern Spain, the French Alps in south-east France and in North Africa. It is hardy in cultivation, although uncommon. It is very tolerant of dry conditions. The bruised foliage has a musty scent.

J. chinensis Linnaeus
Chinese juniper

Tree to 25m. Crown ovoid-conic. Bark brown, peeling in long narrow twisting strips. Juvenile leaves in pairs or 3s, found at the base of mature shoots, on separate all juvenile foliage shoots, less often at tips of adult shoots, dark green on outer face, inner face with the broad white stomatal bands separated by a broad green midrib, very prickly, spreading, 0.2-0.5cm. Adult leaves closely adpressed, blunt, in decussate pairs or rarely 3s, dorsal gland obscure, 0.1-0.15cm. Dioecious. Cone globose or obovoid, irregular, outlines of scales visible, ripening in second year whitish due to a thick glaucous bloom, 0.6-0.8cm; seeds 1-4, usually 2-3. Zone 3.

Chinese juniper is native to most of China, except the far south and west, Inner Mongolia and in Japan from coastal sites around Honshu, Kyushu and Shikoku. It makes a reasonable tree in cultivation and has given rise to a large number of cultivars. Some of these may be the result of hybridisation with other species; often the name *J.* × *media* Van Melle is used for plants allegedly hybrids of *J. chinensis* and *J. sabina*. This hybrid is not accepted here; it is possible that more than one species is present in some of the cultivars but the evidence for their being of hybrid origin is inconclusive. The following is a selection of the cultivars in this group.

Tree Forms

'Aurea' makes an excellent golden-foliaged narrow ovoid-columnar or conic tree slowly growing to 15m. It is a male clone and can be very effective with the massed yellow cones in April. The colour mainly comes from the adult scale foliage, as the juvenile foliage, when carried or on young plants, is much paler. It is worth planting for the admirable combination of habit, foliage and male cones.

'Blue Alps' is a strong upright-growing form with sharp blue-green juvenile foliage set on more or less nodding branches.

'Columnaris' is a very narrow conic plant, to 15m, with awl-shaped, deep green leaves. 'Columnaris Glauca' is similar but glaucous.

'Kaizuka' makes an excellent character plant as it is invariably irregular in growth, often leaning to one side. The foliage is bright green and dense, with round ultimate shoots; it is female and often carries masses of cones. 'Kaizuka Variegata' has splashes of white, contrasting with the green foliage; it is slower and does not have such a character habit.

'Keteleeri' makes a dense, regular narrow conic tree with dark grey-green scale leaves. It is a reliable form for formal use.

'Robusta Glauca' is a slender conical form of slow growth, around 7-8cm per annum, with dense dark blue-green foliage.

'Stricta' makes a narrow conic plant with an acute apex. The dense branches are ascending and carry soft juvenile foliage; this is blue-green and bloomed, becoming steel blue in winter.

Shrub Forms

'Blue Cloud' is a spreading plant of low habit. The steel blue foliage is on thin, almost filamentous, branches.

'Femina' makes an upright bush with yellow-green scale leaves, copiously covered with ovoid yellow-green bloomed cones.

'Globosa' makes a dwarf open shrubby plant to 1m. The light green foliage is composed mainly of scale leaves; it is a female clone.

'Japonica' is a form with very stiff sharp needle

foliage of a glaucous coloration. Scales leaves are only carried on old plants. It makes a small bush.

'Obelisk' makes a slender and rather irregular column to 3m by 1m, with ascending branches and long needle leaves, 1-1.5cm.

'Pfitzerana' is very distinctive with branches which arch out and up at 45° to the horizontal, eventually forming a flat-topped plant with horizontal tiers of foliage, to some 3m high. The leaves are adpressed, sharply pointed and different from adult leaves of the type. It is a male clone and is tetraploid. 'Pfitzerana Aurea' is similar but with golden sprays of foliage. 'Mint Julep' has bright green foliage and a somewhat vase-shaped crown. More compact forms include 'Armstrongii' with grey-green or grey-blue foliage and 'Old Gold' with bronze-yellow foliage, retaining this colour during the winter. 'Golden Saucer' and 'Gold Sovereign' are two recent forms with brighter gold foliage but whose precise habit is as yet unknown.

'Plumosa' is a cultivar with short-spreading branches bearing dense drooping green sprays of mainly scale leaves. It is a male clone and will make a plant a metre or so high. 'Blaauw', with bluish green foliage, is slightly taller. 'Plumosa Aurea' also is more erect, with the foliage green-gold, becoming bronze-gold. 'Plumosa Albo-variegata' and 'Plumosa Aureovariegata' are two small-growing plants, respectively with white and yellow variegations.

'San Jose' is a dwarf prostrate plant mostly with grey-green juvenile foliage.

'Variegata' is a sturdy plant with a large proportion of the new growths creamy white, otherwise green. When propagating it, do not use all green shoots as cuttings, as these will revert.

J. gaussenii Cheng
Gaussen juniper

This tree is closely related to Chinese juniper but differs in the leaves being regularly in 3s, scale leaves 0.2-0.45cm and juvenile leaves 0.6-0.8cm. The cone is ovoid-conic, black and contains only 1-2, rarely 3 seeds. Zone 8.

Gaussen juniper is recorded from Yunnan, where it is a tree to 8m.

J. davurica Pallas
Dahurian juniper

Trailing shrub with stout spreading branches bearing ascending branchlets. Shoots slender, quadrangular, 0.1cm. Fertile shoots have both juvenile and scale leaves; juvenile leaves acicular, spreading, 0.3-0.9cm, mainly 0.4-0.6cm; scale leaves adpressed, rhombic, acute, often a number at the tips of the shoots, distinct dorsal glandular depression, 0.1-0.3cm. Dioecious. Cone flat globose, dark brown and bloomed grey, on recurved peduncle, 0.4-0.6cm long by 0.6-0.8cm wide; seeds 2-4. Zone 6.

Dahurian juniper is found in Heilongjiang province of China, Korea and adjoining areas of Outer Mongolia and Pacific Russia. It makes a low-spreading plant. It has been confused with Chinese juniper, with which it is related, but is most distinct in the brown, broader than long cones carried on shoots with all or much of the foliage juvenile.

'Expansa' (*J. chinensis* var. *expansa* Grootend., *J. chinensis* var. *parsonsii* Hornibrook) is the common form in cultivation, also as 'Parsonsii'. It makes a spreading table-forming but not prostrate plant with green foliage; the cones have 6 seeds. 'Expansa Aureospicata' is a form with the needles yellow variegated. 'Expansa Variegata' has more blue-green foliage with variable patches of creamy white foliage.

J. sargentii (Henry) Takeda
Sargent juniper

This plant is related to *J. chinensis*, of which it is often treated as a variety, var. *sargentii* Henry. It is distinct in the prostrate habit with short creeping flexuous stems and short erect or suberect branches. The leaves, except on young plants, are scale-like, dark bluish green; the juvenile leaves are in 3s and 0.3-0.6cm. The foliage smells of camphor when bruised. The globose cones are dark blue or black, 0.5-0.7cm, with 2-3, rarely 4-5 seeds. Zone 4.

Sargent juniper is found in north-east China, Korea, Sakhalin, the Kurile Islands and probably mainland Pacific Russia and in Japan either near the seashore or in rocky places inland. It makes a useful prostrate plant and is quite distinct from Chinese juniper in the foliage smell and resin analysis.

'Compacta' has a compact habit with light green scale leaves with a dark margin and juvenile leaves dark green on the outer face but very glaucous on the inner face.

'Glauca' is a vigorous clone with blue-green foliage with a more ascending branch habit.

'Viridis' has the foliage without a glaucous bloom and therefore appearing light green.

J. procumbens Siebold ex Miquel
Bonin Isles juniper

This makes a spreading procumbent plant, to 2 m across and up to 0.75 m high. The foliage is nearly entirely juvenile, in 3s, acicular, sharply pointed, stiff, convex on the outer face and light or yellow-green, inner face convex with 2 pale green or slightly glaucous stomatal bands, 0.6 cm to 1.5 cm by 0.2 cm. The shoots are stout and the older branches have smooth red-brown or purple-brown bark. The cone is subglobose, 0.8-0.9 cm in diameter, brownish or blackish, with 2-3 seeds. Zone 4.

This tree is native to southern Japan where it is found around the seashore on the Bonin Islands and on Kyushu. It is widely cultivated as a ground cover, for which it is very effective.

'Bonin Isles' is a mat form with dense foliage.

'Golden' has the branch tips golden yellow on grey-green foliage.

'Nana' is a smaller mat form, less vigorous than 'Bonin Isles.'

'Santa Rosa' is a very dwarf plant.

J. virginiana Linnaeus
Pencil cedar

Tree 15-20 m but occasionally to 30 m in the wild. Crown conic, becoming open with wide-spreading branches. Bark grey-brown or red-brown, with narrow spiral slightly stripping ridges. Shoot becoming dark grey, irregularly arranged; ultimate shoots slender, 0.06-0.08 cm. Juvenile leaves in pairs, convex with a grey-green outer face, glaucous on the concave inner face, pointed, pointing forwards, 0.3-0.6 cm, some at the base and usually apex of shoots; scale leaves in pairs, ovate, pointed, thickened, convex, overlapping, 0.15 cm. Dioecious. Cone ovoid, brownish violet and very glaucous when ripe at end of first year, erect or spreading, 0.4-0.6 cm; seeds 1-2. Zone 3.

Pencil cedar, also known as Eastern red cedar, is native to the eastern half of the USA from the area enclosed within a line from central Texas and northern Florida north to Maine and eastern North Dakota. It just extends into southern Canada in Ontario and Quebec. It is similar in general appearance to some forms of Chinese juniper but, in the absence of the very different cones, can be distinguished by the almost invariably paired juvenile leaves and the acute scale leaves.

In cultivation, Pencil cedar makes an interesting but scarcely attractive tree. It thrives on a wide range of freely drained sites and is frequently the largest juniper. Many cultivars have been named, of which the following are a selection.

Tree Forms

'Burkii' is a dense fastigiate plant with blue-grey foliage which develops a purplish tinge in winter; it will make 6 m.

'Canaertii' is a vigorous plant to 20 m with upswept branching, developing a columnar or conic crown with dark green foliage in dense short shoots. It is female and the plentiful cones can make an attractive display. 'Schottii' has dense yellow-green foliage and a more rounded top to the crown.

'Elegantissima' makes a small open tree or large bush, with the foliage sprays golden at their tips.

'Glauca' is a narrow columnar form with slender round grey-green bloomed foliage. The bark is a rich brown and the cones only 0.3 cm. 'Manhattan Blue' is a similar form, but male, and more blue-green.

'Hillii' has a dense columnar habit with the glaucous leaves taking on a purplish hue in the winter; it will make a plant to 4 m or more. 'Boskoop Purple' is a taller- and faster-growing mutation of 'Hillii' which develops a stronger purplish brown colour in winter.

'Pseudocupressus' is a narrow ovoid-conic form with bright grey-green foliage; it makes 10 m.

Shrub Forms

'Grey Owl' makes a spreading plant with somewhat ascending branches, useful as a ground cover. It was raised from seed of 'Canaertii' and may be a hybrid with *J. chinensis* 'Pfitzeriana'. The foliage is silvery grey with a waxy bloom.

'Hetzii' has grey-green foliage and slowly builds up a mound of tiered branches to 4 m. It is female. 'Sulphur Spray' is a bud mutation of 'Hetzii' with sulphur yellow foliage. Both are often referred to as forms of *J. chinensis* or *J.* × *media* but fit better here.

'Kobold' is a dwarf globose form with a dense crown and dense blue-green needles 0.5-1 cm by only 0.05 cm.

'Silver Spreader' is a flat-growing plant, similar to 'Grey Owl', but with the foliage more greenish silver.

'Tripartita' is a low-spreading shrub with mainly juvenile foliage, attaining 2 m high with time and at least as wide.

J. silicicola (Small) Bailey
Southern red cedar

This tree is closely related to Pencil cedar but

differs in its more pendulous and slenderer foliage, much narrower cones, 0.4 cm long by 0.1-0.2 cm in diameter and in occurring in wet swampy coastal sites along the coastal plain of eastern USA from north-east North Carolina through central Florida to south-east Texas. It is uncommon in cultivation and less hardy, therefore needing some side shelter. It has been treated as a variety of Pencil cedar (*J. virginiana*), var. *silicicola* (Small) Silba. Zone 9.

J. scopulorum Sargent
Rocky Mountain juniper

Tree to 15 m. Crown ranging from an open bush in exposed situations to an irregular rounded tree. Bark reddish brown, furrowed into strips or squarish plates. Branches spreading ascending or drooping, with smooth peeling bark. Scale leaves in pairs, not imbricate, ovate to elliptic-ovate, tips acuminate, glaucous pale grey-green to dark green, 0.15-0.2 cm. Monoecious. Cone globose, maturing in two years, bluish black with a thick bloom, giving a light blue effect, around 0.6 cm in diameter; seeds usually 2. Zone 3.

Rocky Mountain juniper is found along the Rockies from Alberta in Canada to Sonora, Chihuahua and north-west Coahuila in northern Mexico. It is uncommon in cultivation but is hardy and is becoming increasingly available in the nursery trade. It is closely related to Pencil cedar, but most easily distinguished by the cones taking two years to ripen and the more rounded ultimate shoots.

'Blue Heaven' has a conical habit with persistently blue-green foliage.

'Chandler's Silver' makes an open conic plant with narrow awl-shaped leaves, silver-grey above and green beneath.

'Gareei' is a dwarf hemispherical plant to 1.5 m, with spreading horizontal branches. 'Globe' is more globose, to 2 m, with silver and green foliage.

'Gray Gleam' has a symmetrical, dense and finely branched crown with the leaves a bright silvery grey.

'Hillborns Silver Globe' is a globular bush with attractive silvery grey foliage, growing some 4-5 cm per annum.

'Silver King' is a low flat plant, to 50 cm high by over 2 m wide and densely branched. The foliage is silver-blue. 'Silver Star' is similar, with the new foliage bright green, becoming more silvery as it matures.

'Skyrocket' is the form most often planted, although often listed under *J. virginiana* 'Skyrocket'. It has an exceedingly narrow crown of glaucous foliage, with the branches all ascending. Until it gets to 6 m or so tall (or is unhealthy), the ratio of height to crown diameter is about ten to one. It is most useful for making a distinctive column or an exclamation mark.

'Springbank' is a narrow conic form with pendent branch tips and intensely silver-blue foliage.

J. blancoi Martinez
Blanco juniper

This tree to 15 m is closely related to *J. scopulorum* but differs in the 2-3 seeded cones which are often bilobed at the tips, and a tight, not stripping, bark which is furrowed into narrow fissures. It is recorded from Mexico, from north-east Sonora, Durango and Mexico states, but is rare. It should be hardy but has not been introduced. Zone 8.

J. barbadensis Linnaeus
West Indies juniper

This tree to 15 m comes from the West Indian islands of Barbados, Cuba, Hispaniola and the Bahamas. It is allied to Pencil cedar with the cones ripening in the first year, but they are subglobose or kidney-shaped and only 0.4 cm long and the scale leaves are only 0.1 cm, on more slender ultimate shoots. It is not in cultivation and is unlikely to be hardy. Zone 9. It is almost extinct due to over-cutting.

J. bermudiana Linnaeus
Bermuda juniper

Also closely related to Pencil cedar, this species has stouter ultimate branches to 0.2 cm, the scale leaves set in 4 rows and 0.15-0.2 cm long, and shorter juvenile leaves, less than 0.4 cm. It is native to Bermuda where a fungal disease has virtually wiped it out. It has been introduced in the past and proved hardy in mild areas, although very rare. Zone 9.

J. horizontalis Moenchen
Creeping juniper

Flat prostrate shrub creeping over rock faces, eventually forming thick mats of foliage. Juvenile leaves paired or in 3s, slightly spreading, 0.2-0.6 cm. Scale-like, adpressed, in 4 rows, oblong or ovate, with a conspicuous dorsal gland, acute, often mucronate, bluish green or blue-grey, 0.2 cm. Cone light blue, scarcely bloomed, 0.6-0.8 cm in diameter; seeds 1-4, usually 2-3. Zone 3.

Creeping juniper is found in the wild from eastern North America to British Columbia, although it does not reach the Pacific. It makes a low-spreading plant on barren sand dunes or rocky sites and is an excellent ground cover. Where it co-exists with either Pencil and Rocky Mountain junipers, it will hybridise.

A number of clones have been named, of which the following are a short selection.

'Bar Harbor' has steel blue foliage and makes a dense prostrate plant. It is probably a group of cultivars, all coming from Bar Harbor on the coast of Maine where they are exposed to salt spray.

'Douglasii' has glaucous foliage which turns plum-purple in winter. It originated in Michigan, from a sand dune.

'Glauca' has very blue, almost steel blue foliage and long whip-like branches. It does not cover the ground as quickly as other forms, making more of a series of snakes until these coalesce.

'Plumosa' is a spreading flat-topped plant with grey-green leaves, turning purplish in winter. It will build up to a mat 60 cm thick.

'Wiltonii' makes a very low prostrate plant with bluish grey leaves, retaining the colour in winter.

Keteleeria Carriere **Pinaceae**

This small genus is exclusively eastern Asiatic in distribution, with taxa in China, Taiwan and south into Vietnam and Laos. The species are not well known and only three or four are rarely cultivated; these tend to be lumped together under two names. The following account is based on that given in the *Chinese Flora* (see Bibliography) and accepts ten species. Some of these may be better treated as varieties or subspecies when better known; however, when I was in China in 1980 I appreciated just how variable the genus can be over short distances and consider that wholesale lumping of species does not reflect the variability of the plant populations.

The genus is allied to *Abies*; it is characterised as follows:

the cones ripen in the first season and are carried erect, as in *Abies*, but on short leafy shoots; the cones do not break up at maturity; the seeds are unique in the pine family in having hypogeal germination (i.e. the cotyledons stay in the seed below ground and only a true shoot is pushed above the soil surface); also, it is alone in the family in coppicing (I think the two go together, as with hypogeal germination there are buds in the axils of the cotyledons below ground — this is a defence against browsing); male cones are carried in clusters arising from a single bud; the leaves bear a central ridge along the upper surface, as in yew; the bud scales persist as a rosette around the base of the shoots.

Ecologically *Keteleeria* species differ from *Abies* in that they are found in hot dry climates at lower elevations. They occur in China in the pine/oak forests, below the montane Silver firs. In cultivation, they need a hot dry site if they are to flourish; they are better suited to the climate of places like California or Australia, rather than to the moist and sunless British climate. They can be grown in Britain, however, although not making such majestic trees.

The species can be divided into two groups on the basis of whether the cone scales are rounded at the tip and tightly pressed against the ones above when growing, as exhibited by *fortunei, oblonga* and *cyclolepis*, or whether they are rhombic with the apex free and often reflexed, as in the remaining species. In this second group of taxa, the bract scales are often visible between the ovuliferous scales. The genus was named after J.B. Keteleer, a French nurseryman.

K. fortunei (Murray) Carriere
Fortune keteleeria

Tree to 25 m, frequently smaller. Crown conical when young but becoming flat-topped. Bark grey-brown, irregularly fissured and scaly, corky. Shoot glabrous, brown, fairly smooth. Bud ovoid-conic, pointed, slightly resinous, whitish brown, 0.3 cm. Leaves spaced on sterile growth, pectinate below, widely parted above, glossy green, yellowish at pointed tip and tapered petiole, pale green with stomatal bands beneath, leaves on coning shoots shorter, with more rounded apex and less regular arrangement, 1-3 cm by 0.2-0.4 cm. Cones cylindrical, rounded at the top, scales incurved, tight when growing, bright glaucous blue-green when immature, ripening brown, bract scale hidden, 6-25 cm by 5-6.5 cm. Cone scales more or less rotund, auricled, margins finely toothed, 2.5-3.2 by 2.7-3.3 cm. Zone 8.

Fortune keteleeria is the type species in the genus and is found in south-eastern China from southern Zhejiang, Fujian, Guangdong and southern Guangxi; it also occurs on two sites on the south side of Hong Kong island, where it grows within a hundred metres of the South China sea. The mature cones are very striking in their glaucous coloration. It is rare but is in cultivation from seed collected in Hong Kong.

K. oblonga Cheng & L.K. Fu
Oblong-cone keteleeria

This plant has cylindrical cones with incurved rounded oblong cone scales which are around 3.5 cm long but only 2.5 cm wide. It is recorded from west Guangxi at low altitude. A population of plants at around 2,400 m near Kunming in Yunnan, which I saw, appeared to fit the cone of this or the following species; the plants were not *K. evelyniana*, which is the predominant local species. Zone 9.

K. cyclolepis Flous
Round-scale keteleeria

Differs from Fortune keteleeria in the rounded less toothed and not auricled cone scales, and the pubescent shoots with leaves bearing stomata on the upper surface. It is recorded in south-east Yunnan, Guizhou, Guangxi, northern Guangdong, Jianxi, Hunan and south-west Zhejiang. It was introduced recently but may have died out. Zone 9.

K. davidiana (Bertram) Beissner
David keteleeria

Tree to 50 m but in cultivation more usually to 10-15 m. Crown conical in young trees, becoming wide-spreading in older ones. Bark grey, furrowed, scaling in small plates, revealing red-brown within. Shoot chestnut brown, densely pubescent, hairs persist on 2-year branches. Bud globular, reddish. Leaves parted on young trees, acute, less regularly parted on mature shoots, apex rounded, bluntly pointed, obtuse or faintly notched, glossy green above with a few stomata near apex, paler with 2 bands of stomata below, 1.5-5 cm by 0.2-0.4 cm. Cones ovoid-cylindric, 8-21 cm, scales obovoid, bent outwards slightly. Zone 7.

David keteleeria is found in southern Gansu, northern to south-eastern Sichuan, west Hubei, west Hunan and Guizhou. It is the commonest species in cultivation, although all the plants may not be correctly recorded. It was the first species after *K. fortunei* to be named and typifies this group.

In Britain it has made plants to 15 m. It can be damaged by late spring and early autumn frosts.

The species can be propagated by cuttings. These seem to need more bottom heat than other plants will tolerate; cuttings I made during the very hot summer of 1976 only started rooting when the soil temperature reached 40°C!

var. *chien-peii* (Flous) Cheng & L.K. Fu is recorded from Guiyang county in Guizhou province. It is said to differ in the mucronulate leaves.

K. evelyniana Masters
Evelyn keteleeria

This species is recorded from Yunnan, south-west Guizhou and south-west Sichuan. It is in cultivation in Britain from seeds collected by Forrest and in California from those collected by Joseph Rock. It differs from *davidiana* in the more conical cone with the scales more widely-spreading and reflexed. The leaves are mucronate, 2-6 cm long by 0.2-0.3 cm wide. Around Kunming it makes tall domed trees to 25 m, but in Britain it is rather slow. Zone 8.

K. formosana Hayata
Taiwan keteleeria

This taxon is restricted to the island of Taiwan; it is often treated as *K. davidiana* var. *formosana* (Hayata) Hayata. It makes a large tree to 35 m with flat, linear leaves 2-4 cm long by 0.3-0.4 cm. They are obtuse or finely notched with revolute margins, but acute on juvenile foliage. Zone 9.

Taiwan keteleeria is an uncommon tree at low elevations in Taiwan. Seed has been introduced but it may not be in cultivation.

K. hainanensis Chun & Tsiang
Hainan keteleeria

This plant has long narrow lanceolate leaves, 5-8 cm by 0.3-0.4 cm, tapered from about a third the length to both the tip and petiole. The leaves are more spreading than in other species and more spaced on the shoot. The cones are 14-18 cm by 7 cm, with rhombic, erect scales free at the tips. Zone 9.

This plant is restricted to the tropical island of Hainan, off Guangdong province, where it occurs at around 1,000 m. It appears very distinct from the other members of this alliance but will probably not prove amenable to temperate cultivation.

K. pubescens Cheng & L.K. Fu
Hairy keteleeria

This tree has short leaves 1.5-3 cm by 0.3-0.4 cm set on densely hairy shoots and small cones 7-11 cm by 3-3.5 cm. The scales are notched at the apex and pointing forwards. It is recorded from southern Guangxi and south Guizhou and occurs in riverine habitats. It was included by Flous in her *K. chienpeii*. Zone 9.

K. calcarea Cheng & L.K. Fu
Yellow-twig keteleeria

This tree has very short broad leaves which are distinctly squarish and notched at the tip, 2-3.5 cm by 0.35-0.45 cm. The shoots are more or less glabrous and yellow. The cones are 11-14 cm by 4-5.5 cm with the rounded scales reflexed. Zone 9.

It is found in northern Guangxi and southern Guizhou but has not as yet been introduced.

K. roulletii (A. Cheval) Flous
Vietnam keteleeria

This tree is the only *Keteleeria* found outside of China and Taiwan. It makes a conical tree to 25 m. The shoots are red-brown, hairy at first, with oblong-ovate buds. The leaves are 6-8 cm on young trees, 3.5-5 cm on mature ones, with a few lines of stomata above and 2 bands beneath; the apex is acute. The cones are 12-18 cm by 6-7 cm and the scales are rhombic with the apex triangular. Zone 10.

This tree is found in the mountains of south Vietnam but has not been introduced.

var. *dopiana* Flous has narrower leaves to 0.25 cm and cone scales which are as wide as long. It is recorded from southern Laos but has not been introduced.

Lagarostrobus Quinn **Podocarpaceae**

This genus consists of one species in New Zealand and one in Tasmania. It has been included in *Dacrydium* but differs in the following botanical characters: the lax female cones are situated on the decurved tips of branches and consist of 5 to 10 spoon-shaped spreading fertile bracts separated by distinct internodes; the sterile basal bract below the seed becomes swollen and forms a fleshy basal sheath round the seed and half as long. The seeds ripen in the first year.

L. franklinii (Hooker f.) Quinn
Huon pine
(*Dacrydium franklinii* Hooker f.)
Tree to 30 m with a conical crown in the wild but in cultivation an attractive spreading bush. Bark smooth, silvery and grey-brown. Shoot green for two to three years, then brown,

slender, arching and pendulous. Leaves scale-like, spirally set, decurrent with pointed free incurved tips 0.1 cm. Cone lax, open, 1.5 cm. Seed globose, 0.2 cm. Zone 8.

Huon pine is native to the Huon river system and adjoining territory in south-western Tasmania. It is hardy in cultivation although needing sheltered woodland conditions and not suitable for cold areas. It makes a very attractive plant with the sprawling, spreading and pendulous branches bearing dark green foliage.

L. colonsoi (Hooker) Quinn
Westland pine
(*Dacrydium colonsoi* Hooker)
This tree differs from Huon pine in the longer scale leaves on mature plants, which are in the range 0.13-0.25 cm and oblong, obtuse seeds 0.2-0.4 cm. It is found on the western side of South Island and in scattered localities elsewhere in New Zealand. It is very rare in cultivation and has only made a small bush. Zone 8.

Larix Miller **Larches Pinaceae**

The larches are the largest genus of deciduous conifers. The leaves are carried on both long and short shoots, as in *Cedrus*, and the cones are borne only on the short shoots. The leaves are spirally set but on short shoots appear as false-whorls. The cones are erect and ripen at the end of the first summer but persisting on the trees for some time; they open to release the seeds. Larches are amongst the earliest trees to flush in the spring, making a verdant start to the year. They are found in northern Europe, over much of Asia from Siberia as far south as northern Burma and in northern North America. The species generally are local and rather restricted. They will hybridise with other species in cultivation and in the wild where they meet.

The genus divides neatly into two sections.

Section *Larix* is characterised by the bract scales being shorter than the ovuliferous scales and rarely visible in the mature cone, the cones being ovoid, globose or conical and the leaves not keeled above but generally flat. It contains the first seven species in the following account.

Section *Multiseriales* Patschke has oblong or cylindric cones with many scales, with the bract scales longer than the ovuliferous scales. The leaves are usually more or less keeled above and 4-sided. It contains the remaining species.

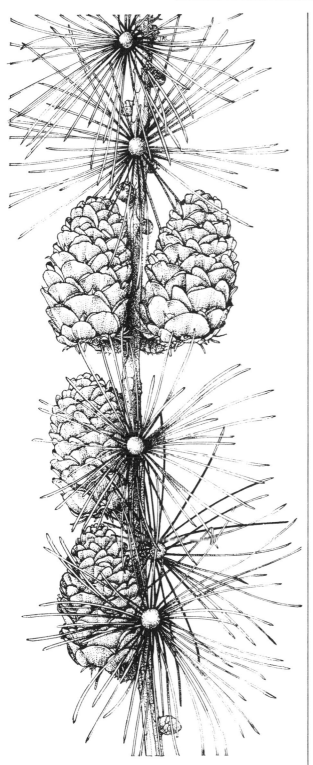

Figure 8.12 Larix decidua. *Foliage and mature cones.*

L. decidua Miller
Larch or European larch
(*L. europaea* De Candolle)

Tree to 50m. Crown conic in young trees, but old trees becoming broader with some wide-spreading horizontal then erect branches. Bark smooth grey in young trees, becoming progressively fissured and scaly, reddish brown, in old trees coarsely ridged and rugged. Shoot glabrous, straw-yellow or yellow-brown but buff-pink or creamy white on some trees. Bud ovoid, golden brown, 0.3cm. Leaves soft, flat above but keeled below, stomata mainly in bands on lower surface, light green, 3.5cm by 0.05cm, but longer on vigorous growths. Male cones yellow. Female flowers erect, green to bright pink or red, bract erect. Cone conic, sometimes cylindric, scales straight or incurved, bract long, exserted, peduncle yellow, 3.5cm or 4.5cm. Zone 2.

European larch is found in the Alps and Carpathian Mountains, forming extensive open forests at high altitudes. It is much planted in forestry for the durable timber of good quality. Young trees are very quick to establish. The leaves are amongst the first to come out in spring. It is useful in the garden context, making a quick but narrow-growing tree with an open crown; the short horizontal branches bear pendent or pendulous twigs. The foliage turns a beautiful golden yellow in late autumn.

Several cultivars have been named but only 'Corley' is of particular merit. It makes a dwarf-spreading plant and arose from a witches broom.

subsp. *polonica* (Raciborski) Domin (var. *polonica* (Raciborski) Ostenfeld & Larsen) is found in northwest Poland and the adjoining parts of the Ukraine. It has smaller cones with more rounded, concave scales.

L. kaempferi (Lambert) Carriere
Japanese larch
(*L. leptolepis* (Siebold & Zuccarini) Gordon)

Japanese larch is closely related to European larch but differs as follows: the shoots are purplish red, covered with a waxy bloom and sometimes hairy; the buds are red-brown and resinous; the leaves are greyish green or occasionally bluish and broader, usually 4cm by 0.1cm; the young female cones have reflexed bracts; and the 3cm cones are ovoid with reflexed scales and short, hidden bracts, on an orange or reddish peduncle. Zone 4.

Japanese larch is native to a small region of central Honshu. It is widely cultivated in Britain as a faster-growing larch suitable for poorer soils than European larch and with greater disease resistance. It will grow on heavier soils than European larch. Trees are very colourful in the spring with the new leaves, in the fall with the autumn gold coloration of the dying leaves and over winter when the one-year shoots are red-purple; massed in plantations, the shoots can make quite a spectacle.

'Blue Rabbit' is a conical form with conspicuously blue-coloured leaves.

'Nana' makes a dwarf plant with a dense global habit; it arose on a witches broom and grows about 5 cm per annum. 'Wolterdingen' is irregular and wider than high; it has blue-green leaves.

'Pendula' can be quite interesting but often is no improvement on a normal seedling. When larches are vegetatively propagated, grafting usually has to be employed; if the grafts of 'Pendula' make a leading shoot, the tree will develop with little more pendulous branchlets than normal but if the graft fails to make a leading shoot but sends out a few horizontally-spreading side branches, these develop curtains of hanging foliage.

L. × marschlinsii Coaz
Hybrid larch
(*L. × henryana* Rehder, *L. × eurolepis* Henry, *L. decidua × L. kaempferi*)

This tree is the hybrid between European and Japanese larches. It occurs regularly where the two species are planted in proximity as there are no barriers to crossing. It is intermediate between the parents and differs in the yellow but slightly waxy bloomed shoots, the reddish brown but non-resinous buds, the conical cones with the scales slightly reflexed and with only a few bract scales visible, set on a yellow peduncle. Unfortunately, the above fairly clear characters are blurred as many plants in cultivation are second or later generations of the cross, or back-cross with either parent. Zone 5.

Hybrid larch is much used in preference to the parents in British forestry as first generation crosses, at least, have hybrid vigour or *heterosis*.

Hybrid larch is usually grown under the name *L. × eurolepis* but this name is invalid and must give way to *L. × marschlinsii*, or possibly to *L. × henryana*. The former name is used here, although there is a slight possibility that it refers to the cross *L. kaempferi × L. russica*.

L. gmelini (Ruprecht) Ruprecht
Dahurian larch

Tree to 20 m. Crown conic, spreading and very broad in cultivation. Bark red-brown, finely scaly. Shoot reddish or yellowish, usually glabrous. Bud globose, slightly resinous. Leaves bright green, blunt at the apex, 1.5-3 cm by 0.07-0.1 cm. Cone ovoid, shiny brown with few scales, 1.2-3 cm by 1-2 cm, on a peduncle 0.5-0.7 cm; scales rhombic with a truncate apex, 1-1.5 cm by 0.8-1.2 cm. Zone 2.

Dahurian larch is native to eastern Siberia and north-eastern China. In cultivation it makes a rather broad tree and may come into leaf as early as mid-winter, when it is often damaged by frosts. It is quite distinctive in the small cones and broad habit. In the wild it varies from a tall tree to a squat bush on less favourable sites.

var. *japonica* (Regel) Pilger has reddish and hairy one-year shoots, shorter leaves and smaller cones (1-2 cm) with more pointed scales. It is native to Sakhalin island, which was partly Japanese at the time it was named.

var. *olgensis* (Henry) Ostenfeld & Larsen (*L. olgensis* Henry) Olga Bay larch has pale brown shoots, densely covered with red-brown hairs, leaves 1.5-2.5 cm by 0.1 cm, ovoid-oblong cones 1.5-2.5 cm, rarely to 4.5 cm, by 1-2 cm. The cone scales are almost round, squarish and faintly notched. It is recorded from swampy areas of north-east China and the Olga Bay region of Pacific Russia. It is close to var. *japonica*, which on Sakhalin also may occur on very wet sites.

L. principis-rupprechtii Mayr
Prince Rupprecht larch

This tree is similar to Dahurian larch and often made a variety of it (var. *principis-rupprechtii* (Mayr) Pilger). It differs in the straw- or yellow-brown, or red-brown, glabrous shoots with a thin waxy bloom, acute needles to 3.5 cm and the ovoid or elliptic cones, 2-3.5 cm by 2 cm, on a peduncle 2 cm, with oblong-ovate notched scales. It is recorded from Hebei province around Peking or Beijing in China. It was first found on the Wutai shan to the west of Beijing. It is in cultivation but like the other species in this group comes into leaf too early in the spring and is often damaged by spring frosts. Zone 4.

L. russica (Endlicher) Sabine ex Trautvetter
Siberian larch
(*L. sibirica* Ledebour)

This tree has bright yellow or yellowish grey,

initially hairy shoots and ovoid cones with the scales hairy on the outer surface, slightly incurved at the apex and about three times as long as broad. It is related to both Dahurian larch, which has glabrous cones scales, and European larch, in which the cone scales are only around twice as long as broad. Zone 2.

Siberian larch is found from north-east European Russia across Siberia and in China from the Altai Shan in Sinjiang province. It requires a climate where spring is regular, not one in which a succession of false-springs occur; in Britain it is severely caught by spring frosts.

L. laricina (Du Roi) K. Koch
Tamarack

Tree 20m. Crown conical, slender. Bark thin and smooth on young trees, dark red-brown and scaly on old ones. Shoot slender, smooth, orange-brown with a pink-grey waxy bloom, later pale brown. Bud small, globose, shiny dark red. Leaves triangular in section, slender, thin, blue-green, 2-3cm. Cone oblong to subglobose, shiny chestnut brown, 1.2-2cm by 1cm; scales less than 20, slightly longer than broad, bract half length of scale except at base of cone. Zone 2.

Tamarack is found across North America from the Atlantic coast to central Alaska; it occurs from just south of the Canadian border to the northern limit of tree growth. At the south of its range, it is mainly found on boggy swamps. Tamarack is quite hardy.

Section Multiseriales

L. occidentalis Nuttall
Western larch

Tree 25m, to 50m in the wild. Crown narrow conic. Bark scaly on young trees, on old trees very thick, deeply furrowed and platy, red-brown to cinnamon brown. Shoot stout, brittle, initially hairy but soon glabrous and orange-brown. Bud chestnut brown, subglobose, 0.3cm. Leaves slender, flat triangular in section, 2.5-4cm. Cones cylindric, purple-brown to red-brown, 2.5-4.5cm; bracts exserted, with a long cusp. Zone 7.

Western larch is native to western North America from south-east British Columbia to north-east Oregon and central Idaho. It makes a majestic tree, sometimes to 60m. It is unusual in section multiseriales in that the leaves are not 4-sided. It is uncommon in cultivation; some introductions have been disappointing, others have made very fine trees, although of slower growth than European or Japanese larch.

L. lyallii Parletore
Subalpine larch

This species is found in Alberta, British Columbia, Montana, Idaho and Washington; this is within the area of Western larch but it occurs at higher altitudes and in regions with a short growing season. It is very different in the densely woolly shoots and cone scales, the 4-sided leaves, the 4-5cm cones with long exserted bracts and a thin, scaly and furrowed bark. It grows at the timberline and makes a tree only to 15m. It is unsatisfactory in cultivation as it is too susceptible to spring frosts. Zone 3.

L. griffithiana Carriere
Sikkim larch

Tree to 20m. Crown narrow conic. Bark purple-grey to brown, fissured into scaly ridges. Shoot orange-brown, finely pubescent at first. Bud ovoid, red-brown. Leaves subacute or obtuse at the apex, 2.5-5.5cm by 0.07-0.18cm. Cone cylindrical or narrow ellipsoid, tapers slightly at ends, purple, ripening purple-brown, 5-11cm (usually 7-8cm) by 2.2-3cm; scales 1-1.5cm broad, bract scale reflexed, exserted portion 0.75-1cm. Zone 7.

Sikkim larch is found from eastern Nepal, through the inner valleys of Sikkim, the Chumbi valley of southern Tibet and Bhutan to Arunachal Pradesh in north-east India. It is uncommon in cultivation but hardy, although susceptible to making its growth too early in the spring. Mature trees of this and other species in this group are quite distinctive in the persistent erect cones held on the branches.

L. speciosa Cheng & Fu
Burma larch

This species has been included in Sikkim larch in the past. It is closely related to it but differs in the broader leaves, 0.15-0.2cm, and the more cylindrical cones, 7-9cm by 2-3cm. The exserted portion of the bract is narrower and the ovuliferous scales are obovoid with a truncate end. It is recorded from north-west Yunnan and north-east Upper Burma. It is probably in cultivation as material was collected by George Forrest on several occasions in 1924/5. Zone 7.

L. mastersiana Rehder & Wilson
Masters larch

This tree has greyish brown irregularly fissured bark, nearly glabrous yellow-brown shoots, leaves 1.2-3.5cm by 0.1cm, oblong cylindric cones only 2.5-4cm by 1.5-2cm with broad obovate scales and reflexed bracts. It is only found in a restricted region of west Sichuan. It has not been introduced but should prove hardy. Zone 7.

L. potaninii Batalin
Potanin larch

Tree to 50m, in cultivation smaller. Crown columnar. Bark purple-grey with long vertical fissures and ridges. Shoot orange-brown to deep orange-brown, becoming grey-brown in second or third season. Bud red-brown, resinous. Leaves with 2 silvery white stomatal bands on lower surface, 1.2-3.5 cm by 0.1-0.15 cm. Cone oblong or ovoid, violet-purple ripening grey or greyish brown, 3-5 cm by 1.5-2.5 cm; scales broad oblong; bracts exserted, erect, exposed part narrow conic. Zone 7.

Potanin larch is native to Gansu and north and west Sichuan province. It is similar in several aspects to Sikkim larch but the cones, and those of the following taxa, have erect, not strongly reflexed, bract scales. It is in cultivation, although possibly only as the following variety.

var. *macrocarpa* Law has larger cones 5-7.5 cm by 2.5-3.5 cm, with the erect bract scales somewhat spreading. The shoots are reddish brown and shiny, almost glabrous. It is found in south-west Sichuan, south-east Xizang and north-west Yunnan. It is in cultivation, although uncommon.

L. himalaica Cheng & Fu
Langtang larch

This tree has yellowish grey shoots, leaves 1-2.5 cm by 0.15-0.2 cm, cylindrical cones 4-6.5 cm by 2.8-3.2 cm, ripening light brown, with the erect bracts about as long as the ovuliferous scales and abruptly narrowed to a rigid tooth. It is allied to Potanin larch but is only recorded from the Langtang valley in central Nepal and adjoining south Tibet (Xizang). It is in cultivation from seeds collected from the Langtang valley. Zone 6.

L. chinensis Beissner
Taibai larch

Tree to 25m. Bark grey-brown or black. Shoot in the first winter light yellow-brown, light yellow or yellow-grey, in the second year grey or dark grey. Cones 2.5-5 cm by 1.5-2.8 cm; scales broader than long, 1 cm by 1-1.3 cm bract with an abrupt cusp. Zone 6.

This tree is recorded from the Taibai shan in southern Shaanxi province. It should be hardy.

Lepidothamnus Philippi **Podocarpaceae**

This genus consists of two species from New Zealand and one from Chile. It has been submerged for many years as part of *Dacrydium* but differs in the erect ovules in the female flowers, the absence of resin ducts in the leaves (found in all other genera in the family), the presence of *Cupressus*-type bordered pits in the wood and chemical differences. The female cones are solitary and terminal, consisting of 3-5 bracts with elongated bases, only 1 or 2 of the bracts being fertile. The seeds mature in the second year and have an asymmetrical membranaceous basal sheath; the bracts usually become fleshy, swollen and pink or red at maturity.

L. laxifolius (Hooker f.) Quinn
Mountain rimu

Prostrate or suberect shrub. Leaves lax, spreading and awl-like 0.5-1.2 cm on juvenile plants, becoming linear-oblong, blunt or acute scale; leaves 0.1-0.2 cm on adult plants. Seed 0.3 cm with a small curved point. Zone 8.

This dwarf plant is found at high altitudes in New Zealand. It makes a very small plant and fruiting specimens barely 7 cm across have been recorded. It is rare in cultivation but should prove hardy, provided it is given sufficient moisture.

L. intermedius (Kirk) Quinn
Yellow silver pine

Tree to 15m. Leaves 1-1.5 cm awl-like, acute and curved on juvenile plants, passing over to dense crowded overlapping scale leaves 0.15-0.3 cm on adult plants. Seeds blunt or minutely pointed, 0.3-0.5 cm. Zone 8.

This tree is widely scattered in New Zealand in montane areas. It has a very resinous and durable wood. It is rare in cultivation but should be hardy, with attention to shelter and choice of origin of the seed.

L. fonkii Philippi
Chilean rimu

This species comes from high montane areas of central southern Chile. It forms a shrub to 30 cm. The juvenile leaves are triangular whilst the adult scale leaves are 0.1-0.15 cm. It is very rare in cultivation but ought to prove hardy. Zone 8.

Libocedrus Endlicher **Cupressaceae**

This genus consists of five species from New Zealand and New Caledonia, although in the past it has been interpreted to include eight others from North America, China, Taiwan, New Guinea and

Chile. The species of *Libocedrus* have flat plumose sprays; the leaves are in facial and lateral pairs, with the facial pairs small and short decurrent. The cones have 2 pairs of valvate scales but only the inner pair is fertile and each bears 1 or 2 unequally-winged flat seeds. The three species from New Caledonia, *L. austro-caledonica* Brongiart & Grisebach, *L. chevalieri* Buchholz and *L. yateensis* Guillaumin, are unlikely to prove hardy in cultivation.

L. bidwillii Hooker f.
Pahautea

Tree to 20m. Crown conical but reduced to a shrub at high elevations. Bark fibrous, flaking off in long strips, light brown. Juvenile leaves with facial pair 0.1cm and laterals 0.3cm, adult leaves triangular, acute, adpressed, 0.2cm, facial and lateral pairs similar except that laterals are longer decurrent. Cone ovoid, 1cm, scales with pointed spreading curved dorsal mucro, seeds single on fertile scales. Zone 8.

Pahautea is found in montane and subalpine parts of both islands of New Zealand. It is a large tree but becomes a small shrub in exposed or boggy conditions. It is the hardiest species in cultivation, but rare and only recorded as a tree to 10m. It could possibly give rise to an interesting range of plants if different and high elevation origins were systematically introduced.

L. plumosa (D. Don) Sargent
Kawaka

This tree differs from Pahautea in the lateral and facial leaves being more markedly different. On juvenile plants, the laterals are up to 0.5cm and the facials less than 0.1cm; on adult plants the respective dimensions are 0.3cm and 0.12cm. The cones are larger, 1-1.8cm. Zone 8.

Kawaka is native to both islands of New Zealand and found at lower altitudes than Pahautea. It is rare in cultivation but appears hardy in mild or sheltered areas and makes a small tree.

Metasequoia Miki ex Hu & Cheng
Taxodiaceae

Metasequoia is a deciduous genus with only one species. It is allied to both *Taxodium* and *Glyptostrobus*, but differs in the cone scales, leaves, buds and deciduous shoots all being in opposite pairs, not spirally set as in the rest of the Redwood family. As in this last respect it is closer to the

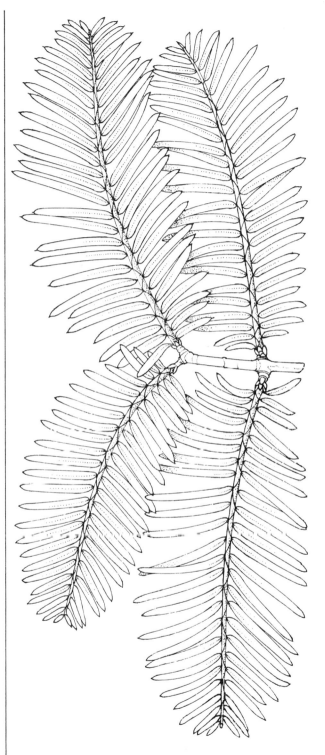

Figure 8.13 Metasequoia glyptostroboides. *Foliage on deciduous shoots.*

Cypress family, it has been suggested that the two families be merged, but this has received little favour and the decussate nature of *Metasequoia* may be of independent origin.

M. glyptostroboides Hu & Cheng
Dawn redwood

Tree to 40 m. Crown narrow conic with ascending branches, in old trees more columnar. Bark fibrous and stringy, orange-brown and red-brown, fissured, bole often deeply fluted at base. Shoots of two kinds: deciduous shoots green, without buds, falling in autumn; persistent shoots with buds, pink-brown or slightly redder. Bud ovoid, 0.2 cm, set with a scar above from the deciduous shoot and below from the subtending leaf. Leaves linear, soft, spreading in 2 ranks, blue-green above, paler below, to 2.5 cm. Cone 2 cm, ovoid, pointed, brown, set on peduncle of 2-4 cm. Zone 5.

Dawn redwood was only found in China in south-west Hubei province and adjoining Sichuan in 1941, which was the same year in which the Japanese palaeontologist S. Miki realised that a number of fossils from various places in the northern hemisphere and previously placed in *Sequoia* differed in the decussate arrangement of the foliage and cones.

Dawn redwood was only introduced in 1948 but has proved hardy and very amenable to culti-vation. Despite coming from southern China it is hardy and makes a very fast-growing tree with feathery fern-like foliage. The autumn colour is a good mixture of yellows, pinks and reds, whilst the bark and habit are attractive at all seasons. Some plants develop butts which are very heavily fluted for the bottom metre or so.

Dawn redwood is fast-growing when young on all soils but sustained fast growth is only achieved on damp sites. It will grow in boggy conditions. It is easily propagated from hardwood cuttings.

A few cultivars have been named.

'Emerald Feathers' is one with greener more fern-like foliage.

'National' is a narrow conical form, of less merit in Britain than most seedlings.

Microbiota Komarov **Cupressaceae**

This is a monotypic genus native to a small region of Pacific Russia near Vladivostok. It has cones with a single seed, as often found in *Juniperus*, but the scales are leathery or woody and open at matur-ity. *Microbiota decussata* is illustrated on page 92.

M. decussata Komarov
Microbiota

Shrub ultimately several metres across. Shoot green for one or two years, then red-brown, finally purple-brown, smooth. Leaves in flat frondose sprays, facial and lateral pairs similar, acute with incurved free tip to 0.3 cm, gland on lower part of scales, mid-yellow-green above, pale yellow-green beneath. Cone globose, with 2-4 scales, only 1 fertile, 0.3 cm by 0.6 cm. Zone 2.

Microbiota is very hardy and makes a useful addition to the range of dwarf conifers. It is prostrate but fairly fast-growing. The foliage is similar in appearance to that of *Thuja* and also turns bronze over the winter period and smells of poppies or ox-eye daisies. The plant, at least the form in cultivation, is monoecious.

Microcachrys Hooker f. **Podocarpaceae**

This is a monotypic genus from Tasmania.

M. tetragona Hooker
Microcachrys

Spreading shrub. Branches prostrate, whip-like, with the spirally set leaves arranged in 4 rows. Leaves scale-like, similar, dark green, margins ciliate, incurved, apex acuminate, 0.15-0.3 cm. Cone ovoid, to 1 cm, with several whorls of 4 round scales, each with a single inverted seed; the scales and arils become fleshy, translucent and bright red or scarlet. Zone 9.

Microcachrys is restricted to western Tasmania. It is uncommon in cultivation but should be hardy in mild regions. The Latin name refers to the very small male cones.

Microstrobus Garden & Johnson
Podocarpaceae

This is a small genus of two species from Australia. They are related to *Dacrydium* and *Microcachrys*, but differ in the small cones, to 0.25 cm, composed of 4-8 scales but without an ovuliferous scale. Each seed has at the base a glume-like scale about as long as the seed.

M. fitzgeraldii (F. Mueller) Garden & Johnson
Blue Mountain pine

Much branched prostrate shrub, rarely to 2 m. Shoots slender. Leaves scale-like, overlapping, set in 4-5 rows, incurved but not tightly adpressed, olive-green with the inner face white with lines of stomata. Zone 9.

This dwarf plant is confined to very damp locations in the Blue Mountains of New South

Wales, where it is found in the spray drift zone at the base of waterfalls. It is rare in cultivation but makes a small dwarf conifer.

M. niphophilus Garden & Johnson
Tasman dwarf pine

This species more regularly makes a shrub to 2 m with short stiff branches. The leaves are short and thick, less than 0.15 cm long and more densely set. It is found in high alpine areas of Tasmania. Zone 9.

Neocallitropsis Florin **Cupressaceae**

This is a monotypic genus allied to *Callitris*.

N. pancheri (Carriere) de Laubenfels
Pancher cypress pine
(*N. araucarioides* (Compton) Florin)

Tree to 10 m. Crown conical. Bark grey. Branches resembling those of an Araucaria with spaced whorls. Leaves lanceolate, loosely imbricate, stiff, in 4-8 rows, margins minutely toothed, 0.5 cm by 0.2 cm. Cone composed of 8 scales in 2 whorls of 4, sessile on short leafy branches, 1 cm. Zone 10.

This tree is confined to New Caledonia where it is found at low elevations on serpentine (very basic or alkaline) rocks. It is unlikely to prove hardy out of doors except in frost-free localities.

Papuacedrus Li **Cupressaceae**

This genus is confined to New Guinea; it is allied to *Libocedrus* but differs in leaf and wood features and in the male cones being set in whorls of 4, not in decussate pairs. Three species have been described but only two are generally accepted.

P. papuana (F. Mueller) Li
Papuacedar

Tree to 50 m. Crown open, domed in mature trees. Bark grey-brown, with broad flat ridges. Leaves in flat sprays, in lateral and facial pairs similar to Fokienia, facial leaves partly covered by laterals, bluntly acute, to 0.17 by 0.15 cm, lateral pairs flat, with a fine acute spreading tip, to 0.3 cm long, dark green above, silvery white below. Cone 1 cm with 4-6 valvate scales, with a small dorsal prickle, only inner pair fertile, carrying 2 very unequally-winged seeds. Zone 9.

Papuacedar is found in New Guinea and the Molucca islands of Indonesia. It is in cultivation but the forms introduced have not proved hardy outside; however, they have been from the lower parts of its range and plants from the top end, near

the treeline at 3,600 m, might prove more hardy. The foliage, particularly of young trees, is very similar to *Fokienia* but the cones are quite different.

P. arfakensis (Gibbs) Li
Arfak papuacedar

This species differs from Papuacedar in the reddish, scaly bark, the larger, blunt lateral scale leaves, to 0.5 cm, the smaller cones, 0.8 cm, whose 4 scales have the small prickle near the base. It is native to West Irian, the part of New Guinea which is in Indonesia. It is found at lower elevations and is unlikely to be hardy. Zone 9.

Parasitaxus de Laubenfels **Podocarpaceae**

This genus is parasitic on *Falcatifolium taxoides* (Brongiart & Grisebach) de Laubenfels.

P. ustus (Vieillard) de Laubenfels
Parasite yew

Shrub to 1.5 m. Leaves succulent, reddish, scale-like, loosely overlapping and spirally set. Cone carried without a fleshy basal receptacle on a nonspecialised branchlet which at maturity envelops the single seed, globose, to 0.4 cm. Zone 10.

This species is found in New Caledonia. It is unique in the conifers in being parasitic. It is unlikely to survive in cultivation.

Phyllocladus L.C. & A. Richard
Celery pines Podocarpaceae

This genus is characterised by the foliar element being modified shoots or phylloclades. Functional true leaves are only found in juvenile plants, being reduced to subulate scales in adult plants. The phylloclades may be either simple or pinnate. The cones are terminal or marginal on the phylloclades; they consist of a number of scales, usually only one to a few of which carry seeds. The plants may be either monoecious or dioecious. The five taxa include one from Malaysia and Indonesia, one in Tasmania and three in New Zealand.

P. alpinus Hooker f.
Mountain celery pine

Tree to 9 m, usually less. Bark brown to dark brown, fissured. Phylloclades simple, rhombic, acute, cuneate, sessile or stalked, margins toothed, 2.5-8 cm by 1.5-2 cm. Scale leaves triangular, less than 0.1 cm. Cones with 2-5 ovules subtended by a pinkish red fleshy scale, seed ovoid, 0.5 cm, greenish black or black, aril white, receptacle fleshy, red. Zone 8.

Mountain celery pine is found throughout the South Island of New Zealand and in scattered localities in the North Island. It is hardy in cultivation but very slow-growing. It makes an attractive curiosity plant of open aspect. The phylloclades are similar to the leaves of celery. It is very similar to Tasman celery pine and is sometimes treated as a variety (*P. asplenifolius* var. *alpinus* (Hooker f.) Keng), although the rank of subspecies might be more logical.

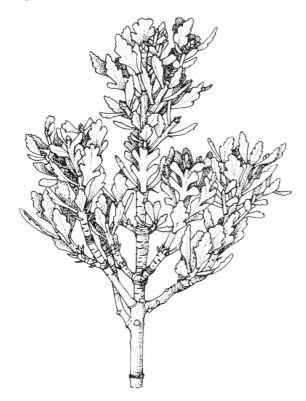

Figure 8.14 Phyllocladus alpinus. *Foliage.*

P. asplenifolius (Labillardiere) Hooker f.
Tasman celery pine

This species differs from Mountain celery pine in the true leaves being subulate or awl-like and 0.2-0.3 cm long and is a larger-growing tree to 18 m. It is confined to scattered places in western Tasmania. In cultivation it is hardy but very slow-growing. Zone 8.

P. glaucus Carriere
Blue celery pine

This species has pinnate phylloclades with 5-12 segments, glaucous beneath. The phylloclades are 12-20 cm, rarely to 30 cm long. The cones are in clusters of 3-5 on each side of the pinnate phylloclades on a short shoot, and occupy the place of the lower lateral segments. The cones ripen 1-1.2 cm and are pinkish red, with 8-20 seeds exserted beyond the thickened scales. The seeds are flattened, black, 0.3-0.4 cm long with a white cup-shaped aril. Zone 9.

Blue celery pine is native to the northern part of North Island, New Zealand, at low altitudes. It is unlikely to prove hardy except in mild areas.

P. hypophyllus Hooker f.
Malaysian celery pine

This tree to 30 m also has pinnate phylloclades but they are only 10-15 cm long with 5-10 segments. The cones are carried in an apical notch on the phylloclades. They consist of around 15 scales but only 2 or 3 are fertile. It is found in the Philippines, Indonesia and Papua New Guinea. Mainly it occurs at altitudes of less than 3,000 m but some populations are found as high as 4,000 m and they might prove hardy. Zone 9.

P. trichomanioides D. Don
Tanekaha

This species makes a medium-sized tree in lowland New Zealand. It has pinnate phylloclades, 8-12 cm with 6-12 segments. It is similar to Blue celery pine in the cones being born laterally on the phylloclades and to Malaysian celery pine in the mature cone having only 1-3 fertile scales and seeds. It comes from northern South Island and North Island of New Zealand but is unlikely to be hardy outside of mild areas. Zone 9.

Picea Dietrich **Spruces Pinaceae**

The spruces are differentiated in the Pinaceae by the following characters. The leaves are entire, never notched, and sit on a distinct projection of the shoot, called a *pulvinus*; when the leaves fall naturally from the shoot the pulvinus remains but if the leaf is torn off, the pulvinus comes away with the needle, therefore leafless twigs of spruce are rough. Leaves are only carried on long shoots. The leaves are set spirally on the shoot but usually twisted at the base to be parted beneath the shoot and imbricate, i.e. pressed down forwards, on the shoot above, unless otherwise noted. The leaves are 4-sided, usually with stomata on all faces. In some species the section is partly flattened, so that in a cross-section, the leaf is rhombic or diamond-shaped; in these species, there often are no stomata on the upper leaf surface and the leaves cannot be rolled in the fingers.

The cones ripen in the first autumn and remain intact, releasing seeds by the scales opening. They are only carried on the uppermost branches and arise from the terminal cluster of buds at the ends of the shoots, not from lateral ones along the length as in *Abies*. At the time of pollination, the female cones are erect, as in *Abies*, but after pollination, they become pendulous.

There are about three dozen species of spruce. They are widely distributed south of the Arctic tundra zones which stretch across Europe, Asia and North America, where a few species occupy vast territories. Further south, they are mainly found in cool montane regions, where the extent of suitable sites is more limited. Only in Asia, on the island of Taiwan, does a spruce cross the Tropic of Cancer, although species nearly get there in northern Mexico.

In the garden, spruces are of value as specimen trees, for shelter and as dwarf conifers. In an open situation, they will retain the lower branches to make complete specimens. They include some of the plants with the brightest blue foliage, and some of the most striking of conifer 'flowers'. They are used for Christmas trees, although less suited for this purpose than other genera. They will tolerate a wide range of sites, especially barren ones but are best on cool moist ones on a medium to rich soil. On thin chalky soils, only a few species will flourish. They will thrive on thin peaty or gleyed (i.e. with a high water table) soils, as generally they make rather shallow surface root systems. It is partly this ability to grow well on poor wet soils that makes the spruces so widely planted in forestry; the other factor being the good quality white timber.

Despite several attempts, no satisfactory classification scheme has been proposed for the spruces; in the following account, I propose to deal with the species in a number of groups.

Group 1   *breweriana*.
Group 2   *omorika, orientalis, maximowiczii, mariana, rubens*.

Group 3   *abies, obovata, wilsonii, morrisonicola, neoveitchii, smithiana, schrenkiana, asperata, retroflexa, aurantiaca, crassifolia, meyeri, koyamae, koraiensis, polita, chihuahuana*.
Group 4   *glauca*.
Group 5   *engelmannii, pungens, mexicana*.
Group 6   *likiangensis, purpurea, balfouriana, bicolor, shirasawae, glehnii*.
Group 7   *brachytyla, spinulosa, farreri, jezoensis, sitchensis*.

Group 1

This group consists of just one species, as below.

P. breweriana Watson
Brewer spruce

Tree to 30 m, although in cultivation only 10 m or so. Crown columnar, conic at the apex, branches level with the branchlets curtaining the branches, seedling trees are very different, see below. Bark grey or purple-grey, smooth, becoming scaly. Shoot slender, hairy, pink-brown. Bud bluntly conic. Leaves thick, blunt, flattened, deep matt or shiny green above, stomata in 2 whitish bands beneath, to 3.5 cm but usually less, arrangement on strong shoots parted below and pressed down forwards above, on weak pendulous shoots radially set and forwards pointing. Cone cylindric, red-brown, resinous, 7-14 cm by 2 cm; scale rounded, entire. Zone 5.

Brewer spruce is native to the Siskiyou Mountains of northern California and southern Oregon, where it is an uncommon timberline tree. It is not closely related to any other North American spruce. It is widely planted for the very attractive habit with the long pendulous branchlets growing a metre or so in length. Seedling trees, however, are very slow to develop either the long thick flat needles or the pendulous branchlets and may not assume the 'characteristic' adult form for 20 or so years. Grafted plants are usually raised for the amenity market; these are much quicker to make an adult tree, although strong shoots must be used for grafting. Despite its popularity and the habit, it is not one of the most attractive spruces.

Group 2

This group consists of five species. They hold together on the basis of the small cones with rounded scales and short needles but the grouping may not be entirely natural. Possibly Caucasian and Maximowicz spruces belong in group 3, or to individual groups.

P. omorika (Pancic) Purkyne
Serbian spruce

Tree to 30 m. Crown a tall narrow spire, branches become more pendent at the base as they lengthen, arching out at the tips. Bark orange-brown, reddish brown or purplish, finely flaky, becoming cracked into square plates. Shoot orange-brown or pink-brown with dark or blackish hairs, becoming darker in second and third years. Bud ovoid-conic, chestnut-brown, with some white resin, 0.2 cm. Leaves at right angles to the shoot below, imbricate above, dark shiny green without stomata above, 2 silvery white bands of stomata below, flattened, apex acute or acuminate and bevelled, 1-1.8 cm by 0.15 cm. Cone ovoid-conic, purplish blue, ripening purplish brown, retained for a year or more on the tree, 3-6.5 cm by 2 cm. Zone 5.

Serbian spruce is native only to the Drina river valley in Yugoslavia, although from fossil remains it was quite common elsewhere in Europe prior to the last Ice Age. It varies in the narrowness of the crown, those plants from the higher altitudes being narrower than the trees from the bottom end of its range. The difference is due to the extent to which the branches become pendulous near the bole. The narrowness of the crown of Serbian spruce reduces the amount of damage by winter snow and gives it a competitive edge over Norway spruce, with which it occurs.

Serbian spruce is very tolerant of site conditions. It will grow at the same steady rate whether on a rich neutral soil, a barren and wet acidic one or on a highly alkaline site. It is most useful as a specimen tree, and will tolerate atmospheric pollution better than most spruces; however, as a genus they are ill-suited to polluted airs. They will move as large plants but they then take the best part of the next decade to come back into form, by which time a small tree would be taller in any case. The Latin name comes from the Serbian word for spruce.

A number of cultivars have been named.

'Expansa' arose as a seedling which failed to make a leader. It will form quite an extensive ground-covering plant, to 4 m by 80 cm high, but will often revert to a normal tree.

'Gnom' is a dense broadly conical dwarf form to 1.5 m. It is said to be very resistant to Red spider mite. 'Frohleiten' is a dwarfer and more open plant, to 40 cm in ten years.

'Nana' makes a broadly conical small tree, slowly reaching 3 m. 'Minima' arose as a witches broom on 'Nana' and is markedly smaller. 'Pimoko' is also a witches broom, making a dense irregular plant to 30 cm high in a decade, with bright green foliage.

'Pendula' is a very narrow selection, due to the pendulous nature of the branches. 'Berliners Weeping' is similar. As the tendency is for the branches to hang down vertically in high altitude origins, other similar plants could be selected.

P. orientalis (Linnaeus) Link
Oriental or Caucasian spruce

Tree to 40 m. Crown of young trees narrow conic, open in whorls, in old trees columnar with a conic top, not narrow, dense. Bark smooth pink-grey, later cracked into small rounded plates. Shoot hairy, orange-brown, becoming grey-brown. Bud ovoid-conic, 0.4 cm. Leaves more or less radial, forwards, parted below on weaker shoots, only slightly flattened in cross-section, blunt, shiny deep green, very short, 0.6-0.8 cm. Male cones bright deep red. Female cones ovoid-conic, pointed, dark purple, ripening brown, 6-10 cm. Zone 5.

Caucasian spruce is found in the Caucasus Mountains of southern Russia and in north-eastern Turkey. It makes an extremely attractive tree, in the shiny green very short needles, the bright red male cones in late April or early May and the columnar habit. It deserves much wider planting, and has the grace and charm so palpably missing from Norway spruce. It will thrive on a wide range of sites.

A number of cultivars have been named.

'Atrovirens' has darker green foliage.

'Aurea' is an excellent tree form, although sufficiently slow-growing to be tolerated in most gardens for a number of years. The buds flush creamy yellow through gold until they change to a normal green after some six weeks; thereafter the tree is scarcely to be distinguished from ordinary seedlings, although sometimes during the winter the leaves on the upper side of the shoots will turn somewhat yellow. It is most desirable, having several seasons of display, yet never being stuck in a single mode like most golden plants. 'Skylands' is similar, except the yellow-gold colour is retained for the entire year. Similarly, 'Aurea Compacta' keeps the upper leaves on the shoots light or dark yellow for the entire season, whilst having a dwarf habit. A number of other cultivars have been named in this group.

'Gracilis' makes a small oval tree with bright green leaves. It is slow-growing, rather than dwarf.

'Nana' is a very small slow globose or ovoid form, to 1 m.

'Nutans' has the branches wide-spread and nodding.

P. maximowiczii Regel ex Masters
Maximowicz spruce

Tree to 20m or more. Crown conical. Bark orange-brown, smooth, finely flaking. Shoot glabrous, yellowish brown or reddish brown, pulvini short. Bud ovoid to globose, red-brown, distinctly resinous, 0.4cm. Leaves radially set, sparse, stiff, acute or obtuse, shiny dark green, 0.8-1.2cm. Cone oblong, shiny brown, 3-5cm. Zone 7.

Maximowicz spruce is a rare tree in its native Japan, occurring only in the vicinity of three mountains, Fujiyama, Fuji and Yatsuga-dake, in Honshu. The plants from the latter two localities are referred to var. *senanensis* Hayashi, which has the needles 1.1-1.5cm long, parted below the shoot and larger cones (4-7.5cm) with fewer bigger scales. The common form in cultivation may belong to this variety, or be of hybrid origin.

P. mariana (Miller) Brittan, Sterns & Poggenberg
Black spruce

Tree to 20m. Crown conical, often with the lower branches layering as a fairy ring around the tree. Bark grey-brown, becoming scaly in thin tight flakes. Shoot pink-brown or yellow-brown, with reddish glandular hairs. Bud ovoid, acute, not resinous. Leaves bluish green above, bluish white on the stomata bands below (some lines above also), blunt, 0.6-1.8cm. Cones persist on the tree, ovoid, incurved on short strong peduncles, grey-brown, 2-3.5cm. Zone 2.

Black spruce is found right across northern North America from Newfoundland to the Alaska coast. It is mainly distributed in Canada but in the east it extends into the USA, as far south as New Jersey and Rhode Island. It is very much a tree of subarctic conditions, being found in barren sphagnum bogs and on drier acid sands. It is unusual in the lower branches naturally layering and this is an important method of reproduction, particularly on the more extreme sites. The cones may take two years to ripen in the far north.

Black spruce makes a neat bluish green tree with a dense crown in cultivation. It does not grow fast, nor large, and can be interesting in the long term if it makes a ring of layered branches around the tree. The common name refers to the dark cones and distant appearance of the trees compared to the sympatric Red spruce.

A number of cultivars have been raised.

'Aureovariegata' makes an irregular conical bush with the new foliage golden yellow, giving a striking effect when overlying the bluish older leaves. 'Aurea' as currently cultivated may be the same plant.

'Beissneri' is a broad conical and dense form, ultimately making 5m. 'Beissneri Compacta' is similar in the bluish green needles but only to 2m. 'Doumetii' also will make 5m in time; it has silvery green needles and will bear cones.

'Nana' makes a dwarf bush to 50cm with a neat habit and short blue-grey foliage. 'Pygmaea' is smaller still.

P. rubens Sargent
Red spruce

Tree to 25m. Crown conic. Bark finely flaky, purplish brown in young trees, grey-brown to red-brown and somewhat scaly in old trees. Shoot orange-brown, initially hairy, smooth. Bud ovoid, acute, red-brown, to 1cm. Leaves slender, crowded on the upper side of the shoot but some below, nearly at right angles, grass green or yellow-green, 1-1.7cm by 0.1cm. Cone ovoid-oblong, red-brown to light brown, falling soon after shedding seeds, 3-5cm. Zone 3.

Red spruce is found in north-east North America from Newfoundland down the Appalachian Mountains to northern Georgia. It is very tolerant of shade and is a long-lived species. Hybrids with Black spruce are occasionally found where the two meet. It is quite distinct in the small cones and wiry yellow-green foliage. It is uncommon in cultivation, although quite hardy and makes a reasonable tree. The name refers to the reddish brown cones.

'Pocono' is a dwarf seedling found in the wild; it has made a plant to 20cm high and across.

Group 3
The species in this group have relatively large cones with woody and usually rounded scales, and needles which are either squarely quadrangular in section or flattened in the vertical, not horizontal, plane. The group consists of two series of species; Siberian spruce leads through Wilson spruce to Taiwan spruce and through Tienshan spruce to Morinda spruce, whilst Dragon spruce, and its associated species, is clearly related to Tigertail and Chihuahua spruces. Norway spruce is somewhat remote from these groupings; morphologically it is closer to Dragon spruce but it hybridises so very freely with Siberian spruce, where they meet, that there are obviously no genetic barriers between them.

P. abies (Linnaeus) Karsten
Norway spruce

Tree to 40m. Crown conic, columnar and rather open in old

trees. Bark red-brown, finely flaky, becoming purple or grey in old trees and slightly scaly. Shoot orange-brown, golden brown or reddish brown, usually glabrous. Bud ovoid, to 0.7 cm on strong shoots, shiny brown. Leaves arranged forwards and mainly above the shoot, dark green, bluntly pointed, quadrangular or sometimes flattened in the vertical plane, especially in young trees, 1.5-2.5 cm. Cone cylindric, scales woody but thinner than in other species in the group, rhombic-ovate, with a truncate, erose or notched apex, 10-20 cm by 3-4 cm. Zone 3.

Norway spruce is found in central and southern Europe, southern Scandinavia and in the Balkans. Plants from northern Scandinavia and north-east Europe differ in the more hairy shoots, deep green leaves and smaller cones with rounded, finely toothed scales and are the product of introgression of genes from Siberian spruce. They are variously treated as a subspecies of either Norway or Siberian spruces or as *P. × fennica* (Regel) Komarov. It is likely that Norway and Siberian spruces have only come together since the Ice Age.

Norway spruce is widely cultivated as a timber tree, and less often as an amenity tree. It has a number of very useful cultivars but is inferior as a specimen tree. Many so used are Christmas trees which have survived the experience, but even as a Christmas tree it is inferior to other conifers. Generally it is a coarse plant.

The following are a selection of the cultivars, grouped by their characters:

Tree Forms — Conical Habit
'Cupressina' has a very narrow tight crown with ascending branches. 'Pyramidata' is broader, and much less appealing.

Tree Forms — Sparse Crowns
'Virgata' and 'Cranstonii' are two plants in which few side buds are produced; the shoots, therefore, are largely unbranched and whip- or snake like. Both make open tall trees; 'Cranstonii' has flattened needles.

Tree Forms — Weeping Habit
'Inversa' is a form with the side branches pendulous but with an erect leader. 'Frohberg' is similar. Both these and other similar plants, like 'Reflexa', can be used as ground cover if they are not encouraged to form a leader.

Tree Forms — Foliage Variants
'Argentospicata' shoots flush white and mature to green.

'Aurea' has the new growths yellowish white; it may be scorched in full sun and be paler in the shade. A number of similar clones have been named. 'Findonensis' is one, with the needles above the shoots remaining a sickly yellow. These plants are all inferior to the somewhat similar forms of Caucasian spruce.

'Coerulea' has the new foliage whitish blue.

Tree Forms — Bark Variants
'Corticata' has bark which is thick and deeply fissured.

'Tuberculata' makes an open tree with the bases of the branches swollen and conical. This is unusual in Norway spruce but a regular feature of old Sitka spruces, and also in one origin of Likiang spruce.

Slow-growing Forms — Conical Habit
'Conica' is a slow-growing plant with a dense conical habit, ultimately making a plant 3-5 m tall. It may represent a group of similar cultivars. 'Mucronata' is similar.

Slow-growing Forms — Globose Habit
'Globosa' makes a large rounded bush; it is rare in cultivation, and probably represented by several clones.

Slow-growing Forms — Weeping Habit
'Acrocona' makes a small tree with an erect leader and pendent branches; it is mainly grown, however, for the large cones profusely carried even on small plants.

'Reflexa' will grow prostrate if not trained to make a stem; it is quite vigorous and will cover several metres, although the foliage is not sufficiently dense to control weeds.

Dwarf Forms — Conical Habit
'Elegans' makes a globose or very broad conical plant with dense and uniform growths.

'Ellwangeriana' has a broad dense habit with ascending branches but no leader. Strong shoots are inclined to produce radial erect growths, giving a rather untidy appearance to the plant. It can be kept small by removing all strong growths, when it will become more spreading.

'Microsperma' makes a broadly conical crown with symmetrical branches bearing clusters of arching shoots at the tips.

'Nana' is an irregular conic plant, to 1.5 m.

'Ohlendorfii' is at first globose but becomes

more conical with age. It has needles 0.4-0.8 cm.

'Pachyphylla' is a curious form with stout shoots bearing thick fleshy leaves. It is slow in growth.

'Remontii' makes a neat cone, very slowly attaining 3 m.

Dwarf Forms — Globose Habit

'Clanbrassiliana' is an old form which arose as a witches broom. It forms a spreading globose plant, eventually making a small tree with a multi-stemmed rounded crown. The leaves are widest in the middle and flattened along the vertical axis.

'Echiniformis' makes a rounded small bun plant. The leaves on long shoots are spaced and sharp, hence the name 'hedgehog spruce'.

'Gregoryana' forms a tight globose plant, similar to 'Echiniformis' but without the occasional long shoots.

'Humilis' makes an irregular dense congested small globose plant.

Dwarf Forms — Flat or Spreading Habit

'Hornibrookiana' makes a flat squat plant with congested shoots.

'Kamon' is slow-growing with silvery blue-green needles; it originated as a witches broom on 'Cranstonii'.

'Maxwellii' arose as a witches broom. Cuttings taken from the slowest-growing portions make diminutive bun-shaped plants, but those from stronger shoots grow more open and larger and are found under the name 'Pseudo-Maxwellii'.

'Nidiformis' makes a spreading to prostrate regular plant, with a nest-shaped depression. The 0.5-0.7 cm needles have a number of fine sharp teeth on the margins (clearly seen under a hand lens), which distinguishes this cultivar. 'Little Gem' is smaller in all its parts and arose as a witches broom on 'Nidiformis'.

'Procumbens' makes a flat-spreading plant; it has longer needles than in similar forms, and they decrease in length along the shoots. 'Pumila' makes a low-spreading bush, with the upper branches somewhat erect, creating a series of layers of rich green foliage. The needles are broadest at one-third of their length. 'Pumila Nigra', with dark blue-green needles, has the upper branches more erect. 'Repens' has a series of level tiers of foliage as it makes a prostrate or spreading plant. 'Tabuliformis' is similar, but always flat at the top, as the upper shoots are nearly horizontal.

P. obovata Ledebour
Siberian spruce

Tree to 35 m. Crown conic. Bark purplish grey, finely flaky. Shoot pale brown to somewhat purplish, becoming dark grey, glandular hairy. Bud ovoid or conic, orange-brown. Leaves pointing forwards along shoot, parted at sides and slightly drooping, leaf below lateral bud often at right angles to shoot, mucronate, shiny green, bevelled, 1.3-2.3 cm. Cone cylindric-ovoid, 5-11 cm by 2-3 cm, scales obovate, rounded, adpressed. Zone 2.

Siberian spruce is found from north-west Europe across northern Asia. It is also reported from north Shanxi in northern China. It makes a small tree in cultivation but some origins may be damaged by late spring frosts.

subsp. *alpestris* (Bruegger) Domin is a form found at high altitude in the Alps. It shows some introgression of Norway spruce.

var. *coerulea* Tigerstedt has glabrous young shoots and radially arranged blue-green needles; it is recorded from the Altai shan of central Asia.

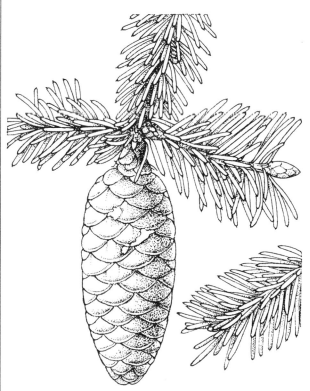

Figure 8.15 Picea wilsonii. *Foliage and mature cone.*

P. wilsonii Masters
Wilson spruce

Tree to 15-20 m, to 50 m in China. Crown conic, columnar in older trees. Bark pink-brown or grey-brown, sometimes flaking in large papery scales. Shoot shiny ash grey or buff-grey. Bud ovoid, bluntly pointed, brown, slightly resinous. Leaves very imbricate above, spreading at sides, parted below, slender or stoutish, 4-sided, bright glossy grass green on all faces, apex blunt or pointed, 0.8-1.3 cm, rarely to 1.8 cm, by 0.1-0.17 cm. Cone oblong, scales rounded obovate with broader flanges, 5-8 cm by 2.5-4 cm, falling soon after releasing the seed. Zone 5.

Wilson spruce is native to northern China from north-west Sichuan along the Qin Ling shan to the Wutai shan near Beijing. It makes a neat tree in cultivation with the grass green leaves set on the distinctive ash-coloured shoots. It is a slow-growing tree, achieving perhaps 30 cm per annum, with a broad conic crown of level branches. The original form introduced by Ernest Wilson from Hubei province had finer shoots and leaves and was named *P. watsoniana* Masters.

P. morrisonicola Hayata
Taiwan spruce

This tree is very close to Wilson spruce but differs in the very slender white shoots, often only 0.2 cm in diameter, and the finer leaves firmly pressed down above the shoot, 0.8-1.4 cm long by 0.1 cm and cones 5-7 cm by 2.5-3 cm with obovate rounded scales. As in Siberian spruce, the leaf subtending a lateral bud projects at a right angle to the shoot. Zone 8.

Taiwan spruce occurs in the high mountains of Taiwan, astride the Tropic of Cancer. It is hardy in cultivation and makes a similar tree to Wilson spruce but needs more winter shelter.

P. neoveitchii Masters
Veitch spruce

This tree may be related to Wilson spruce. It has 1-year shoots which are light yellow or very light brown, in the second and third years, grey or light yellow-grey, sharp dark green leaves 1.5-2.5 cm by 0.2 cm which are laterally compressed, and cones 8-14 cm by 5-6.5 cm with large rounded scales as wide as long, 2.7 cm by 2.7-3 cm. Zone 7.

Veitch spruce is native to western Hubei, southern Shaanxi and adjacent Gansu. It only makes a small tree and does not appear to have been introduced.

P. smithiana (Wallich) Boissier
Morinda spruce

Tree to 40 m. Crown of old trees columnar with spreading horizontal branches and pendulous branchlets, young trees conic. Bark ash grey or purplish grey, becoming scaly. Shoot off-white or pale brown, becoming greyer. Bud ovoid or ovoid-conic, chestnut brown, resinous, 0.7 cm. Leaves more or less radial, especially on weaker pendulous shoots, dark green, incurved, longest of any spruce, to 4 cm by 0.1 cm. Cone cylindric, tapered at both ends, scale rounded, incurved, thick, woody, bright brown, 10-20 cm by 4-5 cm. Zone 6.

Morinda spruce is found in the west Himalayas from Afghanistan to west Nepal and in adjoining parts of south-west Xizang, China. It makes a large and majestic tree with the semi-pendulous foliage and is easily recognised by the large cones and long needles. It will thrive on a wide range of sites, including limestone sites; however, it is slow to get established as a young tree and seems to require an adequate water supply in the early years, suggesting good weed control is essential. Plants from west Nepal with hairy shoots have been named var. *nepalensis* Franco.

P. shrenkiana Fischer & Meyer
Shrenk spruce

Shrenk spruce is similar to Morinda spruce but has shorter, stiffer needles which are pale glaucous green or bright green and less radial in arrangement; the leaves are 2-3.5 by 0.15 cm. The cones are 8-10 cm by 2.5-3.5 cm and dark purplish brown. It has stouter shoots which are finely pubescent and creamy brown conic buds. Zone 5.

Shrenk spruce is recorded from the Tien shan of central Asia, along the border between Russia and China. In the wild it is tolerant of dry conditions. It is in cultivation and hardy, although susceptible to late spring frosts. In cultivation it makes a much smaller tree than Morinda spruce, with a denser crown. Plants from the west Tien shan are sometimes treated as a separate subspecies, subsp. *tianshanica* (Rupprecht) Bykov; they differ in the leaves usually 1.2-1.5 cm but sometimes longer and the small cones, less than 7 cm with broader scales, almost truncate at the apex.

'Globosa' makes a large globose bush.

P. asperata Masters
Dragon spruce

Tree to 20 m. Crown conic or columnar. Bark purplish grey, with moderately thick flaky scales. Shoot stout, prominently ridged with the pulvinus sitting near the front of a ridge, yellowish brown or buff, slightly pruinose, becoming ash grey, glabrous or very sparsely hairy. Bud conic or ovoid-conic, pale brown, slightly resinous, 1cm. Leaves sparser below, assurgent or slightly imbricate, all may be assurent at sides or bent forwards, very stiff, stout, bluntly pointed, not sharp, glaucous blue or blue-green, becoming dull green by fifth or sixth season, stomata on all 4 faces, 1-2.5cm by 0.1-0.15cm. Cone cylindric, fawn brown or dull brown, scales rounded, 5-16cm. Zone 6.

Dragon spruce is native to south-west Shaanxi, eastern Gansu, and northern central Sichuan. It is hardy but variable in the forms in cultivation. Part of this variation is caused by the following four taxa being lumped together under this name. The plants generally make bluish, rather than strikingly blue, trees, very often with clear boles and high somewhat gaunt crowns. However, some plants are much more compact and persistently conical and very much more attractive. The bark is also interesting. Dragon spruce will thrive on a wide range of sites and is reasonably slow in growth.

P. retroflexa Masters
Tapao shan spruce

This tree is close to Dragon spruce but differs in the greyer bark, golden yellow, becoming grey and generally glabrous shoots, the green or glaucous, erect and spreading leaves which are sharp and the slightly shorter and broader cones, 8-13cm by 2.5-4cm, which are shining brown with striated scales. Zone 6.

It is found in west Sichuan in the Tapao shan, to the south-west of the range of Dragon spruce. The plants in cultivation are noticeably greener than Dragon spruce, although Wilson, who found it, described it as glaucous. Its horticultural value is similar.

P. aurantiaca Masters
Orange spruce

This tree differs from Dragon spruce in the strikingly deep orange to dull orange coloured bark of the shoots, turning grey in the fourth or fifth season. The leaves are 0.9-2cm long by 0.15-0.2cm wide and the cones are cylindrical, cinnamon brown or shining brown with rounded but slightly erose (nibbled) scales. Zone 6.

Orange spruce comes from a restricted area to the south-west of Kangting in west Sichuan, and to the south-west of Tapao shan spruce. In the wild, the trees are spire-like with sparse, gaunt, crowns. It is uncommon in cultivation, but thrives

on a shallow chalk soil in southern Britain. It is the most southerly in distribution of the Chinese spruces of this alliance.

P. crassifolia Komarov
Qinghai spruce

This species differs from Dragon spruce in the golden red-brown shoots which are distinctly hairy on the petioles, becoming pale yellow in the second winter, and the leaves which are very broad, by virtue of being laterally compressed, at least in cultivated material; they are in the range 1.2-3.5cm but in cross-section are 0.2-0.3cm (by 0.1cm on young trees, at least). The apex is tapered to an acute, sometimes sharp, tip. The cones are 7-11cm by 2.5-3.5cm and ripen yellow-brown or orange-brown. Zone 5.

Qinghai spruce is found primarily in the Qilian shan (Kunlun shan) which runs along the border between Qinghai and Gansu provinces and also in Ningxia and Inner Mongolia. This is a region with a dry climate. This species is in cultivation from seeds collected by Joseph Rock, although usually recorded as Dragon spruce. It is comparable in attributes to that species.

P. meyeri Rehder & Wilson
Meyer spruce

This tree has the 1-year shoots yellow-brown, or reddish yellow-brown, changing to pale yellow-brown, pale brown or brown for the second and third years. The needles are somewhat flattened, particularly those at the side of the shoot, acute, and 1.3-3cm by 0.2cm. They are glaucous bluish green and arranged mostly above the shoot. The cones are 6-9cm by 2.5-3.5cm. Zone 6.

Meyer spruce is found in Shaanxi, Hebei and adjoining Inner Mongolia. It was confused from the very beginning with Dragon spruce and most trees cultivated as Meyer spruce belong to Dragon spruce. It is in cultivation from seeds collected by Joseph Hers in Hebei, although as Dragon spruce!

P. koyamae Shirasawa
Koyama spruce

Tree to 20m. Crown columnar. Bark purple-brown or grey-brown. Shoot golden brown or orange-brown in the first year, paler or purplish in second year, mainly glabrous. Bud ovoid, bluntly pointed, red-brown, very resinous, 0.4cm. Leaves point forwards, thick, blunt or acute, not sharp, 0.8-1.2cm possibly longer on young cultivated trees, by 0.15cm. Cone ovoid-cylindric or cylindric, scales rounded and minutely toothed, 4-10 cm by 3.5 cm. Zone 6.

Koyama spruce is only known from a single stand of around 100 trees in Honshu, Japan, on Mount Yatsuga-dake. It is very distinct in the short thick needles; these are variable in length along the shoot, being at their longest near the base of the shoot and tapering evenly towards the tip; some of the other species in this alliance may occasionally show this character, but never to the same extent with such short needles. Koyama spruce is in cultivation but is rare; most of the trees so labelled are Korean spruce, which has been confused with it.

P. koraiensis Nakai
Korean spruce

This tree is similar to Koyama spruce but differs in the longer, soft leaves which are bluish green and 1.2-2.2 cm by 0.15 cm, the 1-year shoots which are yellow, pale yellow-brown or pale red-brown, becoming light yellow-brown, brownish yellow or grey-brown in the second and third years and cones with somewhat elongated obovate scales. The leaves are set more widely-spreading on the shoots and the buds are less resinous. Zone 5.

Korean spruce is native to Korea, Pacific Russia and north-east China. In the wild it makes a large tree, to 80 m, although usually smaller. It is uncommon in cultivation, such trees as are grown usually being labelled as Koyama spruce. It shows some variability in Korea and several different species have been named, although they probably warrant only subspecific treatment. They are *P. intercedens* Nakai (*P. koraiensis* var. *intercedens* (Nakai) Lee), *P. pungsaniensis* Uyeki and *P. tonaiensis* Nakai.

P. polita
Tigertail spruce
(*P. torano* Koehne)

Tree to 25 m. Crown conic. Bark purple-brown or grey-brown, scaly. Shoot pale yellow or pale reddish brown, glabrous. Bud ovoid, not resinous. Leaves rather radial, but less below and those above somewhat forwards pointing, rigid, very sharp, dark shiny green, slightly compressed, 1.5-2 cm by 0.18 cm. Cone oblong, yellowish brown, ripens to grey-brown; scales elliptic, thin, margin finely toothed, 8-12 cm by 4.5 cm. Zone 6.

Tigertail spruce is native to central and southern Japan, from central Honshu south to Shikoku and Kyushu. It makes an attractive tree in cultivation, notable for the viciously sharp and rigid leaves.

P. chihuahuana Martinez
Chihuahua spruce

This tree is very similar to Tigertail spruce in the cones (10-15 cm by 3-4 cm) with thin rounded scales, the very sharp needles, noticeably flattened on young trees, although more quadrangular and blunt on coning shoots. The crown is more similar to Morinda spruce with level branches bearing pendulous branchlets. The bark is silver grey and exfoliates in large scales. The leaves, however, are bluish grey and set on very stout shoots. Zone 7.

Chihuahua spruce is found in a score of widely scattered sites in the vast western Mexican states of Chihuahua and Durango. It only occurs near to streams or on moist soils and all the populations are small, with little regeneration. It is not closely related to any other North American spruce, although it was more widespread, particularly in Mexico, in the recent past. It is in cultivation and is hardy except in cold districts. Recently, a small population of trees has been found in Nuevo Leon state, some 640 km to the east. These trees differ in the fresh green foliage and possibly in other characters. This population has also been introduced and appears hardy.

Group 4

This group includes only one species. It has rounded tight cone scales, but they are thin and flexible, as in group 5.

P. glauca (Moenchen) Voss
White spruce

Tree to 20 m. Crown narrow or broad conic. Bark pink-grey, becoming ash brown, scaly with white cracks. Shoot buff-white, becoming pale yellow and then brown, usually glabrous, often bloomed. Bud ovoid, chestnut brown, 0.6 cm. Leaves somewhat parted below the shoot, spreading at the sides, forwards and imbricate above, on strong shoots all assurgent, stiff, 4-sided, apex acute, sharp in young trees, blue-green, 1-1.5 cm by 0.1 cm. Cone long ovoid, tapering at ends, scales rounded and finely toothed, ripening light brown and falling soon after, 2.5-6 cm by 1.2 cm. Zone 2.

White spruce is found right across North America, from the Atlantic to the Pacific oceans, mainly in Canada but just entering the USA in the eastern states and along the Rocky Mountains. It occurs in the forests south of the Arctic treeline, with Black spruce and Tamarack. It is a very hardy tree, but, like many from severe continental climates, is inclined to come into leaf early, although it is more tolerant of spring frosts than other such trees. It makes an interesting small tree of relatively low stature and slow growth.

var. *albertiana* (Brown) Sargent is the form found in the northern Rocky Mountains in Alberta and Montana, where it can attain 50 m. It has a flakier bark, darker and more hairy shoots, longer, more forward-pointing needles to 2 cm with a rounded apex, and smaller ovoid cones 2.5-5 cm with entire scales. It is in cultivation, most frequently as the form 'Conica' or 'Albertiana Conica'. It makes a very neat cone to 2 m and is an excellent dwarf conifer, although susceptible to spider mite in dry years and winter damage if exposed. Several cultivariants of 'Conica' have been named; these include 'Albert Globe' with a globose crown and short needles, 'Elegans Compacta' with bright green leaves, 'Gnom' with grey-green foliage and 'Laurin' with dark green leaves and very slow growth.

var. *densata* Bailey is an isolated population found in the Black Hills of Dakota. It makes a compact tree with light green needles and cylindrical cones 3-5 cm. It is in cultivation.

var. *porsildii* Raup has a broader crown, more hairy shoots and a smoother bark with resin blisters. It is the form from north-west Canada and Alaska.

Several cultivars have been named, including the following:

'Aurea' has the needles golden yellow above.

'Aureospicata' flushes yellow but the foliage matures to green.

'Caerulea' has blue-grey to silver short needles and a dense conical habit.

'Cecilia' originated on a witches broom; it makes a slow-growing upright plant with thick and dense silvery grey needles.

'Echiniformis' makes a flat globose plant, to 0.5 m high and 1 m across.

'Nana' makes a conic or globose plant with the branches spreading and erect. It has large, prominent buds, which distinguish it from 'Echiniformis'.

'Pendula' is based on a plant with pendulous branches.

Group 5

This group is related to group 4 but differs in the cones having thin papery loose scales.

P. engelmannii (Parry) Engelmann
Engelmann spruce

Tree to 40 m. Crown conical with rather short branches. Bark red-brown, becoming cracked into squarish hard scales. Shoot pale orange-brown to pale yellow-brown, later red-brown, finely hairy. Bud ovoid or conic, chestnut brown, shiny, 0.6 cm. Leaves more or less radial and forwards pointing, more parted below on weak shoots, soft, slender, flexible, apex rounded or pointed, glaucous or bluish green, 1.5-3 cm. Cone ovoid-cylindric, light brown, falling soon after ripening, scales flexible, irregularly toothed, 2.5-7.5 cm by 2-2.5 cm. Zone 3.

Engelmann spruce is found in the Rocky Mountains from British Columbia to Arizona and New Mexico; it is commonest in the northern part of this range, occurring in more scattered localities further south. It will grow well on very poor sites and is very hardy. In cultivation, it is not very common, although making a neat tree. It is very distinct in the foliage which is slender and lush, often, but not always, soft to the touch.

'Argentea' has more silvery grey needles.

'Fendleri' makes a tree with pendulous shoots and longer, bluish foliage.

'Glauca' is a very attractive cultivar with the needles a bright blue-green. Both this and 'Fendleri' are worthy of wider planting.

P. pungens Engelmann
Colorado spruce

Tree to 30 m. Crown dense, conic in young trees, columnar conic and open in old ones. Bark purplish grey, scaly. Shoot stout, glabrous, grooved, orange-brown to yellow-brown, later red-brown or purple-brown. Bud ovoid-conic, acute, scales often reflexed with a ring of awl-like scales at the base. Leaves radial but curved up from below, stout, stiff and very sharp, grey green or blue with a thick covering of glaucous wax, becoming greener in succeeding seasons, 1.5-3 cm. Cone cylindric, pale brown to white, scales flexible, notched and finely toothed, 7-12 cm by 2.5-3 cm. Zone 3.

Colorado spruce is found in rather scattered localities in the southern Rocky Mountains from Wyoming, Idaho, Utah, Arizona, New Mexico and Colorado. In the wild it comes from dry hot sites at high altitudes. Populations with green and blue foliage plants exist and it is mainly the latter which have been grown in cultivation. They belong to forma *glauca* (Regel) Beissner. These have been repeatedly selected to give very strongly-coloured blue foliage but suffer from aphids and from the natural tendency of the leaves to become less glaucous as they age. Also, unless the tree is growing vigorously, the strong blue outer foliage contrasts badly with the red-brown bare branches of the inner crown. Despite these drawbacks, the blue selections can make very attractive plants, at least when young. They have to be grafted and therefore may take a few years to get established and start to make erect growth.

The cultivars can be grouped under the following headings:

Blue Foliage — Tree Forms

'Koster' makes a conical tree with whorled branches and silvery blue needles. It was the first form of Blue spruce to be distributed. 'Hoopsii' has very blue-white foliage. 'Thomsen' is similar but with thicker needles. Other forms of Blue spruce commonly offered by nurserymen include 'Endtz', 'Hoto' and 'Spek'.

'Pendula' is a form with the branchlets pendulous, but foliage glaucous blue.

Blue Foliage — Dwarf Forms

'Montgomery' is a compact spreading or conical plant of slow growth and grey-blue leaves. 'Globosa' is probably the same plant.

Grafts of Blue spruce cultivars which fail to make a leader will form prostrate plants, although they may eventually produce a leading shoot. Some such plants have been named as dwarf forms in the past but can only be kept small or prostrate by pruning.

Special Foliage Forms

'Argentea' has the new shoots flushing silvery white, before becoming glaucous blue. The new foliage of most of the blue forms starts off silvery.

'Aurea' has the new growths golden, then changing to glaucous blue.

'Compacta' makes a dwarf, slow-growing plant with dark green needles. 'Globe' is a slow-growing globose form with grey-green foliage.

'Microphylla' is a tree form with short bluish green needles to 1.2 cm.

P. mexicana Martinez
Mexican spruce

Tree to 25 m. Crown conic. Bark whitish, scaly. Shoot pale yellow-brown, glandular hairy, becoming brown in third and fourth years. Bud globose, chestnut brown. Leaves forward and more or less radial, rather sparse, stiff, sharply pointed, 4-sided or compressed, grey-green or bluish green, 2-4 cm, by 0.1 cm or less. Cone ovoid-oblong, light brown, scales papery, thin, finely toothed, bract scale around half length of ovuliferous scale (proportionally smaller in other species), 4-6.5 cm. Zone 7.

Mexican spruce is found in a restricted region of north-east Mexico, in Coahuila and Nuevo Leon states to the east of Saltillo. It is allied to Engelmann spruce and has been treated as a subspecies (subsp. *mexicana* (Martinez) Taylor & Patterson) or variety (var. *mexicana* (Martinez) Silba) but seems sufficiently distinct to be regarded as a separate species. It differs from Engelmann spruce in the longer, stiffer and sharp needles, the paler bark and the large bract scale in the cones. From Colorado spruce it differs in the slender needles, hairy smooth shoots and the smaller cones. It is very restricted in the wild, being found in a few local stands over a small area of country; only discovered in 1962, it was nearly wiped out in part of its range in 1975 by a forest fire. It is hardy in cultivation and is making neat trees with somewhat glaucous blue crowns.

Group 6

This group includes a number of species with somewhat flat needles which have the majority of the stomata in 2 broad bands beneath, although with a few lines of stomata in 2 bands in the upper surface, the leaves usually being distinctly bevelled at the tip and the cones having papery, free scales.

P. likiangensis (Franchet) Pritzel
Likiang spruce

Tree to 30 m. Crown conic or broad conic, open in some forms but tight in others. Bark pale grey, becoming fissured. Shoot buff-brown or pale yellow-brown, glabrous or sparsely hairy. Bud conic, purple-brown, slightly resinous. Leaves rather open, parted below, forwards and slightly imbricate above, bluish with a few lines of stomata above, whitish blue with 2 broad bands beneath, acute, sharp, 0.6-1.5 cm by 0.1-0.15 cm. Female young cones bright red or reddish purple, up to 7.5 cm, erect. Cones cylindrical, purplish brown, scales with wavy margins, 7-15 cm by 3.5-5 cm. Zone 6.

Likiang spruce is found in north-west Yunnan, south-west Sichuan and in the drier parts of south-east Tibet or Xizang. The female cones are carried on young trees, particularly on dry sandy sites!, and are bright red whilst being pollinated. They then become pendent, and ripen through purple. The male cones are more frequent and variously pink or crimson.

Most of the plants in cultivation are from the type locality, the Lijiang or Likiang shan in Yunnan, yet despite this they are quite variable in crown habit, size of cones and hairiness of shoots. Some forms make very narrow conic trees but one form, introduced by George Forrest under his number 6746, has a very broad, open and rather gaunt crown with the base of the branches heavily tuberculated.

Likiang spruce ranks amongst the most beautiful of spruces, both for the young cones and the blue foliage. It is particularly useful for dry sites.

var. *linzhiensis* Cheng & Fu is described from south-east Xizang, north-west Yunnan and south-west Sichuan. It is said to differ in the leaves being without stomata on the upper surface or with only 1 or 2 rows, but is doubtfully distinct.

P. purpurea Masters
Purple-cone spruce

Tree to 30 m. Crown dense, columnar, or broad conic with the tips of the branches forming erect leading shoots. Bark orange-brown, flaky. Shoot pale buff-coloured, densely hairy, slender. Bud conic, chestnut brown, shiny. Leaves pressed tightly down above the shoot, parted beneath, glossy green with a smooth ridge above, usually without any stomata but sometimes with 1 or 2 incomplete lines, pale greyish green below with bands of stomata, apex acute, sharp, or rounded, mucronate, 0.7 1.2 cm by 0.1 0.18 cm. Cone purple from flowering until ripening purple-brown, ovoid, 2.5-4 cm, rarely to 6 cm, by 1.7-3 cm, scales rhombic. Zone 5.

Purple-cone spruce is native to north-west Sichuan, southern Gansu and Qinghai. It has been treated as a variety of Likiang spruce (var *purpurea* (Masters) Dallimore & Jackson) but really is quite different. The plants originally introduced by Ernest Wilson from west Sichuan in 1910 have made much taller, more columnar trees than those introduced by Joseph Rock from Gansu in the 1920s. Either form makes a very attractive green-leafed tree. The cones, unfortunately, are too small to make much of a display, but are attractive in detail. This tree will tolerate a wide range of sites and is quite hardy.

P. balfouriana Rehder & Wilson
Balfour spruce

This tree is very closely related to Purple-cone spruce, differing in the somewhat longer needles which are bluish grey above with a few lines of stomata and a brighter blue beneath and the larger cones, 4-9 cm with more rounded or acuminate scales. Zone 5.

Balfour spruce is found from south-west Sichuan, south Qinghai and eastern Tibet (Xizang), in very dry zones. It is often referred to Likiang spruce, as var. *balfouriana* (Rehder & Wilson) Hillier, but seems to appear to be closer to

Purple-cone spruce; if treated as a variety of Likiang spruce, the name would have to be changed to var. *rubescens* Rehder & Wilson.

Balfour spruce is in cultivation from seeds collected by Wilson and also by Harry Smith. One of the latter's plants at Göteborg Botanic Garden (Sweden) is markedly pendulous in its branching.

Two other spruces have been described from west Sichuan and share many characters with Balfour spruce. They are *P. montigena* Masters and *P. hirtella* Rehder & Wilson. The latter plant is in cultivation but is rare. Both have been treated as varieties of Likiang spruce (as var. *montigena* (Masters) Cheng ex Chen and var. *hirtella* (Rehder & Wilson) Cheng ex Chen), whilst *P. hirtella* has also been referred to as *P. balfouriana* var. *hirtella* (Rehder & Wilson) Cheng. The cultivated plants of *P. hirtella*, from north-west Sichuan, make an attractive densely foliaged grey-blue tree.

P. bicolor (Maximowicz) Mayr
Alcock spruce

Tree to 25 m. Crown broad conic, becoming rather open and gaunt in old trees. Bark purplish brown, becoming cracked into small square plates. Shoot white or pale orange-brown, becoming reddish brown, usually glabrous. Bud conic or rounded. Leaves below the shoot spreading and curved upwards, those above upwards and somewhat forwards, in young trees more imbricate, blue-green above with 2 distinct pale lines of stomata, whiter below, slightly compressed, 1-2 cm by 0.15 cm. Cone narrowly ovoid, scales obovate, rounded or slightly narrowed at apex, irregularly toothed, 6-12 cm by 3-5 cm. Zone 6.

Alcock spruce is native to the central part of the Japanese island of Honshu. It is hardy in cultivation and makes an interesting tree with its open crown.

var. *reflexa* Shirasawa & Koyama has shorter leaves and cone scales which are entire, with a slightly elongated, reflexed tip. It is restricted to the Akaishi range in central Honshu.

P. shirasawae Hayashi
Shirasawa spruce
(*P. bicolor* var. *acicularis* Shirasawa & Koyama)

This tree is very rare on Mount Yatsuga-dake in Honshu province, where it occurs with the equally rare Koyama spruce. It differs from Alcock spruce in the thin greyish flaky-scaly bark, the thicker, longer and more incurved bluish needles and the cones having rounded, obovate, smooth scales. It is in cultivation but is very rare. It may be a stabilised hybrid between Alcock and Koyama spruces. Zone 6.

P. glehnii (Schmidt) Masters
Glehn spruce

Tree to 30 m. Crown narrow conic. Bark purplish brown, fissuring into small flakes. Shoot golden reddish brown, deeply grooved and hairy in the grooves, becoming purplish dark red-brown. Bud ovoid or conic, red-brown, slightly resinous. Leaves spreading below the shoot, forwards and slightly imbricate above, dark green or blue green above with few stomata, stomata in 2 whitish bands below, apex obtuse or acute, 0.6-1.2 cm, longer on young trees, by 0.12-0.15 cm. Cone cylindric, dark purplish, scales suborbicular, entire or finely toothed, 5-8 cm. Zone 6.

Glehn spruce is recorded from the island of Sakhalin, off the coast of north-east Pacific Russia, and in Japan from Hokkaido and one locality on Honshu. It occurs in bogs and on very alkaline serpentine rocks. It is uncommon in cultivation but makes an interesting small tree.

Group 7

This small group consists of species with the flattened leaves bearing the stomata entirely or mainly on the underside (due to a twisting of the pulvinus — what appears as the underside in this group and several other species is, in fact, the upper surface!) and relatively small cones with thin flexible scales.

P. brachytyla (Franchet) Pritzel
Sargent spruce

Tree to 20 m. Crown conic, becoming domed. Bark grey or purplish grey, with reddish cracks, becoming scaly. Shoot white, buff or yellow-brown, sometimes somewhat pruinose, later orange-brown, glabrous or sparsely glandular hairy. Bud ovoid-conic, red-brown, 0.4 cm. Leaves parted beneath the shoot, those above imbricate, forwards pointing, deep shiny green above without stomata, 2 silvery white or bluish bands beneath, apex pointed or rounded, mucronulate, 1-2.2 cm by 0.1-0.15 cm. Cone cylindric or cylindric-ovoid, 6-12 cm. Zone 7.

Sargent spruce is native to central and western China, from Hubei, Sichuan and Yunnan, into east Tibet (Xizang) and south of the Himalayas from eastern Bhutan and Arunachal Pradesh in eastern India. Several forms have been named as species, including *P. complanata* Masters, *P. ascendens* Patschke and *P. sargentiana* Rehder & Wilson, but generally only the first is upheld as a variety, var. *complanata* (Masters) Cheng ex Rehder, with larger cones. The tree is in cultivation from several origins of Chinese seed but the Himalayan plants have not been introduced. It makes a very attractive tree, particularly the forms with the more strongly silver undersides to the leaves, and ranks as one of the best spruces for large gardens. The branchlets are pendent.

P. spinulosa (Griffiths) Henry
Sikkim spruce

Tree to 25 m, taller, to 60 m, in the eastern Himalayas. Crown conic, domed in old trees, branchlets markedly pendulous. Bark pink-grey, becoming fissured. Shoot glabrous, white to pale pinkish brown. Bud blunt, red-brown, ovoid. Leaves widely parted below, forwards along shoot above, radial on weeping shoots, dark shiny green above, 2 bluish white bands of stomata below, apex rounded, acute, 1.5-3.5 cm by 0.1-0.2 cm. Cone cylindric, scales semi-woody rhombic with finely toothed margins, glossy red-brown, 6-8 cm. Zone 7.

Sikkim spruce is recorded from Sikkim and Bhutan and possibly from elsewhere in the eastern Himalayas. The position is complicated in that some, at least, of the plants in Bhutan do not equate with the above description, which is based on the form in cultivation (which probably originated from Sikkimese seed). In eastern Bhutan, both Sikkim and Sargent spruces are recorded growing together, and this just happens to be the locality from which the type specimen of Sikkim spruce was collected; it is possible that there are three species in Bhutan — Sargent spruce, Sikkim spruce and one allied to Likiang spruce. Whatever the true affinities of Sikkim spruce, it makes a very attractive tree for a sheltered moist situation, with its pendulous branches.

P. farreri Page & Rushforth
Farrer spruce

Tree to 30 m. Crown open, conic, branches spreading, branchlets deeply descending or pendulous. Bark greyish, scaly. Shoot olive brown to pale orange-brown, dull or slightly shiny, sparsely glandular hairy, becoming pale tan or yellow-brown, shiny, by third year. Bud ovoid or ovoid-conic, slightly resinous, chestnut brown. Leaves nearly radial around shoot, point forwards, not tightly imbricate, sparse, blue-green, slightly bloomed above, vividly silver below, apex acute, 1.5-2.5 cm. Cone ellipsoid-cylindric, mid-brown, scales irregularly rounded, 6-10 cm by 3-4 cm. Zone 8.

Farrer spruce is only known from the Feng-Shui-ling of Upper Burma, although it may also occur in western Yunnan and parts of Arunachal Pradesh. It makes a very attractive tree with the bright silvery leaves and pendent foliage. It appears hardy, at least in mild areas, although preferring a moist site.

P. jezoensis (Siebold & Zuccarini) Carriere
Jezo spruce

Tree to 30 m. Crown conic, in old trees gaunt with spaced spreading branches. Bark brown in young trees, becoming purplish grey, fissured. Shoot white or pale yellow, shiny, glabrous, becoming orange-brown, rather stout and stiff. Bud ovoid, shining brown. Leaves parted below, strongly imbricate above and pointing forwards, especially on the line of leaves directly over the shoot, acute, mucronate, shiny dark green without stomata above, 2 whitish or bluish bands beneath, 1-2 cm by 0.15-0.2 cm. Cone cylindric, pale reddish brown, scales oblong, finely toothed, very thin, stiff, 4-6.5 cm. Zone 4.

Jezo spruce is native to Honshu and Hokkaido islands of Japan, to Sakhalin, Pacific Russia and to north-east China. It is variable in a number of characters and in the *Chinese Flora* (see Bibliography), vars. *microsperma* (Lindley) Cheng & Fu, *komarovii* (Vassil) Cheng & Fu and *ajanensis* (Fischer) Cheng & Fu are recognised, differing in details of cones and cone scales. The plants from Honshu are also often separated, as var. *hondoensis* (Mayr) Rehder, with the leaves bright silvery beneath and a dark green above. This last plant is the form in cultivation, those from further north suffering from spring frosts due to their coming into leaf too early.

'Aurea' is a form in which the new foliage is golden yellow, fading through brown to green.

P. sitchensis (Bongard) Carriere
Sitka spruce

Tree to 60 m, taller in the wild. Crown conic, with wide-spreading branches, base of branches in old trees tuberuculate. Bark dark purple-brown, becoming greyer in old trees with large scales. Shoot white or buff, glabrous, becoming more orange in second year. Bud ovoid, resinous, blunt, brown. Leaves parted below shoot, imbricate above, stiff, very sharp, bright dark green above with 1 or 2 lines of stomata, below with stomata in white or bluish bands, 2-2.5 cm. Cone cylindric, pale brown or nearly white, scales thin, stiff, irregularly toothed, 5-10 cm by 3 cm. Zone 6.

Sitka spruce is native to western North America from Kodiak Island in Alaska to northern California, but always within 80 km of the sea. It makes a tall tree with a majestic large diameter bole. In cultivation it is widely planted for timber production, tolerating poor, exposed and wet sites. It is less useful as an amenity tree, although where there is space, and a suitably cool and moist climate, it does make a large tree quickly. The underside of the foliage is often displayed, at least in patches on the crown, and can look interesting, although plantations of millions of small trees deaden the effect.

'Compacta' makes a broadly conical dwarf form to 2 m.

'Papoose' is a dense compact form with dark blue-green leaves, silvery beneath; it grows at the rate of 4 cm per annum. 'Tenas' is similar but the upper surface of the leaves is lime-green.

'Strypemonde' is a very slow globose plant with blue-green needles. It originated as a witches broom.

Hybrid Spruces

A number of species hybridise naturally in the wild where they meet, such as Sitka and White spruces (*P. × lutzii* Little), or White and Engelmann spruces or Norway and Siberian spruces (*P. × fennica* (Regel) Komarov). Many other hybrids have been raised in artificial crosses made either to try to breed faster or healthier trees, or to investigate relationships. Only the following, however, has shown any promise as an amenity tree.

P. × mariorika Boom (*P. mariana* × *P. omorika*)

This tree differs from the parents in the broadly conical habit, short pubescent shoots, narrow blue-green needles which have 2 broad bands of stomata below and 0-2 lines of stomata above and smaller cones. It makes an interesting bluish green tree. Zone 5.

Pilgerodendron Florin **Cupressaceae**

This is a monotypic genus, at one time included in *Libocedrus*. It is distinguished by the awl-like (not scale) leaves and the cones with 4 scales but with only the upper pair fertile and each bearing 2 seeds.

P. uviferum (Pilger) Florin
Pilgerodendron

Tree or shrub. Crown conic. Bark thin, exfoliating in long strips. Shoot yellow-green for several years, then bright brown. Leaves in decussate equal spreading pairs, thick, stiff, decurrent, spaced, incurved, triangular and keeled on back, stomata in broad whitish green band on inner face, outer faces yellow-green, 0.5 cm by 0.1 cm. Cone ovoid, ripening brown, fertile scales with incurved 0.3 cm hooked point, sterile scales smaller, 0.8-1.3 cm. Seed with 2 unequal wings. Zone 7.

Pilgerodendron is native to the southern Andes in Chile and western Argentina and makes a tree to 20 m. In cultivation it is hardy, except in cold districts, although it may be damaged by cold weather. It makes a small very fastigiate plant and is exceedingly slow in growth, attaining no more than 8 m. It probably requires a mild and damp situation to flourish. It is rare.

Pinus Linnaeus **Pines Pinaceae**

The pines are the largest and most diverse genus of conifers; they are the most important genus economically and are found throughout the northern hemisphere and, in Indonesia, just across the Equator.

Pines are characterised by the leaves which are of two types. The most obvious leaves, which carry out all the photosynthesis, are in bundles of 2-5, rarely 1 or 6-8. These bundles, normally called fascicles (after the bundle of sticks around the axe which represented the power of the Roman senate) are in fact short shoots and have a minute bud in the centre; only if the main buds are lost in the first year or so can the bud in the short shoots develop further. The needles in a fascicle are segments of a circle and if fitted together will make a cylinder; they are, therefore, a rounded triangle or semicircular in cross-section. Stomata may be carried on all three surfaces or on just the inner two sides. The margins of the leaves are usually finely serrate or toothed. The base of the short shoots and needles is enclosed in a sheath which represents the bud scales; these may be persistent or deciduous within the first season.

The second type of leaf consists of small triangular brown scales; they are set singly and spirally on the shoots. The leaf-bearing short shoots (or male cones) are carried in the axils of these scale leaves and are radial in arrangement. In many species the scale leaves are decurrent on the shoot, which is then ridged and grooved.

Young plants, and in a few species older ones too, produce juvenile leaves. These are solitary, spirally set, linear-lanceolate with toothed margins. Very often they are somewhat glaucous. Morphologically they are the same as the scale leaves.

The male cones are carried instead of the leaf fascicles at the base of the current season's growth; after shedding the pollen, they turn brown and are quickly lost, leaving the basal portion of the shoot bare. Pollination occurs when the pollen is shed in early summer and lands on the receptive female flowers. Female cones usually are set either terminally or at subterminal nodes on the current year's growth in the axils of scale leaves, although occasionally elsewhere on the shoots. Fertilisation of the ovules, i.e. the joining of the two haploid cells, only occurs at the beginning of the second summer (except for two species where it is delayed a further season) and the cones ripen in the next autumn/winter period.

The cones are woody, composed of many scales set spirally along the rachis. The cones expand rapidly in size in the second year after fertilisation, making the mature size in a few weeks. The portion of the cone which represents the pre-fertilisation growth is known as the *umbo* and often ends in a prickle. The umbo may be either terminal or dorsal on the enlarged scale. The part of the cone which is exposed when the cone is shut is called the *apophysis*. Bract scales in *Pinus* are small and insignificant. Species differ in whether the cones open on maturity or after a period, e.g. after a forest fire.

The seeds are relatively large and are edible in a number of species. They may have either an effective wing for wind dispersal or have only a rudimentary wing. The kernel is enclosed in a thick woody shell or *testa*. Germination in all species is epigeal, i.e. the cotyledons are raised above the soil surface and act as the first leaves; the number of cotyledons varies from 4-23. In most species, the seedling makes an erect growing shoot in the first year. However, in some species from the southern parts of the range, there is a 'grass' stage in which the young plant makes an extensive root system but keeps the bud at ground level, surrounded by many grass-like leaves. After a period, the bud grows up to 4 m in one year with a single unbranched stem. A 'grass' stage is considered a protection against grass fires, reducing the time which the young tree spends with the growing point at the susceptible height.

The pines are odd in the way that shoot growth is made. The axis of the shoots elongate over a period, usually of a few weeks, and at this stage all the shoots are erect. Subsequently the needle fascicles develop and only then do the shoots adopt the normal spreading posture (only erect in the case of the leading shoot). The stage when the shoots lengthen is called the 'candle' stage, as the emerging erect shoots look like candles. The trees can be quite attractive, in an odd sort of way, at this time.

The branches are in whorls, without inter-nodal branches. Most pines are uni-nodal, with but a single whorl of branches (i.e. one new node) per annum. A number of species are multi-nodal and produce 2-4 whorls of branches in a season. The female cones are always carried at the nodes.

Pine timber varies in quality between species but in some is very good. Some species also yield resin or 'naval stores', i.e. turpentine or pitch. This is extracted either by tapping the living trees (making a cut through the bark and collecting the flow of resin in a cup) or by distilling chipped wood. The resin yields turpentine, pitch and rosin — the latter product being used to fill or 'size' paper.

In the garden pines can be used as shelter or backcloth planting, as dwarf plants or as ground cover but are most attractive as majestic specimen trees. They are well adapted to dry barren sandy sites, although very happy on richer ones. Some species will tolerate chalky sites but several, such as Scots pine, may become chlorotic after a number of years. They will not tolerate any shading, needing good light, if not full sunlight. Most pines will naturally lose the lower branches but any shading makes the tendency more pronounced.

Propagation is best effected by seed but where this is not available, grafting will probably have to be used. Cuttings can be rooted but are difficult to root unless seedling plants less than ten years old are available to give the cuttings. Single leaf fascicles, with the base of the short shoot, can be rooted but are difficult to get to grow away; disbudding the shoots some weeks prior to taking the cuttings can increase the chance of success.

The genus is divided into three well-marked subgenera.

Subgenus *Ducampopinus* contains but a single species, *P. krempfii*, which is well marked by the 2 needles being very flattened, not semicircular in cross-section, narrowly lanceolate, not needle-like, and relatively broad. The needles contain a single fibro-vascular bundle (see below). It has been treated as a separate genus, *Ducampopinus* A. Cheval.

Subgenus *Strobus* is separated absolutely from the typical subgenus by the needles containing but a single fibro-vascular bundle, and the cones not having a differently coloured band where the scales meet, therefore they are two-tone in coloration. The fibro-vascular tissue is the conductive material which runs along the centre of most conifer needles and contains xylem and phloem elements (i.e. wood and bark tissues); it can easily be seen in a leaf section under a microscope!

However, the subgenus is well marked by the following characters, although with some overlap. The cones are relatively soft, not fully woody and either open on maturity or fall intact; the sheath of bud scales at the base of each fascicle is soon deciduous, although only partly or tardily deciduous in section *Parrya*; the scale leaves are not decurrent on the shoot, the needles are usually in 5s, although species with 1-4 needles occur; the stomata are often only on the 2 inner faces of the needle; the bark is often smooth for several years, only becoming scaly or platy in old trees; the timber is relatively soft with the annual growth rings obscure, and not very resinous. The species in this subgenus are commonly called 'soft pines'. The shoots are uni-nodal, except in *P. nelsonii*. A synonymous name for this subgenus is *haploxylon*, referring to the single vascular bundle.

Subgenus *Strobus* is divided up into two sections. Section *Strobus* has the umbo terminal on the cone scale in the mature cone. It contains two subsections and 21 species. Section *Parrya* has the umbo dorsal on the fully developed cone scales; it contains four subsections and 17 species. The subsections are discussed below.

Subgenus *Pinus* is characterised by the leaves having two fibro-vascular bundles. It is further distinguished by the hard woody and often oblique cones which have the umbo dorsal on the scale; the often decurrent base of the scale leaves; the short shoots containing 2, 3 or 5 needles with a sheath which persists for the life of the fascicle, except in section *Leiophyllae* where it is deciduous; the timber is usually resinous and there is a much more pronounced difference between the wood laid down in spring (soft) and summer (hard) of the one year, hence 'Hard pines'. A number of species are multi-nodal. A synonymous name for this subgenus is *diploxylon*, referring to the two vascular bundles.

Subgenus *Pinus* contains four sections. Section *Pinaster* Koch is characterised by the very hard, woody, serotinous cones reddish in colour with fairly large seeds; long retention (more than two years) of the juvenile leaves; thick platy bark; characteristic curled bud scales. It contains two subsections and six species. Section *Leiophyllae* Vanderburgh is characterised by the deciduous fascicle sheath and contains two species. Section *Taeda* Spach has cones with a distinct spine on the umbo and contains four subsections and 48 species. Section *Pinus* differs from the other subsections of subgenus *Pinus* in the wood ray cells having very large ('fenestriform') pits between the cells, all the other sections having very small such pits. It contains one subsection with 21 species.

The synopsis of the genus presented below follows, with some modification, that proposed by Little & Critchfield (see Bibliography).

SUBGENUS *DUCAMPOPINUS* (A. Cheval) de Ferre
Section *Ducampopinus*
Subsection *Krempfianae* Little & Critchfield
krempfii

SUBGENUS *STROBUS* Lemmon
Section *Strobus*
Subsection *Cembrae* Loudon
cembra, sibirica, koraiensis, pumila, albicaulis.
Subsection *Strobi* Loudon
strobus, chiapensis, monticola, lambertiana, flexilis, reflexa, strobiformis, ayacahuite, peuce, wallichiana, bhutanica, armandii, amamiana, dabeshanensis, dalatensis, fenzeliana, parviflora, morrisonicola, wangii, kwangtungensis.
Section *Parrya* Mayr
Subsection *Cembroides* Engelmann
cembroides, edulis, monophylla, quadrifolia, culminicola, remota, discolor, johannis, maximartinezii, pinceana, nelsonii.
Subsection *Gerardianae* Loudon
bungeana, gerardiana.
Subsection *Balfourianae* Engelmann
aristata, longaeva, balfouriana.
Subsection *Rzedowskianae* Caravajal
rzedowskii

SUBGENUS *PINUS*
Section *Pinaster* Koch
Subsection *Pineae* Little & Critchfield
pinea
Subsection *Pinaster* Loudon
canariensis, roxburghii, pinaster, halepensis, brutia.
Section *Leiophyllae* Vanderburgh
Subsection *Leiophyllae* Loudon
leiophylla, lumholtzii.
Section *Taeda* Spach
Subsection *Taeda* Loudon
palustris, taeda, echinata, glabra, rigida, serotina, pungens, elliottii, densa, caribaea, occidentalis, cubensis.
Subsection *Ponderosae* Loudon
ponderosa, arizonica, engelmannii, durangensis, jeffreyi, washoensis, coulteri, sabiniana, torreyana, montezumae, rudis, cooperi, hartwegii, devoniana, wincesteriana,

pseudostrobus, estevesii, oaxacana, apulcensis, douglasiana, maximinoi.
Subsection *Contortae* Little & Critchfield
contorta, banksiana, virginiana, clausa.
Subsection *Oocarpae* Little & Critchfield
radiata, muricata, attenuata, greggii, patula, pringlei, jaliscana, oocarpa, teocote, herrerai, lawsonii.
Section *Pinus*
Subsection *Sylvestres* Loudon
sylvestris, densiflora, tabuliformis, takahasii, densata, yunnanensis, kesiya, merkusii, massoniana, henryi, mugo, uncinata, nigra, heldreichii, leucodermis, resinosa, tropicaulis, thunbergii, luchuensis, taiwanensis, hwangshanensis.

Subsection *Krempfianae* Little & Critchfield
This subsection contains only the following species.

P. krempfii Lecomte
Krempf pine
Tree 15-30 m tall. Bark red-brown, smooth. Sheath deciduous. Leaves 2 per fascicle, flattened, narrowly lanceolate, sharply pointed, 4-7 cm by 0.15-0.4 cm. Cone ovoid, red-brown, opening at maturity, 5 cm by 4 cm; apophysis pyramidal; umbo dorsal. Zone 10.

This unique species is only recorded from south Vietnam, between Dalat and Nhatrang. It has not been introduced, but could conceivably be hardy in the mildest regions as it occurs at altitudes of up to 2,000 m.

Subsection *Cembrae* Loudon
This subsection has cones which do not open, or dehisce, to release the seeds. Instead, the entire cone drops to the ground where it is broken up, usually by small mammals, and the seeds scattered (or eaten!). The seedwing is reduced to a mere rim. The leaves are in fascicles of 5. The group includes four species from northern Eurasia and one in western North America. It may not justify separation from subsection *Strobi*.

P. cembra Linnaeus
Arolla or Swiss stone pine
Tree to 25 m. Crown narrowly columnar, dense. Bark smooth, dark grey, becoming fissured red-brown and scaly. Shoot densely covered with brown hairs. Bud ovoid-conic, sharply pointed, dull brown with closely pressed scales, 0.6 cm. Leaves in close fascicles, a few lines of stomata on the outer, dark shiny green surface, many stomata on the bluish white inner

faces, only 2 resin canals in the corners of the leaf near the outer side, 7-9 cm. Cone broad oblong-conic, blue or purple-green, rarely green, ripening brown, resinous, falling in autumn of second or third year, 6-8 cm by 6 cm. Scales thick, obtuse. Seed 1-2 cm. Zone 5.

Arolla pine is found in the Alps and Carpathian Mountains of central Europe where it grows from 1,500 m to the treeline. It forms a very neat densely foliage tree, of rather slow growth in cultivation. It will grow in most situations and will flourish on northern aspects or moist heavy clay soils. For optimum development it likes a cool moist site; unthrifty trees are open and not very attractive.

'Aureovariegata' has yellow leaves. It is slow-growing.

'Chalet' makes a dense rounded column of soft bluish green foliage.

'Monophylla' has all 5 needles connate but inclined to throw out the occasional normal shoot. It makes a dwarf plant.

'Pendula' has pendulous branches. At the other extreme is 'Stricta' which has ascending branches and makes a narrow column.

P. sibirica du Tour
Siberian stone pine

Tree to 35 m, or occasionally shrubby. Crown narrowly conical or ovoid. Bud scales glossy brown. Leaves dark green with stomata only on the inner 2 bluish surfaces, 3 resin canals, 1 in each corner, 6-11 cm by 0.15-0.17 cm. Cone 5-12 cm by 3-8 cm. Seeds with a thin shell. Zone 3.

Siberian stone pine is found from the Ural Mountains as far east as 125°E. It occurs along the Altai shan of northern Mongolia and Xinjiang province of China. An isolated population of plants is also reported much further west on the Kola peninsula, near the Russian/Norwegian/Finnish border. It is commonly found in wet situations, in Xinjiang occurring along streams. The seeds are an important food source. In cultivation it is slow-growing.

P. koraiensis Siebold & Zuccarini
Korean pine

Tree to 20 m in cultivation but up to 50 m in its native habitat. Crown columnar with a conic apex. Bark smooth, dark grey, becoming fissured in old trees with scaly ridges. Shoot green-brown, covered by dense orange-brown curly hairs. Bud ovoid, sharply pointed, scales with long free tips, dark brown. Leaves with fascicles tight in first season, opening out in second year, deep shiny green outside with a few lines of stomata, broad band of silvery white stomata on 2 inner surfaces, resin canals 3, 1 in each corner, apex blunt, 6-12 cm. Cone cylindric-conic,

bright green or sometimes purple, 9-16 cm by 6-8 cm; scales rhombic with the acute apex spreading. Seed 1.2-1.6 cm by 0.7-1 cm, cotyledons 13-16. Zone 3.

Korean pine is recorded in north-east Asia from Korea, Manchuria and adjoining Pacific Russia. It is also found on high mountains on the Japanese islands of Honshu and Shikoku. It has a valuable timber and also provides edible nuts.

It is amenable to cultivation, although slow-growing as a young plant and preferring a cool moist climate.

'Compacta Glauca' is a compact but not dwarf form with thick branches and blue-green foliage. 'Silveray' is similar with bluer leaves.

'Tortuosa' is a tree form with the needles spirally twisted.

'Variegata' has the leaves variously entirely yellow or bordered with or partly yellow.

'Winton' has blue-grey leaves and makes a beautiful wide-spreading dwarf form, to 2 m high and twice as wide. It has been suggested that it may be a form of *P. pumila.*

P. pumila Regel
Dwarf Siberian pine

Shrub, often prostrate but rarely a small tree to 6 m. Shoots green-brown, becoming grey-brown in second year, with a dense covering of hairs. Bud cylindric-conic, shortly pointed, resinous, scales lanceolate, tightly adpressed, red-brown, 0.6-1 cm. Leaves shorter than those of P. cembra and less toothed, or occasionally untoothed, dark green without stomata on outer surface, bright blue-green with lines of stomata on 2 inner surfaces, 2 resin canals near the rounded outer margin, 4-6 cm, rarely to 8 cm, by 0.1 cm. Male cones bright red-purple, very showy in late spring. Cone ovoid, violet-purple when growing, ripening to red-brown or yellow brown, 3-6 cm by 2.5-3 cm, scales rounded, adpressed, with a reflexed tip, seed pear-shaped, 0.7-1 cm by 0.5-0.7 cm. Zone 5.

Dwarf Siberian pine, also known as Japanese stone pine, is native to east Siberia, extending to the Pacific ocean, in north-eastern China and in scattered localities in Honshu, Hokkaido and Korea. It forms extensive forests of scrub, rarely making a tree. It is very hardy and in cultivation is useful, though too uncommon, as a blue-foliaged small pine.

'Draijers Dwarf' is a prostrate and compact growing form with blue foliage.

'Glauca' is a bushy slow form (the species never is fast!) with blue-grey foliage. 'Blue Dwarf' is similar, but makes a flat-topped bush wider than high, approximately 40 cm high by 50 cm wide after ten years.

'Globe' is a dwarf globular form with blue foliage. It grows at the rate of 4 cm per annum.

'Jermyns' is a conical form.

'Jeddeloh' is a vigorous nest-forming spreading plant with leaves bright green on the outer surface, blue-white on the inner 2 sides.

P. albicaulis Engelmann
Whitebark pine

Tree to 15 m. Crown spreading on a short bole. Bark whitish grey, smooth, becoming scaly. Shoots reddish brown, stout, hairy, flexible. Bud ovoid, pointed, resinous, with acuminate scales, yellow-brown or red-brown. Leaves bunched at ends of shoot, dull green with stomata on all 3 surfaces, 1-3 resin canals, margins not toothed, 4-7 cm by 0.1 cm. Cone sub-globose, purple-brown, 4-8 cm by 4-6 cm, scales thick, with stout pointed umbos. Zone 4.

Whitebark pine is recorded in the Rocky Mountains from south-west Alberta and central British Columbia south to the Sierra Nevada in central California. It makes a small treeline tree. It is very similar to the sympatric *P. flexilis*, from which reliably it can be distinguished only by the non-opening cones with smaller seeds. Both species are unusual in this section *Strobus* in that the margins of the leaves are not toothed.

Whitebark pine is amenable to cultivation but is not as attractive a tree as most pines.

'Flinck' is a dwarf form which originated from a cone on a witches broom.

'Nobles Dwarf' is a shrubby form of compact habit.

Subsection *Strobi* Loudon
White pines

This group of species share the following features. The leaves are almost invariably 5 to a fascicle, any deviation being an aberration and not constant. The margins are usually serrate, but entire in the species as mentioned below; the sheath is deciduous within the first year, rarely persisting until the beginning of the second summer. The cones are carried on a distinct peduncle, usually of 2-3 cm, but shorter in *P. parviflora* and the species related to it; they are displayed during the first year as long-stalked oblong conelets. They become relatively long and narrow and open at maturity; the umbo is terminal on the scale. The seeds have an adnate wing, this is one which is firmly attached to the seed (unlike the articulate wing found in some other groups which grips the seed by means of two prongs and can be removed and replaced without damaging it); the wing is usually long and functional, although in several species it is short and inoperative.

The species in this group are evenly divided between North America and Asia, with one species in southern Europe. They include some very attractive species, but prefer conditions giving some shelter from strong or cold winds.

P. strobus Linnaeus
Weymouth or Eastern white pine

Tree to 50 m. Crown slender conic in young trees with open upswept branching, in older trees becoming domed and twiggy. Bark dark grey, smooth, as the tree ages becoming darker grey or blackish, deeply fissured and cracked. Shoot slender, olive brown, shiny in the first winter, becoming olive green and grey in later years, smooth and leafless in the third year, weakly hairy on the ridge behind each fascicle in the first year, more generally hairy on weak shoots only, soon glabrous. Bud cylindrical, apex conical, shortly acuminate, scales tight, mid- to pale brown, clusters of 5-10 at the ends of strong shoots, 1 cm. Leaves forwards along the shoot, more spreading in second season, linear, acute, grey-green with 2-3 lines of stomata on the outer face, greyish white with several lines on the inner faces, rarely persisting into third season, 8-14 cm by 0.07 cm. Cone pendulous, tapered cylindric, green, ripening brown, 8-15 cm, rarely to 24 cm. Seed 0.5-0.8 cm with wing 1.8-2.5 cm. Zone 3.

Weymouth pine is found in eastern North America in the area encompassed by the triangle from Newfoundland to south-east Manitoba to northern Georgia. It used to be a very significant element in the broadleaved forests, with trees emerging high above the other trees but over-cutting and White pine blister rust (see page 68) have devastated the species. The species has a very good timber, in the past much used as yellow pine in furniture or for templates as it is easy to work accurately.

Weymouth pine is hardy and fast-growing in cultivation. It is not, however, very attractive as the leaves are usually shed after the second or in the third summer, making the tree very open crowned; also they do not have the attractive colour or length of other species. It is not tolerant of atmospheric pollution.

'Alba' is a tree form with the new foliage whitish green. It is also called 'Nivea'.

'Fastigiata' develops a columnar crown composed of branches which rise at around 30° to the vertical.

'Inversa' has the branches pendulous; in 'Pendula' the branches are horizontal, with the branchlets pendulous.

'Macropin' makes a broad, open rounded bush to 1 m high and across. The leaves are blue-green and shorter, less than 8 cm. It was propagated from a witches broom.

'Prostrata' is a procumbent plant, too open to be useful for ground cover, but with a gravel mulch it will let bulbs show through.

'Pumila' is a dwarf form with silvery green twisted needles. It makes a globose plant, growing at 5 cm per annum. 'Radiata' is similar in the dwarf globose habit but has the leaves arranged more radially, not pendulous.

'Umbraculifera' makes an umbrella-shaped plant, to 2.5 m, and wider than high. The leaves are short and the appearance is less than pleasing.

'Variegata' has leaves variously yellow and green.

P. chiapensis (Martinez) Andresen
Chiapas pine
(P. strobus var. chiapensis Martinez)

This pine occurs at low altitudes in the southern Mexican states of Veracruz and Chiapas and also in western Guatemala and Belize, a distance of some 2,400 km from the nearest Weymouth pine populations. The plant has smaller cones with more rounded scales and shorter needles. Zone 10.

P. monticola Douglas
Western white pine
Tree 35 m, occasionally to 60 m in the wild. Crown narrowly conical in young trees, broadening to columnar in old trees, with horizontal branching. Bark smooth, dark grey, developing squarish or rectangular plates. Shoot rusty pubescent all over, not dense on strong shoots, brownish green or coppery brown. Bud cylindric-ovoid, pointed, scales free at tips, dark orange-brown, 1.2 cm. Leaves with stomata on all faces, few on pale green outer side, more on bluish green inner faces, persist 3-4 years, 7-10 cm. Cone narrow conic, 13-35 cm, usually 15-27 cm. Zone 7.

Western white pine occurs on both sides of the Rocky Mountains from British Columbia south to central California where it is a montane species. It has been severely affected by White pine blister rust but shows a greater degree of inherent resistance.

Western white pine is similar to Weymouth pine, but can be identified by the more general, though on strong shoots sparse, covering of hairs, the leaves lasting three or four years and the generally longer cones. The cones have a different arrangement of the scales in spirals; in Western white pine, starting from one scale, the two spirals come together in one scale after 8 and 21 scales, the respective numbers in Weymouth pine are 5

and 13.

In cultivation Western white pine is uncommon. It does, however, make a much better tree than Weymouth pine, with its more luxuriant foliage.

'Minima' is a dwarf form with short needles; it was propagated from a witches broom.

'Pendula' is a plant in which the branches are pendulous.

P. lambertiana Douglas
Sugar pine
Tree to 25 m but up to 70 m in the wild. Crown conical, developing spaced horizontal branches on a long branch-free bole. Bark thin, smooth, grey-green on young trees, becoming thick with scaly ridges in old trees. Shoot with rusty hairs at first, becoming smooth, orange-brown. Bud cylindric, acute, chestnut brown, to 0.8 cm. Leaves forwards along the shoot, stout, twisted, deep green on outer face, bluish white on inner surfaces, persisting 2-3 years, 5-10 cm by 0.2 cm. Cone large, cylindric, hanging down at tips of branches, 25-65 cm, usually 30-50 cm. Seed 1.2 cm, wing 2.5-4 cm. Zone 7.

Sugar pine is found from western Oregon south to northern Baja California del Norte in Mexico. It occurs on cooler and moister sites than the other western North American pines. The common name refers to a resinous exudation from the bark following injury and which is sweet to eat. It is more susceptible to Blister rust than Western white and Weymouth pines. In cultivation it is uncommon.

P. flexilis James
Limber pine
Tree to 10-25 m. Crown conical, becoming rounded as the tree ceases making height growth. Bark smooth, thin, grey-white, becoming slightly fissured. Shoots pliant, hairy, green, later grey-brown. Bud cylindric-conic, scales free at tips, red-brown, grey at base, to 1.3 cm. Leaves in tight spaced fascicles, forwards along shoots in first year, later spreading, persist 5-6 years, dark green with faint lines of stomata, usually on all faces, margins entire, or a few well-spaced teeth at the apex, 4-9 cm. Male cones red. Cone ovoid-conic, tapers from lower third, 7-15 cm (possibly to 25 cm) by 4-6 cm; scales thickened, tip points forwards or slightly reflexed. Seed with wing reduced to a rim 0.1 cm, 0.8-1.1 cm by 0.6-0.8 cm. Zone 4.

Limber pine is found in western North America along the Rocky Mountains from south-west Alberta to northern Arizona. The exact distribution is unclear as it has been confused with both of the following species and probably hybridises or intergrades with them. It is very similar in foliage (but not in cone) to the sympatric Whitebark pine and the ranges of the two trees are similarly imprecise.

Limber pine makes a small tree in cultivation

but is uncommon. It will thrive on most sites.

'Firmament' is a selection with blue foliage, said to be resistant to Blister rust, which can affect the species. 'Glenmore' has silvery blue foliage, with longer needles.

'Nana' is a bushy dwarf form in which the needles are only 3 cm long.

'Pendula' is a plant which has weeping shoots, including the leader. It can be trained to form a weeping tree, or used to cascade over boulders on the rockery.

'Tiny Temple' is a low plant with green and grey-blue leaves. It will grow at the rate of 10 cm per annum.

P. reflexa (Engelmann) Engelmann
Southern limber pine

Tree to 20 m. Crown columnar-conic. Bark smooth bluish grey on young trees and in upper positions of old ones, becoming cracked in many small square plates. Bud cylindrical, resinous, light brown, small. Leaves slender, flexible, glaucous green, stomata only on the inner 2 faces, margins with small distant teeth, 6-11 cm. Cone bright green when immature, ripening yellow-brown, 13-23 cm; scales usually spreading or slightly reflexed with an elongated apophysis but sometimes adpressed with a rounded apophysis on the same tree, thick. Seed dark brown or black with a rudimentary wing 0.2 cm, 1.5-2 cm by 0.8-1 cm. Zone 6.

This tree occurs from Nuevo Leon and eastern Coahuila in north-east Mexico. Similar plants are recorded from the southern border of the USA and in the northern Mexican state of Chihuahua and Durango. The exact distribution is very confused as the tree has invariably been relegated to synonymy with either *P. flexilis* or *P. strobiformis*. Of the two, it is closer to *P. flexilis*. The above description is based on the plants found on Cerro Potosi in Nuevo Leon state where it occurs on the moister eastern side, near the top of the mountain at above 3,000 m. This plant may not be the same as the one Engelmann described as a variety of *P. flexilis*, in which case a new name may be required.

The tree is variable in cone scales. Most cones have scales which are free during the growing period but a few cones with adpressed scales may occur on the same tree with the other form.

Southern limber pine is in cultivation from seeds I collected on Cerro Potosi. Also some of the older plants recorded as *P. flexilis* may belong here. It should make an interesting tree with green foliage, tolerant of very dry sites and be perfectly hardy.

P. strobiformis Engelmann
Southwestern white pine

Tree to 30 m. Crown conical, in old trees columnar-conic, with level spreading branches. Bark grey-white on young trees, dark brown and ridged on old ones. Shoot with reddish brown hairs at first, becoming glabrous and pruinose. Bud oblong-ovate, to cylindrical, resinous, light reddish brown. Leaves slender, dark to bluish green, stomata only on the 2 inner faces, margins serrate with small spaced teeth, 9-13 cm. Cone sub-cylindrical, resinous, tapers to apex, 15-30 cm, rarely longer; scales dark brown, thick, apophysis prolonged, reflexed. Seed with a rudimentary wing sometimes to 0.8 cm, around 1.5 cm long by 0.7-1 cm wide. Zone 6.

This pine is found in northern Mexico from the states of Chihuahua, Durango, Coahuila, Sinaloa and northern Jalisco. It also occurs in the southern USA along the border with Mexico. Similar plants from southern Nuevo Leon may also belong here. It occurs in moist sheltered sites, usually on rich, well-drained soils.

It has been confused with both *P. reflexa* and *P. ayacahuite*, and has been treated as a variety of the latter, as *P. ayacahuite* var. *brachyptera* Shaw. From *P. reflexa* it differs in the longer cone with the scales having a much longer reflexed apophysis and the slightly longer leaves. From *P. ayacahuite* it differs in the rudimentary wing to the longer seed and the shorter foliage. Recently, plants from north-west Jalisco have been named as a new species, *P. novo-galiciana* Caravajal, but seem to be referable to this species as a variety or subspecies.

P. strobiformis is rare in cultivation, but comes from a part of Mexico where cold winters are experienced.

P. ayacahuite Ehrenberg ex Schlectendal
Mexican white pine

Tree to 45 m, usually smaller. Crown conical, in old trees becoming columnar. Bark smooth, ash grey, becoming fissured and rough, scaly on old trees. Shoot finely pubescent, pale yellow-brown with abrupt ridges in first winter, grey and smooth in the second. Bud cylindric-conic, pale brown, with spreading scales, not resinous, 1.5 cm. Leaves radial, or tending to point forwards and droop below the shoot somewhat, shiny green on outer face without stomata, inner 2 faces with several lines of stomata and whitish blue, margins with regular fine teeth, leaves retained 3-4 years, 10-20 cm, usually around 12-14 cm, by 0.1 cm. Cone cylindrical, apex conical, very resinous, yellow-brown, 20-45 cm; scales thin, somewhat elongated, the basal infertile scales on the cone usually strongly reflexed. Seed less than 1 cm, usually 0.7-0.8 cm, dark grey with brown spots, wing long, functional, 3-4 cm. Zone 7.

This species is found in southern Mexico from the region south of the capital down to northern

Guatemala. It makes a vigorous tree with the foliage appearing bluish. The species has quite a wide altitudinal distribution, in Guatemala occurring at over 3,000 m and plants from this part of the range are hardy, provided not exposed to strong cold winds.

var. *veitchii* (Roezl) Shaw differs in the larger seed, around 1.3 cm, with a wing of around 2 cm which is semi-functional. The bud is ovoid-conic, sharply pointed with adpressed erect or slightly free chestnut brown scales, to 1 cm. The cones have broader, thicker scales which are somewhat rounded triangular. It is recorded from central Mexico, from the states of Hidalgo, Pueblo, Morelos, Michoacan and Veracruz, to the north of the area in which *P. ayacahuite* is found. In some respects it might be better treated as a subspecies of *P. strobiformis*. var. *veitchii* is in cultivation and is one of the parents of *P. × holfordiana*.

P. peuce Grisebach
Macedonian pine

Tree to 30 m. Crown ovoid or columnar. Bark grey-green, smooth, becoming progressively more fissured and grey or purple. Shoot green, glabrous and glaucous in first year, becoming grey or grey-brown in subsequent seasons. Bud cylindric-conic or ovoid-conic, pointed, tips of scales free, directed forwards, to 1 cm. Leaves directed forwards, stiff, not drooping below shoot, grey-green with few lines of stomata on outer face, paler or bluish green on inner faces with more lines, slender, retained 3-4 years, 7-9 cm by 0.06 cm. Cone on a short peduncle of 1 cm, cylindric-conic, curved, composed of few scales, green, ripening red-brown, 7-16 cm; scales obovate, rounded, or with a small blunt triangular umbo, incurved. Seed 0.6 cm, with a long wing 1.5-2 cm. Zone 5.

Macedonian pine is found in the Balkans from southern Yugoslavia, Albania, southern Bulgaria and along the northern frontier of Greece. It is a dense foliage and attractive tree. It is very reliable, growing well on a wide range of sites from barren upland peat sites to frost pockets or limey sites in southern Britain. It makes steady growth, more or less the same whatever the nutrient status of the site.

'Arnold Dwarf' is a clone which develops a formal conical habit, with the blue-green needles slightly twisted.

'Glauca Compacta' is a tight growing form.

P. wallichiana Jackson
Blue pine
(*P. excelsa* Wallich ex D. Don,
P. griffithii McClelland)

Tree to 35 m. Crown with open whorled branches, conical when young, older trees may remain conical or become more rounded, with large ascending branch stems, branches often retained to the base. Bark grey-green, smooth in young trees, becoming darker and fissured into small scales. Shoot olive green, becoming grey-green in second and third years, glabrous, stout. Bud cylindric-conic, scales free at tips, point forwards, pale brown, 1.5 cm. Leaves somewhat floppy, arch below the shoot, kinked downwards near base in second year, retained 2-3 years, margins sharply toothed, colour variable from grey-green to bright glaucous blue, stomata few on greener outer face, more on whitish or blue-glaucous inner faces, 11-20 cm by 0.1 cm. Male cones 1 cm. Cones ellipsoidal, often curved, green, ripening pale brown, 10-30 cm by 3.5 cm, opening to 5-9 cm, the basal infertile scales sometimes somewhat reflexed, as in Mexican white pine. Zone 6.

Blue pine is found along the Himalayan Mountains from Afghanistan to Arunachal Pradesh on India's eastern frontier. It is found in the dry inner valleys and to a lesser extent as occasional trees in moister situations. The trees vary considerably in the blueness of the foliage, with some forms, such as most of the plants in western Bhutan, being rather a plain grey-green with short leaves, but other forms having bright blue foliage, long and very pendulous. It is worth selecting plants before acquisition. Although the species will grow in exposed situations, it is best regarded as an aesthetic flop there and needs reasonable shelter to bring out its full beauty. Soft pines generally do not like exposure, Macedonian pine being a notable exception.

'Nana' is a dense dwarf form with leaves silvery blue. 'Silverstar' has similar foliage but a globose to columnar habit.

'Umbraculifera' is a dwarf form with an umbrella-shaped crown on a short stem, also with the foliage pendulous around the shoot.

'Vernisson' has erect twigs.

'Zebrina' has the needles banded with a yellow strip about 2.5 cm from the apex, otherwise is a normal plant.

P. bhutanica Grierson, Long & Page
Bhutan pine

This tree has only recently been described and introduced. It is related to Blue pine but differs in the following macroscopic characters, as well as some details of leaf anatomy. The branches are sinuous and usually drooping, the young shoots are distinctly glaucous and finely hairy, the leaves are longer, in the range 12-28 cm, pendulous from the base from young, twisted and much more glaucous. The cone is very similar to Blue pine. Zone 9.

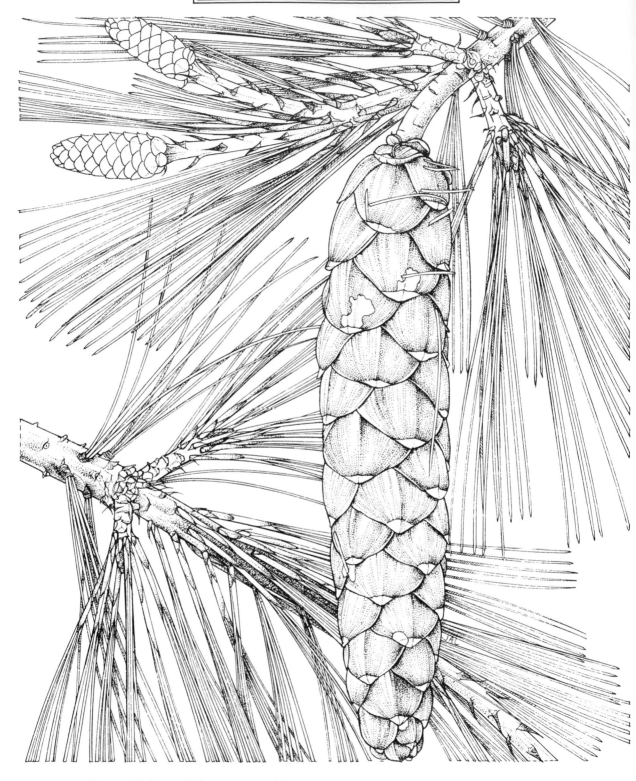

Figure 8.16 Pinus wallichiana. *Foliage, mature and immature cones.*

This tree is found in Bhutan and adjoining areas of Arunachal Pradesh; in Bhutan it is commoner in the east and favours a wetter climate than Blue pine, although the two do grow together. The first introduction was from plants growing at low altitude but it has since been found growing at nearer 3,000 m and these plants should prove hardier. It promises to make an attractive addition to our garden flora.

P. armandii Franchet
Armand pine

Tree 40 m, usually smaller. Crown conical or columnar-conic. Bark smooth, grey, becoming deeply cracked into small squarish plates. Shoot glabrous, mid-green or olive green for first winter, in succeeding years olive brown or green-brown and slightly grey. Bud cylindric or ovoid, with a short conic tip, scales free, point forwards, pale brown, 1 cm. Leaves point forwards and partly hang down, in rather tight fascicles, usually straight but sometimes kinked in second year as in P. wallichiana, outer face without or with few stomata, deep shiny green, inner faces with stomata, pale whitish green to glaucous blue, 10-20 cm. Cone cylindric-conic, green, ripening dull brown, 7-25 cm, mostly 12-20 cm by 5-10 cm; scales incurved, thick. Seed with a rudimentary wing of less than 0.1 cm, 1.3 cm by 1 cm. Zone 7.

Armand pine is found from the Tsangpo valley in south-east Tibet (Xizang) across western China to Hubei province. It may also occur in north-east India in Arunachal Pradesh and northern Burma, whilst a variety is recorded as below. In a number of respects it is close to Korean pine, such as the wingless seeds, but on most characters firmly belongs in this alliance.

In cultivation all origins tried have proved hardy, although disliking exposure to de-icing salt; however, as might be expected with such a wide natural distribution, some forms are much more pleasing and graceful than others; in this respect it is similar to Blue pine. Length, colour and fineness of needles all show marked variations, although there is some indication that the leaves are a brighter blue when grown in shade. It can be a most attractive tree and at its best is well worth extensive use.

var. *mastersiana* (Hayata) Hayata differs in the ovoid cones 9-12 cm, shorter leaves 8-15 cm and the smaller seeds 0.8-1.2 cm. It is restricted to Taiwan but is close to the type. Young trees in cultivation appear hardy.

P. amamiana Koidzumi
Amam pine
(*P. armandii* var. *amamiana* (Koidzumi) Hatusima)

This species differs from Armand pine in the ovoid or ovoid-elliptic cones only 5-10 cm long and shorter rigid needles only 5-8 cm long, set on brownish shoots. It is recorded from two islands (Yakushima and Tanegashima) off the southern coast of Kyushu, Japan. It is probably more closely related to *P. morrisonicola* and *P. fenzeliana*. It is very rare in cultivation but may prove hardy. Zone 8.

P. dabeshanensis Cheng & Law
Dabieshan pine

This tree is closely related to Armand pine, but differs in the leaves being only 5-14 cm long, and the ellipsoidal cone less than 14 cm long by 4.5 cm, with larger seeds 1.4-1.8 cm by 0.8-0.9 cm. It is recorded from the Dabie shan which lies between Anhui and Hubei provinces in eastern China. It has yet to be introduced. Zone 9.

P. dalatensis de Ferre
Dalat pine

This tree is inadequately known but has glaucous brown shoots which bear leaves which are in the range 4-10 cm but only 0.05 cm wide. The cylindrical cones are only 5-10 cm long by 2.5-3.5 cm. It is described from the mountains around Dalat in south Vietnam but is not in cultivation. It has been made a variety of Blue pine (as *P. wallichiana* var. *dalatensis* (de Ferre) Silba) but the characters given above and the geographical separation justify its retention as a distinct species. Zone 10.

P. fenzeliana Handel-Mazzetti
Fenzel pine

Tree to 50 m. Bark scaly, brown. Shoots slender, brown. Bud ovoid, resinous. Leaves 10-18 cm by 0.05-0.07 cm. Cone ovoid-cylindric, 6-10 cm by 3-6 cm. Seed 0.8-1.5 cm by 0.5-0.8 cm with short wing 0.2-0.4 cm long. Zone 8.

This tree is recorded from southern China, including the island of Hainan and from central Vietnam. It has been introduced but may have been lost. It is allied to *P. parviflora* but appears quite distinct.

P. parviflora Siebold & Zuccarini
Japanese white pine
(P. himekomatsu Miyabe & Kudo, P. pentaphylla Miyabe & Kudo)

Tree to 20 m but usually smaller. Crown conic, rounded, but in the usual form in cultivation it is low and spreading. Bark purplish, in old trees scaly. Shoots glabrous or hairy, greyish brown or yellowish brown. Bud ovoid, pale, bright or orange-brown, scales free at tips, point forwards. Leaves slightly curved, outer face deep green, without stomata, inner faces whitish blue or bright blue, 2-6 cm by 0.07-0.1 cm. Cone ovoid-oblong, 5-7 cm, with broad short incurved scales. Seed 1 cm, wing much shorter than seed. Zone 5.

Japanese white pine is recorded from the mountains of southern Japan, from Honshu, Kyushu and Shikoku. The name *P. pentaphylla* has been proposed instead of *P. parviflora* for this species on the basis that the type specimen is a *nomen confusum*, consisting of material of *PP. pentaphylla, himekomatsu* Miyabe & Kudo and *pumila*; this only holds if Japanese white pine is divided into two species (the *P. pumila* element is insignificant) and therefore this treatment is rejected here.

Japanese white pine has been cultivated for a very long period and the common forms encountered are derived from Japanese garden selections, rather than from the wild species. In cultivation it is useful as a small tree with bright foliage but is better for some of its dwarf cultivars, of which many have been named.

var. *pentaphylla* (Mayr) Henry is distinguished by the seed wing being about as long as the seed, and the more regular, less tapered cones with more rounded scales. It comes from the northern part of Japan, from Honshu and Hokkaido and also the Korean offshore island of Utsurio-To. It is uncommon in cultivation.

'Adcock's Dwarf' makes a dense slow-growing form with short grey-green needles, 1.5-2.5 cm, clustered at the branch tips.

'Bergman' is a broadly conical plant with twisted blue-green needles and a growth rate of 5 cm per annum.

'Blue Giant' is a tree form with blue-grey leaves and a regular habit. 'Gimborn's Ideal' and 'Tempelhof' are similar.

'Brevifolia' is a small tree form with sparse open branching and short needles only 2-3 cm long.

'Gimborn's Pyramid' makes an oval cone to 3 m by 2 m. The leaves are an intense blue-green in early summer.

'Glauca' is the commonly cultivated garden form. It makes the low tree with a spreading crown and the foliage is bowed and twisted. It would be more attractive if the cones did not outstay their welcome, as they are dull and dark after ripening and releasing the seeds.

'Kokuho' is a very slow-growing bun-shaped plant with congested blue-green foliage creamy at the tips. It will make growths of around 2.5 cm per annum.

'Kokonoye' makes an irregular dwarf character plant with short greyish blue needles. It grows 4-5 cm per annum.

'Negishi' makes an upright open branched tree with grey-green or blue-green short (3.5-4.5 cm) leaves.

'Saphir' is an irregular-growing plant with short blue foliage.

'Variegata' has the needles irregularly marked with yellow or yellow patches.

P. morrisonicola Hayata
Taiwan white pine

Tree to 25 m. Bark greyish brown, smooth, becoming fissured. Shoot smooth, glaucous. Bud ovoid. Leaves 4-10 cm by 0.06-0.1 cm, bright glossy grass green, stomata on 2 inner faces only. Cone ovoid or oblong-ovoid, scales slightly spreading when shut, 7-11 cm by 5-7 cm. Seed 0.8-1.0 cm, to 2 cm with wing. Zone 8.

This tree is restricted to the island of Taiwan. It has been introduced but is uncommon. Several reference books confuse it with Japanese white pine, to which it is related but differs in the longer leaves, larger cones and smaller seeds with longer wings.

P. wangii Hu & Cheng
Wang pine

Tree to 20 m. Shoots hairy, red-brown in first year, becoming grey-brown in second and third years. Bud ovoid, dark brown. Leaves 2.5-6 cm by 0.1-0.15 cm. Cone oblong-cylindric, 4.5-9 cm by 2-4.5 cm. Seed 0.8-1 cm by 0.6 cm, wing 1.6 cm by 0.7 cm. Zone 9.

This tree is only known from south-east Yunnan province of China. It awaits introduction.

P. kwangtungensis Chen ex Tsiang
Guangdong pine

Tree to 30 m. Shoot glabrous, olive brown in first year, brown or grey-brown in second. Bud cylindrical, conic at the apex, scales free at tips, point forwards, brown, less than 0.5 cm. Leaves radial and point forwards on shoot, fascicles splayed out from first year, twisted, stout, retained for three years, margins very regularly and sharply saw-toothed, outer face shiny mid- or yellow-green, without stomata but with a linear groove, concave, not convex, inner faces whitish or bluish white with bands of stomata, apex rounded, 4-8 cm by 0.15 cm. Cone cylindric-conic, rounded at both ends, 4-9 cm by 3 cm, opening to 6 cm, on a peduncle of 1.5-2 cm. Seed 0.8-1.2 cm. Zone 8.

This small tree is recorded from Hunan, Guizhou, Guangxi as well as Guangdong province, from whence it was first described. It is in cultivation and makes a small tree, noticeable for the stout, very saw-toothed leaves. It needs shelter from spring frosts in southern Britain.

Section *Parrya*

Subsection *Cembroides*
Pinyons or Nut pines

The pinyons or nut pines are a group of eleven species from south-west USA and north and central Mexico. They have large seeds with a very short, easily-detached ineffective wing which remains attached to the cone scale, and in most species are tasty to eat. The leaves are characterised by a semi-persistent sheath, the base of which remains as a curled rosette round the fascicle in most species, though more persistent in *P. nelsonii*. They range from dwarf shrubs to small trees, occasionally to 18 m. All the species come from hot dry areas, with the rainfall falling in summer and the winters dry and cold. In cultivation they will make slow-growing plants and need full sun. They are better sited on dry sandy soils. The species are characterised by the leaves (primarily the stomatal distribution, number of leaves per fascicle and the basal sheath) and by the cones. The following descriptions use that of *P. cembroides* as the reference; where a character is not mentioned, it will be similar to that exhibited by this species.

P. cembroides Zuccarini
Mexican pinyon

Tree 5-8 m, rarely to 18 m. Crown rounded, domed. Bark silvery grey, scaly, with red-brown fissures. Shoot orange-brown, becoming grey-brown, glabrous or hairy. Bud sub-cylindric, scales with long tapering tips, often reflexed, reddish brown. Leaves set radially on shoot, in fascicles of both 2 and 3, dark green on outer face, variably glaucous on inner 2 faces, stomata on all 3 faces, margins entire, 3-6.5 cm by 0.12-0.16 cm. Sheath on newly mature fascicles reflexed through 270°. Cone globose or sub-globose, bright green, ripening reddish or yellowish brown, 2.5-4 cm by 3-5.5 cm wide, peduncle 0.2-0.5 cm; fertile scales 9-13, umbo protuberant. Seed 1.4 cm, the only species with pink endosperm. Zone 7.

Mexican pinyon is recorded from Mexico from Hidalgo state northwards to south-western Texas, with subspecies as below. It is the type species of this complex, and most of the following species have been confused with it or referred to it as varieties at some time or other.

subspecies *orizabensis* Bailey differs from the typical form in the fascicle having 3, or occasionally 4 needles (only very rarely just 2) which are 4-6 cm long by 0.13-0.2 cm, the scale leaves beneath the fascicles soon turning black, and the bark has yellow-orange fissures. The cone has 12-16 fertile scales and is 6 cm by 7 cm. The apophysis of the scales is more angular and flatter than in the typical subspecies.

It is recorded from Puebla, Tlaxcala and Veracruz states of central Mexico. It is uncommon in cultivation but appears perfectly hardy. The tree growing at Kew which is listed in several books as *P. nelsonii* belongs to this subspecies; it is a small neat tree of 10 m.

subspecies *lagunae* (Robert-Passini) Bailey is restricted to a small area in the Sierra de Laguna at the southern tip of Baja California del Sur. It differs in the thinner seeds with more cotyledons, the longer but narrower leaves, averaging 6.75 cm by 0.12 cm and the longer peduncles. This subspecies is not in cultivation.

The chemistry of the resins of all three subspecies differs.

P. edulis Engelmann
Rocky Mountain pinyon

Tree 6-15 cm. Crown compact, irregularly domed. Shoots stiff, orange, turning bluish, bloomed red. Bud ovoid, with coarse scales. Leaves primarily 2 to a fascicle but some single or triple fascicles occur on the one tree, usually curved, dark green on outer face, glaucous on inner faces, persistent 3-9 years, 3-6 cm by more than 0.17 cm. Cone globose or subglobose with a flattened base, 4-6 fertile scales, ripens pale brown or greenish tan, 3 cm by 4-7 cm wide; scales with a small raised umbo with a central depression and a minute prickle; peduncle less than 0.3 cm. Seed 1.1-1.4 cm, dark reddish brown. Zone 8.

Rocky Mountain pinyon is recorded from Colorado, eastern Utah, New Mexico, Arizona and western Texas. It is the common pinyon of the south-west USA and the seeds are much used for food. It has been referred to Single-leaf pinyon as a variety but is clearly separated on the basis of much smaller seeds and cones, with the scales ending in only a short umbo which is depressed in the centre, although the two species hybridise where they meet in the wild.

var. *fallax* Little is a 1-needled variety reported from Arizona, south-west Utah and south-west New Mexico.

P. monophylla Torrey & Fremont
Single-leaf pinyon

Tree to 10 m or a shrub. Crown flat domed. Bark dark brown or grey, smooth, becoming fissured. Shoot stiff, orange, becoming dark brown. Bud chestnut brown, scales obtuse. Leaves set singly or occasionally in pairs, spaced on shoot, round in cross-section (unless 2-needled), curved, thick, rigid, sharp-pointed, grey-green or bluish, persist 4-12 years, 2-5.5 cm. Cone broadly ovoid, 8 cm by 8 cm when open, fertile scales 10-16, apophysis with a pyramidal boss, over 1 cm including thickness of scale, spreading with small recurved umbo. Seed 1.7-2 cm by 0.8-0.9 cm. Zone 8.

Single-leaf pinyon is native to south-western USA from southern Idaho, west Utah, north-west Arizona, Nevada and California, crossing the Mexican border into northern Baja California del Norte. It is very distinct in the short, usually curved foliage and the large cones and seeds. In cultivation it is slow-growing.

P. quadrifolia Parletore ex Sudworth
Parry pinyon

Tree to 10 m. Crown rounded, low. Bark grey, smooth, becoming fissured, scaly and red-brown. Shoots pubescent, orange-brown. Buds brown. Needles mostly 3-4 in a fascicle, some trees with 2 or 5, rigid, incurved, bright green to bluish green, stomata on inner faces only, persist 3-4 years, margins entire or slightly toothed, 3-4 cm. Cone with 6, rarely to 12 fertile scales, ovoid to subglobose, 4-6 cm by 5-6 cm, dark yellow; scales with a central cylindrical boss carrying the umbo. Seed 1.5 cm. Zone 7.

This pinyon is recorded from southern California and northern Baja California del Norte. It is not recorded in cultivation but ought to prove hardy.

P. culminicola Andresen & Beaman
Cerro Potosi pinyon

Shrub to 4 m, usually smaller and spreading. Crown dense. Bark green-grey, scaly. Leaves in dense fascicles of 5 (rarely 4 or 6), outer face blue-green without stomata, inner 2 faces glaucous, margins toothed, apex rounded, 3-5 cm by 0.1-0.13 cm. Cone subglobose, 3-4.5 cm by 3.5-4 cm; fertile scales 10-14. Seed rounded, 1 cm by 0.9 cm wide, endosperm white. Zone 6.

Cerro Potosi pinyon was described from the mountain of that name in Nuevo Leon, north-east

Mexico; it has since been found on the Sierra de Santa Maria on the Nuevo Leon-Coahuila border and in one locality in eastern Coahuila. On Cerro Potosi, it occurs on the moister eastern side of the summit as a low bush, although it will make a larger shrub in pine forest. It is found at higher altitudes than other pinyons. It is fully hardy in cultivation, making a small slow-growing plant.

P. remota (Little) Bailey & Hawkesworth
Papershell pinyon

Shrub or tree to 7 m. Crown irregular. Shoots slender, grey. Buds subcylindrical, with fine long tapered scales. Leaves mainly in fascicles of 2, some of 3, stomata on all 3 faces, mainly on the usually glaucous inner faces, 3-5.5 cm by 0.13-0.18 cm. Sheath on newly mature fascicles only reflexed to less than 180°. Cone with 5-7 fertile scales, fragile, ripen yellow, 2.5-3.5 cm by 3-5 cm; scales with sunken umbo. Seed 1-1.3 cm by 0.9-1 cm, with very thin shell 0.1-0.3 cm thick. Zone 8.

Papershell pinyon is recorded from the Edwards Plateau in western Texas to Coahuila, west Nuevo Leon and east Chihuahua in Mexico. It occurs at lower altitudes than other pinyons, but despite this appears to be hardy. It is one of the recently named pinyons.

P. discolor Bailey & Hawkesworth
Border pinyon

Tree 5-12 m. Crown rounded, spreading. Leaves usually in fascicles of 3, but occasionally of 4 or 5, outer face dark green without stomata, inner faces very glaucous, almost white, margins entire, 3-6 cm by 0.13-0.16 cm. Cones with 8-12 fertile very flat scales, 2-3 cm by 2.5-4 cm; peduncle 0.3-0.6 cm. Seed with white endosperm. Zone 7.

Border pinyon is found close to the USA/Mexico border in south-east Arizona, north-east New Mexico, north-west Sonora and north-west Chihuahua, and also further south in southern Chihuahua, Durango and San Luis Potosi in isolated populations. It is unique in that it is almost dioecious, i.e. with separate male and female trees. It is also striking in the difference between the outer and inner surfaces of the leaves.

P. johannis M.F. Robert
Johan pinyon

Multi-stemmed shrub or small tree to 6 m. Crown rounded. Leaves in fascicles of 3, rarely 4 or 5, outer face dark green without stomata, inner faces somewhat glaucous, 3.5-6 cm by 0.13-0.17 cm. Cones 2.5-4 cm by 3-5 cm. Seed with white endosperm. Zone 7.

This small tree is found in Mexico in north-east Zacatecas, in southern Coahuila and southern

Nuevo Leon. It makes a small tree or shrub on very dry sites, in association with species of *Agave* and other xerophytic plants and at higher altitudes than *P. cembroides* populations. It has recently been introduced and promises to be hardy.

P. maximartinezii Rzedowski
Martinez pinyon

Tree to 10 m. Crown open rounded, branched from base. Bud conical, 1.3 cm. Leaves in fascicles of 5, thin, pale grey-green on outer face, whitish on inner faces, margins entire or toothed, tip acute or obtuse, 9-13 cm (to 20 cm in cultivation). Cone ovoid or oblong-ovoid, mace-like with the ovoid prominent apophyses spreading, 18-21 cm by 11-15 cm; 50-60 fertile yellow scales. Seed dark brown, 2-2.6 cm by 1-1.2 cm, with 18-23 cotyledons. Zone 9.

Martinez pinyon is found in the south-east corner of the Mexican state of Zacatecas. It was discovered due to the very large seeds which were on sale in the local markets; Rzedowski recognised that they must represent a new species and traced them back to the wild plants. The cones are remarkable for being similar in armature to a medieval mace, whilst the number of cotyledons is the highest recorded for any pine. Unfortunately, Martinez pinyon is rather tender and needs either a cool greenhouse or a mild site.

P. pinceana Gordon
Pince pinyon

Tree to 12 m. Crown much branched, rounded. Shoots long, slender, ash grey, smooth. Bud cylindrical, brown. Leaves in fascicles of 3, pale green or glaucous-green, stomata on outer face in southern part of range but only at tip in northern part, stomata on inner faces, margins entire, 4-10 cm. Cones ripen greenish yellow with dark umbos, ovoid, rich shiny cinnamon brown, 6-10 cm; fertile scales 15-25, umbo slightly depressed with small central prickle; peduncle 1-2 cm. Seed 1.3 cm by 0.8 cm, with a fine dark collar separating a pale brown underside from dark brown top. Zone 9.

Pince pinyon, also known as Weeping pinyon, is recorded from Coahuila, Zacatecas, San Luis Potosi, Guerrero and Hidalgo states of northern Mexico. It has the foliage attractively weeping but needs a mild site.

P. nelsonii Shaw
Nelson pinyon

Tree to 9 m, or a shrub with many straight stems. Leaves in fascicles of 3 but connate and thus appearing single, only separated by rolling between the fingers, stomata on inner faces or all faces, dark green, margins regularly toothed, 4-9 cm; sheath persistent for several years. Cones emerge from branch at right angle but stout peduncle curved to hang down, sub-cylindrical, 8-14 cm by 6 cm; fertile scales 30-45; peduncle long, scaly. Seed 1.2-1.5 cm by 0.8 cm, chocolate brown with bright red-brown end. Zone 9.

Nelson pinyon is a rare and local species from Coahuila, Nuevo Leon, Tamaulipas and San Luis Potosi in north-east Mexico. It is unique in the subgenus *Strobus* in the persistent basal sheath to the leaves and is totally different in appearance to any other pinyon. It is in cultivation but may not be very hardy.

Subsection *Gerardianae* Loudon

This group of pines differs from the above subsection in the stouter, glossy needles having a fully deciduous sheath, the cones bearing wrinkled apophyses when mature (smooth in subsection *Cembroides*) and also in the distinctive bark.

P. bungeana Zuccarini ex Endlicher
Lacebark pine

Tree to 20 m. Crown bushy or columnar. Bark grey-green, smooth, exfoliating in small round scales to reveal creamy or pale yellow, gradually darkening through green, olive brown, reddish or purple. Shoot olive green, becoming grey-green. Bud ovoid, pointed, projecting forwards through leaves. Leaves in fascicles of 3, dark yellow-green on outer face, pale with grey-green lines of stomata on inner faces, hard, shiny, 6-8 cm. Cone ovoid, with spined umbos, 4-7 cm by 3.5 cm. Zone 4.

Lacebark pine is native to northern China but planted also in Korea around temples. The bark of old trees in China becomes a very striking white colour; in cultivation, so far it has only achieved the cream and green flaking, like that of a plane tree (*Platanus*). The bark of some of the pinyon pines can be similar when young but is not as attractive.

Lacebark pine makes a beautiful specimen and is fully hardy, although slow-growing.

P. gerardiana Wallich ex D. Don
Chilgoza pine

Chilgoza pine is closely related to Lacebark pine, differing in the longer needles, 5-10 cm, the larger cones 10-20 cm long by 8-12 cm wide with reflexed scales and the longer seed 2-2.5 cm. It is native to the north-west Himalayas from Kashmir, southern Xizang (Tibet), northern Pakistan and eastern Afghanistan. The seeds are important economically. It makes a slow-growing but hardy tree, although the bark is not as spectacular as that of Lacebark pine. Zone 7.

Subsection *Balfourianae* Engelmann
Foxtail pines

This group of three species is charcterised by the short, entire needles in fascicles of 5, rarely 4-6. The seeds have long wings which are articulate. The needles are retained on the trees for at least ten years and the branches are likened to the brush of a fox, hence foxtail pines.

P. *aristata* Engelmann
Bristlecone pine

Tree 3-15 m. Crown with upturned dense branches. Bark dark grey, smooth, becoming reddish brown, fissured. Shoot red-brown or orange-brown, brighter below, with short pale hairs, becoming darker. Bud ovoid, pointed, dark red-brown, 0.7 cm. Leaves in fascicles of 5, very dense on shoot, curved along the shoot in first year, more spreading later, covered with flecks of white resin, bright green with a groove but no stomata on outer face and blue-white on inner faces in first year, darker on outside and grey on inside in subsequent years, 2-4 cm. Cone cylindric-ovoid, brown, 4-10 cm; scales terminating in a narrow bristle-like prickle. Seed 0.6 cm, with articulate wing. Zone 5.

Bristlecone pine is recorded from high altitudes in western Colorado, northern New Mexico and northern Arizona. It is extremely long-lived and slowly makes a gnarled specimen in the hostile regions it inhabits. The flecks of resin come from the bursting of the single resin canals which are placed very close to the margin and can be seen by the naked eye as a groove running along the outer face of the needle.

Bristlecone pine is very hardy and in cultivation makes a slow-growing tree suitable for small gardens. It has proved surprisingly well suited to north-east Iceland and flourishes there.

P. *longaeva* Bailey
Ancient pine

Tree to 15 m. Crown conical in young trees, gnarled in old ones. Bark dark brown, scaly. Shoot red-brown, hairy. Bud ovoid-conic, pointed, chestnut brown, scales with free forward-pointing tips. Leaves tightly pointing forwards at first, more spreading in following years, in fascicles of 5, or occasionally 3 or 4, acute, shiny grey-green on outer surface, whitish on inner surfaces, resin canals visible as 2 grooves along outer surface, flecks of resin few, starting in second year, 2.5-3 cm by 0.11 cm. Cone ovoid, base rounded, rich rusty red, 6-10 cm, umbo with small fragile prickle. Zone 5.

This tree is allied to both Bristlecone and Foxtail pines. It is recorded from the White Mountains of eastern California, from central Utah and southern Nevada. It grows in a very inhospitable dry moun-

tain area and the species includes the oldest living thing. Still living trees have been dated, by counting the rings, to be over 4,900 years old. They are not neat tall specimens, but gnarled and half dead, although aesthetically appealing in their own way. The leaves can be retained for up to 30 years. In cultivation, it has proved hardy and of reasonable growth rate.

P. *balfouriana* Jeffrey ex A. Murray
Foxtail pine

Tree to 15 m, to 25 m in the wild. Crown broadly conical. Bark grey, ridged. Shoots orange-brown, hairy. Bud ovoid, sharply pointed, 0.3 cm, resinous. Leaves in fascicles of 4 or 5, dark green with faint stomata on 2 inner faces only, curved, persist 10-20 years, 2-2.8 cm by 0.1 cm. Cone oblong-cylindric, purplish brown, 8-14 cm, apophysis with a central umbo bearing a short, 0.2 cm, prickle. Seed distinctively patterned light and dark, 1 cm by 0.4 cm, with a pale brown articulate wing. Zone 6.

Foxtail pine is restricted to the Klamath Mountains of northern California. In cultivation it makes an interesting tree with the upswept branches carrying the long-retained needles. Most reference books record the wing of Foxtail pine as adnate but this is an error.

subsp. *austrina* Mastrogiuseppe & Mastrogiuseppe is recorded from central California, being separated from *P. longaeva* by only 35 km. It differs in the cinnamon brown bark, the leaves with a pronounced waxy bloom over the stomata on the inner faces and without a groove on the outer face and the elliptic cones which are less than 10 cm long and ripen rusty red-brown. It may be in cultivation as the type, otherwise it should prove hardy, coming from high altitudes.

Subsection *Rzedowskianae* Caravajal

This recently named subsection contains only the one species discovered in a remote area of Michoacan in 1968; it is in some respects intermediate between subsections *Cembroides* and *Balfourianae*, probably closest to the former group, with very similar foliage but immediately distinguished by the long, effective seed wing.

P. *rzedowskii* Madrigal & Caballero
Rzedowski pine

Tree to 30 m. Crown open, irregular. Bark grey, rugose, fissured. Shoot grey-brown, slightly hairy. Bud conical. Leaves in fascicles of 3-4, flexible, margins toothed, green without stomata on the outer face, with glaucous inner faces, 6-10 cm by 0.07-0.1 cm. Cone bright red-brown, oblong-cylindrical, pendulous, 10-15cm by 6-8.5cm; scale fairly thick, strong with a small pointed umbo; peduncle 1.5-3cm. Seed 0.8-1cm by 0.5cm, wing 2-3.5cm by 1-1.3cm wide. Zone 8.

This very distinct pine is native to Michoacan state of Mexico. It comes from a region where the minimum temperatures are down to −5°C, so may prove hardy in mild areas.

SUBGENUS *Pinus*

Section *Pinaster* Koch

Subsection *Pineae* Little & Critchfield

This subsection consists of a single very distinctive species in which the cones take three years to ripen.

P. pinea Linnaeus
Stone or Umbrella pine

Tree to 20m. Crown conical in young trees but old trees have the branches radiating out from a short bole like the spokes of an umbrella. Bark fissured, platy, orange and brown. Shoot orange-brown. Bud cylindric-ovoid, chestnut-red, 1cm. Leaves in fascicles of 2, sparse, twisted, stout, shiny dark green, 10-12cm. Cone ripens in third year, ovoid, shining brown, 12cm by 9cm; scales rounded, with radiating lines, umbo with 'tide' marks. Seed 1.5-2cm by 1cm, with a short rudimentary wing. Zone 8.

Stone pine, after the edible nuts, or Umbrella pine, after the crown shape, is found around the northern coast of the Mediterranean and Black Seas. Its natural distribution is unknown following extensive planting for the nuts. It is slow to lose the glaucous juvenile leaves. In cultivation it is quite hardy except as a small seedling.

Subsection *Pinaster* Loudon
(including subsection *Canariensis* Loudon)

This subsection resembles subsection *Pineae* in foliage and bark characters but differs greatly in the cone, which is not triennial but (as normal for pines) biennial and has seeds with a long effective wing which may be articulate or somewhat adnate (though not as strongly as in subsection *Strobi*). The leaves are in fascicles of 2 or 3.

P. canariensis C. Smith
Canary Island pine

Tree 25-40m. Crown spreading, often retaining some lower branches. Bark fissured into scaly plates, grey, red-brown or deep red. Shoot glabrous, yellow, becoming buff-brown. Bud ovate, acute, large. Leaves persist 1-3 years, flexible, spreading or somewhat pendulous, grass green, 15-30cm by 0.05-

0.13cm. Cone ellipsoid-ovoid, opening to broad ovoid or ovoid-conic, 9-20cm by 5-8cm; peduncle to 2cm. Zone 9.

Canary Island pine is restricted to the Canary Isles where it makes a large tree. It will retain the glaucous juvenile foliage for a considerable time. It is not hardy in most of Britain but useful for warmer climates or for a cool glasshouse.

P. roxburghii Sargent
Chir pine

This very closely-related tree is found in the Himalayas from north-west Pakistan to Bhutan. It differs in the more prominent umbos of the mature cones and in various minor anatomical details of the leaves and wood; the leaves are 25-40cm. Fossils indicate that the two species once formed a single population stretching from the Canary Isles across southern Europe to the Himalayas. Unfortunately, a hardy provenance of Chir pine still has to be found. Zone 9.

P. pinaster Aiton
Maritime pine

Tree to 40m. Crown domed on a long bole. Bark orange-brown, fissured, becoming deeply fissured and ridged, purple. Shoot pink-brown above, green beneath, becoming dull grey-brown, stout. Bud oblong, fusiform or conical, sharply pointed, with reflexed scales. Leaves stout, somewhat spaced, stiff, acute apex but not sharp, grey-green, becoming deep green, glossy, 10-25cm by 0.2cm. Cone sometimes clustered, ovoid-conic, olive green ripening to rich brown or orange-brown, scales with a transverse ridge and forward curved prickle, 8-22cm by 5-8cm. Zone 7.

Maritime pine is found around the central and western Mediterranean; it is extensively planted along the Atlantic coast of France and also in Spain and Portugal but may not be native to these regions. It makes a vigorous tree for dry sandy sites and is hardy as far north as Edinburgh. In parts of the New Forest it is naturalised. The cones may remain on the tree for some time before opening.

'Nana' is a dwarf form which makes a rounded flat-topped bush to 1m.

'Variegata' has short leaves to 7cm which are a mixture of green and straw-yellow or entirely yellow.

P. halepensis Miller
Aleppo pine

Tree to 20m. Crown conical, becoming rounded in old trees. Bark red-brown, fissured and scaly on old trees, silver-grey and smooth on young ones. Shoot grey-glaucous, remaining grey for several years. Bud conical, red-brown, with recurved scales, not resinous. Leaves slender, sparse, bright fresh green, curved and twisted, persisting for 2 years, 6-11 cm by 0.07 cm. Cones ovoid-conic, deflexed back along shoot or somewhat spreading, orange or red-brown with convex scales, 5-12 cm by 4 cm; peduncle scaly, to 2 cm. Zone 8.

Aleppo pine is found in the Mediterranean, mainly in the western part, although the exact distribution has been obscured by planting. It is a very drought-tolerant species and is planted around the Mediterranean countries in afforestation schemes and for stabilising sandy soils. In cultivation it makes a slow-growing tree.

P. brutia Tenore
Calabrian pine

This tree is closely related to Aleppo pine, of which it is sometimes treated as a variety. It differs in the following features: the leaves are 10-15 cm long by 0.1-0.15 cm wide, darker green and more rigid. The shoots are green and more flexible. The cones are generally larger with thicker bases and set on a stouter peduncle; they are either forward-pointing or wide-spreading, never deflexed. The range of measurements of both cones and leaves is similar to that of Aleppo pine. It is recorded around the eastern Mediterranean from Turkey and Crete, although originally described as being found in Calabria in Italy. In cultivation as a young tree it makes a rather sparse open tree, like Aleppo pine, although dense in mature trees. It is also very drought-tolerant. Zone 8.

Three related taxa which are variously species or varieties of these two pines are: P. eldarica Medwediew known in the wild only from a single mountain in eastern Georgia, USSR, but wildly cultivated (?or native) in Iran, Aghanistan and Pakistan, with short cones with whitish grey concave apophyses; P. pityusa Steven from the Aegean and Turkey, with shorter leaves; P. stankewiczii (Suk.)Fomin. from the Crimea, with narrower leaves and cones with indented umbos. The value of these pines in cultivation is likely to be similar to the main two species; only P. eldarica is rarely encountered.

Section Leiophyllae Vanderburgh
Subsection Leiophyllae Loudon

This small section is unique in the hard pines in having the basal sheath of the short shoots deciduous. The subsection consists of two species.

P. leiophylla Scheide & Deppe
Smooth-leaf pine

Tree to 30 m. Crown rounded, thin. Bark reddish, scaly and rough, but thin and smooth on the young trees. Shoot yellow or reddish brown, pruinose. Bud ovoid, small. Leaves in fascicles of 5, slender, greyish green, 10-15 cm. Cones ripening in third season, persistent on tree, ovate to ovate-conic, 4-7 cm; scales with double or superimposed umbo; peduncles to 1.3 cm. Zone 7.

This tree is native to Mexico from east Sonora down the central and western part of the country to Oaxaca. It is very distinctive in the umbos bearing the 'tide' marks of the two years spent at the conelet stage and the deciduous sheaths. The cones are smooth and egg-shaped. Felled trees will produce coppice shoots but they normally fade out. It appears hardy in southern Britain, at least with some shelter.

var. chihuahuana (Engelmann) Shaw **Chihuahua pine** differs in the thicker and stiffer leaves being in fascicles of 3, 4 or 5, mainly 3. It is found in northern Mexico in Chihuahua, Durango, Sonora and Zacatecas, and also in the southern USA in New Mexico and Arizona. It is often treated as a separate species. It has been introduced into cultivation and should prove hardy.

P. lumholtzii Robinson & Fernald
Lumholtz pine

Tree to 25 m. Crown columnar or conical, with level or hanging branches. Bark reddish brown, scaly and fissured, in old trees grey. Shoot slender, pruinose, becoming chestnut brown. Bud oblong, small, reddish brown. Leaves in fascicles of 3, rarely 2 or 4, hanging vertically downwards from the shoot, bright green, flexible, 18-30 cm, rarely to 38 cm. Cone ripens in second year, narrow ovoid-conic, rounded at base, symmetrical, 5-6.5 cm; peduncle curved, to 1.2 cm. Zone 9.

This tree is recorded from western Mexico from Chihuahua south to Guanajuato. It is incredibly beautiful in the weeping foliage; the plants at the northern end of its range should be hardy but it is not, as yet, in cultivation.

Section Taeda Spach

Subsection Taeda Loudon
(subsection Australes Loudon)

This group has the leaves in fascicles of 2 or 3 on the shoots which are either uni-nodal or multi-nodal. The cones are symmetrical, opening on maturity, and usually are shed without leaving any basal scales on the twig. The species are native to the eastern USA and in Central America and the

Caribbean. They do not rank as the most attractive species in the genus, but some are very important timber and resin-producing trees.

P. palustris Miller
Longleaf pine

Tree to 40 m. Crown small, high, open. Bark orange-brown, in scaly plates. Shoot very stout, uni-nodal, to 2.5 cm thick, orange-brown, prominently ridged. Bud very large, covered with reflexed white scales which give protection from forest fires, 3.5-6 cm. Leaves in fascicles of 3, bright green, flexible, 20-45 cm. Cones cylindric or narrow ovoid, red-brown, scales with spreading hooked umbo, 15-25 cm. Zone 9.

Longleaf pine is native to the south-east USA from south-east Virginia west to eastern Texas. It is distinctive for the enormous white buds and the long spreading or drooping foliage. The timber is of good quality, although the tree is somewhat slow in growth. It occurs on dry barren sandy soils and the seedlings have an extended 'grass' stage as a precaution against forest fires. The cones may be shed leaving some basal scales on the shoot. It is in cultivation but needs a mild location. It also needs planting out when small, as holding plants till a larger, and therefore hardier, size is attained is a recipe for them to blow down after a few years.

P. taeda Linnaeus
Loblolly pine

Tree to 30 m. Crown rounded, dense, on a long clear bole. Bark scaly and black on young trees, becoming grey or red-brown and fissured into plates. Shoot multi-nodal, slender, glaucous, glossy, olive brown, later yellow-brown to red-brown. Bud cylindric-conic, scales red-brown, free at tips, 1.2 cm. Leaves usually in fascicles of 3, rarely of 2, slender, flexible, yellow-brown or grey-green, 15-25 cm by 0.15 cm. Cone ovoid-conic, pale brown, scales with a sharp spreading prickle, 5-15 cm. Zone 7.

Loblolly pine is native to south-east USA from southern New Jersey to eastern Texas and also extends up the Mississippi valley. It is an important fast-growing timber tree. The name 'loblolly' refers to the moist depressions on which the tree is usually found in the wild; it is more tolerant of shading than other south-east USA pines and invasive of dry sandy sites. However, it has no protective mechanism against forest fires. It is hardy in cultivation, except as a small seedling, but the temptation to keep it in a pot for several years must be resisted; I have seen too many trees blown down after a few years because they became potbound before planting out. Plants from the northern parts of the range from Delaware and New Jersey will probably be hardier. A hybrid between Longleaf and Loblolly pines is quite common in parts of their ranges and is named *P × sondereggeri* Chapman.

P. echinata Miller
Shortleaf pine

Tree to 30 m. Crown conical, open. Bark nearly black on young trees, becoming red-brown, flat but fissured into plates in old trees. Shoot multi-nodal, slender, flexible, whitish green and somewhat glaucous, becoming orange-brown or red-brown. Bud small, cylindric-ovoid, red-brown or grey-brown, 0.6 cm. Leaves mainly in fascicles of 2 but some of 3 on the same shoot, slender, flexible, yellow-green or blue-green, often some produced on bole, 6-13 cm by 0.1-0.15 cm. Cone ovoid-conic, dull brown, scales with a sharp spreading prickle, 3-8 cm by 2-3 cm. Zone 7.

Shortleaf pine has a similar distribution to Longleaf and Loblolly pines but occurs further from the coast; it is also found further north, into New York and is missing from the Florida panhandle. It is hardy in cultivation but not very common.

P. glabra Walter
Spruce pine

Tree to 20 m. Crown narrow and long, with level branches. Bark dark grey, smooth until fissured in scaly ridges. Shoot smooth, multi-nodal. Bud ovoid, brown. Leaves in fascicles of 2, slender dark green, 4-12 cm. Cone ovoid, dull brown, scales with deciduous prickle, 4-7 cm. Zone 9.

Spruce pine is found in a band from South Carolina across northern Florida to eastern Louisiana. It is not particularly common but is more tolerant of shading than most other local pines. The bark is smooth for several years. It is uncommon in cultivation and likely to need a sheltered site.

P. rigida Miller
Pitch pine

Tree to 20 m. Crown conic or ovoid, rounded, irregular, with spreading branches. Bark dark grey or dark red-brown, fissured. Shoot multi-nodal, grey-brown. Bud resinous, cylindric-conic, acute, chestnut brown, 2 cm. Leaves in fascicles of 3, thick, stiff, usually twisted, spreading rather radially, dark grey-green, 7-14 cm by 0.2 cm. Cone ovoid-conic, yellow-brown, 3-9 cm by 3-4 cm, opening on maturity but usually persisting on the tree, scales with a spreading prickle. Zone 4.

Pitch pine is found in eastern North America from Maine to south-east Ontario and south to Georgia. It is a mountain species and is not found near the

175

coast except at the northern end of its range. The bole may carry epicormic or sucker growths and cut trees will often throw out coppice growth, but rarely will this survive to fruit. Pitch pine is intolerant of shading. It is fully hardy in cultivation but not common.

P. serotina Michaux
Pond pine

Pond pine is related to Pitch pine and is sometimes treated as a variety (*P. rigida* var. *serotina* (Michaux)Loudon ex Hoopes) or subspecies (subsp. *serotina* (Michaux)Clausen) of it. However, it is ecologically distinct, occurring on swampy and low flat wetland sites and differs in the slender, flexible, yellow-green needles 15-20cm long and the subglobose to broadly ovoid matt yellow cones, 6-9cm by 5-7cm, nearly spherical and broader than long when open, which may remain on the tree for several years without opening. It is found from New Jersey south to Florida. When not in cone, the foliage is similar to Loblolly pine but the very resinous buds should separate them. It usually bears epicormic shoots on the bole and can sprout after forest fire damage. It is rare in cultivation but plants from the northern end of the range should be hardy. Zone 8.

P. pungens Lambert
Table mountain pine

Tree to 24m, although usually much less. Crown rounded, low, irregular. Bark dark brown, scaly. Shoot multi-nodal, green, becoming bright orange. Bud cylindric, apex blunt, resinous. Leaves in fascicles of 2, occasionally of 3, dark green or yellow-green, twisted, stout, with a lemony scent when crushed, 3-8cm by 0.2cm. Cone ovoid, salmon-pink when first ripe, light brown later, often persisting closed, scales with very stout pointed spreading spines, 6-9cm. Zone 7.

Table mountain pine occurs along the Appalachian Mountains in eastern USA. It is a small intolerant tree which invades abandoned farmland. The cones are distinctive in the sharp stout pointed development on the scales. It makes an attractive young tree with interesting cones but is uncommon in cultivation.

P. elliotii Engelmann
Slash pine

Tree to 30m. Crown rounded, dense. Bark orange to dark purple-brown, fissured into plates, flaking off in thin papery layers. Shoot multi-nodal, stout, orange-brown. Bud 2cm with silvery brown scales. Leaves in fascicles of 2 and 3, stout, glossy dark green, 20-30cm. Cone distinctly stalked, ovoid-conic, chocolate brown and very shiny, scales with spreading prickle, 6-15cm by 4.5-5.5cm. Zone 9.

Slash pine is found on the coastal plain of southeast USA from South Carolina to Louisiana. It is intolerant of shading and cannot withstand forest fires. It is a very important and fast-growing timber tree. It is only likely to thrive in cultivation on the mildest sites.

P. densa (Little & Dorman)de Laubenfels & Silba
South Florida slash pine

This tree is restricted to the coast of southern and central Florida and some of the offshore keys or islands. It is closely related to both Slash and Caribbean pines. From Slash pine it differs in the seedlings having a definite 'grass' stage and the shorter needles, 9-24cm, in fascicles of 2 only and the smaller ovoid cones around 4cm long (but possibly to 10cm in parts of its range). It is unlikely to prove amenable to cultivation. Zone 9.

P. caribaea Morelet
Caribbean pine

This species has leaves in fascicles of 3, or sometimes more, narrow ovoid cones which are glossy red-brown, and cylindrical red-brown buds. It is recorded from the Bahamas, western Cuba and the Island of Pines in the Caribbean, and Guatemala and Belize in Central America. The Bahamas tree is referred to as var. *bahamensis* (Grisebach)Barr. ex Golf. It might be hardy in the mildest areas. The Central American plants belong to var. *hondurensis* (Senecluse)Barr. ex Golf. Neither this nor the typical form is likely to prove hardy. Zone 10.

P. occidentalis Swartz
West Indian pine

This tree differs from Caribbean pine in the uninodal shoots, more slender leaves in fascicles of 2 and around 15cm long, and the cones. At the conelet stage they point forwards on the shoot but at maturity they are reflexed, ovoid and 5-8cm. It is recorded from southern Cuba, Haiti and the Dominican Republic, where it occurs in mountains at high altitudes. It is just possible that the highest elevation origins might prove hardy. Zone 10.

P. cubensis Sargent
Cuban pine

This species has the needles in fascicles of 2, dull green, stiff and only 10-14cm long, and ovoid-conic cones around 4.5cm long, the scales of which bear forward-pointing prickles. It is sometimes referred to West Indian pine, either as a synonym or a variety (*P. occidentalis* var. *cubensis* (Sargent) Silba), but it may be closer to Caribbean pine. It comes from eastern Cuba. Zone 10.

Subsection *Ponderosae* Loudon
(including subsection *Sabinianae* Loudon)

This section has leaves in fascicles from 2 to 5 needles, uni-nodal shoots, and more or less symmetrical cones which generally open on maturity and when falling from the shoot leave a few basal scales and the peduncle on the shoot; however, a few species drop the cone with the short peduncle. The stomata are found on all 3 faces of the needles. The trees in this section are amongst the most attractive of the genus, although only suitable in the long term for large gardens. They do, however, need full sunlight, although some also need side shelter.

P. ponderosa Douglas ex Lawson
Ponderosa pine

Tree to 40m, occasionally more. Crown conic in young trees, columnar with a conic apex or more irregular in older trees. Bark very distinctive in old trees with deep fissures and smooth broad plates of yellow-brown, red-brown and pink-grey, in younger trees purple-grey with scaly ridges. Shoot stout, smooth, green-brown, becoming orange-brown and dark red-brown. Bud cylindrical with a pointed apex, red-brown but partly excrusted with resin. Leaves in fascicles of 3, rarely 2 or 5, lying forwards on shoot, dense, rigid, grey-green or yellowish green, 10-25cm by 0.15cm. Cone ovoid to ovoid-conic, dark green-brown, bright brown to pale reddish brown, apophysis with a transverse ridge and a short stout spreading umbo, 6-16cm by 3.5-5cm. Zone 4.

Ponderosa pine is found along the Pacific coast side of the Rocky Mountains from southern British Columbia to central California. It is also known as Western yellow pine. It is a tree with bold foliage and a distinctive bark. Coming from further north and at higher altitudes than other species in this grouping, it is hardy, but lacks the grace of other species. It will, however, make a larger tree.

'Pendula' has an erect leading shoot with hanging branches. Such forms have arisen on more than one occasion.

subsp. *scopulorum* (S Watson)Weber **Rocky**

Mountains ponderosa pine is a form from the drier eastern side of the Rockies, from eastern Montana and Dakota south to Arizona and western Texas. It has shorter grey-green or dark green leaves, 10-18cm by 0.15-0.2cm, with fascicles of both 2s and 3s; the leaves are splayed out and often kinked. The cones are smaller, only 5-9cm. It is sometimes treated as a separate species, in which case the name probably should be *P. brachyptera* Engelmann. It is in cultivation but is less attractive due to the shorter needles.

P. arizonica Engelmann
Arizona pine

Tree to 30m. Crown conic, becoming open and rounded. Bark rough, deeply fissured into reddish plates, on young trees or in upper crown dark to greyish brown. Shoot stout, rough, yellowish brown, slightly pruinose, becoming greyish brown. Bud long ovate, acuminate, reddish brown. Leaves in fascicles of 3, 4 or 5, stiff, medium to dark green, 10-20cm by 0.1-0.15cm. Cone ovoid-conic, yellowish to reddish brown, apophysis raised, with a short decurved umbo bearing a persistent prickle, 5-9cm by 3-6cm. Zone 6.

This pine is found in the USA from south-east Arizona and south-west New Mexico and in Mexico from Chihuahua, Durango, western Coahuila and south to San Luis Potosi. It is distinct from Ponderosa pine where the two are found together in Arizona and New Mexico in the more slender needles on thin glaucous twigs and smaller cones with less prominent prickles but in Mexico (where Ponderosa pine is not found) the twigs are less glaucous. It is probably not in cultivation but should be hardy.

var. *stormiae* Martinez is found in north-east Mexico in eastern Coahuila, Nuevo Leon and Tamaulipas and also in the Chisos Mountains of south-western Texas. It differs in the longer leaves, 17-30cm by 0.15-0.2cm and the larger cones, 8-14cm, which are set on longer peduncles. It may be specifically distinct from Arizona pine and of independent origin. When introduced, it should prove hardy, at least with some shelter.

P. engelmannii Carriere
Apache pine

Tree to 35m. Crown with stiff, thick branches. Bark dark brown or blackish grey, rough, fissured into plates. Shoot grey-brown. Bud conical, resinous. Leaves in fascicles of 3, less often of 5, dark green, rigid, spreading or drooping, persist 2 years, 25-45cm. Cone ovoid to conic, somewhat asymmetrical, scales chocolate brown on inner face, dark brown or black on lower face, apophysis protuberant, subconical, reflexed, yellow-brown, with a strong persistent terminal prickle, 12-

18cm by 5-7cm. Zone 8.

Apache pine is found in North America from southern Arizona and New Mexico south to Zacatecas in Mexico. It has long, bold foliage and makes a very commanding tree. It is in cultivation and appears hardy, provided it is sheltered from strong winds.

P. durangensis Martinez
Durango pine

Tree 20-40m. Crown conic, becoming rounded and dense. Bark rough, scaly, greyish brown to dark grey. Shoot dark grey to brownish, slightly pruinose when young, rough. Bud cylindric-conic, red-brown, scales with free tips, not resinous. Leaves in fascicles of 5 or 6, rarely to 8, pale shiny green, slender and flexible in young trees, stiffer in old ones, 10-23cm. Cone ovoid to ovoid-conic, slightly curved, reddish brown, apophysis keeled with a greyish raised umbo carrying a short persistent prickle, 7.5-10cm. Zone 8.

Durango pine is found in the Mexican states of Durango and southern Chihuahua. It is related to Arizona pine and intergrades with it to some extent in central Chihuahua. It has recently been introduced into cultivation and should prove hardy if protected from cold winds.

P. jeffreyii Greville & Balfour
Jeffrey pine

Tree to 40m. Crown conical or columnar with a conical top. Bark black or dark grey, fairly smooth, with fine deep fissures. Shoot stout, bloomed violet, grey-green, becoming orange-brown. Bud conical or ovoid-cylindric, pointed, red-brown, scales free at tips, slightly resinous, 3cm. Leaves in fascicles of 3, spreading, grey-green or bluish green, 12-26cm by 0.2cm. Cone ovoid-conic with a rounded base, opening to a broad flat base, apophysis with a recurved umbo, pale yellow-grey, rarely darker brown, 13-30cm by 5-8cm. Zone 6.

Jeffrey pine is found in the USA from south-west Oregon through the Sierra Nevada into western Nevada and California and in Mexico in northern Baja California del Norte. It grows under more extreme conditions than Ponderosa pine, of which it has been referred as a variety. It makes a striking tree with the long stout leaves held out from the thick bloomed shoots but is not particularly long-lived in cultivation.

P. washoensis Mason & Stockwell
Washoe pine

This rare and local species differs from Jeffrey pine in the shorter leaves which are 10-15cm long, the shoots being orange-brown and then grey-white and the smaller conical or ovoid cones 5-10cm with a reflexed umbo. It was only discovered in 1938 in Washoe county, Nevada but is also known from Warner county in eastern California. Trees answering its description have been found at a number of high altitude sites further north, in southern British Columbia. Washoe pine is more closely related to Rocky Mountain ponderosa pine from the other side of the Rocky Mountains, rather than to the nearest members of the subsection, and probably should be referred to Ponderosa pine as a subspecies. It is named after the Washoe Indians and has proved hardy but slow-growing in cultivation. Zone 6.

P. coulteri D. Don
Coulter pine

Tree to 30m but often only half as tall in the wild. Bark in young trees grey and becoming fissured, in old trees blackish or dark purple-brown with broad scaly ridges. Shoot green-brown with a purplish bloom, becoming grey-brown in second year. Bud brown, cylindric-conic, often starts elongating in early winter and may be several cm long in the spring. Leaves in fascicles of 3, spaced on the shoot, grey-green or bluish grey-green, held stiffly forwards around shoot, 20-30cm by 0.15cm. Cone 20-35cm, often remaining closed on the tree for some years, ovoid-oblong, light brown or yellow-brown, massive, scales with sharp forward-directed pointed claw; seed large, 2cm. Zone 8.

Coulter pine is native to the mountains and coastal ranges of central and southern California and in the north of Baja California del Norte in Mexico. It has the largest, though not longest, cones in the genus. These weigh at least 0.7kg (1.5lb) but can be up to 2.25kg (5lb). In the wild Coulter pine makes a small tree usually only 15m tall, though up to a maximum of 25m. In cultivation it is usually grown on better sites with more adequate water supply and will grow larger. The foliage is similar to Jeffrey pine (in the wild it may hybridise with it) but the more wide-spreading and open crown and the buds separate out non-coning trees.

Coulter pine is an excellent garden tree, attractive both as a young plant and at maturity, if there is sufficient space. It will flourish on a wide range of sites, including very heavy clay soils and makes an open crowned tree with bold foliage. The cones are not carried with great regularity in cultivation; they are borne on the leading shoot or main branches but somewhat buried amongst the foliage. Consequently they are much more impressive when viewed off the tree.

P. sabiniana Douglas ex D. Don
Digger pine

Tree to 20 m. Crown open, sparse. Shoot more slender than in Coulter pine and with the fascicles more widely spaced, light brown or purple-brown, green with a glaucous white bloom in the first year. Bud ovoid-conic, slightly resinous, expanding from early autumn in cultivation. Leaves in fascicles of 3, blue-green or grey green, flexible, 15-30 cm by 0.1 cm. Cone ovoid, chocolate brown, on a long recurved peduncle, scales with a spreading, deflexed or S-shaped sharp claw, 10-25 cm by 8-10 cm; seed 1-2.5 cm. Zone 8.

Digger pine is found only in California in the coastal ranges and the Sierra Nevada. It is very distinctive in the open aspect of the crown, although as a small tree, the foliage is neat and fairly dense. It is named after the Digger Indians, to whom the large seeds were an important food source. It will thrive on a wide range of sites, including heavy clay soils.

P. torreyana Parry ex Carriere
Soledad pine

Tree to 15 m, although taller in cultivation. Crown conical, narrow in young trees, becoming rounded. Bark deeply fissured into broad flat ridges of red-brown scales. Shoot stout, green with a glaucous bloom, becoming light purple, then almost black. Leaves in fascicles of 5, stout, dark green, 20-33 cm. Cone broad ovoid, yellow-brown, on a long reflexed peduncle, chestnut brown, scales with a small short stout spike, 10-15 cm; seed 2-2.5 cm. Zone 9.

Soledad pine is very limited in its natural distribution, being found only in southern California on two cliff sites near the mouth of the Soledad river in San Diego county and on the nearby island of Santa Rosa. It is less impressive than the two preceding large seeded species and more tender, needing a sheltered site with full sunlight.

P. montezumae Lambert
Montezuma pine

Tree to 30 m. Crown columnar-conic, in old trees a rounded dome. Bark of young trees covered in corky scabs, becoming thick, greyish brown and divided into small squares, ultimately deeply fissured. Shoot very stout, light brown or reddish brown, becoming grey-brown, rough. Bud small, cylindric-conic or ovoid conic, chestnut brown with scales reflexed at tips, to 1.5 cm. Leaves pendent, long, narrow, usually in fascicles of 5, some of 4 or 6, grey-green or fresh green, 15-30 cm by 0.1-0.15 cm. Cone ovoid to ovoid-conic, yellowish brown or reddish brown, apophysis slightly swollen with a strong transverse ridge, umbo raised with a small, deciduous reflexed or spreading prickle, 13-20 cm. Zone 8.

Montezuma pine is found from north-east Mexico south into Guatemala, in a number of differing forms and at varying altitudes. It is most attractive for the long bold pendent foliage which arches out and down around the shoots. With such a wide range, some forms are more hardy than others, and those from north-east Mexico seem to be hardier than most origins further south. In cultivation, all forms will benefit from sheltered woodland conditions and are unlikely to survive exposed situations. Most of the Mexican pines in this group have been referred to or confused with Montezuma pine at some time or other. With knowledge of the appropriate characters, it is possible to separate them out, at least with some measure of confidence.

Var. *lindleyi* Loudon is a much confused variety which differs in the more cylindrical cone with numerous smaller scales. It appears to be intermediate between Montezuma and Endlicher pines.

P. gordoniana Hartweg is close to Montezuma pine and probably should be referred to it as a subspecies. It comes from western Mexico from Tepic and north-west Jalisco. It differs in the ovoid-conic cone which is rounded at the base but only 10-12 cm long, with the apophysis striated and rough. It is in cultivation but is only hardy in the mildest areas. Zone 9.

P. rudis Endlicher
Endlicher pine

Tree to 20 m. Crown high rounded dome, lower branches soon lost. Bark dark grey, rough and deeply fissured. Shoot stout or slender, purple-brown, variably pruinose. Bud cylindric, apex rounded conic, pointed, light brown, scales free at tips. Leaves held out around the shoot, not pendent, in fascicles of 5, rarely 4 or 6, blue-green, grey-green or yellow-grey-green, moderately stout or slender, 10-16 cm, sometimes to 25 cm, by 0.1 cm. Cone long ovoid, slightly curved, tapering to apex, base rounded, dark brown, apophysis with a transverse keel and raised umbo bearing a conical, recurved prickle, 7-13 cm. Zone 7.

This tree is found across central and northern Mexico at fairly high altitudes. It is very distinct in the 'flesh' in the radically spreading leaves and the low rounded umbrella habit, quickly losing the lower branches; however, it has more often been confused with Montezuma and Hartweg pines. It is in cultivation and is hardier than Montezuma pine but the habit is less attractive.

P. cooperi Blanco
Cooper pine

Tree to 30 m. Crown in old trees dense and rounded, with the thick branches pendent at the tips. Bark reddish brown, rough, fissured into irregular plates, in young trees brown and slightly smoother. Shoot glaucous green, becoming reddish brown, rough, red-brown ovate-conic scale leaves beneath the fascicles persistent into second year. Bud cylindric, conic at the tip and short acuminate, red-brown, scales free at tips. Leaves in tight fascicles of 5 but often some of 3 or 4 on same shoot, densely forwards along shoot, stiff, light to bright blue-green, 5-12 cm by 0.1 cm. Cone long ovoid, slightly oblique, shiny reddish brown, apophysis flat, slightly keeled, umbo with persistent reflexed prickle, 5-9 cm. Zone 7.

Cooper pine is found in north-west Mexico in west Durango and south-west Chihuahua. It grows in a region of low summer rainfall and dry cold winters. It was only introduced in the early 1960s but has proved hardy, making a slow-growing tree which loses the lower branches and develops a rounded umbrella crown, like *P. rudis*, to which it is closely related.

var. *ornelasii* (Martinez)Blanco differs in the following features. The leaves are set more distantly on the shoot and droop forwards and down; they are also longer, 10-20 cm by 0.07 cm, and mid- to dark green. The shoots are pruinose, glaucous green becoming brown and the scale leaves are smaller and less persistent. The buds are reddish brown and slightly resinous. Cones light brown, 6-10 cm, apophysis raised, umbo with a fine persistent reflexed prickle.

This variety is also found growing in Durango. It is in cultivation and makes a more vigorous tree with longer, laxer foliage. The strong shoots are quite distinctive in the spaced leaves and glaucous bloom. Both the species and variety tend to drop the cones complete with the peduncle.

P. hartwegii Lindley
Hartweg pine

Tree to 35 m. Crown columnar, domed. Bark greyish, thick and rough. Shoot reddish brown, grooved. Bud long ovoid, acute, reddish brown. Leaves variously in fascicles of 3, 4 or 5, on different populations or sometimes on same tree, stiff, light to slightly glaucous green, 9-15 cm. Cone black or very dark brown, cylindric-ovoid, often curved, 7-16 cm, scales thin, flexible, apophysis bulbous with a prominent umbo bearing forward-pointing prickle. Zone 7.

Hartweg pine is found on the highest volcanoes across central and southern Mexico and in Guatemala and north-west El Salvador. It occurs at the treeline, usually forming pure forests, although at the lower end of its range it is mixed with Silver fir or other pines. It is hardy but rare in cultivation. The seedlings undergo a distinct grass stage before making height growth.

P. devoniana Lindley
Michoacan pine (*P. michoacana* Martinez)

Tree to 25 m. Crown dense, rounded. Bark thick, brown, very rough, in young trees scaly and brown. Shoot stout, light brown, becoming dark brown, very rough. Bud ovoid, acute, resinous, red-brown, 2.5 cm. Leaves in fascicles of 5 or 6, radially arranged, stout and coarse but flexible and drooping, pale shiny green, 25-50 cm. Cone oblong to cylindro-conic, straight or curved, dull brown, 14-28 cm, apophysis bulbous, particularly at base of cone, umbo grey, raised, bearing a small, often deciduous, forward-pointing prickle. Zone 9.

Michoacan pine is found in central and southern Mexico. It is most impressive in the leaves, the longest of any pine species, and the remarkable cones, and makes trees with a bold appearance. In cultivation, it is probably only suitable for the mildest areas but origins from the northern and higher parts of the range might produce hardier forms. It is usually called *P. michoacana* Martinez but this is almost certainly a synonym of *P. devoniana*; for many years this and other species were lumped by botanists under Montezuma pine with little regard to their distinctions and when Martinez started to sort out the taxonomy of Mexican hard pines, he was uncertain of the application of some names, so he gave the most distinctive elements new names. Michoacan pine is related to Hartweg pine.

P. wincesteriana Gordon
Winchester pine (*P. michoacana* var. *cornuta* Martinez)

This little-known tree appears to be intermediate between *P. montezumae* and *P. devoniana*, but differing from both in the frequently even larger long conic cones 20-35 cm by 9 cm, when closed!, which are often curved but sometimes straight, with the scales 1.5 cm broad, stout, with a greatly thickened conic apophysis with a stout umbo bearing a straight or reflexed spine. The apophysis has a strong transverse ridge and is often broader than long (unlike *P. devoniana* in which it is often longer than broad). It may be synonymous with *P. montezumae* var. *macrocarpa* Martinez. Zone 9.

P. pseudostrobus Lindley
Smooth-bark Mexican pine

Tree to 40 m or more. Crown rounded, domed. Bark of young trees yellowish brown, thin, smooth for several years, in old trees thick, rough, fissured, grey. Shoot yellowish green, later reddish brown, slightly pruinose, slender, decurrent leaf bases not persistent, soon smooth. Bud oblong to oblong-conic, slightly resinous, yellow-brown to pale brown. Leaves in fascicles of 5, yellowish green, bright green or dark bluish green, stiff but flexible, pendent, slender, 17-32 cm by 0.1 cm. Cone ovate to oblong-ovate, slightly oblique, reddish brown, on a peduncle 1-1.3 cm, 8-15 cm, apophysis flat or with a low transverse ridge, apophysis flexible, not hard, umbo small with a small deciduous prickle. Zone 8.

This pine is found throughout Mexico except for the northern regions near the USA border and extends south into Guatemala. It is extensively planted in many tropical countries because of its fast growth and good timber quality. Despite this, it is hardy in cultivation, although rare. It is probably necessary to try several plants of different origins to find a hardy individual. The northern origins from southern Nuevo Leon may be hardier than others.

P. estevesii (Martinez)Perry
Esteves pine

Tree to 15-20 m. Crown rounded dome on stout bole, lower branches lost. Bark thick, black and rough. Shoot rather rough, stout. Bud small, ovoid, yellow-brown, resinous. Leaves in fascicles of 5, coarse, thick, drooping, shiny green, 20-30 cm. Cone broad ovoid, scales hard, stiff, apophysis raised, umbo greyish, raised, with a strong persistent prickle, 8-12 cm. Zone 8.

This tree was formerly regarded as a variety of *P. pseudostrobus* but is very distinct in the habit, which is like that of *P. rudis*, in that the lower branches are lost, and the more ovoid cones. It is found in the Sierra Madre Oriental in Nuevo Leon and Tamaulipas in north-east Mexico and should be hardy.

P. oaxacana (Martinez)Mirov
Oaxaca pine

This tree is related to *P. pseudostrobus* but differs very markedly in the cone, which has the apophysis very protuberant, more or less conical and reflexed. There are a number of significant differences in the resins contained in the tree. It is found in Veracruz, Puebla, Guerrero, Chiapas, Mexico and Oaxaca states of Mexico. It has been introduced but is probably only suitable for mild areas. Zone 9.

P. apulcensis Lindley
Apulco pine (*P. pseudostrobus* var. *apulcensis* (Lindley) Shaw)

This species is characterised by the oblong-ovoid, symmetrical yellow-brown cones, 8-15 cm, with stout hard stiff scales. The apophysis is pro-tuberant and slightly reflexed. The foliage is similar to but shorter than that of *P. oaxacana*, 15-25 cm, mostly 20 cm, and sometimes more than 5 to a fascicle. It is probably related to and in some ways intermediate between *P. oaxacana* and *P. estevesii*. It is found in eastern Mexico from the states of Hidalgo, Tlaxcala, Puebla and Veracruz. Zone 9.

P. douglasiana Martinez
Douglas pine

This tree differs from *P. pseudostrobus* in the thinner but stiff leaves, 25-33 cm by 0.07-0.1 cm, which in transverse section have the hypoderm intruding in places through to the vascular bundle, the rougher shoots, the peduncle falling with the cone (not remaining on the tree with the basal few scales). The cones are 8-12 cm by 4-5 cm with thick hard scales; the apophysis is thick, flat or slightly raised, with a flat or slightly raised unarmed umbo. It is recorded from western Mexico from Sinaloa to Oaxaca. It may be in cultivation but is only suited to mild areas. *P. martinezii* Larsen is closely related but has the leaves in fascicles of 6 and the peduncle remains attached to the tree when the cone falls. It was described from Michoacan but its status is uncertain. Zone 9.

P. maximinoi Moore
Thin-leaf pine (*P. tenuifolia* Bentham)

This tree is close to *P. douglasiana* but differs in its finer foliage, with the leaves 15-28 cm by only 0.05-0.07 cm with similar intrusions of hypoderm tissue into the endoderm tissue, in resin content, and the 6-10 cm fragile cones with thin weak small scales; the apophysis is thin and flat, whilst the umbo is flat and unarmed. It is recorded from western and central Mexico from Sinaloa south through Guatemala, Belize, Honduras and into Nicaragua. It is only likely to be suitable for mild areas. Zone 9.

Subsection *Contortae* Little & Critchfield

This group comprises four species which have the following characters in common. The leaves are 2 to a fascicle and short, less than 10 cm. The shoots are multi-nodal and the cones are small, 3-8 cm. The cones in most of the taxa do not open immediately but are 'serotinuous', literally late, meaning that they open some time after maturity, often after a forest fire. The species are very tough little trees, well adapted to hostile sites but not of the first, or second, order of beauty for the garden. They are of value as timber trees.

P. contorta Douglas ex Loudon
Shore pine

This species is divided into four subspecies. The descriptions use the typical form as a benchmark. Cultivars are detailed at the end. Zone 5.

P. contorta subsp. *contorta*
Shore pine

Tree 25 m. Crown ovoid or columnar with a domed apex, young trees conical, bushy at base. Bark red-brown or yellow-brown, fissured into small squares. Shoot greenish brown, becoming orange-brown and shiny. Bud cylindric, pointed, cinnamon brown, very resinous. Leaves tight and point forwards on shoot, dense, deep to bright green, often somewhat yellowish, twisted, 4-5 cm by 0.1 cm. Male cones abundant, even on young trees, yellow. Cone long-conic, yellow-brown or pink-brown, reflexed, persisting on tree, most opening on maturity, scales with a spreading or forward-pointing thin prickle, 2.5-7.5 cm.

Shore pine is found from south-east Alaska to northern California, always along the coastal strip. In the wild it ranges from low bushes to small trees, depending upon the severity of the winds off the sea. In cultivation it has shown considerable vigour, even on the poorest and wettest sites, including pure peats. The crown form tends not to be that good, often developing a basal sweep to the bole.

P. contorta subsp. *latifolia*
(Engelmann)Critchfield
Lodgepole pine

Tree 30 m. Crown conic, open, on a straight bole. Bark more flaky in curled scales. Leaves 6-9 cm by 1.5 cm, more spreading, brighter green. Cone ovoid, prickle shorter, 4 cm, most remaining closed.

Lodgepole pine comes from the Rocky Mountains from the Yukon to southern Colorado. The majority of the cones remain closed until there is a forest fire, although a small proportion may open and shed seed in the normal way. Fires are natural within its range, often started by lightning strikes. Lodgepole and Shore pines intergrade where the two meet. It also hybridises with Jack pine where they meet in the Yukon and British Columbia.

P. contorta subsp. *murrayana*
(Grev. & Balf.)Critchfield
Sierra lodgepole pine

Tree to 50 m. Crown narrow conic. Bark thin, brown, scaly. Leaves rigid, yellowish green, 5-8 cm by 0.13-0.22 cm. Cones open on maturity, soon falling, more symmetrical than in other forms.

This tree is native to the Cascade Mountains of south-west Washington and west Oregon south along the Sierra Nevada through California to northern Baja California del Norte in Mexico.

P. contorta subsp. *bolanderi*
(Parlatore)Critchfield
Mendicino shore pine

Shrub or small tree. Bark black-brown. Leaves under 5 cm, without resin canals (a proportion of leaves lacking resin canals in the other forms). Cone asymmetrical, opening late.

This shrubby form is very local, restricted to Mendicino county of California.

In cultivation, *P. contorta* has proved more useful as a shelter or forest tree on very barren sites, rather than as an amenity tree. The tree is capable of making roots into waterlogged soil profiles and does this by forming air spaces in the tissues to permit the movement of oxygen so that the roots can respire. The leaves tend to become more yellow-green over winter.

A number of cultivars have been named.

'Compacta' has a dense upright habit and dark green needles.

'Frisian Gold' is a mutation with bright yellow-gold foliage and a dwarf habit.

'Spaans Dwarf' is an open bush with erect branches and mid-green leaves only 1.5 cm.

P. banksiana Lambert
Jack pine

Tree to 20 m. Crown irregular, scruffy. Bark fissured, orange-grey or red-brown. Shoot thin, flexible, red-brown or purple-brown. Bud ovoid to cylindric, very resinous, pale brown. Leaves twisted and divergent, stout, yellow-green, 2-4 cm. Male cones yellow. Cone points forwards along shoot, or forwards and widely-spreading, ovoid-conic, asymmetrical, straight or more often curved, remaining unopened for some time, scales variable on the cones, unarmed or with a minute deciduous prickle, 4-6.5 cm. Zone 2.

Jack pine is found across Canada from the Atlantic coast to the Yukon and in the USA along the Canadian border from Minneapolis to New Hampshire. It grows further north than any other American pine, and is found on dry sandy soils. It is curious for the forward-pointing cones but otherwise is rarely handsome.

P. virginiana Miller
Scrub pine

This tree differs from Jack pine in the grey-green leaves which are 4-7cm long, pink-white bloomed shoots and the orange-brown male cones; the cones are oblong-conic, symmetrical, spreading or pointing back slightly, opening at maturity, with a persistent prickle and 4-8cm in length. Zone 5.

Scrub pine is found in eastern USA from New York to Alabama and Mississippi states. It occurs at relatively low elevations. Aesthetically, it is no improvement on Jack pine, although hardy in cultivation and has been recommended for bonsai!

P. clausa (Chapman)Vasey
Sand pine

This tree has thin, hairy, glaucous bloomed shoots, later red-brown, non-resinous buds, slender dark green needles 5-9cm and serotinous dark brown or yellow-brown cones which are 5-8cm and have short sharp prickles. Zone 7.

It is found on coastal sands across northern Florida, just extending into coastal Alabama, and regenerates rapidly after forest fires. Sand pine is rare in cultivation.

var. *immuginata* Ward from the western end of the range differs in the non serotinous cones.

Subsection *Oocarpae* Little & Critchfield

The pines in this group are mainly characterised by the serotinous cones which remain on the trees for several decades and only open to release the seeds after a forest fire. The heat of the fire melts the resin in the cones and they open slightly. They then close when it next rains (ensuring the fire is out!) and open fully on redrying. The seeds are therefore released onto a bare site, covered with a thin layer of fertiliser (ash), and are able to establish before other plants can seed in from outside. The seeds can remain viable for about 20 years in the closed cones. The cones generally are oblique, with the outer scales more woody, and are often in clusters together; these protect the cones whilst they are awaiting a passing fire. The leaves are mostly in fascicles of 3, but 2 in some species and 5 in others. The shoots are mainly, but not exclusively, multi-nodal, uni-nodal shoots being commoner in cool climates.

P. radiata D. Don
Monterey pine

Tree to 40m, occasionally more but small in the wild. Crown narrow conic with open whorls of branches in young trees, rounded dome, dense and on a stout branchless bole when old. Bark black or dark grey, deeply and ruggedly fissured and ridged, on young trees purplish grey. Shoot grey-green, later grey-brown. Bud cylindric, conic at the apex, slightly resinous. Leaves in fascicles of 3, shining bright green, although appearing dark green on the tree, arranged forwards and spreading, slender, 10-15cm by 0.1cm. Cones very oblique, occasionally symmetrical, persistent for 25 years, ovoid, recurved on shoot, around 20 scales (rarely none) on the outer side swollen and bulbous with an obtuse conical umbo, other scales flat, red-brown or yellow-brown but grey after exposure on the tree for some years, 8cm by 5cm to 15cm by 9cm when closed, rarely 14cm by 5cm when resembling Knob-cone pine. Zone 8.

Monterey pine is restricted in the wild to two Mexican islands and three sites on coastal mainland California — Monterey, Cambria and Ano Nuevo, and together these wild populations cover less than 6,500 hectares. By contrast it has been planted as a forest tree over many times greater areas of the world, primarily in New Zealand where over 400,000 hectares have been planted but also in Spain, Portugal, South Africa, Chile and Australia. It has a very fast growth rate, having made 30m in 17 years and 65m in 40 years in New Zealand, and a reasonable timber. Monterey pine can be either uni-nodal or multi-nodal, with up to four whorls of branches on the multi-nodal forms.

In cultivation, Monterey pine is most useful for providing a fast-growing tree for either shelter or scale. It makes a very impressive tree very quickly, although rarely lasting for more than 100 years. The yellow male cones can be very attractive in spring.

'Aurea' has the needles golden yellow.

var. *binata* (Engelmann)Brewer & Watson is a form from the Mexican island of Guadelupe, off the coast of Baja California del Norte. It differs in the needles in fascicles of 2, except on the strong shoots where they are in 3s, and shorter and broader, 7.5-12.5cm by 0.15-0.2cm. About half the trees carry symmetrical cones with all the scales flat. There are about 400 trees surviving on Guadelupe. Rainfall is very low and the trees obtain a high proportion of their moisture supply through the condensation of the frequent fogs. It is in cultivation but is uncommon.

var. *cedrosensis* (Howell) Axelrod is found on Cedros Island to the south of Guadelupe. It has been referred to Bishop pine in the past on account of the 2-needled fascicles but the cones are Monterey pine, although as in the Guadelupe plant, a high proportion carry symmetrical cones with all the scales flat. Plants from Cedros island are in cultivation but are rare.

P. muricata D. Don
Bishop pine

Tree to 30m. Crown either broadly domed with green foliage or narrower and taller with dark blue-grey leaves. Bark dark grey, deeply fissured into long plates. Shoot orange-brown. Bud cylindric, red-brown. Leaves in fascicles of 2, rarely some of 3, crowded, spreading, stiff, colour as below, 10-15cm by 0.2cm. Cone oblique, ovoid-conic, matt or less often glossy, darker brown than in Monterey pine, outer scales with a stout sharp spine spreading or pointing back, inner scales flatter, less spined, 7-9cm by 4-5cm. Zone 8.

Bishop pine is found on seven sites along the coast of California from Humboldt to Santa Barbara counties. The two northern populations differ from the southern five populations in that the trees are taller-growing, especially in cultivation, and have blue-green rather than yellowish grey-green leaves with the cones tending to be narrower with smaller scales and slenderer spines (although with much overlap); there are also differences in the chemical content of the resins. They belong to the var. *borealis* Axelrod. Bishop pine grows very quickly on barren acidic sand soils and shows considerable promise for forestry purposes on soils of low inherent fertility. It retains the closed cones for longer than any other species, up to 70 years, although it is doubtful if the seeds remain viable for much over 20.

P. remorata Mason is a form or related species described from Santa Cruz and Santa Rosa islands off the southern California coast. The true status of these plants is not known.

P. attenuata Lemmon
Knobcone pine

Tree to 25m. Crown conic, often forked with ascending branches. Bark grey, smooth, in old trees fissured and scaly. Shoot green-brown. Bud cylindric, pointed, resinous. Leaves in fascicles of 3, stiff, slender, grey-green, 8-18cm. Cone ovoid-conic, paler yellow-brown than in Monterey pine, 9-20cm by 5cm, elongated, scales on outer portion swollen, conic, with pointed umbo, on inner portion flatter. Zone 7.

Knobcone pine has the widest distribution of the trio of Californian species, extending from south-west Oregon to northern Baja California del Norte. It also occurs away from the coast, on dry hill sites. The conic, not rounded, outer scales clearly

separate it from Monterey pine. It grows fairly fast when young but usually on two or more stems which break up in middle age and therefore it does not make such a useful tree as Monterey pine.

P. greggii Engelmann ex Parlatore
Gregg pine

Tree to 15 or 30m. Crown broad conic, domed in older trees. Bark grey, smooth, eventually becoming rougher. Shoot grey-brown, pruinose on young shoots. Bud oblong, dark brown, not resinous. Leaves in fascicles of 3, stiff, slender, spreading all around shoot, shiny bright green, 7.5-13cm. Cone oblong-conic, yellow-brown, irregular in shape, apophyses raised unevenly, sessile, remaining closed on the trees for several years, 7.5-13cm. Zone 7.

Gregg pine is restricted to north-east Mexico, from Hidalgo, San Luis Potosi, Nuevo Leon and Coahuila. It is related to *P. patula* but differs in the spreading, not drooping foliage and the uneven cones which are roughly cylindrical for the lower half and conical above. It occurs in dry and cold areas. The male cones are located at the base of the second internodal length of shoot and shed pollen in mid-summer, far later than in other species but coinciding with the rainy season in north-east Mexico.

Gregg pine is hardy in cultivation and makes a medium-sized tree. Recent re-introductions have proved less hardy than the original one; whether this is due to inherent tenderness of seedling trees or from the choice of more southerly origins is not clear. Plants from the Coahuila and northern Nuevo Leon populations should be hardy.

P. patula Scheide & Deppe
Mexican weeping pine

Tree to 30m. Crown ovoid, open with level branches. Bark reddish to yellow-brown, scaly, becoming more deeply fissured and greyer. Shoot pale greenish brown, bloomed, becoming redder. Bud oblong-conic, reddish brown. Leaves in fascicles of 3, sometimes 4 or 5, slender, drooping, light green to yellow-green, shiny, 15-30cm. Cone long conic, sessile, yellow-brown to chestnut-brown, 6-10cm. Zone 8.

Mexican weeping pine is found in eastern Mexico, primarily the states of Queretaro, Hidalgo, Puebla and Veracruz but south into Oaxaca and Chiapas; also it may occur in Honduras and Guatemala. It makes a very attractive tree with the bright shiny foliage hanging down from the shoots. It is hardy in mild and sheltered localities in cultivation and well worth trying where adequate shelter and moisture are available, with good sunlight. In subtropical climates it is used as a fast-growing tree for timber production.

P. tecumumanii Schwerdtf. from northern Guatemala may be a form of P. patula in which the cones are not serotinous and are on long peduncles.

P. pringlei Shaw
Pringle pine

This subtropical species has stout leaves, 15-25 cm, and conical cones, 5-10 cm, set on short but distinct peduncles. It is found in central western Mexico. It is unlikely to prove successful in cultivation. Zone 9.

P. jaliscana Perez
Jalisco pine

This recently described tree is close to P. oocarpa but differs in the more slender leaves, only 0.6-0.08 cm wide, and small cones 4.5-8.5 cm by 3.5-5.5 cm. It is recorded from north-west Jalisco state but is unlikely to thrive in cultivation. Zone 9.

P. oocarpa Scheide ex Schlechtendal
Egg-cone pine

This tree, with needles in fascicles of 5 (sometimes of 3 or 4), is most distinctive in the smooth, ovoid or egg-shaped cones which are usually set on a slender peduncle to 3 cm, although sometimes on a shorter and stouter peduncle, though never sessile. The foliage resembles that of P. patula. Zone 9.

It is found in Mexico from Chihuahua to the southern border, and in Guatemala, Belize, Nicaragua and Honduras but is absent from north-east and eastern Mexico. It is widely planted in tropical countries as a timber species. Most origins are not hardy in cultivation, but those from the northern states are likely to prove more amenable, and occasional plants are encountered in collections. In north-west Jalisco in 1984 the trees were shedding pollen in November but I am not sure whether this was abnormal, a local occurrence or characteristic of the species.

P. teocote Schlectendal & Chamisso
Teocote pine

Tree to 30 m. Crown dense, rounded, irregular. Bark greyish brown, rough and deeply fissured, in young trees reddish brown and flaky in thin scales. Shoot pruinose, becoming reddish brown, thin, smooth. Bud cylindric, acuminate, resinous. Leaves in fascicles of 3, rarely 2, 4 or 5, stout, rigid, bright to dark green, 10-15 cm. Cone ovoid to ovoid-conic,
reflexed on a short peduncle, symmetrical or slightly oblique, dark brown to reddish, 4-6 cm, open on maturity but rather persistent on tree, apophysis slightly bulbous or flattish, lightly keeled, umbo ash grey with a deciduous prickle. Zone 7.

Teocote pine is widely distributed throughout Mexico from Chihuahua south into Guatemala. It is, however, probably the least attractive of Mexican pines, having neither a good crown nor bold foliage to commend it. The crown is untidy and the open cones are retained for several years. It is hardy but rare. This species and the following two do not seem to fit easily in this subsection and may justify a separate subsection.

P. herrerai Martinez
Herrera pine

This tree is related to Teocote pine but differs in the longer, soft, very slender and more flexible leaves, 11-20 cm, the cylindrical non-resinous buds and the very small long-ovate cones, 2.5-4.5 cm (the smallest of any Mexican pine), scales small, numerous, similar to but less rigid than in Teocote pine. It is found in subtropical regions of Mexico from Sinaloa to Guerrero. It has been introduced but is suitable only for mild areas. Zone 10.

P. lawsonii Roezl
Lawson pine

This tree differs from Teocote and Herrera pines in the following characters: bark red-brown, finely fissured and scaly; buds cylindrical, non-resinous; leaves glaucous, in fascicles of 3 and 4, less often 5, green or grey, soft, flexible, 13-23 cm; cone ovoid, mid- to yellow-brown, 5-7 cm, apophysis flat or raised, glossy, umbo flattened. The closed cone is much stouter and broader than in Teocote pine, with much larger and fewer scales. sometimes nearly resembling P. oocarpa and P. pringlei. It comes from subtropical and warm temperate parts of Mexico from Jalisco and Hidalgo south to Guerrero and Oaxaca. It has been introduced but is not likely to be hardy outside the mildest areas, which is unfortunate, as it is a beautiful tree with the long soft blue foliage. Zone 9.

Subsection *Sylvestres* Loudon

This section is distinguished by the shoots being uni-nodal, the 2 needles per fascicle (unless mentioned), the symmetrical cones opening on maturity and in some characters of the wood and chromosomes.

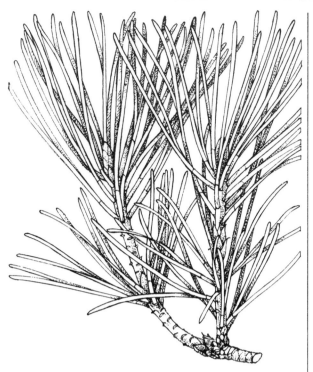

Figure 8.17 Pinus sylvestris. *Foliage.*

P. sylvestris Linnaeus
Scots pine

Tree to 30 m. Crown conical, dome-shaped in old trees. Bark of two types; upper bark exfoliating in thin scaly flakes, red-brown or orange, lower bark deeply fissured with purple-grey ridges which exfoliate in small thick scales. Shoot green-brown, becoming dull pink-brown. Bud cylindric-ovoid, short pointed, red-brown, resinous. Leaves stiff, twisted, bluish or yellowish grey-green, stomata in distinct lines on both surfaces, 5-7 cm by 0.1-0.2 cm. Sheaths orange-brown, becoming blackish brown. Male cones lemon-yellow, globular, pollen shed in May. Cone ovoid-conic, green, ripens pale grey-brown (or red-brown), 3-7 cm by 2 cm when closed; scales rhombic with a small blunt or sometimes raised umbo. Zone 2.

Scots pine has a vast range from Scotland in the west across northern Eurasia nearly to the Pacific Ocean in the east. It extends south to Spain and Turkey.

Scots pine is essentially a tree of continental climates. It will flourish on dry sandy soils and will only grow slowly on wet soils. It tolerates chalk conditions for a period but cannot be relied upon to grow to full maturity on these soils. The foliage of many origins turns yellow in cold weather, which has presented problems in the eastern USA where the tree is used for a Christmas tree. Some origins, such as those from the Caucasus (referred to var. *hamata* Steven) remain blue-green however cold in winter.

Scots pine is an attractive tree, particularly when fully grown with its rounded domed crown; the abrupt change in colour of the bark also adds interest, but grafted plants will almost always only have the upper bark form. Grafted plants also develop more rounded, compact and less vigorous habits. The seeds are an important food source for some birds.

With such a large range, an equally large number of botanical varieties have been named. Detailed description of all these is outside the scope of this work and, apart from the following cultivars, only the following two varieties are discussed.

var. *hamata* Steven includes the plants found from south-east of a line from Albania, along the lower Danube, the Black Sea north of the Crimea, the Sea of Azov and across to the northern end of the Caspian Sea. The populations within this area are rather disjunct but differ in resin composition and some other characters.

var. *mongolica* Litvinov **Mongolian Scots pine** is found in north-east China in Heilongjiang province and in outer Mongolia and adjacent parts of Siberia on sandy soils. It has very smooth grey-green shoots and needles to 9 cm.

'Argentea' is a garden selection with the foliage bluish silver. It makes a neat plant, although because it is grafted, the true basal bark is not formed and the habit will be more rounded and compact. Similar seedlings can be selected amongst many populations and will form better trees.

'Aurea' is a splendid plant. The foliage only turns golden yellow in early winter, remaining so until spring when in April it changes to a nearly normal blue-green with only the hint of yellow. The harder the winter, the more intense the colour, providing some solace for the weather. 'Aurea' will make a plant to 10 or 15 m but 'Gold Coin' is a dwarf, growing to 2 m, with a more intense golden colour. 'Gold Medal' is brighter and smaller, with leaves to 3 cm and makes a plant 1.5 m in three or four decades. 'Moseri' is similar but with longer needles less gold in winter but greener in summer.

'Beuvronensis' is a dwarf form growing to 1 m as a low rounded bush. The annual growths are 6-7 cm and the bluish green leaves to 4 cm. It originated as a witches broom.

'Compressa' is a very narrow conical form making growths of no more than 5 cm and therefore suitable as a dot plant on a rockery.

'Doone Valley' is a witches broom form which makes an upright bush of irregular outline.

'Fastigiata' is an interesting form with a pencil narrow columnar crown. The branches are fastigiate and therefore liable to be damaged by wind when the tree is exposed, hence few are seen more than 6 m tall.

'Inverleith' is a variegated form, with the blue-green needles covered with splashes of white. It originated at the Royal Botanic Garden, Edinburgh.

'Jade' is a dwarf mound-forming plant with the congested foliage a striking jade.

'Saxatilis' has short bluish needles and makes an irregular compact mound.

'Tabuliformis' is a table-forming clone (not to be confused with the following species of this name).

'Watereri' has a pyramidal habit, becoming rounded with time. It makes a large bush, 8 m high and through, although growing the blue-green foliage at the rate of only 10-15 cm per annum.

P. densiflora Siebold & Zuccarini
Japanese red pine

Tree to 20 m, to 30 m in Japan. Crown conic in young trees, becoming wide-spreading and flat-topped in older ones. Bark reddish brown, scaly, fissured and greyish at base. Shoot whitish green, later pink-brown. Bud cylindric-conic, chestnut brown, slightly resinous. Leaves bright green, slender, 8-12 cm by 0.07-0.12 cm. Cone ovoid-conic, sometimes clustered, yellow or pale brown, scales thin, flat on exposed portion, 3-6 cm. Zone 5.

Japanese red pine is found throughout Japan and in Korea, north-east China and adjoining Maritime Russia. It makes an interesting tree, with its bright foliage but otherwise is similar to Scots pine.

'Alice Verkade' is a diminutive plant with fresh green foliage, forming a globe expanding at around 7 cm per annum. A number of other dwarf cultivars have been named.

'Aurea' has the foliage yellow-green during the summer but, as in the Golden Scots pine, the best colour is only developed during the winter when the weather is at its coldest. It makes a harsher yellow than in the Scots pine form.

'Oculus-draconis' has each needle banded with two yellow spots, appearing from above like 'Dragon's eyes'. This effect develops better after good summers.

'Pendula' is a form with weeping foliage. It can be used to make a weeping tree, if trained to form a stem, or for ground cover.

'Umbraculifera' develops a rounded dome-shaped or umbrella crown, achieving 4 m tall by 6 m spread with time.

P. tabuliformis Carriere
Chinese red pine

Tree to 30 m. Crown conic when young, becoming flat-topped and spreading in old trees. Bark similar to Japanese red pine. Shoot yellow-brown, becoming more brown. Bud ovoid-conic. Leaves mid-green, spreading around shoot, 9-15 cm by 0.1-0.15 cm. Cone broadly ovoid-conic, 4-9 cm by 3 cm, scales hard, stiff, woody, flat with small central prickle on the umbo, seed large with relatively short wing. Zone 5.

Chinese red pine is found across northern China from Shandong to Sichuan provinces. It has not made a significant tree in cultivation, although as pleasing as others of this group.

var. *mukdensis* Uyeki is a form from north-east China. It has more widely splayed needles and ash-yellow shoots, becoming grey-brown. It has recently been introduced.

P. takahasii Nakai
Xingkai pine

This tree is related to *P. tabuliformis* but differs in the stiffer glossy green needles, 5-10 cm (slightly longer in cultivation) by 0.1-0.15 cm and the brown first year shoots which are greyish above and become grey-brown with a purple hue in the second year. The conelets are globular with forward-pointing prickles on the umbos; they mature globose to ovoid in shape, 4-5 cm by 2-3 cm. It is in cultivation from seeds collected in north Korea by Wilson under his number 8815 and has made a tree to 18 m. Zone 6.

P. densata Masters
Gaoshan pine

This tree is related to *P. tabuliformis*, of which it is often treated as a variety, and to *P. yunnanensis*. It differs in the yellow-brown shoots, leaves in 2s or in both 2s and 3s on the same shoots (although more often in 2s), cylindric buds with rounded conic tips and free, slightly spreading scales, and the oblique cones with swollen scales bearing a thickened, backwards pointing umbo. It occurs in western Sichuan, eastern Xizang, southern Qinghai and north-west Yunnan. It is in cultivation but is uncommon. Zone 7.

P. yunnanensis Franchet
Yunnan pine

Tree 30 m. Crown rounded dome on mature trees. Bark reddish brown, fissured into plates. Shoot stout, shiny pink-brown. Bud ovoid, red-brown with white fringed scales. Leaves in fascicles of 3, rarely in pairs, pendent, bright green or grey-green, 10-30 cm by 0.12 cm. Cone ovoid-conic, ripening dark brown, apophysis gently rounded with impressed umbo, 6-10 cm. Zone 9.

Yunnan pine is found in Yunnan, south-east Xizang, west Sichuan, Guizhou and Guangxi provinces of China. It makes an attractive hardy tree with long needles. It is related to Chinese red pine, through Gaoshan pine and to the following species.

P. kesiya Royle ex Gordon
Khasi pine

This tree is related to Yunnan pine, differing in the more slender, bright brown shoots, the needles in the range 12-24 cm by only 0.05 cm, and the ovoid, bright brown cones only 4.5-6 cm with the apophysis ridged in the centre and with a thick sharp central umbo. It is found from north-east India across south-east Asia to the north-west Philippines. It has been introduced but is only hardy in mild areas. It is also known as *P. insularis* Endlicher, which may be a better name. Zone 9.

var. *langbianensis* (Cheval)Gaussen is a form from north Vietnam and south Yunnan with broader leaves and cones.

P. merkusii Junghman & de Vrise
Merkus pine

This pine has grey-brown fissured bark, hairy shoots, long narrow brown buds, leaves usually 2 to a fascicle but sometimes in 3s and 17-25 cm by 0.01 cm, and narrowly cylindric cones 6-13 cm by 3 cm. It is found from eastern Burma through south-east Asia to the eastern Philippines and is the only pine to cross the Equator, which it does in Indonesia, to 1°S. It occurs at low altitudes and is unlikely to prove hardy in cultivation, except in very mild areas. *P. latteri* Mason, from Guangdong, Guangxi and north Vietnam, may be identical but is described as having broader leaves and narrow ovoid cones with the apophysis ridged and with a small hooked umbo. Zone 10.

P. massoniana Lambert
Masson pine

Tree 18 m, exceptionally to 45 m. Crown with spreading branches, domed. Bark reddish grey, fissured into small scales. Shoot slender, smooth, orange-brown to yellow-brown. Bud cylindrical, slightly resinous, scales loose, reflexed at tip. Leaves in fascicles of 2, rarely 3, bright green, 12-20 cm by 0.05-0.1 cm. Cone ovoid to ovoid-conic, yellow-brown to dark brown, 4-7 cm by 2.5-4 cm. Zone 8.

Masson pine is found in central and southern China, in Taiwan and in north Vietnam. It occurs at fairly low altitudes but plants from central China are hardy, at least with some shelter.

P. henryi Masters
Henry pine

This tree has prominently grooved branches which are yellow-brown or grey-brown, ovoid-conic red-brown buds, stout leaves 7-12 cm by 0.1 cm and cones ovoid, yellow-grey, 2.5-5 cm, with the apophysis somewhat rounded with a depressed mucronate umbo. It is recorded from west Hubei, north-east Sichuan and south Shaansi. It has been referred to Masson pine as a variety but may be more closely related to Chinese red pine. It is probably not in cultivation but should prove hardy. Zone 8.

P. mugo Turra
Dwarf mountain pine

Shrub to 3.5 m with thick ascending, erect or decumbent branches. Bark grey, scaly. Shoot green, maturing brown. Bud ovoid-cylindric, very resinous. Leaves spaced, tight, dark or bright green, 3-8 cm by 0.15-0.25 cm. Cone symmetrical, ovoid to ovoid-conic, 2-6 cm by 1.5-2.5 cm; umbo in centre or lower part of scale, with a small mucro. Zone 2.

This dwarf tree is common on the mountains of central Europe, the Balkans and the Apennines in Italy. In the wild the thickets of interlocking branches can create impenetrable conditions and are called 'krummholz' in German. It has been used to give shelter for forest plantings in northern Europe. In the garden it can be used as a dwarf conifer or for ground cover. A number of clones have been named. Most of these are more dwarf than the species.

'Compacta' is of more normal stature for the species but makes a denser plant.

'Corleys Mat' is a carpeting form with green needles, growing 6 cm per annum. 'Mops' grows at the same rate but is globose.

'Gnom' makes a squat plant, becoming more globose in time.

'Hesse' has very twisted leaves on a globose habit.

'Kissen' is a bun-shaped plant with short dark green needles.

'Kokarde' has the leaves growing with alternate bands of dark green and yellow, giving a variegated appearance.

'Winter Gold' is an open bush with light green twisted leaves which turn bright yellow in cold weather. This effect is more reliable on the continent of Europe as, whatever British people think of their climate, it usually is not cold enough to make a good display!

P. uncinata Miller ex Mirbel
Mountain pine

Tree to 25 m. Crown conic, rounded at the apex. Bark grey-pink, becoming black as the small squares flake off. Shoot orange-brown. Bud cylindric, with a short point, very resinous, 0.5-0.8 cm. Leaves in stiff, tight pairs, dark green, 6 cm. Cone strongly oblique, ovoid, apophysis prominent on exposed side, recurved-hooked or rounded-hooked, umbo offset, 4-6 cm by 2-3 cm. Zone 6.

This tree is found in the central and west Alps and also in the Pyrenees and central Spain. It has been confused with Mountain pine but is very distinct from Dwarf mountain pine in the cones although hybrids are quite frequent where the species meet. These have been accorded formal rank as follows, depending upon which species they most closely resemble: *P. mugo* var. *pumilio* (Haenke)Zenari has erect branches, smaller cones 4-5 cm by 2.5 cm with the apophysis convex above and concave below with an eccentric umbo, whilst the other form is referred to *P. uncinata* as var. *rotundata* (Link)Antoine with a shrubby habit and rounded or hooded apophyses.

P. nigra Arnold
European black pines

This species includes a number of very distinct geographical elements but which clearly merge in various parts of the range and therefore do not fit well as independent species. They are variously treated as species, subspecies or varieties of *P. nigra*. In accordance with the general trend in taxonomic botany the elements which make up this species complex are treated here at the level of subspecies, although the equivalent name at both the varietal and specific level is also cited. The typical form is described in detail, with only the distinctions of the other forms being listed. Dwarf cultivars are discussed at the end, as for some it is not certain to which taxon they belong. Zone 4.

P. nigra subsp. nigra
Austrian pine

Tree to 40 m. Crown domed with wide-spreading dense but spaced branches. Bark dark brown or black, fissured into scaly ridges. Shoot rich brown. Bud broad ovoid, abruptly sharp pointed, with white papery scales, 1.2 cm. Leaves straight, dense set, rigid, apex sharp pointed, dark or blackish green, 8-16 cm by 0.15 cm. Sheath 1-1.5 cm. Male cones conic, 1.3 cm. Cones ovoid-conic, yellow-brown, ripening brown, scales flexible with a transverse ridge, 5-8 cm.

Austrian pine is found in Austria, central Italy, Greece and Yugoslavia. It often forms a forked tree but can make neat specimens on a single bole. The higher montane origins from central Europe are very tough trees, withstanding poor or exposed conditions.

P. nigra subsp. laricio (Poiret)Maire
Corsican pine (P. laricio Poiret, P.n. var. maritima (Aiton)Melville, P.n. var. calabrica (Loudon)Schneider, P.n. var. corsicana (Loudon)Hyl)

Tree to 50 m. Crown narrow conic, older trees becoming columnar, rarely broadening. Bark pink or grey in young trees, in old ones dark grey, deeply ridged and scaly. Shoot yellow-brown, later orange-brown, grooved. Bud narrow conic, ending in a tapered sharp point. Leaves spaced, flexible, pairs splayed out, twisted, grey-green or green, apex not very sharp, 11-18 cm by 0.12-0.2 cm. Cone ovoid-conic, slightly curved, apophysis with a transverse ridge and a small prickle on umbo, yellow-brown or pale grey-brown, 6-8 cm by 3.5 cm. Zone 8.

Corsican pine is recorded from the island of Corsica, and in southern Italy from Calabria and Sicily. The Corsican and Sicilian plants are sometimes separated from the type of this subspecies. It is the commonest form in cultivation, making a fast-growing tree with a reasonable quality of timber. It is faster-growing than Scots pine and more reliable on chalk sites. On northern upland sites it can suffer from a fungal disease caused by *Brunchorstia destruens*, which will cause dieback of shoots and death; the disease is only a problem where there is insufficient summer heat and insolation.

Corsican pine can be easily separated from Austrian pine by the much more vigorous and open crown with lighter grey-green foliage.

P. nigra subsp. dalmatica (Vis.)Franco
Dalmatian pine

Small tree with broadly conical crown. Leaves rigid, only 4-7 cm by 0.15-0.18 cm. Cones 3.5-4.5 cm.

This small form is found along the coast and

islands of Dalmatia in Yugoslavia. It is rare in cultivation.

P. nigra subsp. pallasiana (Lambert)Holmboe
Crimean pine (*P. pallasiana* Lambert, *P.n.* var. *pallasiana* (Lambert)Schneider, *P.n.* var *caramanica* (Loudon)Rehder)

Crown broadly ovoid. Bark as for subsp. laricio. Shoot shiny yellow-green, becoming orange-brown. Bud conical, whitish brown. Leaves forward-pointing, hard, sharp pointed, stiff, dark green, twisted or irregularly curved, 12-18 cm by 0.16-0.21 cm. Sheath 1.8-2.6 cm. Cone narrowly conic, rough, purplish green, ripening brown, 5-12 cm.

This form is found in the Carpathian Mountains of central Europe, the Balkan peninsula, Turkey and the Crimea. In cultivation, many trees develop a short single bole which then proliferates into several erect stems, likened to the pipes of an organ.

var. *pyramidata* Acatay is a form occurring in a small forest at Tavsanli in Turkey. The trees are very narrow columnar in habit, occasionally conical, with short leaves, 5.5-12 cm and cones 5.5 cm. It is in cultivation.

P. nigra subsp. salzmannii (Dunal)Franco
Pyrenean pine (*P. pyrenaica* Willk., *P.n.* var. *cebennensis* (Grenier & Godron)Rehder)

Tree to 20 m. Crown narrow conical or columnar, in old trees open, domed. Shoot orange-brown, becoming brown by third year. Bud ovoid-cylindric, white with resin encrustation. Leaves slender, not sharp pointed, flexible, grey-green, 8-16 cm by 0.1-0.12 cm. Cone ovoid-conic, base rounded, smooth with flat transverse ridges on apophysis, dull purplish brown, 4-6 cm by 3 cm.

This plant is found in the Cevennes in southern France, along the eastern Pyrenees and in central and eastern Spain. It is distinctive in the narrow slender and not pungent leaves. This subspecies may also occur in North Africa in Algeria and Morocco. It is uncommon in cultivation.

'Aurea' is a tree form with the leaves lemon-green in the first year, becoming greener as they age. It has little to command it, being a poor plant compared to the golden form of Scots pine (although providing colour during the growing season).

'Hornibrookiana' is a dwarf form making a small shrub with glossy dark green leaves set on stout spreading or erect branches. It arose as a witches broom on Austrian pine.

'Jeddeloh' is a very compact and dense plant with short prickly foliage. It may be a form of Dalmatian pine.

'Moseri' is now known to be a cultivar of *P. sylvestris, qv.*

'Nana' is a shrubby slow-growing form. It will eventually make 3 m but only at around 5 cm per annum.

'Pendula' is an erect form with the branches hanging.

'Strypemonde' originated on a witches broom and makes a slow-growing bush with dark green or grey-green stiff needles.

'Variegata' has some straw-yellow fascicles amongst the normal leaves.

P. heldreichii Christ
Heldreich pine

Tree to 20 m, often shrubby. Crown rounded, conical. Bark ash grey, flaking to leave yellowish patches. Shoot glaucous in the first year but soon yellow-brown or brown. Buds green, not resinous. Leaves rigid, spiny-tipped, light green, becoming glossy green, 6-9 cm by 0.15. Cone ovoid, brown, 7-8 cm. Zone 6.

Heldreich pine is found on limestone sites in Albania, Greece and Yugoslavia. It is frequently confused with Bosnian pine but differs in the brown shoots, more open foliage, and the cones with flat scales carrying a short acute prickle.

P. leucodermis Antoine
Bosnian pine

Tree to 30 m. Crown ovoid-conical, narrow and regular. Bark smooth grey in young trees, becoming ash grey and dividing into regular small square plates on old trees. Shoot pale brown with a glaucous bloom at first, becoming white and remaining so for three years, then finally grey-pink. Bud brown, 1.5 cm. Leaves densely cover the shoot, point forwards, apex sharply pointed, rigid, dark green, 7-9 cm by 0.12 cm. Cone beautiful cobalt blue by first summer, retaining this colour when they enlarge in the second year, ripening through purple to dull orange-brown in autumn, ovoid-conic, apophysis conical with a recurved spine, 5-10 cm by 2.5 cm, with thin soft flexible scales. Zone 6.

This tree occurs in the Balkans in Bulgaria, Greece, Albania and Yugoslavia and also in south-west Italy in Calabria. It makes a very neat conical tree with dense green foliage and strikingly white shoots. It produces the exquisite cones at a young age. In the wild it occurs on dry limestone sites and would be worth a trial on chalky sites to see if it would make a long-term tree on these sites.

'Aureospicata' is a slow-growing conical form in which the needles have yellow tips.

'Compact Gem' has very dark, green-black

foliage and makes a small plant, growth slow, of around 2.5cm per annum. 'Pygmy' is a dense globose form. 'Schmidtii' has deep green sharp needles. Young plants are very slow-growing and make an oval dense bush. It was originally found as a mature plant 3m tall and estimated as over 100 years old in Bosnia near Sarajevo.

P. resinosa Aiton
Red pine

Tree 15-25m. Crown conic with upturned stout branches. Bark two-tone, upper bark red-brown as in Scots pine, on the lower bole pink-grey and scaly. Shoot stout, rough, orange to red-brown. Bud 2cm, conical with red-brown scales. Leaves brittle, breaking if bent, slender, straight, yellow-green, persist 4-5 years (other species of Red pine normally 2-3), 10-15cm. Male cones purple. Cone ovoid-conic, chestnut brown, 4-6cm by 3cm, umbo unarmed. Zone 2.

Red pine is restricted to north-eastern North America from Nova Scotia to south-east Manitoba and south to West Virginia. It is very uniform and closely related to Scots pine. The foliage, though, is more likely to be confused with Austrian pine. In cultivation, it has little to commend it over other species of Red pine.

'Globosa' makes a rounded, densely branched, slow-growing form, ultimately to 5m. 'Quinobequin' is a bun-shaped plant raised from seed of 'Globosa'; it makes growths of 9cm per annum. 'Nobska' is similar but smaller.

'Watnong' originated from a witches broom and is a diminutive bun with small narrow dull green leaves.

P. tropicaulis Morelot
Tropical pine

This tree is similar to Red pine but has longer foliage 15-30cm which is occasionally in 3s. The best identification feature is the large resin canals which fill the space between the vascular bundle and the thick margins. Tropical pine is found at sea-level in the Caribbean in western Cuba and the Island of Pines; it is not in cultivation and is unlikely to be hardy. Zone 10.

P. thunbergii Parlatore
Japanese black pine

Tree to 25m. Crown conic when young, in old trees with erratic level branches upswept at the tips. Bark dark purplish grey with narrow fissures. Shoot yellow-brown. Bud cylindric, tapering at the apex to a fine point, covered with white silky scales. Leaves in tight fascicles, thick, apex pointed, spiky, dark grey-green, 7-15cm by 0.15-0.2cm. Cone conic-ovoid,

apophysis flattened, umbo depressed with a small prickle, 4-7cm. Zone 6.

Japanese black pine is found close to the sea around the coasts of south Korea and the Japanese islands of Honshu, Kyushu and Shikoku. It is tolerant of salt-spray, either natural or from de-icing operations on winter roads. It is most distinctive in the silky white buds. The form in general cultivation will produce masses of cones on the shoots where normally the male cones are found; it probably represents a garden form.

'Oculus-Draconis' had the leaves banded with yellow-white. This does not show on young trees and is most apparent in the autumn. 'Benijanome-Kuromatsu' is a form in which the bands are pink in winter but this may not be in cultivation outside of Japan.

'Globosa' makes a rounded bush or small tree. 'Aurea' has some leaves yellow.

P. luchuensis Mayr
Luchu pine

This little known tree differs from Japanese black pine in the smooth shoots, the late formation of rough bark on the bole and the leaves being 12-16cm long. It is recorded from the Ryukyu or Luchu islands between Japan and Taiwan. The following two species have been referred to it by various authorities. It is not in cultivation. Zone 9.

P. taiwanensis Hayata
Taiwan black pine

Tree to 15m in cultivation but to 35m in Taiwan. Crown with horizontal branches. Bark fissured into purplish square scales. Shoot green-brown. Bud with long free scales. Leaves rigid, 8-11cm. Cone oblong-ovoid, 6-7cm. Zone 8.

This tree is restricted to the mountains of Taiwan. It has been introduced in the past but is rarely met with.

P. hwangshanensis Hsia
Hwangshan pine

This tree has been included as a synonym of Taiwan black pine but plants in cultivation from seed sent out a few years ago by the Chinese Academy of Forestry seem distinct at the present time. They have yellow-brown shoots with a pinkish tinge, cylindrical buds with an abrupt sharp conical tip and chestnut brown scales, and fresh green or yellow-green leaves. The conelets have umbos with abrupt mucronate prickles. In the mature cone, the umbo is depressed. The plant is hardy and appears more similar to Japanese red pine. It is recorded from eastern China. Zone 8.

Pine hybrids

A large number of hybrids have been made in artificial crossing experiments to investigate affinities between species or to try to improve the disease resistance or growth rate of pines. Also, hybrids often occur in the wild where related species meet. However, only a small number of these hybrids are of any horticultural significance.

P. × hakkodensis Makino
(*P. parviflora* × *P. pumila*)

This hybrid occurs in northern Honshu where the two parents meet. It has longer, coarser and more twisted needles than *P. pumila*. It makes an attractive low slow-growing plant. Zone 6.

P. × holfordiana Jackson
(*P. ayacahuite* × *P. wallichiana*)

This hybrid arose in cultivation in England at Westonbirt Arboretum. It differs from *P. ayacahuite* in the less reflexed cone scales and the smaller seeds and from Blue pine in the slightly hairy shoots, buds and wider cones. The first generation plants are closer to the *P. ayacahuite* var. *veitchii* mother plant, but seedlings raised from the hybrid show much greater variation, as is to be expected. It makes a medium to large tree. Zone 7.

P. × hunnewellii Johnson
(*P. parviflora* × *P. strobus*)

This makes a small tree with blue-green leaves set on hairy shoots. It is vigorous and colourful, though not neat. Zone 7.

P. × schwerinii Fitchen
(*P. wallichiana* × *P. strobus*)

This hybrid has been raised on several occasions as a means of introducing the resistance of *P. wallichiana* to White pine blister rust into Weymouth pine. It makes a vigorous tree, although less graceful than the parents. Zone 7.

Platycladus Spach **Cupressaceae**

This genus is related to *Thuja* but differs in the cones being rather fleshy and only having 2 pairs of fertile scales which each bear 2 large wingless seeds. The cones are glaucous and have pronounced recurved hooks. The genus is often included in *Thuja* or as *Biota*, which is a later name for *Platycladus*. On an olfactory level, the crushed foliage of Biota is almost scentless whilst that of all true *Thuja* species is strongly aromatic.

P. orientalis (Linnaeus f.)Franco
Biota (*Thuja orientalis* Linnaeus f., *Biota orientalis* (Linnaeus f.) Endlicher)

Tree to 15 m. Crown irregular, often on several stems with rounded masses of foliage at the top and bare at the base, splaying out, in young trees conic. Bark fibrous, stripping, red-brown. Leaves in vertical sprays irregularly arranged, facial pairs only slightly smaller than laterals, with a groove, bluntly pointed, matt dark green or yellow-green, usually becoming bronze or brownish over winter. Cone upright flask, grey bloomed, scales with dorsal reflexed hook near the tip, 2 cm. Seed 0.3 cm, ovoid. Zone 6.

Biota is cultivated throughout China and in Japan. Its exact distribution is lost but probably extended across northern China and south to the drier parts of Yunnan along the Tibetan (Zixang) border. It may also be native to parts of Iran.

Biota is rather slow-growing. It makes a tree tolerant of dry dusty sites and good for polluted townscapes. Mature trees are scarcely beautiful but have a degree of charm. Seedlings often will regenerate in old walls, and survive to make trees some metres tall growing out of the top of quite high walls.

A large number of cultivars have been named, including the following.

'Athrotaxoides' makes a dwarf form with a rather irregular globose habit of twisted branches, ultimately making 3 m.

'Aurea Nana' is a dwarf plant to 60 cm in which the leaves are yellow-green, paling as they mature and becoming bronze over winter.

'Bonita' has a conic habit with blue-green foliage.

'Conspicua' makes a small column or cone to 1.5 m; the foliage is a bright light green.

'Elegantissima' is a broad conic plant making 5 m with time. The foliage is golden yellow, becoming yellow-green, and then brown in winter. Plants very similar to this are cultivated in Yunnan.

'Flagalliformis' is a tall-growing form with the yellow-green foliage whip-like.

'Meldensis' retains the juvenile leaves and makes a globose or broad conic plant to 1 m. The leaves are dull green but become purple-brown over winter. There is only a thin veneer of live foliage covering the dead brown inner leaves and, if not growing well, it can look unpleasant.

'Minima' is a very dwarf globose form. The foliage changes with the seasons from yellow-green through dark green to bronzy brown in winter.

'Pyramidalis Aurea' is a tall-growing form; as a young plant it is narrowly conic but broadens with time. The foliage is a persistent yellow-green, not bronzing in winter. 'Semperaurea' likewise does not turn bronze, but is a smaller ovoid plant to 3 m with golden yellow new growths and yellow-green foliage.

'Rosedalis' is a dwarf ovoid and dense form with juvenile foliage of a golden yellow colour when it flushes, later only bright green. 'Sanderi' also has juvenile foliage but of a bluish grey in summer and purple-blue in winter.

Podocarpus L'Heritier ex Persoon
Podocarps Podocarpaceae

The Podocarps are found in the Americas from Mexico southwards, in central and southern Africa, Asia from the Himalayas to Japan and in Australasia. The genus has been restricted in recent years to a more clearly defined group but it remains the second largest genus of conifers. They are characterised by the female fruit being produced on an axillary shoot, set on a naked peduncle with an enlarged basal receptacle formed from the fusion of two bracts. The seed is single and inverted; at maturity it is enclosed in the leathery fertile scale. Generally the species are dioecious.

Of the 90 or so species in the genus, most come from tropical or warm temperate regions and are not suitable for cultivation. Only the following species, which are hardy in cultivation, are discussed here. A number of the other species, especially some from Papua New Guinea and northern South America, are recorded from high altitudes and might be hardy if tried in suitably sheltered areas.

P. alpinus R. Brown ex Mirbel
Tasman podocarp

Shrub to 2 m with a spreading dense hemispherical crown. Shoots green, later brown, glabrous, slender, crossing. Leaves more or less parted, linear-oblanceolate, tip rounded, often apiculate, not sharp, dull green above with 2 greyish stomatal bands beneath separated by keeled green midrib, 0.6-1.2 cm by 0.15-0.2 cm. *Fruit bright red, 0.6 cm, containing 1 seed. Zone 8.*

This species is native to Tasmania, Victoria and New South Wales. It is hardy and makes an interesting low shrub, of very slow growth. The fruits are attractive when carried.

P. nivalis Hooker f.
Alpine totara

This plant is very similar to Tasman podocarp but differs in the longer and broader, more rigid leaves, 1-2 cm by 0.3-0.45 cm, which are set more radially on the shoot. It comes from New Zealand where it is found on both islands. It is of similar value as Tasman podocarp. Zone 7.

P. macrophyllus (Thunberg)D. Don
Kusamaki

Tree to 15 m but usually seen as an erect shrub 1-2 m. Leaves spirally arranged, crowded, erect or spreading, linear, rounded or tapered at tip, of firm leathery texture, bright green above with 2 broad glaucous stomatal bands beneath, 6-10 cm by 0.6-1 cm. Zone 7.

This species is native to Japan and eastern China. It is generally used as a tub plant but is hardy, at least with suitable shelter in southern Britain.

'Aureus' is a form in which the leaves have yellow margins or stripes. 'Argenteus' is similar but with white variegations.

P. salignus D. Don
Willowleaf podocarp

Tree to 20 m. Crown columnar or broad conic, with spreading then pendent branches. Bark red-brown, stripping in fibrous ridges. Shoot green, becoming grey-brown in second or third year. Bud minute, with brown filamentous scales. Leaves clustered near the tips of the current year's growth, persisting 2-3 years, arranged forwards and spreading flat, narrow-linear or strap-like, often falcate (sickle-shaped), tapers gently at base and abruptly to acute apex, shiny mid-green with a central ridge above, pale or yellow-green below, 5-11 cm by 0.4-0.8 cm. Fruit on 2 cm peduncle growing on current year's growth, receptacle 0.5 cm, bearing 1 or 2 ellipsoidal seeds 0.8 by 0.4 cm, receptacle and seeds green or dark violet. Zone 7.

Willow podocarp is native to central southern Chile where it occurs as a minor element in the *Nothofagus obliqua* forests. The common and Latin names both refer to the willow-like leaves, which are typical of most Podocarps. It is hardy in the milder areas, although it will survive in colder areas with shelter; in Britain this means it is hardy at least to the regions along the west coast and south

of London. It makes a very attractive tree with the long soft foliage held on pendent branches and the red-brown stripping bark.

P. totara D. Don ex Lambert
Totara

Tree to 20 m. Crown ovoid bush or a conic tree. Bark grey-brown or orange-brown, peeling in grey strips. Shoot olive brown, becoming pale yellow or grey-brown in fourth year. Bud small, ovoid. Leaves pectinate below, more or less parted above with a few recurved along shoot, lanceolate, slightly falcate, tapered to a shiny apex, grey-green above, yellow-green beneath, more so in third year, 3 cm by 0.5 cm. Cone with orange-red or crimson receptacle and 1 or 2 subglobose seeds. Zone 8.

Totara is found in New Zealand throughout the North Island and in the north-eastern parts of the South Island. It makes a tall tree in its native habitat with a good timber. In cultivation, it only attains tree-like dimensions in the milder areas, but is hardy as a shrub elsewhere.

'Aureus' is a form with golden leaves.

P. hallii Kirk is similar to Totara but has a thinner more papery bark and longer juvenile leaves. It generally occurs at greater elevations in New Zealand; it is in cultivation but is rare. Zone 8.

P. nubigenus Lindley
Chilean totara

This tree differs from Totara in the purplish brown bark, the more perpendicularly arranged leaves which are broadest above the middle and bright green with 2 broad white stomatal bands on the lower surface. It is native to Chile south of 41°S and also adjoining Argentina. It makes a better tree in the western parts of Britain, probably as it requires a moist climate for sustained growth. Zone 8.

P. lawrencei Hooker
Lawrence podocarp
(*P. acutifolius* Kirk)

Tree to 10 m but more usually a spreading shrub. Bark thin. Shoots slender, olive green, becoming grey-buff. Leaves spreading, linear, hard with a pointed sharp tip, dull, bronzed grey-green, with 2 indistinct stomatal bands beneath, 1-2.5 cm by 0.2-0.3 cm. Fruit solitary or rarely in pairs, on a short peduncle, receptacle comprising 2 fleshy red scales. Seed narrowly ovoid. Zone 8.

This small tree is native to the South Island of New Zealand. It is related to Totara and is uncommon in cultivation but hardy.

Figure 8.18 Podocarpus alpinus *(above). Foliage and fruit;* P. salignus *(below). Foliage and male cones.*

Prumnopitys Philippi **Plumyews**
Podocarpaceae

Prumnopitys differs from *Podocarpus* in the leaves lacking a hypoderm layer of cells and with only a single resin canal placed above the vascular tissue and in the female cone lacking the enlarged basal receptacle. It has been included as two sections, *Stachycarpus* Endlicher and *Sundacarpus* Bucholz & Gray, of *Podocarpus*. The genus comprises ten species but only one is well represented in cultivation. The other two discussed here are suitable for mild areas, but some of the other species might be as hardy if introduced.

P. andina (Poepell ex Endlicher)de Laubenfels
Plumyew
(*Podocarpus andinus* Endlicher)

Tree to 20 m. Crown ovoid or conic, usually on several stems. Bark smooth, grey-brown. Shoot green for three years, then dark grey-brown or blackish, slightly ridged along decurrent leaf-bases. Bud ovoid, pointed, green, 0.1-0.2 cm. Leaves widely parted below, the same above on shaded shoots but more assurgent when grown in full light, dull bluish green, subshiny above with 2 pale whitish stomatal bands below, linear, with a faint raised midrib, tapered to acute tip, soft, 2-3 cm by 0.2 0.25 cm. Fruit yellowish white, plum-like and surrounded by a thin fleshy layer which is edible and tasty, 2 cm. Zone 7.

Plumyew is native to the Chilean Andes and also to adjoining parts of Argentina. In the wild it is now rare, but formerly the seeds were eaten by the local Indians. It is hardy and quite common in cultivation. It is slow-growing but will make a neat but often bushy tree with yew-like foliage and is tolerant of a range of sites.

P. ferruginea (D. Don)de Laubenfels
Miro

This tree to 25 m is found in scattered localities in New Zealand but may need a sheltered spot in the milder parts of the country to thrive. It has fruits which are purplish red with a bluish bloom and 2 cm long. The leaves are 1.5-2.5 cm by 0.25 cm with revolute margins; on drying they assume a rusty coloration, hence the specific name. Zone 9.

P. spicata (Mirbel)Masters
Matai

This tree of up to 25 m differs from Plumyew in the following characters: the bark is bluish black and exfoliates in large scales; the branches are pink-brown and purple, very slender and pendulous; the leaves are distant or clustered at the tip of the shoots, green above and bluish below, blunt or shortly pointed, 1-1.3 cm by 0.15 cm; the fruit is on a peduncle 2.5-5 cm, black, globose, to 1 cm.

Matai is native to both islands of New Zealand but is rare in cultivation and only suited to the milder areas. Zone 9.

Pseudolarix Gordon **Pinaceae**

This genus of a single species has deciduous leaves as in the larches but the cones differ in that they break up at maturity to release the seeds.

P. amabilis (Nelson)Rehder
Golden larch

Tree to 20 m. Crown broad, open with level branches. Bark grey, cracked into plates. Shoot ripens pink-brown or purple, later greyish, spur shoots curved. Bud ovoid, terminal ones with free filamentous scales. Leaves spirally arranged on long and short shoots, soft, fresh green, turning a beautiful golden orange in autumn, stomata below only, 2-5.5 cm by 0.15-0.4 cm. Cone light green or yellow-green, ripening brown, ovoid, erect, spiky with tips of scales free, scales deltoid with an auricled base, 6-8 cm by 4-5 cm. Zone 4.

Golden larch is native to southern China from southern Jiangsu, Zhejiang, Fujian, Jiangxi, Hunan and Hubei. It is a most attractive tree, with the brilliant autumn colour of the foliage and deserves much wider planting. It is difficult to germinate and slow to establish, however.

Pseudotaxus Cheng **Taxaceae**

This genus of one species is similar to *Taxus* but differs in the structure of the leaf epidermis, in having sterile scales in the male cones and the female cones being on an unbranched shoot with more sterile scales subtending the ovule.

P. chienii (Cheng)Cheng
White berry yew

Shrub to 4 m. Leaves 1-2.5 cm by 0.25-0.45 cm, lacking the characteristic but microscopic papillae found on leaves of all true Taxus, apex abruptly rounded with a long acuminate point. Flowers on separate male and female trees. Fruit surrounded by a white aril. Zone 7.

This interesting shrub is found in Zhejiang, Jiangxi, Hunan, Guangdong and Guangxi provinces of China. It has not been introduced but should prove hardy, at least in sheltered areas.

Pseudotsuga Carriere **Douglas firs** **Pinaceae**

Douglas firs are related to Spruces and Hemlocks in the general cone characters such as the cones being erect at the time of pollination but thereafter pendulous, not breaking up on maturity and ripening in the first year; they differ markedly in the very long exserted bract which is usually trident-shaped at the tip. The leaves are more similar to Silver firs, being set on a small depression on the shoot, not on a distinct pulvinus. The buds are quite different from other members of the Pine family, being ovoid-conic and sharp pointed. The genus is found in western North America and eastern Asia, although fossils have been recorded in Europe. The North American plants all have entire, usually bluntly pointed leaves, whilst those from eastern Asia have rounded, notched leaves, never entire.

P. menziesii (Mirbel)Franco **Douglas fir**

Tree to 60m. Crown broad conic with open whorls when young, older trees becoming denser with wide-spreading branches. Bark thick, corky, ridged, grey-brown with rich red-brown fissures, on younger trees smooth, grey-green to purple-brown, with resin blisters. Shoot yellow-green, becoming bright brown, slightly hairy. Bud red-brown. Leaves loosely parted or somewhat forwards, more clearly parted on shaded shoots, soft, tapering to a bluntly pointed apex, green above, stomata below in 2 white bands, 1.5-3cm by 0.15-0.2cm. Female flowers before the leaves, from terminal buds on strong shoots of upper crown, pale yellow-green. Cones ovoid-conic to ellipsoid, dull brown, with long exserted trident bract, 7-10cm by 2.5-3.5cm. Zone 5.

Douglas fir is found from south-west British Columbia south to central California. It makes a dominant tree occasionally to 80 or 90m tall in the temperate rain forests of the north-west Pacific coast. The tree has a very valuable timber and is widely planted in temperate regions. As an amenity tree, it can be very attractive when mature with the thick corky bark but lacks the grace and charm of many other conifers. It is, however, a very vigorous species, although it can be caught by late spring frosts.

Interestingly, this species had 13 pairs of chromosomes, which is one more pair than in all the other species in the genus. All the other members of the pine family also have only twelve pairs, except for *Pseudolarix* which has eleven pairs.

Two geographical forms are recorded. Var. *menziesii* is as above.

Var. *glauca* (Beissner)Franco Blue douglas fir differs in the smaller cones, 4.5-6cm, with reflexed, not erect, bract scales, and bluer leaves covered with a glaucous bloom. The bark generally is thinner, grey or blackish and scaly. This form is found from the interior of British Columbia south as far as the Pico de Orizaba, the highest mountain in Mexico, on the borders of Puebla and Veracruz states. It is not so impressive a tree, although the blue foliage can be attractive and the cones are more interesting in detail. It is susceptible in Britain to a leaf-cast fungus, *Rhabdocline pseudo-tsugae*, but may be more resistant to the aphid, *Adelge cooleyi*, which can cause the green form to look unhealthy. Plants from the northern part of its range, in interior British Columbia, are sometimes separated as var. *caesia* (Schwerin)Franco, with grey-green leaves and erect cone bracts. Plants in Mexico are also often segregated out, under the names *Ps. guinieri* Flous, *Ps. flahaultii* Flous, *Ps. macrolepis* Flous and *Ps. rehderi* Flous. On foliage characters these taxa generally fit this variety, but the cones are very variable; however, it is not clear whether the variation is in any sense consistent, or possibly just due to differing climates. All four taxa are in cultivation, the most distinct appearing to be *Ps. macrolepis*. A better understanding of the plants in Mexico and of their chromosome counts might lead to general acceptance of some of these taxa.

Numerous cultivars have been named, the following being a selection.

'Albospica' has new leaves nearly pure white, later greening.

'Anguina' is a form with few side branches. It arose at Endsleigh, near Tavistock and is similar to the *Picea abies* cultivar 'Virgata'.

'Blue Wonder' is a selection which forms a conical tree with intensely blue-green leaves.

'Brevifolia' is a slow-growing plant, ultimately a small tree, with dense short leaves, to 1.3cm.

'Densa' makes a dwarf spreading flat-topped bush with short foliage. 'Hillside Pride' and 'Little Jon' are similar, but smaller and slower, growing no more than 3cm per annum.

'Fletcheri' makes an attractive rounded or flat-topped bush with the needles 2-3cm and set radially. It may, eventually, make 3m. 'Nana' and 'Cheesemanii' are similar and arose from the same batch of seed.

'Fretsii' is a slow-growing small conical tree with very short, parted, dull green leaves.

'Moerheimii' has somewhat bluish foliage on a slow compact habit.

'Stairii' is a tree form with the new foliage partly yellow or yellow-green.

'Tempelhof Compact' is a small, slow-growing dwarf form, the original was 60cm after 20 years.

P. macrocarpa (Torrey)Mayr
Bigcone douglas fir

This tree differs from Douglas fir as follows: bark dull grey with orange fissures, later red-brown; leaves longer, 2.5-5cm, rarely to 8cm, stiffer; cone ovoid-cylindric with the bract only just longer than the thick ovuliferous scales, 9-18cm. It is very distinct in the cone and reasonably so in the foliage. Significantly, it has one pair less chromosomes than *Ps. menziesii*. It comes from southern California and is in cultivation, although needing some shelter. Zone 7.

P. forrestii Craib
Forrest douglas fir

Tree to 16m. Crown very broad conic, open. Bark grey-brown, scaly. Shoot olive brown or buff-brown, hairy in the weak grooves. Leaves parted, sparse, apex rounded, notched, yellow-green with a distinct groove above, 2 greenish white stomatal bands below, 2.5-5cm by 0.15-0.2cm. Cone broad ovoid, heavy, woody, scales orbicular, 2.5-3.5cm by 3-4cm. Zone 8.

Forrest douglas fir comes from north-west Yunnan and south-east Xizang. It has been confused with Taiwan douglas fir but the nearly round cone scales and the longer leaves distinguish it. It is in cultivation but very rare. It has a very broad, open crown and is susceptible to late spring frosts.

P. wilsoniana Hayata
Taiwan douglas fir

This tree differs from Forrest douglas fir in the shorter narrower leaves, usually 1.5-2.5 by 0.1-0.15cm (rarely to 4.5cm), the glabrous shoots and the thinner cone scales which are oval with a sub-cordate base and only 1.5-2cm long by 2-2.5cm wide. It is restricted to Taiwan and is uncommon in cultivation. Zone 8. *P. xichangensis* Kuan & Zhou is a newly described species from Sichuan, differing in the more pointed buds and larger seeds.

P. japonica (Shirasawa)Beissner
Japanese douglas fir

This differs from Forrest douglas fir in the glabrous shoots, shorter leaves, 2-2.5cm by 0.15-

Figure 8.19 Pseudotsuga japonica. *Foliage and mature cones.*

0.17 cm, which are blue-green above and with white stomatal bands and in the small cones 3.5-4.5 cm long. It is confined to two small areas in southern Honshu and to Shikoku islands of Japan. It is rare both in the wild and in cultivation. Zone 6.

P. sinensis Dode
Chinese douglas fir

This species has leaves 1.3-3 cm, usually 2-2.5 cm by 0.2 cm, which are shiny green, and cones which are as large as in Forrest douglas fir but with flabellate, auricled scales. It is found in Yunnan, Sichuan, Guizhou, Hunan and Hubei provinces of China. It is in cultivation but makes a rather poor weedy plant and is tender. Zone 8.

P. brevifolia Cheng & Fu
Shortleaf douglas fir

This taxon from south-west Guangxi is not in cultivation and may not be hardy. It has short broad leaves, usually 0.7-1.5 cm by 0.2-0.32 cm, although up to 2 cm long, and ovoid-conic cones, 4-6.5 cm by 3-4 cm. It looks quite distinct in the drawing in the *Chinese Flora* (see Bibliography). Zone 9.

P. gaussenii Flous
Gaussen douglas fir

This tree has leaves 2-3 cm by 0.2 cm and ovoid-conic cones 3.5-5.5 cm by 2-3 cm. The cone scales are very distinct, being very broad, 2 cm long by 3.5 cm wide, half moon shaped with spreading flanges. It comes from southern Anhui and west Zhejiang but is not yet in cultivation. Zone 9.

Saxegothea Lindley **Prince Albert yew**
Podocarpaceae

This is a monotypic genus, as below.

S. conspicua Lindley
Prince Albert yew

Tree to 15 m. Crown slender conical in mild areas, slower-growing and more bushy elsewhere, branches whorled. Bark purple-brown, smooth, somewhat flaky and fluted. Shoot green for 3-4 years, then brown. Bud globose, small, green, 0.1-0.2 cm. Foliage in whorls at end of shoots, rather pendulous or outspreading. Leaves rather irregular, parted above and below the shoot, open, not crowded, persistent for six or more years, straight, twisted or falcate, linear or narrow lanceolate, taper to twisted base and abruptly to pointed apex,

with prominent raised midrib above, dark subglossy green above, flat below with broad pale green margins as wide as the 2 dull white or silvery white stomatal bands and a narrower green midrib, to 3 cm by 0.4 cm. Male cones in pairs in leaf axils, ovoid, short stalked, pollen grains unwinged. Cone globose, mace-like, to 1.5 cm on scaly leafless stalk 1-1.5 cm, composed of around 15 overlapping triangular pointed scales, glaucous green and becoming fleshy when ripe, the upper scales bearing 2 inverted ovules but only around 6 mature. Zone 7.

Prince Albert yew is native to southern Chile and adjoining parts of Argentina. It was named in honour of Queen Victoria's husband, Prince Albert of Saxe-Coburg-Gotha. It is similar in some respects to yew but clearly separated by the irregularly arranged foliage and the fruit. It is unique in the Podocarpaceae in the unwinged pollen grains.

In cultivation Prince Albert yew has proved hardy throughout the British Isles, although needing some woodland protection in northern Scotland. It is shade-tolerant and makes a neat small tree or shrub with its spreading and arching foliage sprays. In the milder parts of Britain, particularly in woodland conditions, it will grow into a narrow crowned upright tree.

Sciadopitys Siebold & Zuccarini
Taxodiaceae

This is a monotypic genus. The cone clearly places it with the Redwood family but the foliage is unlike any other conifer.

S. verticillata (Thunberg) Siebold & Zuccarini
Japanese umbrella pine

Tree to 20 m. Crown narrow conic on a single bole or if on several stems, broader conic. Bark red-brown, peeling in narrow vertical strips. Shoot brown. Bud small, red-brown. Foliage in whorls at the ends of shoots. Leaves in two kinds; whorls at the end of the shoots of long linear organs which are kept for three years, grooved above, deep green, slightly notched, deeply grooved below with a white or golden yellow band of stomata in the groove, and which are subtended by a brown scale leaf at the base, 5-12 cm by 0.3 cm; scale leaves also set spirally along the shoot below the whorls. Male cones clustered at ends of shoots, in catkins 2.5 cm. Cones on a stout peduncle, ripening over two years, ovoid, composed of many spirally set scales, each with 5-9 flat seeds, 5-8 cm by 3-5 cm. Zone 6.

This remarkable tree is confined to southern Japan, from south Honshu, Shikoku and Kyushu but in earlier times was widespread in the northern hemisphere and fossils are very frequent in certain

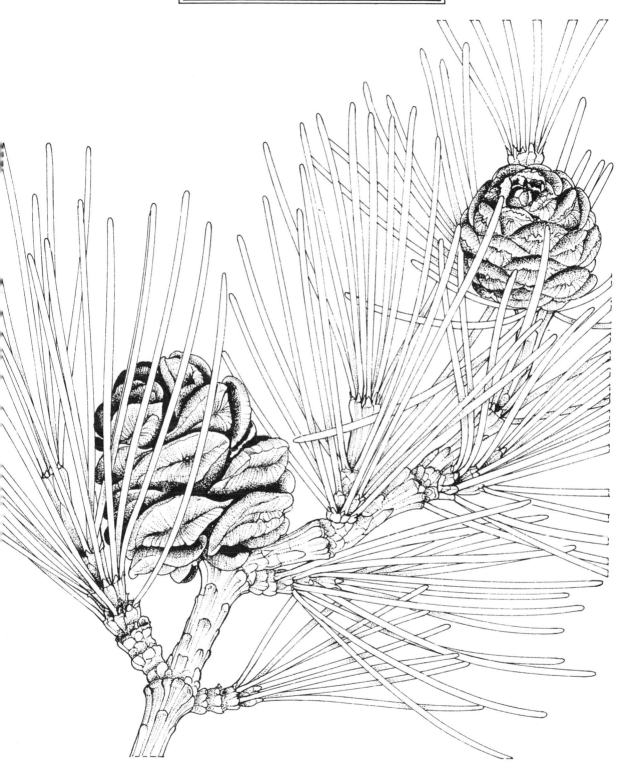

Figure 8.20 Sciadopitys verticillata. *Foliage, ripe and green cones.*

coal formations in Germany. The whorled foliage is most distinctive. Opinions differ as to whether the 'leaves' are two true leaves fused together on a short shoot as in *Pinus*, or whether they are cladodes, that is modified shoots; they are borne on a short peg-like structure and subtended by a brown scale leaf.

The name is derived from the similarity of the foliage whorls to the spokes of an umbrella, the narrow habit of the tree more approximating to a folded one!

Sciadopitys makes a slow-growing tree which will thrive in all conditions, except limey ones. It is good near to water and will tolerate a wet site. It will take some shade but is best placed in an open position in full sun. The seeds can be difficult to germinate.

Sequoia Endlicher **Coastal redwood** **Taxodiaceae**

This monotypic genus holds the record for the tallest tree in the world (although not the fattest). Claims that certain Eucalypts (*Eucalyptus* species) from Tasmania were taller have not been substantiated. Unauthenticated rumours abound that taller Coastal redwoods and Douglas firs used to exist, but the tallest tree currently flourishing on the planet is a Coastal redwood in the Redwood Creek grove and it is 112 m tall. The genus is named after Sequoiah, the son of a British trader and a Cherokee squaw, who invented an alphabet for the Cherokee language; his name is now commemorated in the names of three conifer genera!

S. sempervirens (D. Don)Endlicher **Coastal redwood**

Tree to 45 m. Crown columnar conic with level branches slightly downswept and up at the tips, in young trees regular conic. Bark thick, very soft, red-brown, deeply fissured and ridged. Shoot green with decurrent leaf bases for first year, becoming bright red-brown in second. Bud ovoid-acute, green, with free scales, 0.3 cm. Foliage in flat sprays. Leaves of two kinds; those on the strongest and coning shoots scale-like, radial; on ordinary shoots, arranged distichously (spreading above and below the shoot), linear, acute, with a twisted decurrent base, rather hard, pale green, stomata mainly on 2 silvery white bands on the underside, 2 cm. Male cones small, globular, shedding yellow pollen in early spring. Cones ripen during first year, pendulous, rounded oblong, 3 cm, with around 20 peltate scales, each bearing 5-7 seeds. Cotyledons 2. Zone 7.

Coastal redwood is restricted to a narrow band

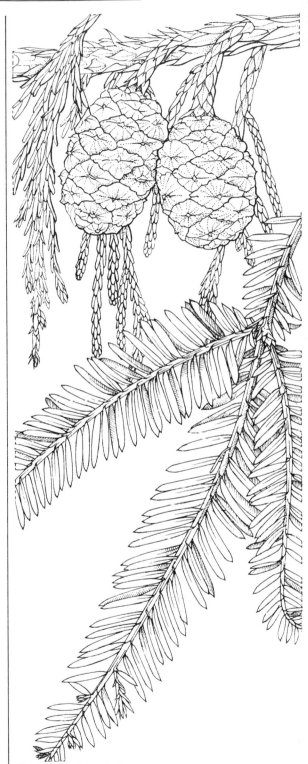

Figure 8.21 Sequoiadendron giganteum *(above). Foliage and cones;* Sequoia sempervirens *(below). Foliage.*

along the Pacific coast from the southern corner of Oregon to Monterey in California. Fossils indicate a much wider distribution in geological times. It is only found within 30 or so kilometres of the sea, in the zone characterised by frequent summer fogs. It receives a substantial proportion of its moisture from the fog which condenses on the foliage, but the logistical problems of supplying moisture to the crown 100 m above the soil level still must be immense. The tallest trees are only found in valley bottom sites, which form only a very small proportion of the natural stands.

In cultivation, Coastal redwood makes a very fast-growing tree but for optimum development it requires a sheltered valley site in the wetter parts of Britain. The foliage is likely to get severely browned by cold winds during harsh winters, although the trees will not be adversely affected. The species is unusual amongst conifers in its ability to coppice, i.e. make new growth from the stump if it is cut down. The combined fast growth rate (few trees are faster when young) and the great beauty of immature trees permits it to be enjoyed even in small gardens, as the tree can be coppiced every time it grows too large, in the certain knowledge that it will regrow (the number of stems will need to be thinned out).

The tree is relatively long lived, taking some 400 or 500 years to reach full maturity, although coning at a much younger age. The tallest trees are estimated to be around 1,200 years old, with a maximum lifespan of 2,000 years,

The bark is thick and very soft. It is easily distinguished from that of Wellingtonia because it is much softer. Both can comfortably be punched with a clasped fist but only Coastal redwood can be repeatedly punched without feeling discomfort; with Wellingtonia, the hand is sore after the third punch!

Several forms have been named, but only the following are worthy of note.

'Adpressa' makes a very interesting small tree, although if the leading shoots are cut out it can be kept dwarf. The foliage is short (to 1 cm) and broad and is loosely adpressed, as in coning shoots. The new foliage is creamy white and gives the tree an extra appeal. With time, it can make a tree 20 m, but is slower-growing than the normal form and worth considering.

'Cantab' is another form which can make a dwarf if the erect leading shoots are removed. Otherwise it makes an open small tree with very wide and rather short glaucous leaves, 1.3 cm by

0.5 cm. It is a cultivariant of 'Prostrata', a spreading form which arose as a witches broom on a plant at the Cambridge Botanic Garden and has similar broad leaves.

'Pendula' is a name mentioned in the literature. Trees with downturned branches are quite common but do not appear to represent a single clone. The character is only developed on old trees.

Sequoiadendron Buchholz
Taxodiaceae

Formerly included in *Sequoia*, this monotypic genus differs in only having scale leaves, in the naked buds, larger cones with around 30 scales each with 3-12 ovules ripening in the second year, and in having 3-5 cotyledons.

S. giganteum (Lindley)Buchholz
Wellingtonia Big tree or Sierra Redwood

Tree to 50 m, in the wild it is up to 80 m. Crown conic, becoming broader in old age or when the top is lost in lightning strikes. Bark thick, red-brown or dark brown, often fluted, fissured and strongly ridged, thick, moderately soft. Shoots green, becoming red-brown during the second season. Buds naked, minute. Foliage in rather wiry sprays set all around the shoot. Leaves awl-like, radial around the shoot, pointing forwards, slightly incurved, not udpressed, grey-green, darkening and becoming shiny, stomata dotted over the surface, not in pronounced bands on the lower surface, to 0.7 cm. Male cones shed pollen in spring, sessile, terminal. Cones green, ripening brown or green in second year, woody, persisting on the tree, ovoid, 4.5 cm. Zone 6.

Wellingtonia is native to the western slopes of the Sierra Nevada range in California. The species includes the largest living beings, and an alternative name is simply 'Big tree'. The largest 'Big tree' is named 'General Sherman' and is estimated to weigh some 6,000 tonnes; it is 83 m tall and 10 m in diameter at the base; yet this mammoth plant grew from a seed weighing one two-hundredth of a gramme (one 5,500th of an ounce).

Wellingtonia is restricted to about six dozen groves in the Sierra Nevadas between 36° and 39°N and at altitudes of from 1,500 m to 2,500 m. The stands are mainly found in the southern half of its range, those in the northern part being smaller and widely scattered. This region is much colder and drier than that occupied by the Coastal redwood and Wellingtonias (or Sierra redwood) are better able to tolerate winter cold and dry sites. Wellingtonia has a fast growth rate and in the 130 years since they were discovered, cultivated trees have made 50 m with butt diameters of up to 3 m. They are damaged by only two agencies, lightning, which often kills the top couple of metres, and honey fungus, which can kill the entire tree.

The thick bark of this, and Coastal redwood, serves to protect the trees from the effects of forest fires. It can be up to 60 cm thick in old trees. Without fires, the young trees are not able to compete with White fir and other conifers.

Wellingtonia is long-lived and trees up to an estimated 3,500 years exist. This pales in comparison to the 5,000 years measured for *Pinus longaeva*, but is far longer than for any other tree, except possibly *Chamaecyparis formosensis*.

In cultivation, it will thrive in any soil, site or exposure, although the best trees will develop in moist valley sites; it does not like heavy shade. Mature specimens will often establish a ring of layered branches around the base but, unlike Coastal redwood, it will not coppice; a tree once cut down is finished.

A number of cultivars have been named.

'Aureum' has young shoots a deep yellow. It is a slow-growing form to 20 m but is rarely seen.

'Glaucum' is dismally misnamed, as the foliage is scarcely any bluer or brighter than the normal plant. It is, however, an excellent cultivar and well worth planting for the attractive narrow conical habit it develops; it is slightly slower than seedling forms in growth, but with a crown only a third the diameter.

'Pendulum' is a real character plant. The habit involves a central main axis, from which fine and absolutely pendulous side branches develop. If the tree happens to grow vertically, it makes a narrow column with its weeping foliage. But more often the trunk grows erratically at some angle to the vertical and snakes across an open space, when the hanging foliage makes curtains beneath the stem; often extra leaders emerge from the upper side to create an even more bizarre picture. Most beautiful if you can take it, although a few stuffy types find it too hard to accept!

'Pygmaeum' is a dwarf clone. As befits the largest tree in the world, it is not exactly small, rather will grow only slowly (around 10 cm a year), ultimately making a rounded bush 3-4 m tall.

Taiwania Hayata **Taxodiaceae**

This genus is composed of two taxa, usually treated as separate species from the island of Taiwan and from China. The juvenile foliage is very similar to *Cryptomeria* in its awl-like leaves but the coning shoots have much smaller scale leaves and cones which are similar to a *Tsuga* cone.

T. cryptomerioides Hayata
Taiwania

Tree to 60 m in Taiwan but smaller in cultivation. Crown columnar. Bark grey-brown, fibrous, peeling in strips. Shoot green for several years due to decurrent leaf bases. Leaves on young trees radial, incurved, falcate, tapering to a point, grey-green with a broad band of blue-green stomata on each side, to 2 cm; on coning shoots the leaves are triangular, scale-like, incurved and covering the shoot, stomata on all 3 surfaces, to 0.4 cm. Male cones in clusters of 5-7, terminal on shoots. Cones globose or ovate, to 1.2 cm, with 15-21 scales, each with 2 seeds. Zone 8.

Taiwania is native to the island of Taiwan where it forms enormous trees to 60 m or more and 10 m in butt diameter. Despite coming from relatively low altitude (1,800-2,400 m) on the Tropic of Cancer it is surprisingly hardy; in light woodland it survives as a small tree of 4 m as far north as Aberdeen, although making much larger plants in milder conditions further south. Mature cones and foliage have not been produced on the trees in cultivation. The juvenile foliage is similar to that of *Cryptomeria* but is harsher to the touch and slightly longer.

T. flousiana Gaussen
Coffin tree

This is the form of *Taiwania* found in China. It was in fact discovered first, by Anderson in Yunnan in 1868 but his specimen was logged at Kew as *Cryptomeria*. It differs most significantly in the more numerous scales in the cones, in the range 21-39. This makes the cone cylindrical in appearance and 1.5-2.2 cm long. The juvenile foliage of cultivated trees is softer, grassy green, with grey-green stomatal bands, not glaucous green. It is recorded as a tree to 75 m, making it the tallest tree in China. Zone 8.

This species is found in Yunnan and along the border with Burma. It was also found in the same general area as *Metasequoia* in southern Hubei province and has been recorded from Guizhou. The plants in cultivation are from the seeds collected at the same time as *Metasequoia* was introduced. They are as hardy as the Taiwan plant. In Yunnan the timber was highly prized by the Chinese for coffin boards and it is mainly this tree which was involved in the coffin trade mentioned by Kingdon-Ward, Farrer and Cox in their writings, although the Coffin juniper (*Juniperus recurva* var. *coxii*) was probably also used.

Taxodium Richard **Swamp cypresses Taxodiaceae**

A genus of three deciduous conifers restricted to south-east USA and Mexico. It differs from *Metasequoia* in the alternate buds and twigs and from *Glyptostrobus* in the cone.

T. distichum (Linnaeus)Richard
Swamp cypress

Tree to 30m. Crown in young trees columnar, becoming broader in old trees with long level branches. Bark dull pale brown, shallowly fissured, slightly shredding, often fluted. Shoot in two kinds; persistent shoots green, maturing to brown, deciduous shoots green. Bud rounded, small, only found on persistent shoots. Leaves radial, on persistent shoots scale-like, small; on the deciduous shoots (which arise from buds along the current and previous season's persistent shoots) twisted to spread in 2 flat ranks, linear, pale green, 2cm. Male cone pendulous, at branch tips in late autumn and lengthening from 5cm to 20+cm, shedding pollen in early spring. Cones green, ripen to brown during first season, globose, 3cm, on a stalk 0.3cm. Scales few, with a central thorn but lacking the arc of triangular teeth found on Glyptostrobus, each bearing 2 unwinged, triangular warty seeds. Zone 5.

Swamp cypress is found in south-eastern USA from the coast of New Jersey to Texas and up the Mississippi valley but may be absent from most of Florida. It grows naturally on wet sites which are under water for at least part of the year. On these sites it will produce aerial roots, commonly called 'knees' or 'pneumatophores', and these are believed to assist with the oxygen supply to the roots growing in anaerobic conditions.

Swamp cypress, also called Bald cypress, is hardy in cultivation but late to come into leaf. The first signs of new foliage appear in May but the tree is not in full leaf until June. The foliage turns brick red in late October and hangs on throughout much of November, giving a valuable late display of autumn colour.

Swamp cypress will thrive in any soil, only needing a copious water supply to germinate the seeds and sustain them for the first few weeks. It will, in fact, grow much faster on normal soils. It enjoys an ecological advantage on wet sites as few other plants can compete. The curious knees,

which are hollow conical brown structures and may grow up to a metre high, are only produced by trees growing in or very close to standing water. The tree can be planted in standing water but is not so well adapted to that environment as *Glyptostrobus*.

The wood of Swamp cypress is brittle and trees are often damaged by storms. They suffer little harm and are able to regrow satisfactorily; the species will also coppice.

T. ascendens Brongniart
Pond cypress

Tree to 20m. Crown narrowly conic, domed. Bark dull brown, fissured. Deciduous shoots arise radially on the persistent shoots but are curved erect, bearing leaves which are radial, adpressed, subulate, 0.5-1cm. Zone 7.

Pond cypress has a more restricted distribution from south-east Virginia to southern Florida and west along the coast to south-east Louisiana. It generally makes a smaller tree and occurs at higher altitudes than Swamp cypress, although the two are sometimes found growing together. The foliage shoots are stiff. Knees are rarely produced, even by trees growing in water.

'Nutans' is the common form in cultivation. The erect foliage sprays become nodding or pendulous as the season develops. This may be fairly normal for the species but this clone also differs in making a tight conical tree to 15m; however, as the branches are as brittle as those of Swamp cypress, it is inclined to become a little ragged.

T. mucronatum Tenore
Ahuehuete or Montezuma cypress

This tree differs from Swamp cypress in pollination occurring in the autumn and in the more elongated and warty cones. The foliage may be slightly shorter and is semi-evergreen or persistent. Knees are rarely produced. Zone 8.

It is found throughout most of Mexico, extending south into Guatemala and just crossing the Rio Grande into extreme south-west Texas. It is hardy in cultivation, although presumably shows some variation in hardiness over its range and I would expect the plants in north-east Mexico, from Nuevo Leon, to be hardier than those from some other parts. It is a very long-lived tree and specimens are dated as prior to the Spanish conquest of Mexico in the early sixteenth century. The largest tree in the world for girth is an Ahuehuete growing in the churchyard at Santa Maria del Tule south of Oaxaca in southern Mexico. It is 41 m tall and has a girth at 1.5 m of 36 m, or a diameter of 11.45 m; it may have arisen as the fusion of three trees.

Taxus Linnaeus **Yews Taxaceae**

The yews are a group of closely allied allopatric species; it has been said of the *T. baccata* cultivar 'Adpressa' that it is more distinct from its parent species than are all the other species. They could in theory all be kept as subspecies but this would scarcely add to our understanding of them and all the normally recognised taxa are here retained as species, although the differences between them are somewhat hard to quantify.

The yew are characterised by the red fleshy aril which subtends each fruit. The aril is the only part of the yew which is not poisonous and is intended to be eaten by birds, who fly off and disperse the seeds. The seed itself is poisonous, but surrounded by a tough seedcoat which does not break down during the passage through the bird's gut. The species are dioecious.

T. baccata Linnaeus
Yew

Tree to 25 m, usually much smaller. Crown broadly conical, becoming progressively more obtuse and domed. Bark purple-brown, smooth, scaly, fluted. Shoot green for several years due to decurrent leaf bases, becoming brown in the third or fourth year. Bud small, ovoid, scales obtuse, not keeled, persisting around the base of the branches for one year, 0.2-0.3 cm. Leaves in the shade parted either side of the shoot, in increasing amounts of natural light or vigour the 2 ranks becoming more erect, forming a narrow V groove, although somewhat erratic, dark glossy or matt green above with a ridge along the midrib, pale green with 2 indistinct bands of stomata below, linear, abruptly tapered at base to twisted petiole, gradually tapered to a fine sharp point above, 2-3 cm, rarely to 4 cm. Male cones clustered along the undersides of the previous season's branches, from buds in the leaf axils, globose head 0.4 cm across, on a stalk 0.3 cm, shedding pollen in late March/April. Female cones at end of last year's shoots, consisting of a single ovule surrounded by small bracts. Aril (red, rarely yellow) develops from the disk on which the ovule sits, swells as the fruit ripens and at maturity excloses seed except at apex, contains a sticky sweet juice, to 1 cm by 0.6 cm. Seed broad-ellipsoid, slightly compressed, 2- or rarely 4-sided, olive brown, 0.6 cm. Zone 6.

Yew is found in Britain, east across Europe to northern Iran and in North Africa in the Atlas Mountains.

In Britain, yew forms forests on chalk down-

Figure 8.22 Taxus baccata. *Foliage and ripe fruit.*

land, although being just as happy to grow on other soils. It is one of the few plants which will flourish under Beech (*Fagus sylvatica*) and is remarkably tolerant of shade.

It makes a small tree, although is slow-growing, and will withstand clipping very well. It has been used for hedges for a very long time and also for topiary. Large yew trees are found in many churchyards and, in some instances, may predate the Christian use of the site, as the tree was held in some esteem by the Druids. The tree is very long-lived, specimens to around 1,000 years old being recorded. This species, as are all yews, is described as being dioecious, i.e. with separate male and female plants, but occasionally a tree will produce a branch of the other sex or make a complete change!

Yew contains poisonous alkaloids in all parts except the fleshy aril. It is poisonous to man, if eaten, and has caused intermittent poisoning of cattle and horses; it would appear that the foliage is more poisonous when dried but individual trees may vary in the content of alkaloids, as it is reported that the following species is fed to cattle in parts of Pakistan without ill-effect. The foliage is eaten happily by deer, without any apparent harm.

Very many cultivars have been named and the following is a selection.

'Adpressa' has leaves short (less than 1.2 cm long), wide (between 0.2 and 0.4 cm) and abruptly pointed. It is a female form and makes a wide-spreading plant of dense growth habit. It is quite striking and very distinct from normal yew. 'Adpressa Variegata' is a smaller plant with the leaves golden at the tips or golden variegated. 'Adpressa Stricta' makes a more ascending bush.

'Amerfoort' has radially arranged leaves which are less than 1 cm long and approximately half as wide, oblong or oblong-elliptic with a rounded, mucronate apex. It slowly develops a stiff upright growth habit.

forma *aurea* Pilger covers all the plants with the foliage margined or tinted with yellow. It does not represent a clone.

'Dovastoniana' makes a small tree or large bush. The branches are wide-spreading with pendulous branchlets and the foliage is a very dark green. Similar in habit is 'Dovastonii Aurea' except for the leaves being yellow-margined on golden yellow shoots. The two plants are quite attractive.

'Fastigiata' is a common form with all the foliage radial, like in the erect leader of a normal plant. It makes an upright columnar tree, so far to 15 m; as the erect shoots crowd each other, it becomes broader with time. It is known as the 'Irish yew' and was found at Florence Court in Eire in the last century. It is a female plant, although it has produced the occasional male-flowered branch. A number of similar plants have been raised, some independently, others with Irish yew as one parent; in the latter category is 'Fastigiata Aurea', which is similar in habit but with golden or gold-variegated foliage. A further selection of this is 'Fastigiata Aureomarginata' in which the leaves have bright yellow margins, although they fade later; it is a male clone. 'Standishii' is a slow-growing fastigiate form with leaves of a rich golden yellow. It is female and fruits freely.

'Fructu-luteo' is a plant in which the aril under the seed is orange-red; it can be effective against the dark green foliage.

'Nana' is a name applied to a number of dwarf cultivars. They are all characterised by the slow growth rate. 'Nana' itself makes an open irregular bush with dark green glossy leaves to 2 cm by 0.2 cm and variously curved away from the shoot or are adpressed along it. 'Nutans' makes an upright or squat bush with shorter leaves and a more regular habit. 'Compacta' makes a compact oval or conical plant with annual growths of 4-6 cm bearing radially arranged leaves around 1 cm in length. It may develop a spread of 1.3 m at the base. 'Knirps' is a very slow-growing form, attaining perhaps 30-50 cm in two decades, with brown branchlets and makes a broad irregular bush. 'Pygmaea' is a very small plant of dense conical or ovoid habit and leaves 0.5-1 cm by only 0.1 cm.

'Repandens' is a low form which develops long, wide-spreading branches. It creates a somewhat undulating mass of ground covering of bluish green foliage. It will grow up to 60 cm or so high and spreading 5 m or more. A number of other similar clones exist. As yew is loath to form a leader from a side cutting, similar plants can be raised by choosing prostrate cuttings and by removing any leaders which do develop.

'Semperaurea' has steeply ascending branches with massed side shoots. The foliage is golden and retains this colour for two seasons, hence 'evergold'. It makes a bush wider than high and will make 3 m by 5 m in about 30 years.

'Washingtonii' has new foliage golden, later becoming yellowish green, and makes a large shrub with a broad sprawling habit.

T. wallichiana Zuccarini
Himalayan yew

This tree is similar in general appearance to common yew. It is found along the Himalayan mountains from east Afghanistan to the Chinese border and also occurs in southern Tibet. It differs from yew in the usually falcate leaves which are covered with microscopic papillae on the underside and have rolled margins. The apex is acuminate and the leaves are generally longer and narrower, although the range is very similar, from 1.5-2.75 cm by 0.2-0.25 cm. The seed is slightly longer, to 0.7 cm, compressed, to 0.5 cm in width, somewhat abruptly tapered to a mucronate apex. The male cones are larger, ovoid, to 0.8 cm. Zone 7.

It is often treated as a subspecies of *T. baccata*, but is as distinct as any yew species. Similar plants are recorded across China to the Philippines, which may belong to the following taxon.

Himalayan yew is rare in cultivation but should be hardy.

T. chinensis (Pilger) Rehder
Chinese yew

This tree is sometimes treated as a variety of *T. wallichiana* (var. *chinensis* (Pilger) Florin) but is upheld as a separate species in the *Chinese Flora*. It has similarly papillose leaves with the margins slightly recurved but differs in their being more abruptly acuminate, shorter and relatively broader, usually in the range 1.5-2.2 cm by 0.3 cm. Zone 7.

It is similar in aspect to common and Himalayan yews and is found across a belt of China from Yunnan and Sichuan to Hubei and Guangxi. It may not be in cultivation. It has been confused with the next taxon but the plants I saw on the Emei Shan in Sichuan province in 1980 were clearly in the *baccata-wallichiana* alliance and quite different from cultivated trees grown from seeds collected by Wilson under his number 4053, which I take to be the next taxon. The name *T. chinensis* may be invalid and therefore have to be replaced.

T. mairei (Lemee & Leveille) S.Y. Hu ex Liu
Maire yew

This tree is treated as a variety of *chinensis* in the *Chinese Flora*, which cannot be correct as it has priority over *chinensis*. Also it appears very different, judging by the living material I have seen. Three other names which have been proposed for this one taxon are: *T. speciosa* Florin, *T. celebica*

(Warburg) Li and *T. sumatrana* (Miquel) de Laubenfels, the last two based on specimens collected in Indonesia. Zone 8.

The plant in cultivation from Wilson's 4053 is a small shrubby tree to 5 m with a spreading crown. The shoots are slender, with bare patches and bear sparse open foliage which is pale yellow-green, shiny above and matt below. The male cones are only 0.2 cm across on 0.1 cm stalks. It is recorded from Sichuan in the west to Fujian in the east. The plants from the Philippines and Indonesia may or may not be the same. In Indonesia, the plant is recorded as crossing the Equator, to 1°S.

The cultivated plants are unique in the openness or sparseness of the foliage.

T. yunnanensis Cheng & L.K. Fu
Yunnan yew

This plant only recently has been described; previously it has been lumped with *T. wallichiana* but from the drawing appears distinct. It differs from Himalayan yew in the longer and more open foliage, with markedly falcate leaves usually in the range 2.5-3 cm, although up to 4.7 cm, by 0.2-0.3 cm, and in the more ovoid tapered seed. It makes a tree to 20 m and is recorded from northwest and west Yunnan, south-west Sichuan and south-east Tibet; it is probably found in adjoining parts of Burma and north-east India as well. It is not recorded in cultivation, although may be lurking in some collection as specimens, and probably seeds, were collected by George Forrest. Zone 9.

T. cuspidata Siebold & Zuccarini
Japanese yew

Small shrub in cultivation, although a large tree to 20 m in the wild. Shoot green for three years, becoming brown in stages. Foliage radial, often twisted into 2 ranks which are frequently erect with a narrow V groove between, linear, 1.5-2.5 cm by 0.2-0.3 cm, abruptly narrowed at both ends, apex spiny, petiole 0.1 cm, dark green above with prominent midrib, tawny or yellow-green below. Fruit carried along the undersides of the shoots, aril scarlet (rarely yellowish around a greenish seed in var. luteobaccata Miyabe & Tatewakiana). Zone 4.

Recorded throughout Japan and in eastern China from Shandong to Jiangsu provinces, it only makes a small shrub in cultivation. The northern populations from Hokkaido are very hardy and preferred in the north-eastern USA over *T. baccata*. The foliage may take on a reddish brown hue in cold weather.

var. *nana* Rehder is a wild dwarf form from the

Japan Sea region of Honshu. It makes a small plant to 2 m with radially set foliage and erect shoots. In cultivation it has made 4 m.

T. canadensis Marshall
Canadian yew

This species makes only a low shrub with a straggling habit, only occasionally up to 2 m tall. The bud scales are more or less lanceolate and rather loose. The leaves taper abruptly to a fine point, are less than 2 cm long, shortly stalked and dark glossy green or yellow-green.

It is recorded from eastern Canada across to Ontario and south-west Manitoba, south to Virginia and Tennessee. It is rare in cultivation and only worth growing in areas with too severe a winter for common yew or out of curiosity. Zone 2.

T. floridana Chapman
Florida yew

This rare tree only grows on limestone bluffs along the Apalachicola river in northern Florida, where it is found with *Torreya taxifolia*. It differs from Pacific and Canadian yews in the dark green falcate leaves in the range 2-2.5 cm. It is in cultivation but is rare. Zone 8.

T. brevifolia Nuttall
Pacific yew

Tree to 15 m, or a large shrub. Crown conical, open, with slender drooping branches. Bark scaly, red-purple. Buds with loose yellowish pointed scales. Leaves parted either side of the shoot, linear-lanceolate, retained for 5-12 years, 1.2-2.5 cm. Zone 4.

Pacific yew is found from south-east Alaska south to northern and central California and inland in the Rocky Mountain region from south-east British Columbia to northern Idaho. It is the only North American yew to make a respectable tree, although usually a shrub. Like other yews, it is very shade-tolerant. It is rare in cultivation.

T. globosa Schlechtendal
Mexican yew

This shrub or small tree has a wide but scattered distribution from Nuevo Leon in north-east Mexico south to Guatemala and El Salvador. The foliage is light green. The fruit is quite distinct, at least in the plants I collected in Nuevo Leon and is larger than in other species with the aril globose and over 1 cm in diameter. It is in cultivation and

should be hardy with suitable shelter. Zone 8.

T. × *hunnewelliana* Rehder
Hunnewell yew
(*T. canadensis* × *T. cuspidata*)

This hybrid differs from the *cuspidata* parent in the narrower, light green needles which have light green (not yellow or golden green) stomatal bands beneath and assume a paler reddish colour over winter. The habit is more slender and it is faster-growing, which also separates it from Canadian yew. It is commonly planted in the USA as a winter hardy evergreen. Zone 4.

T. × *media* Rehder
Hybrid yew
(*T. baccata* × *T. cuspidata*)

This hybrid is also planted as a winter hardy evergreen in the eastern USA. It is intermediate between the parents. From Japanese yew, it differs in the distinctly 2 ranked and often pectinate foliage arrangement, and the olive green shoots; from common yew, it differs in the stiffer, broader leaves which abruptly widen at the base. Zone 5.

Numerous forms have been named and are cultivated in America. One which is in cultivation in Britain is 'Hicksii' which makes an open version of Irish yew but with yellow-green foliage and a more spreading vase-shaped crown; it is a seedling of *T. cuspidata nana*. 'Hatfieldii' is similar, but more conical in habit.

Tetraclinis Masters **Cupressaceae**

This is a monotypic genus related to *Callitris* and *Widdringtonia*, but differing in the flattened *Thuja*-like sprays which are articulated where the 4 rows of scale-leaves come together, and the cones with 4 scales.

T. articulata (Vahl)Masters
Tetraclinis

Tree to 15 cm. Crown conical. Foliage in erect, compact sprays. Leaves in 4 rows, with the lateral and facial pairs coming together in false whorls, lateral pair larger, partly covering facial leaves, pointed, incurved, tips free. Cones terminal, solitary, rounded, angular, with 4 thick glaucous woody scales, only the outer pair fertile, each bearing 2-3 winged seeds. Zone 9.

Tetraclinis is the only genus of conifers exclusively native to the Mediterranean region. Its main distribution is in North Africa in Morocco and

Algeria but it also occurs in one locality in south-east Spain and as a rare plant on the island of Malta. It is too tender for general cultivation in Britain, although will survive for a period of time with some protection. It is well suited to regions with pronounced dry periods. It has a valuable timber and also produces a resin used in the varnish industry.

Thuja Linnaeus **Thuja Cupressaceae**

Thuja is a small genus of five species. They are restricted to North America and north-east Asia. The small woody cones which have the scales hinged at the base to release the small winged seeds characterise the genus. Two (rarely 3) small, winged seeds are carried on each fertile cone scale, of which there are 2, rarely 3, pairs. The foliage is in flat sprays with very different lateral and facial pairs; the crushed foliage is strongly and individually scented.

T. occidentalis Linnaeus
White cedar

Tree to 20m but usually smaller. Crown rounded conic, with slightly billowing branches. Bark orange-brown with vertical shredding ridges. Shoot green, covered by decurrent leaf bases, soon brown. Leaves scale-like, in flat sprays, thick, yellowish green above, pale or greyish green beneath, laterals pointed, keeled, overlapping facial leaves, up to 0.2cm, facial leaves in the centre bearing a prominent raised round gland, crushed foliage smells of apples, the foliage generally takes on a bronze coloration over winter. Male cones ovoid, black, 0.1cm. Cones ovoid, erect, later pendulous as the branches bend under their weight, yellow-green, ripening brown in autumn, 1cm. Scales 8-10, smooth, only the central 2 pairs fertile. Zone 2.

White cedar is native to eastern North America from the Atlantic coast across to Manitoba and in scattered localities south to Tennessee. In the wild it occurs on a range of barren or wetland conditions. In cultivation it is a slow-growing tree and rarely looks thrifty, but has given a number of very useful cultivars, amongst the many named. These can be discussed under the following headings:

Tall-growing Forms — Columnar Habit
'Columbia' makes a narrow tree to 15m in which the new growths flush white, and then become conspicuously white again in winter.
'Columna' has a very narrow columnar habit and will make only 5m or so.
'Fastigiata' is a conic or ovoid plant with the foliage in vertical sprays, retaining the green colour over winter; it has made 15m.
'Hetz' Wintergreen' is a fast-growing conical form in which the foliage remains green over winter.
'Malonyana' is a very slender and vigorous form with dark green foliage which remains that colour in winter; it has made 20m.
'Skogholm' is a dense columnar form with bright green leaves.

Tall-growing Forms — Pendulous
'Pendula' has pendulous twigs with blue-green foliage (greyer in winter) set on an upright but tortuous plant to 5m.
'Filiformis' is a mound-forming plant to 8m in which the foliage is in whip-like sprays and pendulous.

Tall-growing Forms — Contorted Branching
'Cristata' is a lax plant to 3m in which the penultimate divisions of the foliage are very contorted.
'Spiralis' is an erect tree to 15m in which the foliage is carried in fernlike spirals.

Tall-growing Forms — Distinctive Habit
'Buchanii' makes a small narrow-crowned tree to 6m which has open, spaced slender branches.
'Mastersii' is a compact conical form with the foliage in vertically-held sprays. 'Wareana' is similar but more robust, to 7m. Both these forms have been raised from seed in the past and show some variation. 'Smargard' is a more recently raised but similar plant with a loosely branched conical habit and bright glossy green foliage throughout the year.

Dwarf Forms — Globose or Ovoid Habit
'Caespitosa' is a very slow-growing cushion or bun-shaped form which is broader than high; it will only make about 30cm by 40cm in 15 years. The twigs are short, thick and upright with adpressed needles.
'Globosa' is of compact globular habit with grey-green foliage; it will make a plant 1.5m through and high.
'Little Gem' is a dwarf slow-growing form with a spreading crown of somewhat upright dark green foliage; it will make a plant up to a metre tall and more than 2m across.
'Umbraculifera' makes a bun-shaped bush 1m high and half as wide again, with glaucous foliage.

Dwarf Forms — Conical Habit
'Holmstrup' has a regular conical habit with the attractive green foliage arranged in vertical sprays; it will make 4m or so, with time. 'Holmstrup Yellow' is a bud mutation with yellow foliage.

'Rosenthalii' is a very slow-growing densely branched columnar form, to less than 3m in 50 years. The stiff branches have more or less vertical sprays of dark green foliage.

Coloured Foliage Forms — Yellow
'Aurescens' has young shoots which are an attractive golden yellow; the plant develops a narrow conical habit to 5m.

'Lutea' makes a medium-sized form with foliage golden yellow throughout the year. It makes a very neat tree, with time to 15m. 'Lutea Nana' is a dwarf form to 2m.

'Rheingold' is a most attractive plant with golden yellow foliage which is mainly juvenile. The new shoots have a rosy tint, and the leaves adopt a bronzy yellow hue over winter. It will make a plant to 1m and is excellent for associating with heathers and as a golden dwarf conifer. It is confused with 'Ellwangeriana Aurea', which has mixed juvenile and adult foliage and arose as a bud mutation on the green 'Ellwangeriana'. This is larger-growing, making either a broad conical plant or more often, when several leaders are formed, a multipeaked mini-forest. It too is an excellent plant, making 3-4m in 15 or so years. It may be that 'Rheingold' is a cultivariant of 'Ellwangeriana Aurea', taken from the foliage with more juvenile leaves. Whatever the origin, both are excellent plants.

'Semperaurea' makes a dense conical plant with outspreading branches, to 10m. The foliage is glossy green with golden yellow tips and assumes a more yellow-brown coloration in winter.

'Sunkist' is a fast-growing and conical plant with dense golden yellow foliage. It needs to be grown in full sun, else the foliage is rather pale and greenish.

Coloured Foliage Forms — White Variegated
'Alba' has the new foliage conspicuously white variegated at the tips. It makes a conical plant to 5m with spreading branches but is more attractive when young.

'Beaufort' has the young growths white variegated; the growth habit is like the species.

'Wansdyke Silver' is a small columnar form to 1.5m in which the short sprays of light green foliage are splashed creamy white.

Coloured Foliage Forms — Brown
'Beteramsii' has the new foliage reddish brown until late summer, when it becomes green. It makes a normal tree.

Juvenile Foliage Forms
'Ericoides' is a form with soft juvenile needle leaves, to 0.8cm. The habit of young plants is compact but as they age this neatness is lost. The foliage is dull green, becoming medium brown in the winter.

'Ohlendorfii' has leaves mainly juvenile, to 1.2cm, carried on stiff erect stems; this foliage is spreading but incurved. Also borne are a few thick shoots with small adult foliage. Cuttings taken from the juvenile portions of this plant will retain a dwarf and compact habit with juvenile foliage, whilst those made of more vigorous growths will produce mainly adult leaved plants. The foliage is two-tone in effect, part dark green, part pinky brown. It makes a dwarf plant of irregular habit, to 1m.

T. plicata D. Don
Western red cedar
Tree to 50m. Crown columnar conic, branches rather billowing, in old trees pendent and layering around the bole to create a forest of new trees, never very dense. Bark red-brown, with a purplish hue, fissured with the ridges exfoliating in narrow strips, often fluted at base. Shoot green from decurrent leaves, turns reddish or purplish brown in second year. Foliage in flat sprays, level or slightly hanging. Leaves in flat shoots, lustrous mid- or dark green above, paler with whitish green bands beneath, with small translucent glands showing when held up against the light but not prominent as in occidentalis, facial pairs much smaller, keeled, obovoid with acute free tip and small lateral band of stomata on lower leaf, lateral leaves incurved, acute, overlapping, stomata on lower side only. Male cones ovoid, 0.1-0.2cm, shedding pollen early spring. Cones flask-shaped, erect, with 8-10 scales of which 2-3 pairs are fertile, 1-1.5cm. Scales with a small spreading terminal hook. Zone 5.

This majestic tree is native to western North America from south-east Alaska to north-west California and in a separate inland region in the Rocky Mountains from south-east British Columbia to northern Idaho. In the wild it occurs on a variety of sites, mainly on rich soils with abundant moisture. Because of its tolerance of anaerobic soil conditions, it also occurs on waterlogged 'muskeg' sites, where few other plants can grow.

Figure 8.23 Thuja plicata. *Foliage and open cones.*

Western red cedar can look similar to Lawson cypress but in the absence of cones it can be distinguished by the fragrant and broader foliage. The trees are more conical in outline and never as dense; looking at a tree from the side, one can always see some daylight through it. Also they have erect leading shoots. The foliage may turn bronze-coloured in winter, but not as strongly as with White cedar.

In cultivation Western red cedar thrives on all soil types although its best development is made on moist soils or in wetter regions. It makes a very useful hedging plant, withstanding clipping. It will grow well on chalk and the ability to grow on anaerobic sites makes the species a practical plant for use around fuel or heating oil tanks, as it is more likely to survive a spillage than most others.

The timber is used for garden sheds and roofing shingles, whilst the fragrant foliage is very useful as foliage in wreaths and floral decorations. It, along with other *Thuja* species, may be attacked by Keithia disease, caused by the fungus, *Didymascella thujina*; this kills individual leaves but it is only of any consequence in young nursery plantings where it can lead to serious losses.

Compared to White cedar, only a modest number of cultivars have been named, suggesting that the number of cultivars is inversely proportional to the beauty of the tree! The following is a selection.

'Atrovirens' is a form with dark green foliage. It is of no special merit.

'Aurea' is a tree form with golden yellow foliage and makes quite an effective plant.

'Fastigiata' makes a columnar tree with ascending branches bearing dense but normal foliage. It is useful where a tall screen is needed, as the narrow habit obviates the need for much trimming, but can also make a neat columnar specimen. 'Excelsa' has a similar narrow crown but with short horizontal branches and darker leaves. It has a more open aspect.

'Rogersii' is a dwarf plant making a broadly conical or ellipsoidal bush a metre or so high. The foliage is golden yellow, bronzing in the winter. 'Stoneham Gold' is a more vigorous and less dense form in which the new leaves are bright gold, changing to dark green inside the plant. It will make 2 m, with a narrower habit than 'Rogersii'. Both are seedlings from 'Aurea'.

'Semperaurescens' is a tree form to 20 m with mossy yellow green foliage.

'Zebrina' has the foliage banded with whitish yellow. It is quite attractive from a distance when the green runs into the gold to give a uniform golden green colour. The trees in cultivation appear to belong to more than one clone, as some are much better than others; part of the variation could be explained by the growing conditions, as the older (usually shaded!) foliage is light green, or the position of the cutting could be involved (see page 47). It makes a large tree, to 30 m and is quite common in cultivation but less attractive than 'Aurea'.

T. koraiensis Nakai
Korean thuja

This small tree or large shrub is chiefly characterised by the bright silvery glaucous stomatal bands on the foliage; they completely cover the underside of the sprays, except for the keel in the centre of each facial leaf and a narrow yellow-green margin on the sides of the lateral pairs. The foliage is more open than in Western red cedar and thicker. The foliage has a strong aroma, variously described as of acetone or almonds. The cones have 4 pairs of scales but only the middle pairs are fertile. Zone 5.

Korean thuja is native to Korea and to Jilin province in north-east China. It makes a small tree, no more than 10m in 50 years, and is most beautiful.

T. standishii (Gordon)Carriere
Japanese thuja

Tree to 20m. Crown broadly conic with open branching. Bark red, in large plates, shaggy. Foliage coarse in dense nodding sprays. Leaves matt, dark grey-green or yellow-green, greyish-green with the lower part faintly glaucous beneath, scales with incurved obtuse points, with a sweet scent of oil of citrinella. Cones oblong, 1cm. Zone 7.

Japanese thuja is found in the islands of Honshu and Shikoku. It makes a neat tree and the foliage is often bloomed blue-grey as it emerges. The scent of crushed foliage is good, but the leaves lack the brilliant silvery undersides of Korean fir.

T. sutchuenensis Franchet
Sichuan thuja

This small tree is said to have obtuse, glandless leaves and cones with 8 scales, free at the tip. The facial leaves have a central groove. The bark is reported as dark grey. Zone 7.

This tree was found by the Revd Paul Farges in 1892 in north-east Sichuan, where it is very rare. Apparently it has recently been introduced into New Zealand(?) where the young plants are described as having the foliage silvery glaucous; I have not seen material and suspect that the true species is extinct.

Thujopsis Siebold & Zuccarini **Hiba**
Cupressaceae

This is a monotypic genus closely related to *Thuja* and *Platycladus*, from which it differs in the thick foliage which is silvery glaucous beneath and the cones which are subglobose with six fertile woody scales, each bearing 3-5 seeds.

T. dolabrata (Linnaeus fil.)Siebold & Zuccarini
Hiba

Tree to 30m, in cultivation smaller, often on several stems and sometimes shrubby. Crown broadly conical to cylindrical, depending on vigour and number of stems. Bark brown or red-purple brown, shredding in small grey strips. Foliage in flat sprays, heavy. Leaves thick, shiny bright green above, silvery white beneath with dark green margins, lateral leaves broad, spreading, boat-shaped, with incurved mucronate tip, facial leaves grooved, tip raised. Cones blue-grey, ripening in the first year, to 1cm. Scales leathery or woody, with an acute upturned central prickle. Zone 5.

Hiba is native to Japan, with the typical form, var. *dolabrata*, occurring in southern Honshu, Shikoku and Kyushu. It is unusual in the stoutness of the foliage, which is silvery beneath, and distinguished by it from *Thuja* species. The foliage is usually retained to the ground and it makes a neat, although very slow-growing, tree or large shrub. The Latin name, *dolabrata* — a hatchet, refers to the leaf shape.

var. *hondae* Makino differs in the denser branchlets composed of smaller leaves and the larger and more globose cones, in which the scales lack the prominent prickle. It occurs in 'northern Honshu and Hokkaido.

'Laetevirens' is a dwarf form to 1m but often wider. The foliage is light green. It is also called 'Nana'.

'Variegata' has creamy white patches on the foliage. The coloured portions are rather erratic in their occurrence so the effect is not strong.

Torreya Arnott **Nutmeg trees**
Cephalotaxaceae

This genus has in the past been placed in the family Taxaceae but is here included in the Cephalotaxaceae, which like it has the fruit entirely enclosed in the fleshy aril. In both genera, the leaves and shoots are subopposite and the cotyledons are morphologically similar. *Torreya* differs in the leaves being hard and spine-tipped and the fruit taking two years to ripen. The germination is hypogeal, i.e. with the cotyledons remaining underground.

Torreya consists of seven species found in southern USA, Japan and across China. Three of the Chinese species are placed in a separate section, *Ruminatae* Hu, because of the large ruminated edible seeds.

T. californica Torrey
California nutmeg tree

Tree to 20m. Crown broadly conic with open whorls of branches. Bark red-brown, flaky, in old trees forming narrow scaly ridges. Shoot green with decurrent leaf-bases, becoming red-brown in second year. Buds conic, pointed, green and brown, scales persist as a ring at base of shoot. Leaves set radially but twisted to give 2 wide-spreading ranks, linear-lanceolate, tapering from near base to spine-tipped apex, dark shiny yellowish green and slightly convex above with a central ridge, pale bright green beneath with whitish bands of stomata in 2 narrow grooves, 3-5cm, occasionally to 8cm, by 0.3cm. Male cones solitary in leaf axils, consisting of whorls of 4 stamens, 1cm. Fruit drupe-like, obovoid or ellipsoidal, to 4cm, enclosed in green, purple-streaked, aril. Zone 8.

California nutmeg is restricted to scattered stands in central California where it is found on moist bottomland sites. The name 'nutmeg' is an allusion to the similarity of the fruits to those of the commercial nutmeg. It makes an impressive tree and is the most commonly cultivated *Torreya*, flourishing best in wetter parts of the country.

T. taxifolia Arnott
Stinking cedar

This tree differs from California nutmeg in the shorter, very sharp and rigid needles, to 4 cm, which are quite strongly convex on the upper surface, and when crushed have an unpleasant odour. The branchlets turn yellow-brown in the second and third years and as the aril degenerates it gives off a foetid smell. Zone 8.

Stinking cedar is only found growing in moist bottomland habitats at the foot of limestone bluffs along a very limited stretch of the Apalichicola river in north-west Florida and extreme south-west Georgia. It is very rare, having been badly depleted by a fungal disease. The tree is represented in cultivation and appears to be hardy, at least in southern Britain.

T. nucifera (Linnaeus)Siebold & Zuccarini
Naya

Tree to 15m. Crown thin, rather open. Bark pinkish brown, finely ridged. Leaves as for California nutmeg, shorter, 1.5-2.5cm, rarely to 3cm, by 0.2-0.3cm, sometimes falcate, with a narrow ridge running along the upper surface, deep glossy green above with 2 white stomatal bands below, crushed foliage emits a pungent aromatic odour. Fruit narrowly ellipsoidal, 2.5cm. Zone 7.

Naya is restricted to moist valley bottom sites in southern Honshu, Shikoku and Kyushu. In cultivation it is similar to California nutmeg but easily separated by the closer set and much shorter leaves which arch down and by the more orange-brown third year shoots.

var. *radicans* Nakai has erect shoots to 3m and makes a bushy plant which spreads by the branches rooting. It occurs in high mountain areas in Honshu.

'Prostrata' and *T. californica* 'Spreadeagle' are two ground-hugging plants. They probably are cultivariants, formed from cuttings of side shoots which have never made a leader. As with many other conifers, *Torreya* is reluctant to make a leading shoot from a cutting taken from a weak side branch.

T. grandis Fortune ex Lindley
Chinese nutmeg tree

This tree is similar to Naya but has thinner, generally shorter, leaves which are virtually scentless if crushed, and the shoots remain green for at least two years, becoming yellow-brown or greyish. The fruit is variable in shape but has a short mucronate point at the apex. Zone 8.

This tree is native to the Chinese provinces of Zhejiang, Fujian and Jiangxi and was introduced by Robert Fortune from the former. It has made a tree to 10m but is uncommon in cultivation. In China, a number of different forms based on the fruit shape are recognised as cultivars.

T. fargesii Franchet
Farges nutmeg tree

This tree is similar to *grandis* but differs in the deeply ruminated seed, which is globose-ellipsoidal and lacks the mucronate apex. The foliage is more gradually tapered, flatter above and with the deeply indented stomatal bands red-brown, at least on dried material. The leaves are 1.3-3cm long by 0.2-0.3cm wide. Zone 8.

It is native to west Hubei and east and northeast Sichuan.

T. jackii Chun
Jack nutmeg tree

This is a very distinct species from southern Zhejiang province and has subopposite leaves 3.5-9cm in length and broad obovoid fruits which are 2-3cm long and apiculate. Unfortunately, it has yet to be introduced. Zone 8.

T. yunnanensis Cheng & L.K. Fu
Yunnan nutmeg tree

This tree is similar to *T. fargesii*, but differs in the apiculate globose fruit and the leaves 2-3.6cm long by 0.3-0.4cm wide. The fruit is less ruminated than in the above species. Zone 8.

It is native to north-west Yunnan. Although not recorded in cultivation, herbarium material was collected by George Forrest, although seed may not have been introduced.

Tsuga Carriere **Hemlocks Pinaceae**

This is a genus of ten or eleven species which are related to *Picea* in the cones and in the shoots having a short peg-like projection, or *pulvinus*, at the base of each needle; the *pulvinus* is very much smaller than in *Picea* and the leaf is much constricted into a short petiole which sites on the *pulvinus* and is usually adpressed to the shoot, the needles are notched, only rarely pointed, with the arrangement somewhat parted above the shoot and the leading shoot is pendulous or leans over at an angle. The species alive today are restricted to North America and Asia from the Himalayas eastwards. Prior to the last Ice Age, species of *Tsuga* were extant in Europe, including Britain.

The genus is divided into three sections.

Section *Heopeuce* Keng & Keng fil. has erect cones with exserted bract scales and foliage like a *Keterleeria* species; it contains only *T. longibracteata*.

Section *Hesperopeuce* Engelmann also contains only one species, *T. mertensiana*. It has larger cones to 8 cm and thicker needles convex and with stomata on both sides, carried radially around the shoot.

Section *Tsuga* contains the remaining species; it is characterised by the flat needles, much broader than thick, arranged more or less parted either side of the shoot and the small pendulous cones rarely larger than 3 cm. This section can be further split into two groups on the basis of the leaf margins, which are finely toothed in three species — *T. canadensis, heterophylla, dumosa* (best seen under a hand lens) and entire in *sieboldii, diversifolia, chinensis, formosana, forrestii* and *caroliniana*, although *chinensis* may have a few small teeth towards the apex of the needles, especially on seedlings. The first three species also have much more floppy leading shoots; in the latter group, they are more inclined to arch stiffly outwards.

Hemlocks are very useful as amenity trees; they are very adaptable to soil and site, being especially good on acidic sands and for shady situations. They can be used for hedges.

T. canadensis (Linnaeus)Carriere
Eastern hemlock

Tree to 30 m, usually smaller. Crown broadly conic, usually on several stems. Bark purplish grey with thick scaly ridges. Shoot slender, grey or grey-brown, with long curly hairs. Bud small, conic. Foliage in pendent sprays. Leaves parted below the shoot, less so above with a line of short leaves adpressed along shoot above and showing the white stomata, taper from rounded base to rounded blunt apex, margins finely toothed, dark green above, with 2 white bands of stomata beneath, to 1.8 cm. Male cones yellow, in spring. Cones ripen light brown during first autumn, oblong-ovoid, 2 cm. Zone 4.

Eastern hemlock is found in eastern North America from the Atlantic seaboard inland as far as Ontario and south down the Appalachian Mountains to northern Alabama. It is very distinct in the line of leaves lying along the upper side of the shoot; these leaves are upside down and show the white stomatal bands.

It grows on cool moist sites, either in pure groves or in a mixture with other conifers or broadleaved trees. The species is extremely tolerant of shading. All the current season's growth, including the leading shoot, is pendulous and this is considered to be an adaptation to shady sites, as it allows an increased interception of the available light. The leading shoot only becomes firm and woody during the autumn/winter period, when the broadleaved trees are leafless.

Eastern hemlock usually makes a specimen with several trunks and remains clothed to the ground. It has given rise to a large number of cultivars, of which the following is a short selection. When purchasing dwarf forms of any *Tsuga*, it is important to ensure that the plants are raised from cuttings; all these species will root readily. A few nurseries resort to grafting these dwarf forms, as this makes a saleable plant more quickly but grafted plants (of these forms) acquire vigour from the rootstock and will not make the neat compact forms described or intended.

Small-leaved
forma *microphylla* (Lindley)Beissner is a group name to cover all the plants with the leaves shorter than in the wild form. They are generally less than 0.6 cm long. The plants make interesting small trees, to 10 m.

Gold Leaves
'Aurea' is a plant with the new foliage and needles yellow-gold, changing to green in the second season. The plant is a moderately slow-growing form, making a conical tree, useful for brightening up a shady vista. It is possible that 'Everett Golden' is now grown as 'Aurea'; it is similar but less regular in outline.

Variegated Leaves
'Albospica' has the new growths white, changing later to green; it is slow-growing and of compact habit.

'Dwarf Whitetip' is a similar broadly conical form with graceful arching branchlets.

Weeping Habit

'Pendula' has the shoots all pendulous and retaining this habit unless trained; if the branches are trained upwards before becoming woody, a pleasant dome-shaped or mound plant can be made. As a well-grown specimen, it can be very effective.

'Gables Weeping' makes arching growths which support weeping lateral shoots and eventually produces a plant 1-2m high and through. It is a very attractive larger dwarf form.

Dwarf Habit — Procumbent

'Cole' is a completely prostrate plant, making a wide-spreading ground cover. 'Prostrata' is similar.

Dwarf Habit — Vase-shaped

'Bennett' is a dwarf plant in which the branches arch out, leaving a hollow nest inside. It is broader than high and compact. The leaves are short and light green. 'Fantana' and 'Jeddeloh' are similar.

Dwarf Habit — Globose

'Minuta' is a very small plant, to no more than 45cm. The leaves are less than 1cm in length and dark green. 'Pygmaea' is similar, with shorter leaves.

'Nana Gracilis' makes a dwarf mound-forming plant which is flat-topped; the habit is graceful with the arching branchlets. It will make 50cm in width after ten years.

'Warners Globe' makes an upright oval form to 80cm by 50cm. The leaves are up to 1.5cm and dark green.

Dwarf Habit — Conical

'Boulevard' is one of a number of compact conical forms with densely arranged deep green needles. 'Compacta' is similar, eventually making a bush 3m tall; it is somewhat coarser in its foliage.

Dwarf Habit — Irregular

'Hussii' makes a rugged slow-growing plant with thick congested branches bearing short dark green foliage. The annual growths are usually under 2.5cm.

'Verkades Recurved' has unusual recurved foliage and will form a flat-topped plant, making 50cm in a decade.

T. heterophylla (Rafinesque)Sargent
Western hemlock

Tree to 50m. Crown narrow conical, with open level branches pendent at the tips. Bark purple-brown, cracked into small ridges, in young trees smoother. Shoot brownish grey, with long brown hairs. Buds ovoid-conic, pale brown, 0.15cm. Leaves of varying lengths, widely parted below, more erect above the shoot, parallel to a blunt rounded apex, margins finely toothed, dark green above with 2 silvery bands of stomata below, to 2cm. Male flowers crimson, shedding pollen in late spring. Cones ovoid, pale green, ripening dark brown, 2cm. Zone 6.

Western hemlock is native down the Pacific coast from Alaska to northern California and inland in the Rocky Mountains from south-east British Columbia to northern Idaho. It makes a tree up to a maximum of 70m and is extremely shade-tolerant. The butt is frequently affected by the decay fungus *Heterobasidion annosum* (see page 67), which degrades the otherwise valuable timber. The species will flourish on a wide range of sites; it is particularly useful on acidic sandy soils where it is fast-growing. It will only withstand a limited amount of exposure to wind.

It is one of the most beautiful of trees, with the neat conical habit of horizontal branches arching down at the tips and a pendulous leading shoot; this beauty is best displayed by small trees under 10m but often larger trees are as neat. Young trees less than 4m tend to have rather flat open crowns.

The common name 'hemlock' was given to the species because the foliage is alleged to have a smell similar to that of the true hemlocks and for want of a better name, it has stuck.

Western hemlock has given rise to very few cultivars:

'Argenteovariegata' has the new shoots white.

'Conica' has a dwarf broadly ovoid habit to 3m.

'Laursen's Column' develops a narrow upright crown, eventually making a sizeable columnar tree.

'Dumosa' is a bushy form to 60m. 'Iron Springs' is similar.

T. dumosa (D. Don)Eichler
Himalayan hemlock

Tree to 50m in the Himalayas but only to 15m in cultivation. Crown conic, bushy when on several stems. Bark pink-brown, scaly, in old trees with scaly ridges. Shoot whitish brown, pink-brown later, finely hairy. Bud globular, 0.2cm. Leaves pectinate below and less so above, taper from rounded base, apex acute or obtuse, margins minutely toothed, often falcate, groove above along full length, bluish green above, with 2 silvery stomatal bands and blue-green margins below, 1.5-

3 cm by 0.15-0.3 cm. Cones broadly ovoid, shiny brown, 1.5-2.5 cm, scales rounded or obovoid, to 1 cm wide. Zone 7.

Himalayan hemlock is recorded from Uttar Pradesh in north-west India along the Himalayan Mountains into south-east Tibet, northern Burma, Yunnan and south-west Sichuan.

Himalayan hemlock is easily recognised by the pointed or obtuse leaves which are usually minutely toothed along the margins and have silvery white stomatal bands. It makes a very fine tree in the wild but most introductions have proved somewhat tender in cultivation in Britain. More careful selection should, however, result in the introduction of hardier forms of this attractive hemlock; introductions from the Chinese end of its range are more likely to be hardy, although in the inner parts of the Himalayas, as in central Bhutan, the tree occurs in cold temperate zones at heights of up to 3,300 m and should be hardy.

Plants are sometimes found in cultivation under the name *Tsuga yunnanensis* (Franchet)Pritzel. This name is applicable to *T. dumosa* but the cultivated plants are probably all *T. forrestii*.

T. sieboldii Carriere
Southern Japanese hemlock

Tree to 20 m, or less. Crown broadly conic, open, on several stems. Bark dark grey, smooth, becoming cracked into small square scales. Shoot glabrous, shiny, buff, darkening to brown in second year. Bud ovoid, dark orange. Leaves irregular in length, parted above the shoot, irregularly so below, grooved and dark glossy green above, 2 broad white or pale stomatal bands beneath, apex notched, margins entire, 0.7-2 cm by 0.2 cm. Cone oval, dark brown, 2.5 cm. Zone 6.

This tree is native to Japan from central Honshu south to Shikoku and Kyushu. It is well marked by the glabrous shoots. In cultivation it makes a slow-growing tree with an attractive broad habit. It will grow on most sites, although preferring protection from exposure. *Tsuga* is the Japanese name for this species.

T. diversifolia (Maximowicz)Masters
Northern Japanese hemlock

Tree to 15 m. Crown broad and dense dome, on several stems. Bark orange-brown, shallowly cracked. Shoot orange, becoming dull brown, with fine short hairs. Bud obovoid. Leaves pectinate below and parted above, dense, broader, towards rounded notched tip, short from 0.5 cm to 1.2-1.5 cm by 0.2 cm, deep shiny green above, 2 broad white bands of stomata below. Male cones red-brown. Cones ovoid, shiny broad. Zone 5.

This slow-growing tree is native to the northern part of Japan, from central Honshu to Hokkaido. It makes a very bushy tree and is similar to *T. sieboldii* but differs in the dense, more regular leaves and the darker-coloured hairy shoots.

'Gotelli' is a dwarf form which makes growths of only around 2.5 cm. 'Nana' may be the same plant, as it was originally labelled *T. sieboldii* 'Nana'.

T. chinensis (Franchet)Pritzel
Chinese hemlock

Tree 15 m or more. Crown conic, or broad conic on several stems. Bark orange-brown with grey-green flakes. Shoot pale or whitish brown, ridged on decurrent leaf bases, with a red-brown patch on the crest of the ridge just behind the leaf base, shiny with short black hairs in grooves. Bud globose, red-brown, 0.2 cm. Leaves pectinate beneath the shoot, irregularly arranged above with a narrow parting, broadest near the base, apex rounded, notched, groove along upper surface, fresh green above, 2 pale or whitish stomatal bands below with broad flat entire or sometimes toothed margins, 0.5-2.5 cm by 0.2-0.3 cm. Cone ovoid, yellow-brown, 1.5-2.5 cm. Zone 6.

The typical form of Chinese hemlock is recorded from the mountains to the north and south of the Yangtse river in China. It is uncommon in cultivation but makes an interesting tree.

No cultivars are recorded, but three varietas are recognised in the *Chinese Flora* as follows. At least one of these forms is in cultivation, and all three may be so, as in the past they would have been recorded simply as the species.

var. *oblongisquamata* Cheng & Fu which is distinguished by the cone scales being distinctly longer than broad. It is recorded from Sichuan and west Hubei, and has recently been raised to *T. oblongisquamata* by Cheng & Fu.

var. *robusta* Cheng & Fu has larger, more rounded cone scales with a larger obdeltoid bract scale; it is recorded from north-east Hubei.

var. *tchekiangensis* (Flous)Cheng & Fu was described from Zhejiang but is also found across south-east China from Fujian to southern Yunnan. It differs in the cone scales being circular with a cuneate base and two small auricles and in the leaves being more tapered from the rounded base with two bright stomatal bands. Plants are in cultivation from southern Zhejiang.

T. forrestii Downie
Forrest hemlock

Tree to 15 m. Crown broadly conical. Shoot red-brown, becoming shiny and pink-brown, with open hairs, more hairy on weaker shoots. Bud globular, 0.2 cm. Leaves irregularly

Figure 8.24 *Tsuga forrestii. Foliage and cone.*

pectinate below, parted above, broadest near cuneate base, tapered to acute, bluntly mucronate or notched apex, margins not toothed, groove runs along lower half of needle only, top half rounded, shiny or subshiny above and bloomed, with 2 silvery glaucous stomatal bands and relatively narrow dark green margins beneath, to 2.5 cm by 0.3 cm. Cones ovoid-oblong, tapered, yellow-brown, 2-4 cm. Zone 7.

Forrest hemlock was described from the Lijiang (or Likiang) range in Yunnan and is also recorded from Zhongdian county to the north-west and from Muli in south-west Sichuan province. It shows similarities to both *T. chinensis* and *T. dumosa* but is quite distinct in the hairy red-brown shoots and the foliage. It is in cultivation from seeds collected by Forrest under his number F.10293 from the Lijiang range.

T. formosana Hayata
Taiwan hemlock
Tree to 50m in Taiwan but smaller in cultivation. Bark grey, furrowed. Shoots pale yellow, later grey-yellow, hairy in grooves. Leaves parted above and below the shoot, linear, base cuneate, apex rounded notched, dark green above with a groove, 2 whitish stomatal bands beneath, 1.5-2.5 cm by 0.2-0.3 cm. Cone ovoid, yellow-brown, shiny, 1.5-2.5 cm, scales

suborbicular or half moon, margins finely toothed. Zone 8.

This plant is confined to the island of Taiwan where it forms forests in the higher mountains. It is allied to *T. chinensis*, of which it is often treated as a variety (var. *formosana* (Hayata)Li ex Keng) but seems reasonably distinct in a number of characters. It is in cultivation but is uncommon.

T. caroliniana Engelmann
Carolina hemlock
Tree 15-20m tall. Crown conical or ovoid, twiggy and open. Bark red-brown, becoming purple-grey with shallow fissures. Shoot red-brown, shiny, hairy in grooves. Bud ovoid, 0.3 cm. Leaves pectinate below, irregular above, sparse, linear, grooved above, apex rounded, blunt, slightly notched, margins entire, deep shiny green above with 2 white bands beneath, 1-2 cm by 0.2 cm. Cones ovoid to elliptic, 2.5-3.5 cm, scales oblong, longer than wide. Zone 4.

Carolina hemlock is found along the southern Appalachian Mountains from south-west Virginia to north-west Georgia. It is easily separated from *T. canadensis* and *T. heterophylla* by the red-brown shoots and the untoothed leaves. From its Asiatic relatives, it is separated by the combination of shoot colour, often longer leaves with obtuse or slightly notched tips and bright white stomatal bands and the oval-oblong cone scales. It makes a small bushy tree in cultivation.

'La Bar Weeping' is a dense-foliaged little plant with a pendulous habit; the original is 1m tall by 0.65 m.

T. mertensiana (Bongard)Carriere
Mountain hemlock
Tree 20-30m but at the treeline reduced to a stunted bush. Crown narrowly columnar-conic. Bark purplish to red-brown, breaking into large rectangular scales. Shoot pale red-brown, becoming grey-brown, hairy for 2-3 seasons. Bud acute, red-brown, 0.3 cm. Leaves spreading radially on long and short spur shoots, pointing forwards, thick, linear, bluntly pointed, often with groove on upper surface but both surfaces convex and bearing stomata, margins not toothed, glaucous blue-green or grey-green, often on adjacent trees in the wild, 1.5-2.5 cm. Male cones purple, pendulous. Cones oblong-cylindric, yellow-green to purple, ripening to dark brown, scales oblong-obovate, on open cones spreading at right angles or reflexed, 4-8 cm. Zone 5.

Mountain hemlock is native along the Pacific coast of North America from southern Alaska to British Columbia and then in the mountains south to central California and also in the Rocky Mountains from south-east British Columbia to northern Idaho. It is usually found at or just below the treeline, ranging from sea level in Alaska to over 3,000 m in the Sierra Nevada in California.

Mountain hemlock is unique in the genus in the radially arranged foliage which is thick and with stomata on both surfaces. The cones are very large for a hemlock and the species is close to *Picea*; the pendulous leading shoot and main branches serve as a quick distinguishing feature. Apart from the long shoots, foliage is also carried on short whorls on the upper side of the shoot, similar to the short shoots of *Cedrus*. The ripe cones often have the scales completely reflexed when fully open.

Mountain hemlock makes an attractive slow-growing tree of neat conical habit with its bluish grey foliage. It needs a moist site for optimum development and dislikes atmospheric pollution. It warrants much wider planting.

There is some variation in the colour of the foliage and the best blue plants belong to the forma *argentea* (Beissner)Rehder; this form occurs naturally within the range of the species. 'Blue Star' is a selection of this form. 'Glauca' is also applied to blue-foliaged plants but seems super-fluous.

'Cascade' is a very compact plant with shorter, denser foliage. The growth rate is only some 3.5-5 cm per annum. 'Sherwood Compact' is a different but similar plant.

'Elizabeth' is a spreading dwarf form, growing about twice as wide as high.

T. × *jeffreyi* (Henry)Henry
Jeffrey hemlock *T. heterophylla* × *T. mertensiana*

This hybrid was first raised in Britain from wild collected seed but has since been found growing in Washington east of the Cascade Mountains where the two species meet. It was originally named as a variety of the Mountain hemlock parent, to which it is much closer, differing in the somewhat parted yellow grey-green foliage which is open and the more slender and flattened needles with finely toothed margins, to 1.5 cm. Zone 6.

In cultivation, Jeffrey hemlock has made a tree to 15 m. It is interesting in its origin but lacks the beauty of either parent.

T. longibracteata Cheng
Bristlecone hemlock

Tree 30 m. Crown in young trees narrow conic, with very pendulous leading shoot, older trees domed. Shoots yellowish brown, becoming grey, glabrous. Bud ovoid-conic, acute, chestnut brown, 0.2-0.4 cm. Leaves somewhat radial or parted

above and below, rather sparse, rounded at base, linear or taper gradually to bluntly pointed apex, groove along upper surface, margins not toothed, mid- to dark glossy green above, paler below with whitish bands of stomata, 1-2.5 cm by 0.1-0.25 cm. Cone carried erect on a short stalk, cylindrical, chestnut brown, 2-6 cm, scales oval, broader than long with lateral auricles, 0.9-2.2 cm by 1.2-2.5 cm, bract scale spathulate, exserted, erect, about two-thirds length of ovuliferous scale. Zone 7.

Bristlecone hemlock was first found in north-east Guizhou in the 1930s. It is now also known from southern Hunan, north Guangdong, north-east Guangxi and Fujian provinces of China. It is very distinct in the leaves, which are sparse and bright green and in the cones carried erect on shoots 1-3 cm long. The aspect of the foliage and cones is of a diminutive *Keteleeria* species, but the very pendulous leading shoot indicates *Tsuga*. The only plant I have seen was cultivated unnamed at Canton and caused me to think hard! Unfortunately this desirable species awaits introduction to cultivation outside of China.

Widdringtonia Endlicher **Cypress pines**
Cupressaceae

The Cypress pines are a group of three evergreen species restricted to southern and eastern Africa. They are similar to *Callitris* in general, differing in the paired adult leaves (in 3s in *Callitris*) and the cones which have a whorl of four (rarely 5-6) unequally sized scales; each scale carries 1 to several seeds and the cones ripen in the second year. The juvenile foliage is long and needle-like and set spirally on the shoot, whilst the adult leaves are scale-like and in decussate pairs. The species are tender except in mild climates but are very tolerant of dry conditions. In Britain, only small plants can be grown out of doors in the mildest areas.

W. cedarbergensis Marsh
Clanwilliam cedar

Tree in the wild usually to 5 m, rarely to 20 m. Crown conical, spreading with age. Bark reddish grey, scaly. Juvenile leaves 1-2 cm by 0.1-0.2 cm. Adult leaves adpressed, ovate, 0.2-0.4 cm. Cones globose, with warty papillae along the margins where the scales meet, 2.5 cm. Zone 9.

Clanwilliam cedar is found in the Cedarberg Mountains of south-west Cape Province, South Africa at altitudes of 1,000-1,600 m.

W. *nodiflora* (Linnaeus)Powrie
Sapree-wood

Tree 10-40m. Crown columnar-conic, dense. Bark grey, exfoliating in thin strips to reveal red-brown beneath. Shoots divided into joint-like segments. Juvenile leaves glaucous green, spreading, lanceolate, 2.5cm by 0.2cm. Adult leaves incurved, bluntly pointed, 0.1-0.12cm long by 0.05cm. Cone subglobose, smooth or wrinkled, without warty papillae where the scales meet, 2cm. Zone 9.

Sapree-wood is found from South Africa through Mozambique, Zimbabwe and into Malawi. It occurs at elevations of up to 2,600m and might be hardy it suitable origins were tried.

W. *schwarzii* (Marloth)Masters
Willowmore cedar

Tree 15-40m. Crown conical or columnar. Bark reddish grey, flaking. Shoots round, threadlike. Juvenile leaves glaucous, 1-2cm by 0.2cm, retained for only a short period. Adult leaves in 4 ranks, ovoid, incurved, with a dorsal gland, 0.1-0.15cm. Cones 2.5cm, scales with warty papillae on valve margins. Zone 9.

Willowmore cedar is restricted to the Willowmore district of Cape Province and is found at lower altitudes than the other species.

Zone 1	below −50F	(below −45C)
Zone 2	−50F − −40F	(−45C − −40C)
Zone 3	−40F − −30F	(−40C − −34C)
Zone 4	−30F − −20F	(−34C − −29C)
Zone 5	−20F − −10F	(−29C − −23C)

Zone 6	−10F − 0F	(−23C − −17C)
Zone 7	0F − 10F	(−17C − −12C)
Zone 8	10F − 20F	(−12C − −7C)
Zone 9	20F − 30F	(−7C − −1C)
Zone 10	30F − 40F	(−1C − 5C)

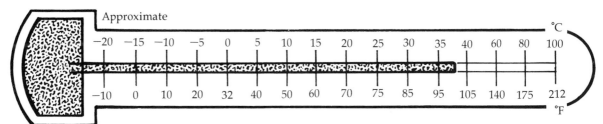

Appendix 1:
Hardiness Zones of
Europe and North America

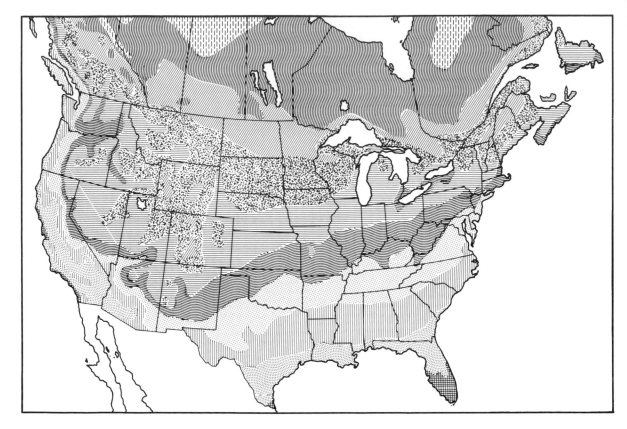

Appendix 2: Metric/Imperial Conversion Table

Bold figures in the centre columns can be read as either metric or British measures eg: 1 inch = 2.54cm, or 1 metre = 3.27 feet.

in		cm	ft		m
.039	**1**	2.54	3.27	**1**	0.91
.079	**2**	5.08	6.54	**2**	1.83
.118	**3**	7.62	9.81	**3**	2.74
.158	**4**	10.16	13.08	**4**	3.66
.197	**5**	12.70	16.35	**5**	4.57
.236	**6**	15.24	19.62	**6**	5.49
.276	**7**	17.78	22.89	**7**	6.40
.315	**8**	20.32	26.16	**8**	7.32
.354	**9**	22.86	29.43	**9**	8.23
			32.70	**10**	9.10

Conversion Formulae

To convert Imperial or Metric multiply by Factors shown in outside columns

Imperial to Metric			*Metric to Imperial*	
Multiply Imperial by			Multiply Metric by	
2.540	Inches to	Centimetres	to Inches	0.3937
0.3048	Feet to	Metres	to Feet	3.281
0.9144	Yards to	Metres	to Yards	1.094
1.609	Miles to	Kilometres	to Miles	0.6214
28.35	Ounces to	Grams	to Ounces	0.03527
0.4536	Pounds to	Kilograms	to Pounds	2.205

Bibliography

The following books are either referred to in the text, or provide more information on one or more aspects of conifers.

Anon, *European Garden Flora*, vol. 1 (Cambridge University Press, Cambridge, 1986). Record of main conifers cultivated in Europe, including keys to species

Bean, W.J. *Trees and Shrubs Hardy in the British Isles*, 8th edn (4 vols., John Murray, London, 1970-80). Reference work on plants in general cultivation in Britain

Cheng, W.C. & Fu, L.K. *Gymnospermae* (1979), tome 7 of *Flora of the People's Republic of China* (Beijing). Herein called *Chinese Flora* (and refers to this volume on Conifers)

de Laubenfels, D.J. 'A revision of the Malesian and Pacific Rainforest Conifers, 1: Podocarpaceae', *Journal Arnold Arboretum*, 50 (2-3) (1969), 274-369. Splits the family into several genera, as largely followed here

— 'A taxonomic revision of *Podocarpus*', *Blumea*, 30 (2) (1985), 251-78. Gives a revision of *Podocarpus*, including a key

Garden, J. 'A revision of the genus *Callitris* Ventenat', *Contributions New South Wales Nat. Herb.* 2 (5) (1956), 363-92

Garner, R.J. *The Grafter's Handbook* (Faber & Faber, London, 1947)

Grierson, A.J.C. & Long, D.C. *Flora of Bhutan*, vol. 1, part 1 (Royal Botanic Garden, Edinburgh, 1983)

Hillier, H.G. *Hillier's Manual of Trees and Shrubs* (David & Charles, Newton Abbot, Devon, 1972)

Krussmann, G. *Manual of Cultivated Conifers* (Batsford, London, 1985). Comprehensive guide to named cultivars. First edition published in German, 1972. 3rd revised edition published 1984

Little, E.L. & Critchfield, W.B. *Subdivisions of the Genus Pinus*, US Department of Agriculture Miscellaneous Publication 1144 (Washington, DC, 1969)

Mitchell, A.F. *Conifers in the British Isles*, Forestry Commission Booklet 32 (Edinburgh, 1972). Records taller-growing conifers in Britain

Phillips, D. & Burdekin, D. *Diseases of Forest and Ornamental Trees* (Macmillan, London, 1982). Detailed discussion of tree diseases, with particular reference to Britain

Silba, J. *An International Census of the Coniferae*, Phytologia Memoirs 7 (New Jersey, 1984). Useful, as it lists the place of publication of many conifers, but exceedingly restricted in interpretation and inclined to lump species together without satisfactory reason

Welch, H.J. *Manual of Dwarf Conifers* (Theophrastus, Rhode Island, USA, 1979). Reference work on dwarf conifer cultivars

Whitmore, T.C. 'A monograph of *Agathis*', *Pl. Syst. Evol.*, 135 (1980), 41-69

Glossary

These definitions relate to their usage when applied to conifers, which may be more restricted than the use of the word in relation to plants in general.

abaxial   the side of a lateral organ away from the main axis, e.g. the underside of a leaf; the description imagines the item lying erect along the axis; *see* adaxial

acicular   needle-shaped

acuminate   with a slender drawn-out point

acute   sharp-pointed, making an angle of less than 90°

adaxial   the side of a lateral organ closer to the main axis, e.g. the upper surface of a leaf; see abaxial

adnate   united with another part

adpressed   lying close to and parallel to a surface, but not joined

allopatric   occurring in a different country, i.e. having a geographical separation

anthesis   the period when the pollen is shed and the ovules are ready for pollination

apex   tip

apical   occurring at the tip

apiculate   contracted into a small point

apophysis   the exposed outer portion of a pine cone

aril   a usually fleshy outgrowth from the tissue at the base of the seed, partly or wholly enveloping the seed

articulate   jointed

assurgent   all leaves rising above the level of the shoot

auriculed   with earlike lobes at the base

axil   the upper angle between a leaf stalk or bract and the subtending shoot

axillary   occurring in the axils

awl-shaped   tapering from the base to a stiff slender point

basal   found at the base or lower portion

bevelled   sloped off at the apex, as in the tip of some spruces

bifid   deeply divided into two points

bract   a scale subtending a seed-bearing scale in its axil

butt   the lower portion of the stem

ciliate   fringed with hairs on the margin

cone   term used to describe the reproductive organs of a conifer, originally derived from the shape of the fruit of pine species, now used to include all conifers and both male and female organs

conic   shaped like a cone

connate   joined together at the base

cotyledon   seed-leaf

cuneate   wedge-shaped at the base

cusp   a sharp pointed projection at the apex of a broader structure

cuticle   protective layer around the leaf

cylindric   in the shape of a cylinder

decumbent   more or less horizontal but with the tips semi-erect or erect

decurrent   running down onto the next structure at the base, e.g. a leaf decurrent onto a shoot

decussate   in opposite pairs at right angles to the succeeding pairs

deflexed   bent downwards

deltoid   triangular in outline with the point of attachment along the base

dimorphic   occurring in two different shapes or forms

dioecious   with the male and female cones on different plants

distichous   arranged in two parted ranks

dorsal   positioned on the back surface

drupe-like   like a drupe, a seed with a fleshy outer covering and a hard bony seed

ellipsoid   shaped like an ellipse but in three dimensions

elliptic   shaped like an ellipse and two-dimensional

endoderm   layer of tissue in a leaf which lies between the vascular central portion and the outer protective layers, where the photosynthesis is carried out

endosperm   food storage tissue found in many seeds

epicormic buds   dormant buds which are found on many conifers and which grow from the outer layer of the live bark; they may grow later and are especially found on the main stem where they often have the radial foliage arrangement of leading shoots

epigeal   commonest form of germination in which the cotyledons are raised above the ground as the first leaves

erose   with a nibbled or wavy margin

exserted   sticking out or projecting

falcate   flat and curved at right angles to the flat surfaces, e.g. as in a sickle

fasciated   bunched

fastigiate   with erect branches and habit

filamentous   threadlike, unbranched

filius, f.   the son, used in conjunction with the authority to a name where both the father and son have named plant species, e.g. Hooker and Hooker f.

flabellate   fan-shaped

flexuous   pliable or bendable

flower   used to denote the stage of the cones, both male and female, at and around the time of pollination; these are not technically flowers in the strict botanical sense

frondose   in fern-like sprays

fruit   used to denote the mature female cone

fusiform   broadened at the middle, spindle-shaped

glabrous   smooth; in English descriptions usually referring to the absence of hairs but not exclusively, especially in Latin names (*glabra*)

glaucous   with a bluish or blue-grey waxy coating

globose   rounded

helical   in an ascending spiral, like in a spring

heterosis   hybrid vigour following the crossing of two related species

hypoderm   thick-walled cells forming a layer beneath the cuticle

hypogeal   mode of germination in which the cotyledons remain underground and are not involved in photosynthesis

imbricate   pressed down above

incurved   bent inwards

internode, inter-nodal   the length of stem between two nodes

juvenile   relating to the immature state of the plant, although this state may be retained on certain fruiting plants

keeled   with a narrow ridge, suggesting the keel of a boat

lanceolate   3-4 or more times longer than wide and tapering towards the tip, broadest in lower half

linear   narrow and parallel-sided

megasporangiate strobilus   the cones bearing the large spores, or ovules, i.e. the female cone

membranaceous   thin and soft

meristem tissue   cells from which growth is made, primarily in the buds and at the tips of roots

micropyle   a pore in the surface of an ovule through which the pollen enters

microsporangiate strobilus   the cone which bears the pollen or small spores, i.e. the male cone

monoecious   both male and female flowers carried on the same tree, in conifers the individual flowers are normally of a single sex

mucro   a short narrow abrupt point at the apex

mucronate   bearing a mucro

mucronulate   bearing a fine mucro

multi-nodal   with more than one node of growth in a single growth flush

node   the point on a stem where a radial cluster of buds and branches are attached (in others plants used to refer to the attachment of a leaf)

notched   an indentation at the top of a leaf or other structure

obdeltoid   deltoid with the point of attachment at the apex of the triangle

oblanceolate   lanceolate with the broadest point above the middle

oblong longer than broad, nearly elliptic but with the sides more or less parallel

obtuse bluntly pointed, making an angle of more than 90°

ovate with the flat outline of a hen's egg, broadest below the middle and often pointed at the tip

ovoid as for ovate but three-dimensional

ovule the body of cells from which the seed develops after fertilisation by the pollen

ovuliferous scale the scales in the cone which bear the ovules

papilla small blunt protuberance on a structure, e.g. a leaf

pectinate spreading on either side, as in a comb

peduncle the stalk at the base of a cone

peltate shield-like, with the point of attachment a central stalk on one face

petiole the stalk of a leaf

phloem the conductive tissue in the bark, also found in the leaf (where it denotes the abaxial side), concerned mainly with the downward conduction of the products of photosynthesis

phylloclade a flattened shoot performing the functions of a leaf

pinnate a compound leaf-like organ with the parts borne on opposite sides of a rachis

plumose feathery

pneumatophore refers to the breathing roots produced by Swamp cypress

primordia an organ at the earliest stage of its development

pruinose with a waxy bloom

pubescent bearing hairs

pulvinus a swollen portion on the stem upon which sits a leaf, e.g. in the spruces

racemose a simple inflorescence bearing stalked flower parts along a single axis

rachis (rhachis) an axis bearing leaves or flower parts

radial arranged spreading around a central axis

radicle the portion of an embryo below the cotyledons, i.e. the primary root produced by a growing seed

receptacle the tip of an axis onto which the floral parts are attached

reflexed bent backwards

resinous with blobs of resin

revolute rolled downwards or backwards

rhombic with the outline of an equilateral parallelogram, with the place of attachment at an acute corner

rhomboidal as for rhombic but three-dimensional

rufous reddish-brown

rugose wrinkled or covered with impressed or sunken lines

ruminated appearing as if chewed, used to describe the deeply indented flesh in seeds of *Torreya* or Walnut

scale a) a minute leaf or a leaf-like organ, used in describing the cone parts and also for the leaves which lie at the base of the foliage leaves of pines and some other conifers;
b) relationship between elements of differing sizes

serrate with saw-like teeth

sessile sitting directly on the lower organ, without a stalk

sheath bundle of budscales which surround the base of a fascicle of pine needles

spathulate with a rounded apical portion which gradually narrows towards the base

stoma, plural stomata the pores through which gases are exchanged on a leaf

striated marked with raised or sunken parallel lines

strobilus catkin-like structure

subdistichous distichous but not fully parted

subglobose broader than round, not perfectly rounded or globose

subobtuse making an angle only slightly larger than 90°

suborbicular not perfectly orbicular, slightly broader than long

subsessile with a short stalk, nearly sessile

subulate awl-shaped, narrowly cylindric and tapered towards the apex

terete round in cross-section

ternate in threes

tetraploid with the normal cells containing four sets of chromosomes

tracheid an elongated closed cell in the xylem involved in the conduction of water solution and in giving support

truncate abruptly cut off at the apex

tuberculate bearing small wart-like protuberances

umbilicate with a navel-like depression, used to describe the depression at the apex of a cone in some Silver firs

umbo part of the apophysis of a pine cone, representing the exposed portion at the stage of development of the cone during the first year of growth prior to the fertilisation of the ovules, usually of a different colour than the rest of the apophysis

uni-nodal with a single node and internode of growth during one growing season

valvate opening by valves, hinged at the base as in *Thuja* cones

warty with wart-like protuberances

witches broom the fasciated growths developed by many conifers in response to some causal agent, often making dwarf conifers if vegetatively propagated

xylem woody tissue in the stem and leaf which provides support and is mainly involved in the conduction of water from the roots to the top of the tree

Index
Botanical and Cultivar Names

Index
English Names

This index gives the page on which each species is described in the Gazetteer section (pages 71-217). Unlike the botanical index, a name mentioned in the text of chapters 1 to 7 is not indexed. The index uses the last element in the name, e.g. for Taiwan douglas fir, go to *fir* and then to the t's to find *Taiwan douglas.*

Ahuetuete 203

Big tree 201
Biota 192
Bunya-bunya 90

Cathaya 93
Cedar
  Atlas 93
  Chilean incense 91
  Chinese incense 93
  Clanwilliam 217
  Cyprus 95
  Deodar 95
  Fortune 106
  Incense 92
  Japanese 194
  of Goa 114
  of Lebanon 94
  Pencil 132
  Smooth Tasmanian 90
  Southern red 132
  Stinking 212
  Taiwan incense 93
  Tasmanian 91
  Western red 209, 210
  White 208
  Willowmore 218
Coffin tree 202
  juniper 122
Cunninghamia
  Taiwan 107
Cypress
  Alice Holt 108
  Arizona 112
  Baker 114
  Bald 203
  Bentham 114
  Bhutan 111
  Cayamaca 112
  Cheng 111
  Chinese swamp 118
  Chinese weeping 110
  Gowen 113
  Guadelupe 113
  Hinoki 101
  Italian 109
  Kashmir 111
  Lawson 98
  Leyland 107

Macnab 114
Mexican 114
Monterey 112
Montezuma 203
Moroccan 110
Nootka 104
Ovens 108
Patagonian 116
Piute 112
Pond 203
Saharan 110
San Pedro 112
Santa Cruz 113
Sargent 114
Sawara 102
Smooth 112
Swamp 203
Taiwan 103
Tecate 114
Tsangpo 112
West Himalayan 111
White 104
Yunnan 110

Diselma 115

Fir
  Algerian 75
  Balsam 83
  Beshan 77
  Bigcone douglas 197
  Bornmueller 74
  Caucasian 73
  Cheng 80
  China 106
  Chinese douglas 198
  Cilician 75
  Coahuilan 84
  Delavay 78
  Douglas 196
  Durango 84
  European silver 73
  Faber 79
  Farges 79
  Flaky 80
  Forrest 79
  Forrest douglas 197
  Fraser 83
  Gamble 76
  Gaussen douglas 198
  Grand 84
  Greek 73
  Guatemalan 85
  Hickel 86
  Japanese douglas 197
  Khinghan 81
  King Boris 73
  Korean 82
  Low 84
  Manchurian 77
  Maries 77
  Mexican 85

Min 76
Momi 75
Moroccan 75
Mount Shasta 86
Nikko 76
Noble 85
Oaxaca 87
Pacific 77
Pindrow 76
Red 85
Sacred 86
Sakhalin 81
Salween 77
Santa Lucia 72
Shensi 77
Shikoku 82
Shortleaf douglas 198
Sibirian 81
Sicilian 74
Sikkim 78
Spanish 74
Subalpine 82
Taiwan 82
Taiwan douglas 197
Tazoatan 75
Tienshan 81
Trojan 74
Veitch 81
Vejar 86
Webb 78
White 84
Fokienia 116

Ginkgo 117

Hemlock
  Bristlecone 217
  Carolina 216
  Chinese 215
  Eastern 213
  Forrest 215
  Himalayan 214
  Jeffrey 217
  Mountain 216
  Northern Japanese 215
  Southern Japanese 215
  Taiwan 216
  Western 214
Hiba 211

Juniper 120
  Alligator 125
  Ashe 127
  Azores 122
  Bermuda 133
  Black 124
  Blanco 133
  Bonin Isles 132
  California 126
  Canary Islands 122
  Chinese 130
  Coffin 122

Comitan 127
Cory 126
Creeping 133
Dahurian 131
Durango 126
East African 128
Flaky 122
Gamboa 127
Gaussen 131
Grecian 128
Himalayan weeping 122
Jalisco 126
Komarov 129
Kunlun shan 129
Luchu 122
Mekong 124
Mexican weeping 125
Mountain 128
One-seed 127
Persian 128
Phoenician 124
Pinchot 126
Ping 123
Prickly 121
Przewalski 125
Rocky Mountain 133
Russian 129
Saltillo 127
Sargent 131
Shore 121
Sichuan 125
Spanish 130
Standley 128
Stinking 129
Syrian 119
Temple 121
Tibetan 128
Utah 126
Wallich 124
West Indies 133
Western 127
Xinjiang 124

Kahikatea 115
Kawaka 141
Keteleeria
  David 135
  Evelyn 135
  Fortune 134
  Hainan 135
  Hairy 135
  Oblong-cone 135
  Round-scale 135
  Taiwan 135
  Vietnam 136
  Yellow-twig 136
Kusamaki 193

Larch
  Burma 139
  Dahurian 138
  European 137